D0934721

Marie von Ebner-Eschenbach
The Victory of a Tenacious Will

Studies in Austrian Literature, Culture, and Thought

Doris M. Klostermaier

Marie von Ebner-Eschenbach
The Victory of a Tenacious Will

ARIADNE PRESS
Riverside, California

Ariadne Press would like to express its appreciation to the Austrian Cultural Institute New York for assistance in publishing this book.

Library of Congress Cataloging-in-Publication Data

Klostermaier, Doris M.
  Marie von Ebner-Eschenbach : the victory of a tenacious will / Doris M. Klostermaier.
      p.   cm. -- (Studies in Austrian literature, culture, and thought)
  Includes bibliographical references and index.
  ISBN 1-57241-038-8
  1. Ebner-Eschenbach, Marie von, 1830-1916--Biography. 2. Authors, Austrian--19th century--Biography. I. Title. II. Series.
PT1853.Z5K55 1997
833'.8--dc20
[B]   96-34901
                                                CIP

Cover design:
Art Director and Designer: George McGinnis
Photo ©Bildarchiv der Österreichischen Nationalbibliothek

For Klaus

CONTENTS

PART FIVE

THE PUBLIC HAS A NOTION (1899-1909)

PART SIX

TO STRIVE UNTIL THE END (1910-1916)

LIST OF ABBREVIATIONS

AW   Marie von Ebner-Eschenbach, "Altweibersommer," *Erzählungen. Autobiographische Schriften.* Vol. 3. Winkler, 1978.

BI   Anton Bettelheim, *Marie von Ebner-Eschenbach.* 1900

BII   Anton Bettelheim, *Marie von Ebner-Eschenbachs Wirken und Vermächtnis.* 1920

BC   Robert A. Kann, ed. Marie von Ebner-Eschenbach - Dr. Josef Breuer. *Ein Briefwechsel.*

BF   Marie von Ebner-Eschenbach und Hieronymus Lorm. "Aus Briefen an einen Freund."

BP   Marie von Ebner-Eschenbach, "Betty Paoli."

DS   *Die Dioskuren.*

EB   *Encyclopedia Britannica.*

EETL   Jiri Vesely, "Marie von Ebner-Eschenbach und die tschechische Literatur."

EF   *Enciclopedia Filosofica.*

EG   Marie von Ebner-Eschenbach, "Meine Erinnerungen an Grillparzer." *Erzählungen. Autobiographische Schriften.* Vol. 3. Winkler, 1978.

ELF   Marie von Ebner-Eschenbach, "Louise von François."

EME   Marie von Ebner-Eschenbach, Ed. "Aus den Erinnerungen des k.k. Feldmarschall-Leutnants a.D. Moriz Frhrn. Ebner von Eschenbach."

ESD   Jiri Vesely, "Marie von Ebner-Eschenbach, Saar, David: Tschechische Elemente in ihrem Werk und Leben."

FM   Anton Bettelheim, ed. *Louise von François und Conrad Ferdinand Meyer.*

HC   Ebner-Eschenbach/Heyse correspondence in: Mechtild Alkemade, *Die Lebens- und Weltanschauung der Freifrau Marie von Ebner-Eschenbach.*

KL   Marie von Ebner-Eschenbach, "Aus meinen Kinder- und Lehrjahren," in *Kritische Texte und Deutungen.* Vol. 4. Ed. Christa Maria Schmidt.

MK   Marie von Ebner-Eschenbach, "Meine Kinderjahre." *Erzählungen. Autobiographische Schriften.* Vol. 3. Winkler, 1978.

NBV   Nationalbibliothek Vienna.

NDB   *Neue Deutsche Biographie.* Ed. Historische Kommission bei der Bayrischen Akademie der Wissenschaften.

NÖB   *Neue Österreichische Biographie.*

RV   Rathaus Vienna.

TBI   Karl Konrad Polheim, Ed. *Tagebücher I.*

TBII   Karl Konrad Polheim, Ed. *Tagebücher II.*

ZT   Marie von Ebner-Eschenbach, "Aus einem zeitlosen Tagebuch." *Erzählungen, Autobiographische Schriften.* Vol. 3. Winkler, 1978.

INTRODUCTION

The idea for this biography had its genesis several years ago, when I happened to read Marie von Ebner-Eschenbach's statement: "Blessed be my will to suffer! To it I owe my inner peace, my courage in the battle of life, my strength and my vigor" (Vesely 217). This remark aroused my curiosity.

I had studied quite a few of Ebner-Eschenbach's works during my high school and university years in Germany and knew that she was considered Austria's most prominent nineteenth-century woman writer. I had also learned in class that she was a member of her country's social elite, that she had had a happy and harmonious marriage and that she had been venerated by the public as a symbol of kindness and compassion. Having lived such a fulfilled life, why did she have to suffer?

From Anton Bettelheim's two biographies of 1900 and 1920 I learned that Ebner-Eschenbach's goal had been to become a dramatist of note and that, after many failures and disappointments in the theater world, she resigned herself to writing prose, a genre in which she finally succeeded beyond her most daring dreams. I now saw that, indeed, she had had to suffer and to struggle for her art, and that, due to various obstacles, like family and public prejudice, physical ailments, and the maliciousness of critics, her life really had been hard.

Ebner-Eschenbach now began to interest me as a person and as a writer. But the longer I read in Bettelheim's biographies in search of Marie von Ebner-Eschenbach, the true human being, the more it dawned on me that he had presented a statue, an idol, a superwoman, to whom I found it difficult to relate. I asked myself whether it would be possible to discover, behind the public façade, the private woman with her likes and dislikes, her strengths and weaknesses, her frustrations, sorrows and joys. The more I thought about it, the more I became determined to search for the real Ebner-Eschenbach, and one day I decided to write her life.

In his first biography Bettelheim, voicing his own view and that of his contemporaries, states: "Whoever wants to get to know Marie Ebner-Eschenbach's life will find the most important and most valuable information in her creations. One just has to be able to search for it" (B I 10). And this is what I have set out to do. I gradually realized that Ebner-Eschenbach was an exceedingly private person who did not believe in confessional writing. She thought it strange that Grillparzer had revealed intimate details about his private life, and therefore she wholeheartedly approved of the fact that Anna Fröhlich had burned her sister Kathi's diaries, in which she had described her relationship with the great dramatist (EG 916).

Marie Ebner-Eschenbach herself destroyed many autobiographical documents when she put her "literary house in order" (Schmidt 171) and consigned many manuscripts to the fire. She destroyed many letters and diaries and asked her closest friends, among them Marie Kittl and Louise von François, to burn her correspondence. Ebner-Eschenbach held the firm conviction that artists should be understood through their work. In "Lotti, die Uhrmacherin," she points out that the essence of master Fessler, the gifted watchmaker, is clearly reflected in his watches; one only has to look carefully for it (865). And in "Ob spät, ob früh" she has the baroness explain to her son: "You know my disgust with newspaper gossip; half of it should not be read, half of it should not be believed. That is how I handle it. Kolberg's compositions delight me. From them I draw the information about the man which is precious to me, and the rest I can do without" (398).

Bearing this in mind, I embarked on a careful study of Ebner-Eschenbach's oeuvre, in the hope of catching a glimpse of the inner life of the woman who had been so eager to protect her privacy. I also remembered the following statement by Christopher Gillie in his monograph on Jane Austen: "[A]n imaginative writer lives in his works, and if a reader has only these by which to shape his judgment, he usually has nearly all that is essential" (19).

The first discovery I made was that in quite a few works the writer uses her own name for her female characters. There is a Marie in "Nach dem Tode," a young, serious-minded woman, cultivated, efficient, and her husband's equal in intelligence. She deeply loves him, but he does not reciprocate her affection. He ridicules her compassion with the underprivileged, neglects her and finally leaves her for his personal interests. When he returns after many years, his wife is dead and finally, all too late, he begins to appreciate her. She has left him a daughter, little Marie, a "sad, withered plant" (64), who trembles in fright of her father and only gradually attaches herself to him.

In "Die Unverstandene auf dem Dorfe" we meet a Marie whose parents have obviously had an unhappy marital relationship. She has "an expression of deep sadness in her dark eyes" (531), sees herself as a "pious martyr" (543) and feels like an outsider. She further has an inkling "that a creature of her worth may not be happy in this wicked world" (553). Marie of "Wieder die Alte" is an artistic but rather unattractive, outspoken and radical teenager, the offspring of an aristocratic family in which harmony and serenity are sorely missing. This youngster pesters and challenges her long-suffering governess with tricky questions regarding history and religion. But ultimately, repenting of her cruelty to the helpless woman, she adopts her as her confidante and shares her most intimate secrets with her. The protagonist of "Unsühnbar," Maria Dornach, likewise artistic and uncompromising in her outlook on life, longs for her early lost mother and, at the mercy of an authoritarian, uncomprehending, overly status-conscious father, burdens herself with guilt and suffering, before she finds her true self. Finally there is a Marie in the story "Im Zauberbann." She has been engaged as a reader in an aristocratic household and comes across as a skeptical lady who has a good understanding of literature and a penchant for patronizing people. She does not shy away from voicing her opinion, even at the risk of being at variance with the views of her employers.

I discovered that all these namesakes of Marie von Ebner-Eschenbach and many other female characters—like Rosa of *Bozena*, Paula and Muschi of *Zwei Komtessen*, Elika of "Die arme Kleine"—bear a strong resemblance to the portrait Ebner-Eschenbach has painted of herself in her semi-autobiographical story "Die erste Beichte" and in her autobiography *Meine Kinderjahre*. There she says about conceiving her literary figures: "I elaborated on their colorful plays, their games and their fights; I put myself into them, I lived in them" (799). In the same quotation she mentions that she identified not only with her female, but also with her male characters, endowing them with her ideals and her longings. I analyzed several male protagonists and detected in them as well some of their creator's characteristics. Edinek of "Unverbesserlich" for instance clearly resembles the young Marie Dubsky in his radicalism, his vehemence and his desire to overcome habits considered repulsive by those around him. Likewise, Dietrich Brand of "Rittmeister Brand," this "fireball" (767) with his deep compassion and his love of children, and Josef of "Die arme Kleine," who hates being tied to the house and makes life difficult for his tutor—both bring the young Marie Dubsky to mind.

My next question was: which of her experiences had Ebner-Eschenbach transmitted to her fiction? Her writings reveal that she must have witnessed unhappy marriages at close range and that she had to have been in contact with men of a rather mercurial temperament, easily given to outbursts of anger. Her autobiography discloses that she felt isolated and little understood in her family and that she suffered from the reality that children in her time were not taken seriously. Her essay "Aus meinen Kinder- und Lehrjahren" shows her anger at the brutality of the feudal system and at aristocratic condescension and prejudice. It further makes the reader aware that even as a young girl Marie Dubsky tried to assert herself against a repressive society that ridiculed girls with an intellectual bent.

From Bettelheim's biography I knew that she had vented part of her frustrations about her ill-fated dramatic career in the story "Ein Spätgeborener" (B II 148); but were there other profound experiences she had described in her work? My question was answered when I read Ebner-Eschenbach's diaries, especially the ones published by K. K. Polheim in 1989 and 1991. They, like the excerpts brought out by Jiri Vesely in 1971, disclose information about the writer's life which she probably thought would never come to the fore. I now learned about her parents' unhappy marriage, about her father's quarrelsomeness and his way of tyrannizing the family. I found that in younger years she did not have a high regard for her second stepmother and that her relationship with her was rather cool and formal. I also realized that Moritz von Ebner-Eschenbach did not get along well with his uncle and father-in-law, and obviously, like the latter, had a penchant for being contentious. I further became aware that Ebner-Eschenbach's marriage was not as happy as she and her husband had led outsiders to believe.

A comparison of factual materials of her life with episodes in her fiction persuaded me that Ebner-Eschenbach had sublimated personal conflicts by depicting them in her work and thus had liberated herself from her complexes and fears. In "Aus meinen Kinder- und Lehrjahren" Ebner confirms that she had poured the tale of her "endeavors" and her "sufferings" into "the most modest form, the form of the narrative" (KL 279). So far critics have assumed this statement to refer to the story "Ein Spätgeborener"; yet Marie von Ebner-Eschenbach may in fact have meant all her prose works. Writing in general became therapy for her, a means to come to terms with her life and her environment (Necker 112).

Ebner-Eschenbach was a biographer at heart. The goal of her work was, as she put it: "to tell the life history or a piece of the life history of a human being, whose fate has aroused a particular interest in me"

(B II 12). Unfortunately, her plan to write a biography of the actress Anna Marie Adamberger, née Jacquet, who had deeply impressed her by her assertiveness toward her authoritarian father, came to nothing. Yet her reminiscences of Grillparzer, a biographical sketch that may be counted among her best works, show Ebner-Eschenbach's remarkable skill in this genre. Her forte was characterization and psychological penetration of the figures she described. Accordingly she herself deserves a biography that focuses as much as possible on her inner life.

In 1871 she commented in her diary about Gotthelf's story "Uli der Knecht," remarking that she enjoyed each character in it, especially because she could see him "feel and think" (Vesely 218). Finally, in "Aus einem zeitlosen Tagebuch" Ebner-Eschenbach claimed: "To measure the distances of the stars, to be intimately familiar with their course, to be able to distinguish the color of their light is not enough —one also has to be able to hear them sing" (744). In other words, amassing all the facts about my biographee's life was not sufficient. I had to breathe fresh life into her and throw new light on her inner state of being. Outwardly the course of her life was rather uneventful. The drama of her life was mainly private and had to be investigated through isolated incidents and inference.

I present here the first full-length English biography of Marie von Ebner-Eschenbach. It is not the "definite life" but focuses mainly on the writer's inner state, her emotions and psychological struggles, and her relationships with family and friends. It is meant as the framework and preliminary groundwork for a later full-scale biography. Such a work will require an investigation into the various genres Ebner-Eschenbach employed, a thorough textual analysis of all her works, a critical evaluation of her dramas, poetry and fiction and a discussion of their ranking in the larger context of nineteenth-century Austrian and German literature. Very desirable and valuable would also be a psycho-linguistic analysis of Ebner's oeuvre.

The last German life of the writer was published seventy-six years ago and needs a revision. Anton Bettelheim, Ebner-Eschen-bach's authorized biographer, portrayed her according to the conventions of the Romantic biographical tradition. He used documents in order to present his subject according to the feminine and artistic ideal of the time. Both had been shaped by the neo-classicist Friedrich Schiller, for whom a woman had to resemble "der lieben Frau Sonne" (B I 155), symbol of warmth, serenity and healing power, and an artist's personality had to reflect the highest purity and perfection. Bettelheim's Ebner-Eschenbach is without fault as a person and as a writer; contemporary readers must have been in awe of the venerable monument he had created.

Marie von Ebner-Eschenbach eagerly strove to conform to the public image her friends and admirers had fashioned of her. Privately she was a "Gemperlein," a rather pugnacious, outspoken, and uncompromising nature. She united within herself two characteristics that have been described as typically Austrian: a romantic penchant for dreaming that leads to a constant longing for something indefinite, and a propensity for nagging and criticizing (Lothar 5). She was a delightfully humorous and sarcastic person who probably never said and wrote anything without that certain malice which her friends Enrica von Handel-Mazzetti and Fritz Mauthner appreciated so much. I have tried to portray the writer with her admirable qualities as well as with her character weaknesses. My goal has been to illustrate her struggles for self-realization and her victory, due to her talent and persistence.

I have collected as much factual material as possible in order to acquaint the English-speaking reader with my subject's life and work and to provide information from German sources. I have studied all the monographs and major essays about Marie Ebner up to 1992 and have read and photocopied numerous unprinted materials—unpublished correspondences, note book entries and reviews—currently held in the two archives in Vienna. I have integrated Marie Ebner's life and work, since I believe they form a unity. I have discusssed her major works but focused especially on *Das Gemeindekind*, because so far it has been considered her most important achievement. I have further dealt with the people who were significant for Ebner-Eschenbach's life and career, and I have concentrated on the historical events that directly affected and concerned her.

My method combines a chronological with a thematic, associative approach. Part One comprises the years 1830 to 1848. Part Two describes the period from 1849 to 1873. Part Three goes from 1874 to 1883. Part Four begins in 1884 and ends in 1898. Part Five discusses the period from 1899 to 1909, and Part Six covers the time span of 1910 to 1916. Within each part I have proceeded thematically, dealing for instance with Ebner-Eschenbach's physical ailments in one chapter, even though she suffered from them all her life. I have further employed the technique of anticipation and flashback, partly because Ebner-Eschenbach uses these devices in her work, especially in her autobiography, and partly because my subject, like all human beings, synthesized in her mind anticipation of future events with memories of the past.

Writing this life I have been mindful of the biographical principle that the subject has to be in the foreground and that everything described in the biography has to relate to her (Maurois). I have been careful not to bury Marie Ebner beneath mounds of facts but rather to recreate her as a lively, thinking and feeling personality. I have tried to show her character through her actions (Hinz). Anecdotes are cited to show her humor, and the quotations from letters and notebook entries have been used to allow her to speak for herself. I made an effort to see the world through her eyes and to convey her perceptions to the reader. I have further heeded Leon Edel's advice that a biographer, though bound by facts, should still be as imaginative as he pleases in his quest for the hidden life myth, as long as he does not invent his material ("Biography and the Science of Man").

While Anton Bettelheim merely refers to the fact that Ebner-Eschenbach's life can be found in her creations, I have gone a step further and shown, by quoting from her work, which experiences and emotions expressed in her autobiography and diaries she actually transferred to her fiction. Marie von Ebner-Eschenbach has wrongly been stereotyped as "Dichterin der Idylle" (Reuter), an attribution that has prevented many twentieth-century readers from familiarizing themselves with her work. Kurt Benesch in the preface to his 1966 fictionalized biography *Die Frau mit den hundert Schicksalen* says that Ebner now has the reputation of a "sentimental, mawkish soul, to whom one does not concede any special literary talent" (IX). Heidi Beutin in her 1980 essay on *Bozena* claims that the name Ebner-Eschenbach usually conjures up memories of the dog story "Krambambuli" and that otherwise the writer's major accomplishments have sunk into oblivion (246). I hope to present a truer picture of her significance

Marie von Ebner-Eschenbach's work deserves close investigation, especially in regard to her keen psychological insights into human nature. Stories like "Uneröffnet zu verbrennen," "Poesie des Unbewussten," "Ihr Traum," reveal her as well familiar with the intricacies of the human psyche. In certain ways Ebner may be linked with George Eliot, whose psychological-social novels resemble her own, and with Henry James who, like her, was influenced by Gustav Fechner's philosophy and by Turgenev, the Russian master of the psychological narrative.

As Robert A. Kann has pointed out, Ebner-Eschenbach's correspondence influenced Josef Breuer's thinking (BC 12), and Breuer in turn had a great impact on Sigmund Freud. Long before the latter discussed the phenomenon of the "split ego," Marie von Ebner-Eschenbach had written her story "Ein Traum," in which an old countess, unable to accept the untimely death of her two dearly beloved grandsons, waits day and night for their return and only in lucid moments admits to herself that they are no longer among the living.

Scholars in America, Austria, the Czech Republic, Slovakia and Germany are currently researching Ebner-Eschenbach's life and work. I have contacted many specialists in the field and have received valuable information. I have also corresponded with Countess Aglae Schönfeldt, the great-grandniece of the writer, who has lent much encouragement to my work.

Where not otherwise indicated, I have used the three-volume Winkler edition for the quotations from Ebner's works. All translations are my own, unless otherwise indicated. I have tried to render the German text as literally as possible and as idiomatically as I felt necessary. All mottos used in my biography are aphorisms of Ebner-Eschenbach and have been taken from the Reclam edition, from Rieder's *Weisheit des Herzens*, and from Needler's English translation of some of them. I am aware that the most authentic materials are Ebner-Eschenbach's letters, notebook entries and the diary entries that have not been edited by the writer, by her family or by Anton Bettelheim and have been designated "A" in K. K. Polheim's edition. I have, however, also quoted from diary entries, marked as "B," which were revised by Marie von Ebner-Eschenbach in her old age. A compa-rison of these unedited and edited entries shows that the latter leave out information of a more private nature but coincide with the original entries in the description of general events.

It is interesting to observe that even in her presumably spontaneous diary notes (version "A") Ebner-Eschenbach is not completely open. She often uses the initials "N. N." instead of revealing people's names and expresses herself ambiguously, especially where she makes disparaging remarks about her second stepmother. The confessional attitude was painful to her. She also assumed that her husband, her "dear old man," would one day read her diaries (TB I 187). Ebner-Eschenbach is not consistent with the spelling of names. She writes Zdislawitz in four different ways: Zdisslawitz, Zdiszlawitz, Zdislavic, Zdislawitz, and I have chosen the last spelling. She also writes Moritz mostly without "t," Adolph with "f" and Viktor with "c." I have used the spelling of official documents of the time.

In order to recreate my subject's personality and character through my work I have at times employed Ebner-Eschenbach's metaphors, as she has used them in her autobiographical materials and in her fiction. I have described her childhood and youth quite extensively, not only because I had ample sources in her descriptions of her childhood in her autobiography, but also because she firmly believed that her life had been predetermined in her formative years (MK 792).

Writing this biography has been an enriching and exciting experience. At times I felt like a detective searching for clues and interpreting cryptic hints. Marie von Ebner-Eschenbach, reticent and reserved, was at one with her famous music director of "Ob spät, ob früh," who avoids people, "because he cannot pretend" (408). She also maintained that "perfect, unspoiled happiness" could be gained "only in the realm of the imagination," and she therefore eagerly strove to keep the outside world at bay (KL 277). Still, despite and partly because of her elusiveness, Marie von Ebner-Eschenbach has left us a great legacy, not only in her works, but in the very way she conducted her life.

At the end of this introduction I wish to express my gratitude to those who in many ways have supported me and made the writing of this work possible. My special thanks go to the librarians and the staff of the archives at the Rathaus in Vienna, the Österreichische Nationalbibliothek, the Österreichische Staatsarchiv, the Israelitische Kultusgemeinde in Vienna, and the national archives in Prague.

I am further indebted to Professors Victor Doerksen, Evelyn Hinz, and Kenneth McRobbie at the Universirty of Manitoba, Professor Günther Pöltner at the University of Vienna, Dr. Agnes Cupkova-Hamernikova, Prague, and Dr. James Lanoway, Winnipeg, for their interest, generosity and advice.

I would also like to thank Dr. Kenneth Hughes, Dean of Graduate Studies at the University of Manitoba, for his generosity and encouragement. Very special thanks are due to Countess Aglae Schönfeldt for her interest in my work. Ms. Shelley Coveney has earned my gratitude for the many ways in which she has made research and technical work easier for me. Special thanks go to my editors Donald G. Daviau and Richard H. Lawson for their patience and advice. Further I want to thank my husband, Klaus, for his invaluable support. My gratitude for his generosity and kindness goes beyond words. Finally I wish to show my appreciation to my daughters Sonja, Cornelia and Evelyn for bearing with me while I was working on this biography and for generously accepting Marie von Ebner-Eschenbach into our midst.

PROLOGUE:

"To grow old means to
gain vision"

Marie von Ebner-Eschenbach spent the winter of 1905 in Rome, the
city of her dreams. She corrected the galley proofs of her
autobiography, *Meine Kinderjahre*, which now appeared insignificant to
her beside the mighty symphony of the Eternal City with its awe-
inspiring past. Yet, as trivial as her own life-story may have seemed to
her, compared to Rome's monumental history, she was aware that she,
too, had fought a long and valiant battle and that she, too, had won her
victories. At seventy-five, as a highly acclaimed writer, she now could
explore her roots and the sources from which she had been able to draw
strength. With the sharpened perception of old age, which allowed her
to focus on significant moments that stood out in the steady flow of a
long career, she thus returned to the origins of her life and of her work,
her country estate Zdislawitz.

Her whole being was tied to this place. It was the soil that had
nourished her ancestors and that forever connected her with them. It
embodied the matrix in which her talent had grown and developed. As
a child she had explored every part of the extensive park of Zdislawitz;
she had known every tree and every shrub and had received inspirations
for her dreams and her stories. She had returned to her "old nest" time
and again not only in her yearly migrations from Vienna but also in her
dreams and her reminiscences. Many of the places she had described
under different names were slightly changed descriptions of Zdislawitz.
Like her forebears she was attached to the soil, a sacred trust to be
cultivated and to be passed on to future generations. Zdislawitz was
more than a place, it was a state of mind, a movable environment she
always carried with her, a symbol for a world that knew suffering, pain
and death but which was ultimately redeemed and made whole again.
Her goal was to immortalize it in her work, to preserve a way of life
inherited from her ancestors and to share it with her readers as a
common spiritual home.

Her maternal great-grandfather, Anton Valentin Kaschnitz von
Weinberg was elevated to the baronetcy in 1786. In 1789 Emperor

Joseph II made him an Imperial Councillor and awarded him the estate of Zdaunek in recognition of his services for the country. After his retirement Baron Kaschnitz became a prominent gentleman farmer in the area of Zdislawitz and was recognized among professionals for his contributions to improvements in the field of agriculture and livestock breeding. He was especially renowned for his expertise in sheep breeding, his flock being known far and wide (Wurzbach, vol. 9, 21). His daughter Marie married Baron Siegmund von Vockel, whose family, belonging to the service nobility, had come from Saxony.

Siegmund von Vockel's grandfather, Johann Paul Vockel, a lawyer, was auditor general at the Polish-Saxon court and in 1741 received the title of Privy Councillor. He was elevated to the nobility in 1746 and became a baron in 1749. He retired to Vienna where he died in 1766. Siegmund von Vockel's father, Friedrich Siegmund von Vockel, was a general and became an envoy of the County of Hesse-Darmstadt at the Imperial Court of Vienna. He was married to the daughter of Imperial Privy Councillor Freiherr von Moll.

Baron Siegmund von Vockel grew up in Vienna and received his education at the Theresianum, founded by Empress Maria Theresia as a high school for the social elite. After his graduation he embarked on an educational trip through Germany, as was customary for young men in his circles. In 1795 he moved to Saxony to take charge of the country estate Manschatz, which he had inherited from his parents. But life away from Austria was not to his taste. He decided to move back to the country where he had grown up and had put down his roots. Upon the advice of a friend, Baron Ferdinand von Geisslern, the owner of a country estate in Hostiz, Siegmund von Vockel devoted himself to the study of agriculture, a field in which he came to excel. In 1800, after his marriage to Baroness Marie Kaschnitz von Weinberg, Siegmund von Vockel bought the estate Zdislawitz from his father-in-law. Soon after, Vockel became a member of an association for the advancement of forestry, agriculture and cattle breeding. All the gentlemen farmers and owners of the manors of Littenschitz, Hostitz, Zborowitz, Zdaunek, Napagedl and others were members of this association, founded in the eighteenth century and especially renowned as one of the best sheep-breeder clubs in Austria (Wurzbach, vol. 51, 122).

When Vockel bought his estate he knew that his future lay in livestock breeding. Grain growing was no longer profitable because of the huge imports from America. In a short time he increased the herd of three hundred and fifty sheep bought from Baron Kaschnitz to a herd of sixteen hundred of the finest quality. He annually sold up to three hundred ewes to all parts of the monarchy, as well as to Prussia, Saxony and Mecklenburg. Sheep breeding became his passion. Once asked why he kept his sheep in a luxurious stable he replied: "With this stable I express my gratitude to these animals, and I return part of what they earned for me. My heir will more gladly take over a beautiful stable than a bad one" (ibid).

Vockel also introduced improvements in the areas of cultivation and production of cattle feed and in the enhancement of soil productivity. He ordered the draining of wetlands and constructed useful buildings on the estate. He enlarged the living quarters in the manor house and embellished the park and the orchard. As a member of the Mährisch-Schlesische Landwirtschaftsgesellschaft Vockel regularly wrote articles on sheep breeding and became a widely known consultant on the subject. When Counts Salm and Auersperg appoached him in 1816 to cooperate with them in founding a provincial museum in Brünn, Baron Vockel collected the funds and made a donation of a collection of thirteen thousand maps of the area inherited from his mother's family.

In his personal life Baron Vockel experienced great tragedy. His young wife died in childbirth in 1801, leaving him his infant daughter, Marie. He became a doting father to her, eager to share with her his love for the estate, for nature, for music, the sciences and the Bible. He taught her himself and instilled in her his cherished principles of enlightened Josephinism. He believed in providing a good education for his daughter so that she later could teach her children and become a force for good in her family. Eventually Baron Vockel married Marie's governess, a Countess Piatti, who vied with him in devotion to the motherless girl. In later years he suffered from a chest complaint for which he vainly tried to find a cure at various resorts in Pistjan. He died in 1829 at the age of fifty-six, the same year in which his first grand-daughter Friederike, named after him, was born. Marie von Ebner-Eschenbach, his second granddaughter, never knew her grandfather, since he died before she was born. But she admired him all her life for the circumspectness with which he had administered Zdislawitz and was grateful to him for the education he had given her mother. The latter had worshiped her father and after his death had continued life on the estate according to his social and ethical principles.

Marie Vockel's husband, Baron Franz Dubsky von Trebomyslic, was a widower seventeen years her senior, and a member of an old, high-aristocratic Moravian family. The Dubsky line can be traced back to the early fifteenth century, before the Thirty Years' War, which wiped out most of Central Europe's archives. In 1406 a Wilhelm Dubsky of Trebomyslic is mentioned as the first Earl of the royal Moravian Castle of Karlstein. In 1576 another Wilhelm Dubsky married a Moravian aristocrat. He became wealthy and distinguished and was ennobled in 1608. During the Thirty Years' War the Dubskys were wrongly accused of siding with the Protestant enemies of the Catholic Habsburgs in the Battle of the White Mountain in 1620.

The Habsburgs finally won the fight and expelled the rebels from the country. Many properties were confiscated and given to those who had proved faithful to the victors. The Dubsky properties were turned over to the Jesuits, the initiators of the Counter Reformation in Austria. Still, the Dubskys rose to some prominence again with Baron Ferdinand Dubsky (1650-1721), who was Grand Prior of the Maltese Order and Privy Councillor. He also was the first published writer in the family, defending the rights of the Maltese Order in Latin pamphlets.

Financially the Dubskys were not well off, in spite of their titles. In 1767 Maximilian August Dubsky died in poverty in a Vienna hospital. His brother Johann Carl had to seek refuge in Vienna, and his five sons had to earn a living in the service of an estate administrator. One of these, Franz Karl Dubsky, the great-uncle of Marie von Ebner-Eschenbach, managed to enter the Civil Service, to acquire through marriage the estates of Lissitz and Dirnowitz in Moravia and to be elevated to the rank of Count in 1810. A year later he became county chief of justice in his province (B II 45).

His brother, Baron Johann Nepomuk Dubsky (1752-90), Marie von Ebner-Eschenbach's paternal grandfather, became a translator of oriental languages on General Laudon's staff. He translated Kadi Omer Effendi's Turkish report of the campaign in Bosnia (1737-39). This soldier-diplomat-translator was married to Johanna von Moskop of Koblenz, the descendant of an ennobled family of civil servants. When he died at age thirty-eight he was survived by his wife, three sons, and a daughter. They lived in very straitened circumstances, since state pensions were minimal. Helene stayed with her mother until her marriage; her brothers all joined the army. The oldest, Joseph, died in the Battle of Dresden in 1813, the youngest, Fritz, died in a battle near Parma a year later. Franz Dubsky, Marie von Ebner-Eschenbach's father, was seriously wounded near Cléry (France) and in 1815 had to retire from active military service. Seven years later he married Konradine von Sorgenthal, the daughter of a prominent industrialist in Vienna. She brought the "Rabenhaus" on the Rotenthurm Straße into the marriage as a dowry. She died childless in 1825.

The Napoleonic Wars took their toll of lives and deeply affected the peoples of Europe. The tragedies of the Dubsky family certainly matched the misfortunes of the Vockels. But what characterized all of Marie Ebner's ancestors was their strong will and their determination to survive. They had shown endurance and resilience in the face of adversity and had not given up, but achieved recognition by dint of hard work and dedicated service. Typically, her father said after the death of his second wife: "If the heavens destroy my home I have to see to it that it is rebuilt" (EME II,3).

There is an old Roman saying *Nomen est omen*. The name Dubsky means "of the oaks."[1] The oak is the toughest and strongest of the trees that grow in Central Europe. All her life Ebner-Eschenbach showed some of the strength of the oak, a strength which no doubt she had inherited from her ancestors. She also knew that she owed gratitude to all those relatives and friends who had supported her in her fight for her art. She was aware that writing as such had given her fortitude. It had been therapy in times of trial, a welcome outlet for her agony.

At seventy-five Marie von Ebner-Eschenbach could calmly look back at her life with a sense of accomplishment. She felt proud of her origins, of her genealogical as well as her spiritual roots. She surveyed the events and the people that had helped and hindered her on her way to realizing herself as a writer. She could now confirm in *Meine Kinderjahre*, the galley proofs of which were lying in front of her:

> The healing power of time helped turn to good what appeared wrong-headed at the outset. The harder and the more obstreperous the soil proved to be, in which the tender tree of my art had to take root, the firmer it stood: and the more cruel the failures were that accompanied every step at the beginning of my career, the closer grew the covenant between myself and my much-contested talent. (851)

She had fought bravely like her soldier ancestors, and she had finally won her battle.

NOTE

1. I received this information from Dr. Eva Kushner, former President of Victoria University in the University of Toronto. I gratefully acknowledge her help. It is noteworthy that Marie Ebner uses the metaphor of the oak-tree in the context of women's writing. In a letter to the writer and editor Baron Emmerich du Mont, in which she complains about discrimination against women writers, she states: "I stand for it, that every hen in Germany is glad not to have to cackle and that every one who has not been relieved from cackling thinks: 'If only it had never sung to me in your leaves, you blessed oak.' But it did sing, the call did take place, and the hen has to follow it" (B II 277).

PART ONE

CHILDHOOD AND YOUTH (1830-1848)

"Fate hammers us either
soft or hard; it depends on
the material"

CHAPTER 1:

"FOR THIS LITTLE GIRL THERE WAS NO MIDDLE ROAD"

The year 1830 was marked by agitation and insurrection in Europe. In the wake of the July Revolution in Paris peoples of various nations started to rebel against feudal laws and demanded the right to self-government. Metternich's Restoration Period was coming to an end, and the Austrians, encouraged by the example of the Belgians, the Poles, and the Italians who had revolted against absolutist regimes, likewise began to oppose a system that held them in political and intellectual captivity. Freedom from censorship and the right to self-determination were no longer seen as merely abstract ideals.

On September 13 of that very year, on the Moravian estate Zdislawitz, a girl was born who would highly value her freedom and would empathize all her life with people craving justice and autonomy. This girl would one day use her narrative talent to describe the fate of those who were oppressed, and she would admonish her peers to adapt to the changing reality in order to avoid the demise of the Austrian aristocracy.

Marie Dubsky von Trebomyslic was named after her mother who died sixteen days after Marie's, her second daughter's, birth. In her semi-autobiographical story "Die erste Beichte" Ebner-Eschenbach later described herself as "sickly and feebly born and during baptism Father Joseph thought her life would slip away under his blessing hand" (465). Marie Dubsky, née Vockel, had been the soul of Zdislawitz, the country estate where she had grown up, and which she had inherited from her father. She had cared for the staff of the manor and for the villagers as for a large family. In return they adored her and mourned her deeply when she died at the young age of twenty-nine (MK 750).

A life-size portrait of Marie Vockel adorned the room of "Großmutter Vockel," the stepmother of the deceased, and those who had known her kept reminding her daughter, little Marie, of the love and respect her mother had commanded. From the painting by Agricola, a well-known portraitist of the time, Marie sensed how beautiful and astute her mother was. "The lovely face suggests deep peace; the brown eyes have an alert and intelligent expression and they radiate the mild light of a mind that is as clear as it is profound" (MK 750). Moritz von Ebner-Eschenbach, her nephew, mentions in his memoirs: "I remember the delight with which I listened to her limpid piano-playing, her attractive voice, and I recall the precious evenings, when she read to me stories and fairy tales" (EME I,2).

Admiring her mother and hearing her admired by everyone who knew her, little Marie strove to be like her, to look like her, to be loved like her. All her life Marie thought of her name as being a bond with her late mother, whom she never got to know personally but with whom she kept a close spiritual relationship.[1] In her autobiography *Meine Kinderjahre* she later wrote: "We had been given to understand that she would keep watch over us from heaven and that she would be with us in hours of sickness or danger. I will never forget with what confidence and what mysterious bliss the awareness of her presence often filled me" (750/51). How close she felt to her is also revealed in "Die erste Beichte," where the protagonist, closely modeled after the author, treasures "a golden necklace that once belonged to her mother" (477) as her highest good and plans to leave this world in order not to sin any more and to be united with her in heaven.

For Marie her late mother would always be the perfect mother and the perfect wife. In her view she was the only one of her father's four wives to whom he had truly felt congenial and who had really understood how to deal with him. In *Meine Kinderjahre* she would later claim: "She lovingly and caringly protected all that was good and noble in him. She pushed the deficiencies of his character back into the shadows and tried to smooth out his rough angles. The years when she was at his side were the crown of his life and he always kept her memory sacred" (770).

Baron Franz Dubsky was devastated when he lost his second wife and was left with his two infant daughters. Had not a relative prevented him he would have committed suicide. He was fortunate in having his mother-in-law, Baroness Vockel, who was willing to move with him into the Drei-Raben-Haus in Vienna and to help him raise his two orphaned girls, Friederike, fourteen months and Marie, the new-born baby. The baroness was devoted to her granddaughters. She was a quiet, intelligent and rather reserved woman, who bore life after her husband's and her stepdaughter's untimely death with a stoic calm. "People called her indifferent. Only those nearest to her knew what that great soft heart had suffered and lost, till it had steeled itself to this external indifference" ("Beichte" 466).

She rarely complained, rarely expressed a concern, but was generous with her praise. Some of her standard phrases, used when the children approached her with their hurts and fears, unfailingly were: "Be still, be reasonable," and "Everything passes, everything will be all right" (MK 752). Her stoicism was probably as much a result of her eighteenth-century upbringing, in which discipline and self-control were highly valued, as of the resignation following the death of the most precious persons she had had. She had seen much imperfection in her life and had come to rather uncomplimentary conclusions about humankind in general. In Zdislawitz "Großmutter Vockel" occupied a room which overlooked the yard with the mausoleum on one side and the fields with the mountain range in the distance on the other. Above her desk was an oil painting of her dog, who had been very close to her. She kept the household accounts and was always seen knitting and crotcheting clothes for her grandchildren and for the poor in the village. She advised her son-in-law in the administration of the estate but was secretly afraid of his hot-tempered and rather violent ways. She tried to help where she could, but never interfered. She became the children's substitute mother, and especially Marie formed a strong bond with her. All the qualities of wisdom, strength, courage and generosity of spirit that Marie would later admire in women were those she had encountered in Großmutter Vockel's character.

Although she did not talk much to her grandmother, Marie always knew that she was a kindred spirit. As she recalled in *Meine Kinderjahre*: "The quiet understanding between grandmother and grandchild strengthened their ties. Hardly ever were fewer words exchanged between two who loved each other, and never did two people understand each other better" (851). When Friederike, called Fritzi, was down with measles one year, the six year old Marie stayed at Großmutter Vockel's apartment on the second floor of the Rabenhaus. In the morning, Marie, awake much earlier than her grandmother, entertained herself by peeling the coating off the wall. She had a marvelous time watching the bubbles burst as they gradually bared the wall, leaving a space "like an ocean on a map" (MK 873). The maid was horrified and outraged when she saw what Marie had done, yet Großmutter Vockel was not perturbed. Her only comment, "[we] will have it repainted" (ibid), showed that she understood children and never made a fuss about their little pranks.

When in 1832 Baron Dubsky decided to remarry, Baroness Vockel worried about her two granddaughters: "Now we would no longer amount to anything . . . we would be set back" (MK 752). She may have feared the same for herself. So far she had been living in the mansion which her stepdaughter had owned and, taking care of her son-in-law's children, she had a position of some authority in the family. A new woman at the head of the household, totally unrelated to her and the family, would jeopardize all that. Fortunately for the children as well as for Baroness Vockel, the new wife did not justify the stereotype of the vicious stepmother.

Maman Eugénie, as the children called her, was a Baroness Bartenstein, a descendant of a family in the vicinity of Zdislawitz, one of whose ancestors, Johann Christoph Bartenstein, a professor's son from Strasbourg, had converted to Catholicism and had become a leading Austrian statesman under Empress Maria Theresia (Siegert, 59). Eugénie was a warm and kind woman who particularly liked children. She bore two sons, Adolph in 1833, Viktor in 1834, and a daughter Sophie, a year later. She treated all her children, including those she had inherited from Baron Dubsky's former marriage, with the same love and understanding.

Marie adored her "much, much loved" (MK 782) Maman Eugénie and vied with her siblings for her affection. Since she had not formed an emotional tie with her biological mother, she accepted Eugénie Bartenstein as her "Maman" and in those years never felt deprived of motherly affection and care. In contrast to some of the aristocratic ladies described in Ebner-Eschenbach's work, who seldom saw their children and, preferring their social commitments to childcare, left them totally in the charge of their maids, Eugénie insisted on her children's company. She took them along on her outings to the Prater in Vienna and spent as much time with them as she could. The children in turn were deeply attached and considered it a cruel blow when they had to be separated from her.

In 1836 a cholera epidemic broke out in Moravia. Many people in and around Zdislawitz caught the disease, and many lost their lives. Dr. Engel, the Jewish doctor, together with Father Borek, the Catholic parish priest, worked indefatigably to save lives and to comfort the bereaved. Baron Dubsky established a soup kitchen in his courtyard, where the villagers came together to get their meals. Despite precautions, Eugénie and the two-year-old Viktor caught the disease and had to be separated for weeks from the rest of the family. In *Meine Kinderjahre* Ebner-Eschenbach recalls the joy she felt when one day the nursemaid came running into the yard to tell the children to look up at the window of the nursery, which had been transformed into a sickroom, where they would see a surprise. "It was easy to guess what

that would be. The little one! The little one—and perhaps even Mama!
. . . It was a miracle that our longing did not pull us up to them as if
with ropes" (807).

Baron Dubsky, just then coming out of the house with Dr. Engel,
saw the joy in the faces of his children and gratefully embraced the
family doctor, who had saved the two patients. Having lost many loved
ones in his life, Baron Dubsky must have been particularly relieved
about his wife's and his son's recovery. But he did not often show his
affection. He considered the exhibition of love a sign of sentimentality,
usually preferring to appear in the role of the stern and distant authority,
whose command everyone in the family had to obey. Fritzi and Marie
especially feared their father who, due to his explosive irritability, could
hold the whole family in a state of constant apprehension. He seldom
saw the children, except in the morning when they were taken to his
study by the nursemaid to greet him with a curtsy and a handkiss.
According to aristocratic tradition he left the upbringing of his children
to nursemaids, governesses and tutors and saw himself as the ultimate
authority in the family, imbued with absolutist and patriarchal notions
of manhood and fatherhood.

The military school, which he had entered as a very young man,
and the battlefields, where he had received his decisive character
formation, may have helped him to develop "the manly virtue of
justice," for which his daughter Marie would later praise him (MK 769),
but it did nothing to enable him to relate to his children.

> The hot-blooded man, the brave Austrian officer, who
> had spent his youth in warfare, had retained his
> soldierlike and rather violent attitude also in civilian
> life. "You need not love me but you should fear me,"
> were the words which his subjects often heard from
> him. He did not ask whether his children loved him.
> He considered it his children's duty to love their
> parents, and it was understood that his children would
> do their duty. (MK 466)

To Marie her father appeared as a tyrant with whom she had a
relationship resembling that of the Russian Tsar to his subjects. While
he had unlimited power, they had to submit to him unconditionally (MK
765). Amiable as he could be in his benevolent moments, he was
terrible in his incomprehensibly easily provoked anger, and the children

were terrified by him (MK 757). Baron Dubsky was also known for his unpredictability. In *Meine Kinderjahre* Marie von Ebner-Eschenbach reports an incident where her older sister Fritzi had broken a window-pane while playing ball.

> "Here comes Papa, Papa," she cried in mortal fear, kneeling down on the floor, wringing her little hands, folding them and sobbing that it rent one's heart . . . She was already turning blue in her face, her breath came out in little bursts, tears flowed like rivulets down her cheeks. (757)

Her grandmother had obviously intervened with the dreaded father, for when he came in, he picked Fritzi up, tried to console her and, to everybody's surprise, smashed another window in order to demonstrate how little he cared for the broken glass. "Papa was dancing around with his little daughter in his arms, and we cheered him and shouted for joy" (758). But if Marie thought she had understood her father's logic, she was mistaken. The next day she felt emboldened to smash an old much-detested coffee pot, in the hope that Papa would throw the equally hated milk jug after it. It did not work that way. Instead of Papa's support, Marie received severe punishment from Pepinka, the nursemaid.

As much as Marie abhorred her father's fierce moods, his aggressive and sometimes even abusive ways, she also admired him for his courage. During a cattle drive one of the bulls separated from the herd and began furiously to run about the farmyard. Everyone jumped for cover—but not Count Dubsky. He fearlessly faced the animal, sternly admonishing it: "You, here!" The bull accepted the command of someone who obviously possessed authority, and it trotted back to the herd (MK 769).

Marie also enjoyed her father's stories and anecdotes from the Napoleonic wars, especially the story of the generous Frenchman who had given him his own coat for protection against the cold (MK 768). As a storyteller Baron Dubsky could fascinate all the children, especially Marie, who appreciated this gift of his the most. In her collection of diary entries "Aus einem zeitlosen Tagebuch" she later preserved an anecdote of her father that must have been among her favorites: A businessman had sent to his brother a particularly beautiful and intelligent parrot from Australia. Upon his return to Austria he asked his brother and family how they had liked the bird, whereupon he received the reply: "It was a bit tough." Amazed and shocked the businessman inquired: "For heaven's sake, you did not cook and eat it? It spoke fourteen languages." His brother, somewhat abashed, retorted: "Why, then, did it not say something?" (725/6).

Baron Dubsky, an excellent equestrian himself, also taught his children to ride and to hunt. Marie learned from him how to treat the horses in the stables of Zdislawitz and she became a passionate rider. She also went hunting with her father but never really cared for it, for she loved animals too much to see them killed. The protagonist of "Komtesse Paula," who talks about her outings with her father, echoes Marie's feelings: "We take long rides together; formerly we used to go hunting together, and he was pleased when I shot a rabbit—more than I was. As far as I am concerned, all rabbits can stay alive at the expense of the young nursery plants and the cabbages" (Harriman 49). In the same story the father emerges as a man the protagonist thinks "frightfully dear" and whose tyranny makes her suffer. Time and again Paula refers to her "fear of her beloved father," a theme that is repeated throughout Ebner-Eschenbach's work.

Marie's dread of her father changed from being afraid of his punishment in younger years, to being afraid of his outbursts of temper when she was an adult, but the dread of him remained. This ambivalent relationship with her father, consisting of love and fear, affected Marie so much in her childhood that it took her all her life to come to terms with it. Writing became a means of analyzing her father and her feelings towards him, feelings that gradually changed from anger and reproach to pity for the man who had once bullied his whole family, and who had in the end become lonely and dependent.

In her 1875 story "Die erste Beichte," written shortly after her father's death, Marie von Ebner-Eschenbach accuses her father of authoritarianism, arrogance, suspicion, and lack of understanding. In her 1889 novel *Unsühnbar* she has the protagonist excuse her authoritarian and arrogant father by saying: "The strong man was helpless in the grip of his passions. Was that not reason enough to pity him?" In her 1901 story "Die Reisegefährten" she has the narrator say about a father who had terrorized his family:

Today he appears to me in a somewhat mellower light
than then . . . Just as repugnant, but less loathsome.

> He was actually not an evil man, he did not oppress
> his peasants, did not mistreat his servants. He was
> deceitful, narrow-minded and egotistical . . .
> Wherever he showed up, there was nothing but him,
> no other individuality found due recognition, everyone
> lost his right to be his own self. (Harriman 110)

In her 1903 story "Die arme Kleine" the father who has never much cared for, nor tried to understand his children, is pitied by his dying son: "We did not love Papa enough. He is good, much better than we knew" (754). Finally, in *Meine Kinderjahre*, Ebner-Eschenbach, while still admitting her father's character flaws, goes out of her way to portray his virtues and strengths: "What was lacking was balance and a perception for the emotional life even of those who were closest to him. However, in the final analysis, he was a man with a warm heart, strong in body and mind" (770).

Having been deeply influenced by this hot-tempered, authoritarian father in her formative years, it is no wonder that Marie later modeled many of her male characters after him. Her stories abound with despotic and irascible men who tyrannize their wives and children. Her father's character emerges in many literary figures and some even have his physique. In "Die erste Beichte" she mentions her father as having thick short hair "which stood upright on his head like a brush and which grew into a sharp point in the middle of his brow" (469) making him appear extremely strict and fear-inspiring. In "Maslan's Frau" the medical doctor has the same kind of hair growing onto his forehead (455), and in "Glaubenslos" Leo Klinger's father has a similar physique and also resembles Baron Dubsky in his attitude to his fellow men:

> His iron-colored hair grew deep into the low and flat
> brow, the dark gray eyes looked sullen and haughty.
> The corners of the mouth were drawn down and sur-
> rounded by an expression of invincible pigheaded-
> ness. Against the assertions or orders which fell from
> these lips, an inferior or a weak person would hardly
> have dared to object. (290/1)

No wonder then, that Baron Dubsky's authority was regularly evoked by Pepinka, the Czech nursemaid, when she feared losing control over the five Dubsky children. When they behaved badly they were simply told "Wait, I'll tell your father and then you'll see" (MK 757) — a threat which, given the baron's penchant for losing his temper, must have amply fulfilled its purpose. The fiery, black-eyed maid, known outside the nursery room as Josefa Navratil, was for the children the "goddess of fate" (MK 753). She kept her world in order with a strong and well-aimed hand and did not shy away from physical punishment when she thought it appropriate. Little Marie calmly accepted what she called a *demonstratio directa* (MK 752). She respected Pepinka's authority and agreed with the maxim that a wicked deed had to be followed by punishment, a principle she would later also advocate in her work.[2]

In her autobiography Marie Ebner remembers that once a year Pepinka, called "Pepi," was bled by the village barber. The children, not knowing what it meant, were always struck with great horror because the next day their maid would invariably have a bandaged arm, but would never explain what had happened. How much affection Marie had for her nursemaid can be seen from the many loving descriptions of maids in her work, most prominently the portrayal of the eponymic heroine of *Bozena*, her first major work. Like Pepinka, Bozena Ducha is a strong, simple-minded character and a dedicated mother figure, dearly loved by the child in her care. In spite of the fear which Pepi must have instilled in the children's heart, they dearly loved her. Marie maintained lifelong contact with her, and even supported her financially in her old age. On October 3, 1866 Ebner-Eschenbach wrote in her diary:

> Called on old Pepi in Kremsier. She has become very old, small and frail —"shrunken" the Viennese say—but she does not look ill. My visit made her happy and her joy did me good. The poor, poor old woman. She can barely make ends meet. She lives with her son Aloys in a small ground-floor room; two beds, a table, two chairs are all that she possesses by way of furniture. I will not wait another four weeks before sending her something. (TB I 121)

Upon learning of Pepi's death in September 1868, she entered in her diary: "Death of our old nursemaid Pepi: with the loyal old woman a part of our childhood has been buried; her care and loyalty have not been adequately appreciated, neither by us nor by her own child" (TB I 235).

If Pepinka represented Tyche in Marie's early universe, Anischa, Marie's wet nurse, represented the Muses. She was "the bright star of our nursery, always friendly and good to us" (MK 753). Marie mentions Anischa's prettiness and her fondness for fine dresses, but more than that she stresses her admiration for two incomparable qualities: Anischa was the children's refuge and consolation in all their woes and tribulations, and she was a fascinating storyteller. She ignited the spark of Marie's imagination, making her aware of the uncanny realm of the mysterious: "O what a storyteller our Anischa was—she understood how to describe, to build up tension, to portray clearly and vividly the creations of her fantasy, to let them arise, float by and disappear" (MK 754).

Remembering the rich delights experienced through Anischa's wonderful stories, Marie von Ebner-Eschenbach in old age laments the deprivation of children for whom fairy tales are banned "on principle," as it often must have been the case in the progressive, science-oriented, late nineteenth century. In contrast, at the tender age of four, Marie learned "to see and hear what others do not hear and see"—the voice of the "water sprite in the gargling sounds of a spring, the rushing of elves in the rustling of leaves, the flashes of light spirits in the shimmer of wheat fields" (MK 755). Marie must have shown great courage early on. She was chosen by Anischa to hear fairy tales too frightening for her siblings. She became privy to the gruesome exploits of *zla hlava*, a fearful head with bushy hair, a flaming beard, devilish eyes and gigantic ears (MK 756). With determination she declared: "I am not afraid. I do not know what it means to be scared. I have great courage" (MK 756).

Anischa stayed in the Dubsky household till she was married to an imposing young officer who came to visit occasionally. Losing Anischa was Marie's first deep sorrow. She was indignant that the nursemaid had left without saying goodbye and offended that Pepi, by telling her Anischa would soon be back, had lied to her (MK 776). Marie never forgot her beautiful wet nurse who had lovingly shown her the way into the fascinating world of fancy and fairy tale. She made it a point to remain in touch with her by regular correspondence. The maid, unable to write, faithfully replied by dictating her letters to her parish priest.

By way of signature she put a little black cross at the end of her letters
(MK 776).

Marie received her first formal introduction to reading and writing
from Mr. Volteneck, the administrator of the estate of Zdislawitz.

> He had a round figure and a head which seemed
> squashed at the temples, and from a distance he
> looked like a top hat with a small cucumber on it. His
> basic colors were brown and yellow; brown were the
> clever, soft eyes, the artless wig, the area near the
> nose which incessantly asked for snuff, and the tips of
> the fingers, which delivered the aromatic dust. The
> small hands and the small face were yellow. The
> color of this man's soul could only have been the
> most delicate apple-blossom pink. (MK 759)

She had repeatedly heard some malicious gossip about him. Her
description certainly is proof (if such is needed) of the acute powers of
observation which children possess at any age. But she liked her first
teacher. She admired his beautiful handwriting and the many different
scripts he knew. But she made only slow progress in reading under his
tutelage. When, after six months of instruction, her father found out that
she could not yet read, he summoned her for a "test." She failed
miserably, not least of all because she was frightened to death when he
tried to examine her. Although Marie later devoured books, at first she
hated reading because it deprived her of her freedom to roam around in
the park and in the fields of Zdislawitz.

Among upper-class families it was customary to employ a
governess for the girls, once they had outgrown the nursery. She was
supposed to supervise the children's behavior as well as teach some
subjects suitable for young girls, usually French and history. At age five
Marie was given her first French governess, an event which she awaited
with great trepidation. Warned by Pepinka that from now on she would
have to sit still, be quiet all day and stay close to a woman whose
language she would be unable to understand, she went into a panic.
Waiting for this monster of a governess was a nightmare. When
Mademoiselle Hélène Hallé finally arrived, Marie threw a temper
tantrum and had to be carried into the governess' room to greet her.
Fortunately for both, this first impression did not last. Very soon the
young, friendly woman won her charge's heart and was able to exert a

lasting influence on her. In no time Marie considered it a privilege to be with Mademoiselle Hallé, and she and Fritzi were able to speak and read French remarkably fast.

Marie resented that besides reading and learning French she also had to busy herself with needlework. Right from the start she had a strong contempt for what were then deemed womanly skills. To have to sit in a room and knit was for Marie another restriction of her highly valued freedom. While the birds flew from tree to tree and her little brothers and her youngest sister were able to play, she had to spend her time learning what was then considered one of the most important pastimes for women. Her grandmother and all the women in the family regularly busied themselves with needlework, producing garments for the villagers in Zdislawitz. Likewise, women in Ebner-Eschenbach's later fictional work would often be described as knitting in their leisure time. Yet she herself rebelled against this occupation, seeing it as a straitjacket, which not only deprived her of the privilege to roam the countryside, but also of the freedom to use her imagination. Knitting had been recommended for young girls for the very reason of preventing them from indulging in flights of fancy considered unbecoming at the time (Kössler 71).

It was felt that the sooner a girl learned to submit to authority the better for her in later life. Marie knew that lamenting and rebelling against paternal decree was useless. Therefore she also had no say when, after two happy years, Mademoiselle Hallé left the Dubskys to return to France, and a new governess was engaged, who had no interest whatsoever in the children. How much Marie suffered under this "dragon" (MK 777) is recorded in several of her stories. In "Die erste Beichte" Mademoiselle Henriette is rendered as a vain and unrelenting governess whose main concern is to make herself attractive to her employer. She lacks affection for the children entrusted to her care. In "Ein kleiner Roman" the narrator echoes Marie's suffering: "It is diffcult for a child to always have to be together with a person to whom she cannot warm up" (18).

To be forced to spend all day with a woman she hated was a traumatic experience for the seven-year-old girl, an experience which may have taught her to become more reserved with people and distrustful of human relationships. Having by now lost two caregivers to whom she had been deeply attached, she began to withdraw into herself. Later in life she would often be accused of not being open (ZT 730), of not trusting people enough. The seed of this reticence may have been planted in those sad years under the rule of "the dragon." Marie's aversion to her was so strong that one day, when the governess dared to make fun of a concert the Dubsky children had attended, she felt like slapping her face (MK 791). No wonder that governesses in Ebner-Eschenbach's work are mostly described as taking sides against their wards. They stand sentry ("Erste Beichte," "Resel") and give away their charges' secrets of the heart ("Nach dem Tode"). Even as a septuagenarian Ebner-Eschenbach remembered with an aching heart that because of this governess she and her brothers and sisters "learned most thoroughly how profoundly unhappy children can be who consider themselves handed over defenseless to an evil power" (MK 778).

As Marie von Ebner-Eschenbach later recalls in her autobiography, her misery would have been ended had Maman Eugénie not been ill. In the spring of 1837 she had borne a baby girl who died soon after, and Baroness Dubsky never recovered from her confinement. When Marie later thought of her "Maman" one event stood out in her mind, which haunted her so much that she had to mention it in her autobiography. "I was then in my seventh year, and today I am in my seventy-fifth. But when the memory of that hour arises, a reflex of that pain awakes in me, that tore my heart apart as a child" (782). Maman Eugénie, already close to delirium, wrongly accused Marie of lying, and the latter was unable to justify herself, since she had been told by her aunt that the patient "must under no circumstance be excited by any kind of contradiction. The physician had strongly advised it. And so, since I had insisted on coming to her, I would have to accept silently the accusations against me, I would have to ask for forgiveness and then go away" (MK 781).

This unfortunate encounter with her stepmother left a deep and lasting impression on the little girl, an impression which she later translated into fiction. In "Das Schädliche" she has the narrator say about Lore at her mother's deathbed: "It was horrible. The child could not wring a motherly feeling out of her. And when the child clung with passionate tenderness to her and the dying woman looked down upon her with secret horror, it crept up my spine" (617). Lore, who no longer begged and also had given up crying out of "inexpressible bitterness" (617), is a sketch of Ebner-Eschenbach herself.

Marie felt particularly hurt about being called a liar, because she always deeply desired to be honest. Admonished by her father, who called himself a "knight of truthfulness," and who was known in his circles as a man who did not hesitate to speak his mind, Marie likewise tried strictly to cling to the truth. In her essay "Aus meinen Kinder- und Lehrjahren" she describes an incident in which as a child she gave a teacher, who hated steel pens, her word never to use an implement like that again. Unable to fulfill her promise, because her father provided only the very pens her teacher had disdained, Marie suffered qualms of conscience. These were heightened by the fact that the teacher, to whom she had given her word of honor, died at just around this time (Schmidt 271). It is, therefore, not astonishing that many of Ebner-Eschenbach's protagonists, like Bozena and Maria Dornach, to name but a few, have an oversensitized conscience and suffer terribly when unable to reveal the whole truth.

Maman Eugénie's death was a tragedy with sad consequences for the family. Baron Dubsky, shaken by the loss of his third spouse, dropped his usual mask of reserve and strength and cried with his children "like a child" (MK 783). Henceforth deep melancholy would rule the family. While Maman Eugénie had been a warm and cheerful person, Tante Helene, Baron Dubsky's sister, who now took charge of the household, had a tendency to fall into depressions (MK 783). She sacrificed her independence by giving up her own meticulously run household to take charge of her brother's ménage and to help raise his five children.

They, however, were still too young fully to realize the impact of the tragedy that had befallen the family. They wore black clothes, continued their games and only gradually understood what a sad void Maman Eugénie had left behind. In the summer all five went to the crypt in Zdislawitz to pray for the departed who had been buried next to their biological mother (KL 273). Marie was by now well acquainted with death. She had lost her mother, she had seen many villagers succumb to cholera, her first teacher in Vienna had been taken from her by sudden death, and finally her dearly loved stepmother had left her forever. When Eugénie's new-born baby had died and the "sinister miracle of death" had taken place in the family, the children were told that the deceased would now "belong to the dear God" (KL 273) and would be transformed into an angel in heaven.

All these experiences shaped Marie Ebner's outlook on death and may well have been the reason why she would later claim that she herself was never afraid of dying, of entering into the realm of the omniscient God ("Schattenleben" 464). Her work abounds with people who die or are mentioned as having died before the actual story begins, and especially mothers are often reported as having died, leaving their

young daughters behind to face the struggle of life. Marie von Ebner-
Eschenbach's experience with death has filtered into the story "Der
Fink," in which she describes little Pia who has found a newborn finch
that has fallen from its nest and looks as if it is going to die. "Terrible,
terrible, death is something terrible, and I have it here, feel it . . . A
horror crept over her and she whispered to the bird: 'Don't die, don't die
in my hand'" (Harriman 99). And later, when the bird has safely reached
the tree, where its mother has been anxiously waiting for it, Pia envies
its joy of being reunited with its mother: "She paused suddenly and
looked thoughtfully into the distance and slowly repeated: 'with its mother.' She had not known what that meant. She had been so tiny at the
time . . . but it must be wonderful for a bird—and a child" (Harriman
100).

The longing to join her mother was also one of the subconscious
reasons why Marie once tried to commit suicide. As she later recorded
in the same story, "Der Fink," to be with one's mother meant to be
saved from all foes. After Maman Eugénie's death the presence of the
hated governess, Marie's declared enemy, must have been particularly
painful, causing the seven-year-old girl more than once to have thoughts
of escape from this sad reality.

Father Borek, the parish priest of Zdislawitz, a kind and lenient
man, taught religion twice a week. He also had the task of preparing the
Dubsky girls for their first confession. Marie, taking the absolution
formula quite literally, resolved rather to die than to offend God again.
As we read in *Meine Kinderjahre*:

> Someone who wants to die jumps out of the window
> and this version of fleeing into the Beyond was to be
> mine. That our house had only one story and that my
> fall need not be fatal I did, however, not consider. I
> was removed from the obvious, was floating in
> heavenly spheres, coming close to the presence of
> God, into my mother's open arms. (804)

Yet Marie's "ascension" failed. Instead of jumping out of the window
and being reunited with her mother after her first confession, she
crashed her head against the mullion and fell back into the room. In
"Die erste Beichte" the episode is rendered in the following way: "The
window at which Clary had stood the night before in the sunset was

open; in front of it was a toppled chair and on the floor lay the child, bleeding from a wound on the forehead. She had wanted to throw herself down—and hit the mullion . . . Praise be to whoever protected her" (479).

In this story Ebner-Eschenbach mainly blames her autocratic father for forcing her as a seven-year-old, far too immature child, to make her first confession. She points out that he insisted on women being instructed in religion, a means to teach them obedience and also to protect the feudal *status quo*. Yet in her autobiography Marie von Ebner-Eschenbach puts the blame on herself, a willful child, who caused the good-natured priest much worry. That she was exuberant and rather radical is not only confirmed by her autobiography but also in "Die erste Beichte," where Ebner-Eschenbach portrays herself in the following way: "One thing was certain; for this little girl there was no middle road; she always moved in this or that extreme. Gay abandon or dark melancholy, dull indifference or a veritable melting with love, incompetence to understand the most simple things and surprising insight into difficult matters . . ." (465). Edinek, the orphan boy of "Unverbesserlich," is likewise "always ready to rush headlong into extremes" (196) and shares with his author the devotion to a parish priest: "full of contradictions as he might have been, in one thing he never changed, in his affection for the pastor" (185).

Marie loved Father Borek and felt even more attached to him after the near-fatal accident. She tried to please him, to make good for the many lapses of attention during catechism classes. She also attended the little village church in Hostiz with special devotion and awe. It fascinated her to observe Father Borek celebrate mass. She studied his every movement and then played at celebrating mass at home with her sister Fritzi in attendance as server. Father Borek was, however, not amused when once invited to such an event (MK 803). The priest may very well have considered Marie an intruder into a sphere where women had no right. Little did he know that by adopting the role of a priest she symbolically anticipated her future career. As a writer she later always considered herself as having priestly responsibilities, a thought she also expressed in her aphorism "An artist—a priest" (Reclam 53). From childhood on Marie was more at home in the male world, preferring racing with her brothers in the park of Zdislawitz to sitting by herself in the house, tied down to feminine occupations.

When her brother Adolph was six and Viktor five they were given a French tutor, M. Just Dufoulon, who soon became a member of the family and was treated by the children like an older brother and playmate. Marie had a special affection for him, making it a point to compete with him in sports and games. When he beat her in their races her pride was hurt so much that even in old age she vividly recalls her antipathy to "male superiority, painfully felt for the first time" (Schmidt 129).[3] She loved to imagine herself as Atalanta, the beautiful, swift-footed girl, who was superior to most men (MK 703). Marie's relationship with "Monsieur Just," who in her view sometimes treated her like "a silly child," has been recorded with modifications in "Die arme Kleine," where Elika experiences her first love for Levin Bornholm, the owner of Valahora, who seems to consider her a "stupid little child" (744).

Much to the sorrow of the children, M. Just had to leave the Dubskys a few years later and tragically died soon afterwards in France of typhoid fever. He had been his widowed mother's only child. Upon learning of their beloved friend's death, Marie and Fritzi went to a ravine where, next to a spring believed to have miraculous powers, a wooden statue of St. Anne had been placed on an old beech tree. There M. Just had once carved his name, and now the children, eager to show their affection, put a little cross beside it as a sign of their loving memory.

Thus Marie lost another loved one through death. From an exuberant, vehement, prankish child she gradually developed into a contemplative girl, susceptible to pain and sorrow and often given to melancholy and pessimism. A few years earlier she had already begun to create her own imaginary world, a dream world into which she could escape when reality around her became too harsh. Once she had conquered her initial horror of those black letters whose meaning she could not grasp at first, she turned into a voracious reader. History began to fascinate her. It was especially the *Histoire universelle* by Louis Richard which became an endless source of joy and inspiration to her (MK 785). With great enthusiasm she memorized the fables of La Fontaine and immersed herself in various French poems. Yet her greatest delight were the fairy tales of the late eighteenth-century French moralist Charles Perrault, who became a major influence. He considered fairy tales "seeds that one throws out, which first bring forth the emotions of joy and sadness, but which inevitably bloom later in the form of feelings" (Barchilon 120). He concludes his story "Peau d'Âne" (Donkey Skin) with the following admonition: "Teach children that they should suffer the worst of troubles rather than fail in accomplishing their moral duties, that the righteous path can bring about much misfortune but eventually it crowns the virtuous with success" (Barchilon 68). Marie must have been deeply impressed by it, because she later advocated these very tenets in her work.[4] From Perrault she also may have learned the importance of lively and dramatic dialogue as a means to arouse the readers' empathy.

On Sundays after mass, when Großmutter Vockel read in her devotional books, Marie was perched on top of two chairs, meant to look like a chariot, and dreamed about the heroes and heroines of her favorite fairy tales. As she recalls in *Meine Kinderjahre*: "Sometimes, when there was prolonged silence in my corner, grandma turned to me and asked: 'Are you still there? What are you doing?' Apparently I did nothing. In reality I had just killed a dragon or had thrown stepmother Grognon into a vat filled with poisonous snakes" (787). In those blissful hours, when her grandmother's presence gave her the security to fly away on the wings of her fantasies, Marie felt that she belonged to the same universal order as the heroes and heroines with whom she identified. All her desires, fears and hopes found expression in this world, a world where she could develop her personality. Her memory of this happy time is reflected in the description of Elika of "Die arme Kleine" who, like herself, loves history and fairy tales (661-662).

Dreaming about heroic adventures and creating a world of her own would remain Marie's lifelong occupation. For quite a while she believed that she was surrounded by a void and that she created reality only when looking at the objects around herself.[5] She wanted to test reality: "I ran, as fast as I could, into the garden up to the fence and there, quick as lightning, I turned round . . . But everything had by then been put again into place, the shrubs, the trees, the flowerbeds and the meadows. My eyes were always too slow, they were always late" (MK 798-799).

When the sixty-two-year-old Ebner-Eschenbach wrote her prose poem "Schattenleben" she had gained the conviction that "everything is, except the void" (464). But she still had a strong desire to dream and to step out of reality to become an onlooker at her life as the shadow of herself. Daydreaming did not mean the idle wandering of the mind, which her family so much condemned, it signified wish fulfillment, reminiscing, pondering and artistically creating a world where personal problems and psychological conflicts could be solved.[6] In *Meine Kinderjahre* she writes:

> Sometimes I took bold decisions. If people do not really exist, if I just imagine them, I will imagine them as they ought to be, so that I can get along with them . . . I will imagine a Papa of whom I am not frightened, a governess who does not torture me. I then approached my imagined father and a Mademoiselle Henriette, who in my imagination consisted of boundless friendliness and love, with such uninhibited confidence that it provoked irritated astonishment and resulted in many a punishment for me. (MK 798)

By creating this dream world Marie was able to cope with her life. Her fantasy transported her to a place "beyond the mountains and a big ocean" (MK 798). There she also fashioned her first literary figures, men like gods and women like fairy queens and, most of all, children whose privilege it was to be "perfectly free like young foals on boundless pastures" (MK 798). All the freedom Marie herself was missing, all the emotions she could not vent on the people around her she invested in her imaginary characters. She had found a place where she could be herself. She lived in her characters, she identified with them (MK 799).[7]

Soon Marie not only invented her characters but also began a correspondence with them. From the start, writing had been great fun for her. Like a boy playing with his tin soldiers, she dealt with her letters, carefully lining them up in rows. She also fabricated little notebooks into which she entered her daily observations (Schmidt 127). Indefatigably she wrote miniature epistles, greeting her imaginary friends and congratulating them on the carefree life they were able to spend in her fantasy land.[8] Over and over she copied and recopied those letters and finally entrusted them to the wind.

> I was always sure to find the envoy there who would take and deliver my messages. It was most beautiful when there was a strong wind . . . With delight I

> entrusted my paper messenger-pigeons to the storm. I held them up and was happy when they were torn away and then appeared just as little white dots in the sunshine . . . They flew and flew—and my thoughts traveled with them. (MK 800)

She never told anyone in the family about this correspondence, out of fear of ridicule from those who were closest to her but understood her the least. "Perhaps I was guided by an undetermined fear, or a doubt, a put-down, which would have shaken the filigran edifice of my dreams or would have darkened its sheen, even if with a breath" (MK 800). She had discovered herself and instinctively knew that she had to withdraw into a dream world in order to gain strength and to preserve her identity.

CHAPTER 2:

"ONLY A GIRL"

When Marie was nine she and Fritzi were occasionally taken to the Karl Theater, where her father had a box. The playhouse, located in the Leopoldstadt, a suburb of Vienna, had been founded in 1781 by Karl Marinelli as Leopoldstädter Theater. In 1845 it was remodeled by Karl Bernbrunn and reopened under the name Karl Theater. It became one of the most popular stages in Vienna, due to its much-appreciated comic repertoire and its outstanding actors (Nadler 300). Long before inviting the girls to actual performances, Baron Dubsky had often told them about his favorite comedy writer, Ferdinand Raimund, and about one of his most beloved protagonists Herr Rappelkopf. Of Raimund's works Marie liked best the *Mädchen aus der Feenwelt*, a play which stimulated her to start writing for the stage. "Totally intoxicated I came home; the direction in which my fantasy would henceforth stretch its wings was decided. I became inexhaustible in inventing theater pieces . . . " (MK 809).

Ever since her first governess, Mademoiselle Hélène Hallé, had taught her French, Marie had written French verses, and even after her teacher had left the family, she had continued to compose her poetry in this language. The letters Marie had entrusted to the wind for her imaginary friends beyond the mountains were also in French and now, after composing hymns to the Virgin Mary, she invented French stage plays to be performed at her home with her sister and some playmates. In *Meine Kinderjahre* Marie von Ebner-Eschenbach records that she once played the part of a wrathful uncle who later revealed himself as a harmless, warm-hearted man. She amused her audience with her temper tantrums but unwittingly caused paroxysms of laughter when she tried to portray him as a touching old man (810).

Soon, however, the other children tired of these plays, and Marie, the initiator of the performances, was again left alone with her little notebooks to which she confided her verses. "My theater pieces, thought out in bright enthusiasm, shared the fate of my poems—nobody wanted to listen to them. Thus my little copybooks became once more my only confidants" (MK 811).

For a while she kept quiet about her poetic endeavors, but she needed an understanding audience and hoped to find it in her older sister. Yet Fritzi also proved a disappointment. As long as Marie had memorized someone else's poetry, she thought it beautiful, but as soon as she learned that her sister was actually reciting her own verses, she

found her "queer," entreating her to give up this "strange" occupation
(MK 808). As Ebner-Eschenbach records in her autobiography: "I
believe that a dark suspicion told her that to make verses was a
dangerous thing which one should better not attempt. She never asked
me to recite my poems a second time and anxiously avoided every
discussion" (808).

Still, Marie always remained very close to her sister.
Notwithstanding Fritzi's lack of enthusiasm for Marie's poetic
outpourings she remained her best friend, perhaps because she
complemented her temperament. Fritzi was beautiful, shy, timid,
submissive, accomplished in the skills expected of a young lady, and
usually did what Marie wanted her to do. In spite of strong misgivings
Fritzi had "celebrated" mass with Marie that time as her faithful
attendant (MK 803). The two had often played with dolls together and
once, suspecting that these dolls had been stolen by a woman in the
neighborhood, they tried to throw ink at the presumed thief from their
window (MK 774).

Yet the two girls, being so close in age, were also rivals. In *Meine
Kinderjahre* Ebner-Eschenbach admits that she was not "as beautiful
and radiant" as Fritzi (MK 565) and that her sister, a much better
student in virtually all the academic and artistic subjects, received much
higher marks for her conduct and achievements. But Marie, by nature
competitive, soon tried to establish her own identity over against her
sister. After a much loved governess, Marie Kittl, had left the family
and the two girls still hoped she would soon return, Marie decided that
if Fritzi would show her joy and relief, she would pretend indifference,
in spite of her perhaps even more burning desire to be reunited with the
departed teacher (MK 844).

By measuring herself against her sister, Marie found out what she
was *not*: she was not compliant, not submissive, not interested in typical
"womanly skills," and not timid. The "de-identification" worked,
because Marie found her true self in the process without disrupting the
bonds of blood and affection that tied her to her siblings.

As Fritzi and Marie grew older, the differences in their characters
became more sharply defined and each reacted in her own way to the
experiences of everyday life. But they always remained close friends.
Later, when Fritzi was married to Count August Kinsky, a member of
a very prominent Moravian family, and living on her estate in
Bürgstein, she attended performances of her sister's plays in nearby

Prague and kept her informed about their reception. Marie regularly visited Fritzi and helped out when her children were ill. Her diary entries of these visits reveal how close the sisters were also in later life. Once Ebner-Eschenbach confided: "My sister Fritzi is a saint. Claudius once said 'I have never known a saint who was a good person.' He did not know my sister Fritzi" (TB I 196).

As a ten-year-old girl Fritzi, however, may have been jealous when she realized that the younger sister could compose beautiful verses, a talent denied to her. As the oldest of the Dubsky children she may have tried to surpass Marie and may have believed she could claim seniority rights. After the birth of Maman Eugénie's last child the two girls vied for possession of the infant. Fritzi felt that she should own the baby, because she was the older of the two (KL 273).

Fritzi also knew that her family did not appreciate Marie's writing poetry. If her friend Fannie's mother allowed her to write stage plays and was even proud of her daughter's talent, in the Dubksy family things were different. Aristocrats generally thought little of people who indulged in composing verses, and her father especially abhorred people who had an intellectual bent. In the preliminary sketch to her autobiography Marie von Ebner-Eschenbach later admitted: "He was a decided enemy of all book learning and he lived in the belief that it was lurking behind the door when one took a book in hand, ready to jump at any moment, turning a practical person with common sense into a stupid scholar" (Schmidt 130). He wanted his daughters to be educated in the accomplishments befitting their station and to later on make a desirable marriage.

Fritzi therefore implored her sister to stop writing poetry (MK 811). As much as Marie tried to deny herself and to pray for release from her creative urge, her longing to make her mark as a professional writer increased. One winter Sunday after mass, when Marie was with her grandmother at the Rabenhaus, she confessed that she wanted to devote her life to writing (MK 813). She told Großmutter Vockel that she wrote poetry and that she aspired to a professional writing career. The result was as unexpected as it was devastating. Baroness Vockel, usually calm and lenient, interrupted her, made it clear that she was bitterly upset and told her granddaughter to leave the room. In her eyes it was a sin to want to do something that was not in keeping with traditional aristocratic convention. Marie never understood why her grandmother had become so angry, why she had treated her as if she had done a great wrong.

Baroness Vockel's behavior showed the extent to which aristocratic prejudice against women's literary endeavors had taken root. In her circles writing poetry and publicizing it was not considered respectable. If an aristocratic woman tried to do so by flouting the rules, strict measures had to be taken. The baroness may have believed, as many did in her time, that women who busied themselves with intellectual occupations ran the risk of becoming barren. Another notion was that women who wrote professionally were considered almost like whores, who sold themselves with their publications. For an aristocrat exhibition in public life was considered a strict taboo, a severe offense against the code.

When Baroness Vockel grew up in the eighteenth century, the majority of women were excluded from higher learning and were relegated to the home and the religious sphere. Her life had been spent looking after her family, knitting for the poor, helping her husband and later also her son-in-law with the administration of the estate. On Sundays she had read and still did read in her devotional books. That her little granddaughter wanted to deviate from this lifestyle must have appeared to her like a crime. She further may have feared that Marie might not marry, another great wrong in the eyes of an aristocrat, to whom the propagation of the family was of the utmost importance. She knew that the aristocracy could only remain intact if its women behaved traditionally and assumed the role of wife and mother. Finally, the baroness may have been shocked to find out that Marie had other than "normal" womanly interests. She knew that this would entail suffering in a society that largely denied women's individuality and placed the highest importance on their reproductive function. A woman who broke out of her conventional role ran the risk of being ostracized.

Seeing her grandmother's indignation, Marie felt stigmatized and desolate. In her anguish she turned to God for help: "If only heaven would have pity on me and deliver me from this sinfulness, or whatever it might be. Deliver me, deliver me! I cried to the Almighty, and to Him and my most loyal friend, my sister, I was looking for help in my confusion, which came quite close to despair" (MK 814). Yet Fritzi did not cooperate. She anxiously begged Marie not to talk about her "problem" anymore, hoping it would vanish. She, like Großmutter Vockel, now began to consider Marie's urge to write as an incorrigible evil.

Ebner-Eschenbach's memory of this tragic time may be revealed in the description of Edinek of "Unverbesserlich," where Emanuel, the priest, tells him that there is no such thing as an "it." He insists that human beings have a free will and are able to master their nature. Edinek, overcome with remorse, concedes: "It may be true, people may be right to call me a son of hell . . . It may be the case, the damned thing which compels me must be the devil" (196). Like Edinek, Marie could not deny her nature. "It" did not disappear. She had to accept it as her fate. Gradually she saw herself chosen by God for martyrdom from which she derived strength and a certain vanity. From now on she wrote secretly, creating her own imaginary world. The self that was denied her by her family came to life through her writing. Henceforth she would lead a double life.

In 1841 the fifty-seven-year-old Baron Dubsky married for the fourth time. His bride was Xaverine Kolowrat-Krakowsky, a descendant of an old aristocratic family and twenty-four years his junior. Großmutter Vockel and Tante Helene had been apprehensive when learning about his engagement and obviously were not happy about Baron Dubsky's choice of a wife. When he had asked the children how they would like a new mother, Marie, shocked and frightened, spontaneously burst out: "Don't bring us a new mother, we don't need one" (MK 820).

The first reception Countess Xaverine Kolowrat-Krakowsky was accorded when she and her mother introduced themselves to the Dubskys was decidedly cool. Großmutter Vockel excused herself from the meeting. Tante Helene, bravely holding the fort, gave them a lukewarm welcome, but the relationship between the three ladies remained within the confines of bare courtesy. Toward the children the new stepmother did not show any special friendliness (MK 821). Fritzi's reaction to the first encounter was: "If only there were not *five* of us!" (MK 821). She intuitively knew that her father's new wife would not find it easy to relate to so many adopted children. After the wedding in Vienna, Baron Dubsky brought his bride to Zdislawitz—following a two-days drive under extremely bad weather conditions. The Countess, not used to her new husband's temper, experienced the first taste of his intemperate and insensitive ways. She aroused his anger, because she feared driving in the dark on drenched dirt roads and screamed when the horses were stuck in the mud (MK 826). Countess Xaverine's arrival in tears was a bad omen. Not only the trip from Vienna to Zdislawitz at Baron Dubsky's side—honeymoons were not the fashion in those days—but her whole life with him was to be marked by quarrels and bitterness. The children, long used to Tante Helene's depression, now had to adjust to their stepmother's unhappiness.[9] They often found her in tears. She suffered from homesickness and from various difficulties endemic to her position (MK 826).

As it later turned out the spouses were incompatible. Their relationship echoes through the story "Der Herr Hofrat," where the protagonist's marriage had been a battle "from the start."[10]

> Two equally strong individuals were facing each other and fought for the same right, the right to develop according to their own, innermost law . . . The hours of warm tenderness were followed by days of resentment, of rebellion. Be different! he demanded of her, she of him, don't blame what I admire and don't ridicule what I adore . . . There were soft hours when love spoke: "Bend down, accommodate, deny yourself." And it happened, but at the expense of sincerity; it was a lie and the price was too high, the lie had its revenge. The quarrel became ever meaner and uglier. (458-459)

How much Marie suffered on account of her parents' marital rows and her father's irksomeness is revealed in the diaries she wrote in the 1860s. Time and again she pitied her stepmother, whose nerves suffered badly in her unhappy marriage. On April 24, 1865 we read: "Poor mother! She was asleep when I called on her before noon. How tired she is, how she suffers! Her nerves have been excessively sinned against" (TB I 45). On March 14, 1867 she writes: "(I stayed) all day long with my parents. Oh, how sad it is there. Poor Papa so restless, poor mother so tired and tormented" (TB I 163). The entry of December 29, 1867 reveals: ". . . poor good mother, she is carrying a heavy cross" (TB I 215). And after Xaverine Dubsky's death in 1869 we learn: "Early in Papa's apartment. I was deeply moved to enter these rooms again. How much our poor mother suffered here! How heartbreaking is the thought of her" (TB I 281). Years later she noticed her brother Viktor's similarity to her father and remarked in her diary: "How he resembles poor Papa: There won't be peace in his house. It will be difficult to feel comfortable at his side if this continues" (TB II 423). The situation in her parents' house was often so bad that Marie hated to go there. No wonder that her work abounds with unhappy couples and with wives whose husbands torment them with their constant quarrelsomeness.[11]

"Mama Xaverine," as she was called by the children, felt superior in rank to the family into which she had married. She slowly transformed the household into one that expressed the values of the social stratum from which she herself had come. She placed great emphasis on social graces, proper entertainment, and the cultivation of the *talents d'agréement*, which she herself possessed. She enjoyed singing and had the older girls accompany her on the piano when she performed French songs. She also painted. Her oil paintings—scenes from the castle and courtyard where she had grown up—delighted the children and served as an inspiration for their own budding drawing skills.

The Countess also introduced changes in the girls' education. The old dance master, Monsieur Minetti, had regularly accompanied them on his guitar when they practiced Spanish dances to entertain their father on his birthday. Now considered old-fashioned, he was replaced by an elegant young French lady who made every effort to teach them manners and the latest of pirouettes. Even as a child Marie hated dancing. Later she avoided the detested balls as best she could. With some sarcasm she recalled the French woman's lessons: "O my young ladies, you must know this well, if you want to possess good manners. Good manners matter a great deal and are almost everything. If Napoleon had had good manners he would have been a very great man indeed" (MK 829).

Dancing was considered a means to shape the female body. The better it was trained the more perfectly a girl's sensitivity was thought to develop (Kössler 48). Countess Xaverine also hired a new piano teacher who, in contrast to the first teacher, Frau Krähmer, introduced a lighter tone, teaching the girls potpourris from operas instead of the all too serious classical music. The time was past when Frau Krähmer hit a trembling Marie's finger with an ivory stick as soon as she played a wrong note (MK 788). But the damage had been done. Treatment like this could hardly turn the children into enthusiastic musicians. Although Marie had a good ear for rhythm and would later enjoy her husband's musical evenings, music never played a prominent part in her life. She seldom went to opera performances and rarely attended concerts. Theater and visits to art galleries were much more important to her. Vienna in her time was the musical center of the world, attracting some of the greatest composers, but we learn little about this in Ebner-Eschenbach's work. We know, however, that in 1847, when the famous singer Jenny Lind performed in Vienna, the young Marie Dubsky attended her concert, after which she received an autograph as well as a kid glove from her as a token of friendship.[12]

When reminiscing in her autobiography about the educational changes her stepmother had effected, Marie von Ebner-Eschenbach sounds rather sceptical, claiming that they had moved from the more solid to the flashy and superficial (828). Yet she gives her stepmother credit for introducing her to literature, especially to German poetry. Anastasius Grün's "Der letzte Ritter," a cycle of poems centering on the Emperor Maximilian I, had a lasting influence on her. "I found this noble poem extraordinarily charming, and if the content formed in my mind only a diffuse picture, the verses penetrated my soul with resounding play and powerful rhythm" (KL 275). Stimulated by Grün, Marie started to compose her own verses and recited them with great pathos, unperturbed by Fritzi's invariable criticism.

Marie also preserved a lifelong gratitude to her stepmother for giving her Schiller's complete works as a present on her twelfth birthday. Receiving the oeuvre of her most venerated poet was for Marie "perhaps the most memorable event" of her childhood (MK 832). Unable to read at first because of sheer excitement, Marie kept her eyes glued to the precious book and, instead of reading it, admired her hero's portrait on the cover. "The appearance so powerful, so full of greatness and strength and the beautiful head bent under the weight of the heavy wreath. Although the luxurious ornament was truly earned, it nevertheless now weighed him down" (MK 833).

When Fritzi saw her sister immersed in such raptures she teased her, remarking ironically: "I bet she thinks that one day she will have such a wreath on her head and stand like this"(MK 833). All her life Marie von Ebner-Eschenbach admired Schiller's work, his style, his themes, his ideals. Through him she became acquainted with "the world," with the working of politics, with conflicts outside the domestic sphere. His ethical values became her own. By him she also saw confirmed what her father had taught her, namely that women's first duty was to obey. Schiller's influence has filtered into "Bettelbriefe," where the countess states: "I did not even know that a woman could have a will of her own. Obedience was taught in the convent, and obedience was demanded by my uncle as my legally appointed guardian. Obedience is a woman's duty, said my adored Schiller" (640).

In 1869, when asked to contribute a work to a Schiller celebration Marie Ebner-Eschenbach gladly obliged. And in old age, when repelled by modern literature because of its seemingly pessimistic and decadent worldliness, she gratefully turned to Schiller, with whose principal values and conceptions of art she had always wholeheartedly agreed.

In 1843 Xaverine Dubsky obtained an Imperial decree conferring the rank of count upon her husband, who by birth had only been a baron. From now on the Dubskys adopted a more aristocratic lifestyle in contrast to their former rather bourgeois way of life and moved in higher social circles. The Countess expected her first child at that time and hired a young nursemaid in place of Pepinka, who had to retire. Fortunately for Marie, her stepmother also employed a new governess after she had learned how much the children had chafed under the regime of Mademoiselle Henriette. With Marie Kittl, the daughter of an Imperial Councillor and the sister of the director of the Prague Conservatory, a very happy time began. In Kittl's presence Marie found the peace and the understanding she otherwise missed in the family. "Like a little Isle of the Blessed the memories of the time, which we then lived through, stand out before me. It was the most beautiful, the most peaceful time of my childhood" (MK 824).

Although physically not as attractive as the former governesses and of a rather stout and dowdy appearance, Marie Kittl, a young woman in her twenties, immediately captured the children's hearts (MK 821-822). She was young enough to seem a comrade and old enough to be a source of counsel, providing a stable basis for the children. Their interest always came before her own. She sang with them, had them recite poetry, took part in their games and watched over them when they were sick and convalescing. Marie felt particularly close to the governess because Kittl understood her literary ambitions. She therefore confided to her all her secret longings. Finally she had found a kindred spirit to whom she could express herself spontaneously and unreservedly, always knowing that she was loved and understood.[13] She could tell her everything and could come to her with all her doubts and worries. Marie Kittl "never used the weapon of derision, which grown-ups are so fond of using against children" (MK 883).

Unfortunately, after only two years, Marie Kittl left the Dubskys, because her father and her brother in Prague had caught typhoid fever and needed her to nurse them back to health. As at the time when Anischa, the nursemaid, resigned, the children were told she would surely come back, yet nothing was further from the truth. The Dubskys, afraid that the governess could spread typhoid in their home, never asked her to return. What upset Marie the most was the fact that her parents had not been honest either. "Did these people not know better than to lie to us and cheat on us? How could they keep us in such suspense and let us live a whole year in the hope of our friend's return, though she had long been torn away from us?" (MK 844). While Marie and Fritzi had still been hoping to see their adored governess again, Marie Kittl had already accepted a position in Paris in the house of Princess Arenberg. Later she became governess, reader and companion at the Belgian court.[14]

Left alone in her family where nobody really understood her, Marie resorted to writing long letters to her confidante. "The correspondence we maintained was for me a support and a staff during an important time of transition. I talked about everything that happened to me, I reported every crazy idea, I received often well-earned admonition and accepted it without demur," Ebner-Eschenbach later recalled in her essay "Aus Meinen Kinder- und Lehrjahren" (276). Marie Kittl learned that her young, ambitious friend intended to be "the Shakespeare of the nineteenth century" (MK 864) and that she was determined "either not to live or to become the most prominent woman writer of all nations and times" (KL 276), a message which filled her with particularly great concern. Yet she wisely never discouraged Marie from writing and even boosted her young charge's ego by affectionately calling her "une petite styliste . . . une jeune personne délicieuse" (MK 852). Marie therefore tried to do her best, even exaggerating her accomplishments, to deserve Marie Kittl's admiration. Years later when reading her letters to her motherly friend Marie von Ebner-Eschenbach felt embarrassed about having boasted so much in order to make herself more interesting (MK 852).

It was the time of puberty, a time when Marie often felt depressed and began to miss her biological mother.[15] She had already lost many loved ones through death or through their dismissal from service in the Dubsky household. She now tried to cling to something stable, something no one could take away from her. Thus she began to focus more on her late mother to whom she had always felt close in spirit. She had experienced how her friend Fanni's mother had encouraged her daughter to write stage plays and to cultivate her creative drive. She had learned that in her family these things were frowned upon, because the Dubskys were members of the aristocracy. She also began to realize how much she longed for her biological mother, who surely would have

sympathized with her urge to write. Something of this longing rever-
berates through *Unsühnbar,* where Maria Dornach says to her late
mother: "You would have been happy with me . . . You would have
known that I only needed to want it in order to become an artist. But
I shall not want to, I must not want to. Someone like us must not do
such a thing. Would you have agreed, mother?" (369).

   Her mother, artistically gifted and intellectually trained by her own
father, would have understood Marie. Had her mother been alive, Marie
would have been spared the loneliness and isolation that she henceforth
experienced more and more. In her letters to her former governess
Marie often expressed her sorrow about not having been raised by her
biological mother. She also felt that she had been destined to become
a martyr (B II 79). Although Marie Kittl tried to comfort her as well as
she could, her young friend continued to crave her mother. In "Ein
kleiner Roman" she later expressed the deep conviction "Nobody on
earth can replace a mother. Nobody!" (9). And in her novella *Margarete*
she claimed that a motherless child cannot even be happy in the
hereafter (136).

   In many of Ebner-Eschenbach's stories and novellas where young
girls lose their mothers, they are deprived of the love and emotional
support which would have made it easier for them to make important
decisions. These girls, as the protagonists of *Bozena, Unsühnbar,*
"Rittmeister Brand" and "Oversberg" are then totally under the control
of tyrannical fathers who exert their patriarchal rights and force them
to succumb to selfish paternal wishes. In "Schattenleben" Marie von
Ebner-Eschenbach refers to her "poor, motherless childhood" (464),
wondering how she could have been so cheerful without any reason.
After Marie Kittl's departure there was no one left in the family in
whom she could confide her deepest longings. The young girl was
painfully aware of the void.

   In later years she visited her former governess who tried to follow
what she thought her true vocation: writing. Marie Kittl had sacrificed
her position, her savings, her reputation for a wrong perception of her
true self. In her autobiography Marie von Ebner-Eschenbach sadly
recalls how her friend, obsessed by her passion to see herself in print,
had published book after book at her own expense, deaf to all
suggestions and admonitions, hoping that the breakthrough to fame
would arrive one day: "She suffered the most bitter fate that I know of:
she carried a burning wish in her soul which could not be fulfilled"

(868). The sad experience regarding Marie Kittl's fixation on writing is reflected in "Wieder die Alte," where Ebner-Eschenbach has Bretfeld say: "Luckily I am not obsessed by the hot and demonic ambition which is often paired with insufficient talent" (107). Such dilettantes are further mentioned in *Bertram Vogelweid,* yet they, in contrast to Ebner-Eschenbach's former governess, listen to reason and their friends' well-meant advice.

Once Marie Kittl had left the Dubskys, a strange procession of governesses moved through Marie's life. A young, well-mannered but extremely vain and lazy Bohemian lady was followed by a kind but uneducated French woman, who in the young girl's opinion "far surpassed me as far as ignorance was concerned" (MK 839). The fate of this governess, whose parents had bequeathed to her and her brother a considerable liability after their death, is reflected in "Wieder die Alte," where Claire endures exploitation by selfish aristocrats in order to pay off her parents' debts.

Since it was the fashion in the Austrian aristocracy to speak English in the context of riding and horse racing, the young countesses had to receive some lessons in this language. Marie Kittl had recommended an Englishwoman who had taught at a college in England and was married to an executive of an English company in Vienna. When Marie and Fritzi learned that the English teacher also tutored the celebrated comedian Louise Neumann, they began to venerate her for actually being able to meet the Burgtheater star. One day the girls asked their teacher to deliver a note to Louise Neumann, which she promised to do. The children then anxiously waited for a reply. Weeks went by and it never came. Finally the English teacher dropped the remark that the actress was far too busy to waste her precious time writing to two young girls.

Yet one day the English woman was suffering from a cold and carried more handkerchiefs in her handbag than usual. By accident it burst open, scattering the children's undelivered letters on the floor. Marie and Fritzi could not believe their eyes, and were aghast at the deception. The teacher, however did not even find it necessary to apologize. Years later Marie von Ebner-Eschenbach still remembered with sadness and indignation that so much love and pain had been wasted—for nothing (MK 843). Incidents like this made an indelible impression on the young girl and entered the life of her imagination.

More and more she realized how little respect was given to children in her society, how vulnerable they were in their dependence on ruthless superiors. Once she had experienced how a serf had been severely beaten by an overseer on her father's estate. She had rebelled against this abuse by screaming and losing her temper, but to no avail. She had been helpless in the face of injustice and, although she would have liked to slap the brutal man, she knew that, instead of achieving justice, she only would have been punished for it. Adults were always in a stronger position (KL 274/5). Since Marie could not smack her dishonest and henceforth disdained English teacher, she could try to castigate her with words, but even this did not make an impression (MK 842).

Marie von Ebner-Eschenbach never treated children condescendingly. On account of the deep hurt she herself had endured in her early years she always empathized with the little ones. She made it a point in her fictional work to try to penetrate children's souls and to understand their psychology. Marie Ebner's work abounds with very sensitive and artistic children who are tyrannized and misunderstood by narrow-minded adults. The most tragic case is Georg of "Der Vorzugsschüler," who ultimately seeks death in order to escape his brutal and ambitious father.

Ebner-Eschenbach must have felt vindicated when she finally had the opportunity in the 1850s to meet Louise Neumann personally. The two became great friends. The famous actress later married a Count Schönfeld who likewise became a close friend of the Ebner-Eschenbachs. On the occasion of the actress' eightieth birthday Marie von Ebner-Eschenbach, twelve years her junior, dedicated a poem to her, in which she praised her as a great artist and friend. We do not know how long the English teacher lasted in the Dubsky household, but we know that the ignorant French governess was soon replaced by a young German who obviously was not as callous as her predecessor.

Fräulein Karoline was well versed in the subjects she taught, yet Marie had an irrepressible urge to make life difficult for her. She still felt very hurt that Marie Kittl had been dismissed; the experience with the dishonest English teacher had likewise left a scar. Poor Fräulein Karoline, therefore, became the scapegoat for Marie's revenge. The favorite battleground was history, where the fourteen-year-old had acquired a solid knowledge and could dare to challenge the governess. Determined to be rebellious, she made it a point to admire the very people her governess considered villainous, while she denigrated those whom her teacher praised as heroes. Fräulein Karoline had a trying time with her abrasive student, but gradually managed to win her over through patience and kindness. In later years Marie von Ebner-Eschenbach still felt ashamed about how she had behaved toward this bashful young woman. "Fräulein Karoline was noble and good. She forgave me everything. She did not hold against the adult what the child had done to her. But I do not feel relieved by her generosity. Even today I blush for shame when I think of the bad tricks which I played a harmless and helpless creature" (MK 845).

These rows with the poor governess left a lasting impression on Marie, so much so that she recorded them in modified form in several stories. Marie, the second daughter of Count Meiberg of "Wieder die Alte," bears a striking resemblance to the insubordinate Marie Dubsky of that time. She challenges her governess, behaves aggressively but ultimately repents and, eager to be reconciled, confesses: "I haver never loved a person more than you, please do count on me from now on" (141). Josef of "Die arme Kleine" likewise reminds us of Marie, as he torments his tutor, Herr Heideschmied. Again, the teacher gains the student's pity and admiration through patience and benevolence. Josef felt "a last surge of opposition against a warm, loving feeling, then came a complete submission. He ran towards Heideschmied and embraced him. 'You are a noble old man,' he said, turned round and left the room with long, emphatic steps" (651).

As much as Marie later regretted her behavior towards Fräulein Karoline and considered those squabbles with her as signs of immature antagonism, they sharpened her wits and forced her to study history seriously in order to win her arguments. Thus the young governess helped her to become a critical and independent thinker.

Another teacher who exerted a lasting influence on Marie was Josef Fladung, a retired court official and a respected amateur mineralogist. She instantly took to him because of his friendliness, his humor and his impeccable manners. As a sign of her confidence in him she showed him some of her secretly written poems. They impressed him so much that he spoke to her parents, urging them to cultivate her talent. To have found someone who believed in her literary accomplishments was a great comfort for Marie at the time. Apart from her grandmother she had no confidante in her family, and even with her she was not allowed to talk about what was most important to her: her poetry and her dramatic efforts.

Yet one day Marie took heart and confessed to Baroness Vockel that she still engaged in writing. Astonishingly enough, the old lady had mellowed, this time only warning her granddaughter to just be "prudent." In her autobiography Ebner-Eschenbach recalls: "Thus I was rid of the awful pressure on my heart caused by the consciousness of secretly doing something of which she disapproved" (851). Her grandmother soon got very ill and died of pneumonia in the spring of 1844. How empty the Rabenhaus in Vienna now seemed without her cherished presence!

Marie was later asked to catalogue the books her grandmother had left to her and Fritzi, so that they could be sent to Zdislawitz. This was a task she thoroughly enjoyed. She read in her grandfather's Bible, she leafed through the works of Thomas à Kempis and Herder and was captivated by a biography of Lessing. Reading the first chapter of his life suddenly made her aware how insufficient her own education was in comparison with that of the celebrated author. "My high opinion of my own talent, of my eagerness to learn, of my urge to know experienced a pitiful blow by comparing myself with the child Gotthold Ephraim Lessing" (MK 876). He had been able to attend schools, he had studied the classics, had met important people from whom he could learn and benefit. What would Marie have given "to be like him for just one day, for just one hour, to communicate with immortals as with friends and to enter into their shining world of thoughts" (MK 877).

For the first time she sadly realized that boys were privileged because they received a much more thorough education than girls. When her brothers Adolph and Viktor were nine and eight they were sent to a boarding school to prepare themselves for their future careers. At that time a devastated Marie had written in her notebook: "My brothers are gone today. I have a pain in my heart which is square and has sharp edges. It also has spikes" (MK 832). At that time she thought it cruel of her parents to send the little boys away to strangers, to an institution they were frightened of. Now she envied Adolph and Viktor for having been given the chance to prepare themselves for a professional career. They attended the Schotten Gymnasium which provided the most élite education in Vienna. It offered a humanities curriculum with emphasis on Greek and Latin for students planning to enter university, the civil service, or to embark on a professional career. The course of studies also comprised German language and literature, history, geography, mathematics, sciences, religion as well as the electives French and English (Rozenblit 101).

Yet Marie was "only a girl" and knew that such an education was out of the question for her. Aristocratic girls did not attend schools but

were instructed at home and expected to forge bonds with other
aristocratic families. Besides, girls were not admitted to institutions of
higher learning because it was feared that they would distract the male
students from their work (Rozenblit 120).[16] In her autobiography Ebner-
Eschenbach, sadly aware of the discrimination, ponders her fate:

> I was only a girl. How many things are considered
> unbecoming for a girl, improper, inappropriate. The
> walls grew sky-high around me, walls between which
> my thinking and my expectations had to move, the
> walls which—pacified me. Not a good word in this
> application. "Pacification" fits only the cemetery, in
> which the dead lie; the living are robbed of their
> peace, if they are confined within too narrow
> boundaries . . . They will attempt to break out, they
> will always assault the walls and believe: this time
> they will give way. (877-878)

Her discontent with her superficial education filtered into many of
her fictional works. In *Aus Franzensbad* she shows her contempt for
aristocratic girls who have never learned to think. In "Komtesse
Muschi" she ridicules the lack of knowledge these daughters of the
social élite often display. In "Komtesse Paula" she criticizes aristocratic
fathers for insisting on their daughters' superficial education. In "Lotti,
die Uhrmacherin" we likewise hear about the thin cultural veneer young
Austrian countesses were given. As Halwig says: "They know
something about horses in spite of a Maquignon, they talk like jockeys
and—are charming. Yes, I must confess that I find them charming,
charming. Although I do not have the slightest illusion concerning their
stupendous superficiality" (896). A girl who enjoyed reading and
studying was derogatively termed a bluestocking and ran the risk of
being ostracized and ridiculed as lacking elegance and finesse.

Yet Marie was not discouraged by this prejudice. She continued to
cherish her books and devoured whatever works she found in her
grandmother's library. There were the dramas of Shakespeare, Racine,
Corneille, Goethe and Kleist. There was also a work by Madame de
Motteville that particularly fascinated her. Its hero, Cinq Mars, would
preoccupy Marie's imagination for many years to come. Her mind was

preparing itself to build its own dwelling. The "covenant between herself and her talent" was made (MK 851).

CHAPTER 3

"UNMISTAKABLE TRACES OF TALENT"

Baroness Vockel's death had left a deep void in Marie's life, a void that could not be filled for a long time. After Marie Kittl's departure the children had attached themselves more to their grandmother. Now she was gone, and the adults who would henceforth take care of them were only employed as instructors. Emotionally they remained aloof. Count Dubsky, never bothering much about his children's emotional life and sensitivities, left their upbringing solely to teachers and governesses. He was only concerned that they obeyed and did their duty. Mama Xaverine in due course gave birth to a girl named Julie and a boy named Heinrich. According to aristocratic tradition she entrusted the children at first to nursemaids and later to governesses and tutors, so that a close relationship between her and the children never developed.

Aristocratic parents and their offspring lived in different spheres. Social obligations played a prominent part in the life of adults, as Marie Ebner would later record in many of her works. Sarah, the protagonist of *Das Waldfräulein*, is sent away to be brought up in the country to enable her mother to dedicate herself wholly to her social commitments. Paula, the heroine of "Komtesse Paula," meets her mother only when the latter has some visitors to whom she likes to introduce her dolled-up child. In "Ein kleiner Roman" the governess is instructed never to complain to her aristocratic employers about their child, since they do not want to be bothered (11).

Missing the emotional closeness she had enjoyed with Maman Eugénie and with Großmutter Vockel, Marie now valued all the more the opportunity to keep up her correspondence with Marie Kittl, to whom she poured out all her joys and sufferings. She often felt lonely, deprived of a kindred soul who was really able to understand her ambitions and drives.

There are many lonely children in Ebner-Eschenbach's work, all of them quite likely reflecting some of her own sense of loneliness in those early years. About Rosa of *Bozena* the narrator says: "With what bitter pain did she feel the saddest of all kinds of loneliness, being alone among people who should be the closest" (111). All the more Marie attached herself to her brothers and sisters. The "troop of the seven upright ones" forged a bond which made them stick together throughout their lives (KL 305). Adolph and Viktor regularly came home from their boarding school for feast days and for the summer holidays, which the family spent at their country estate.

Around the middle of May the Dubskys used to pack their suitcases, and the whole household, including the servants, moved to Zdislawitz. Especially the children looked forward to spending their holidays in the country. While they arranged their belongings they sang verses Marie had composed to the tune of the old folksong "Da droben auf dem Berge" (High upon the mountain). To see their castle and the inhabitants of the village again filled them with great joy and excitement.

In her novella "Ein kleiner Roman" Marie von Ebner-Eschenbach later described the trip from Vienna to the country, which took three days and three nights. In those days they traveled in six coaches, each drawn by four horses. "In front of each post station which we reached, twenty-four horses were standing ready to move us on. The drivers jumped from their carriages, unhitched the steaming, tired horses, and replaced them with new, well-rested ones" (15). The arrival in Zdisla-witz was always a special event. Marie appreciated not only the warm welcome by the people but also the greeting offered by homely well-known nature, the fields, the pastures, the flowering trees at the road-side, and by every reed and shrub in the garden. "There was no more beautiful welcome than by that of our avenue of linden trees, our favo-rite playground on hot summer days—how eagerly I often wished to be a giant with enormous arms so as to be able to embrace all those tree tops and to press them to my heart" (MK 784).

The park where Marie knew every bird and tree always held a special place in her heart. The castle, her "old nest," scat of her maternal ancestors, played an immensely important part in her life. In "Die erste Beichte" she describes it as follows:

> The castle with its gardens was situated on a high plateau which offered a free view towards the south of the open country, the well cared for fields and meadows, watered by little rivulets. Toward the north it was bordered by a threefold chain of wooded mountains. A multi-turreted tower crowned the corner of the left wing of the castle, for which the steep walls of mighty basalt rocks served as an under-pinning. Their dark pyramids emerged barren up there. Further down the valley they were overgrown with short but thick vegetation. Between their mosses

and small shrubs rose single spruce and pine trees, the
fringe of the nearby forest. (475)

To stroll between the trees and to recite Schiller's verses was one of
Marie's favorite pastimes. "How often those old, dear linden trees of
ours had to hear the oak forest roar! How often did I call to them, who
certainly marveled at it, 'I have lived and loved'"(MK 833).

When Adolph and Viktor came home from boarding school to
spend their summer holidays in Zdislawitz Marie would use every free
minute to be with them and join in their games. The children from the
village came to watch the Dubsky children playing together on the
sports grounds. Yet these onlookers were not always friendly. In "Die
arme Kleine" a battle between the children of the castle and the village
youth is described that may well reflect certain events during Marie's
summer holidays. The villagers trampled down flowerbeds in the castle
garden and tore branches from the trees. They also threw stones at the
boys in the courtyard, and a bitter fight between village and castle youth
erupted. "Next day many youths in the village were walking about
limping and with bandaged heads, and Heideschmied marveled at the
bruises which covered his pupils" (665).

All the Dubsky children enjoyed riding, and they all participated in
hunts. Yet Marie always pitied the animals and in later years tried to
avoid hunting. Much of what she thought of pursuing helpless deer has
found its way into the description of a hunt in *Unsühnbar*.

> The ground is filling up with dead, dying, mutilated
> animals. They fertilize the soil with their blood; they
> are broken and strangled; the chasers tie their hindlegs
> and load their poles with the twisting loot. Marie had
> averted her eyes. Nausea, antagonism, wonderment
> filled her; those who found delight in the suffering of
> a poor creature were all good people. (466)

Instead of chasing animals Marie liked to play with them and care for
them. She was especially fond of dogs and birds and would later
lovingly describe them in her work.

She also enjoyed walking with Fritzi through the woods and calling
on relatives at a nearby castle. For the children the summer always
passed too quickly. Soon the boys had to return to their institute,

leaving their sad sisters behind (MK 858-859). In late autumn the whole household was moved back to Vienna to the Rabenhaus where the winter routine began. "Our house," Ebner-Eschenbach writes in *Meine Kinderjahre*, "had the shape of a long-tailed piano; its narrow end stretched from the Haarmarkt through two small lanes up to the so-called Rabenplatzl. There it towered above its two neighbours at the right and the left—very ancient, large houses . . . It was not very gay and lively around here, least of all on Sundays, when the shops were closed" (811).

The Dubskys lived on the second floor in an apartment that hardly admitted any sunlight. Family life, overshadowed by Count Dubsky's ill humor and outbursts of temper, lacked harmony. With his suspicion and want of sensitivity he easily offended his family and regularly quarreled with his wife, so that the marriage remained forever strained. Something of the couple's relationship may have filtered into "Glaubenslos":

> In the short conversation between husband and wife behind each word mountains of accusations seemed to loom. How often there must have been similar exchanges before to irritate and outrage to such a degree as was evident. These same nerves, constantly pulled at in the same way, jerked traumatically at the slightest occasion, the wounds in the souls opened ever faster, were bleeding ever longer and never had time to heal. (260)

Marie, at a very impressionable age and by nature already extremely sensitive, suffered from the tensions in her family, to which she later referred in her work. In "Wieder die Alte" she describes an aristocratic family, where "the cheerful element was missing" and where the count "surrendered himself to his bad moods with the obstinacy of a child and the perseverance of a man" (138). Count Dubsky's ill humor was known and even proverbial in his circles, where, as Marie Ebner recorded in her diary, the saying went that "one does not marry a Dubsky" (TB I 79). When the family members were all together they often felt bored; serious interests were missing, everyone was afraid of making a remark which might arouse the Count's wrath. It is therefore not astonishing that the writer described men mostly as exhibiting "Zorn" (wrath) and as being prone to outbursts of temper. The boredom which likewise must have deeply affected Marie is recorded in several of her works. Muschi of "Komtesse Muschi" says: "We are bored like mopes" (306) and in "Die arme Kleine" the narrator explains: "Boredom! Boredom! It was crouching with ashen wings on the ceiling and as soon as people entered the room which it had chosen for its domicile, it let itself glide down the walls and fell on their chests" (622).

It was a convention in the Dubsky family to stay up till ten o'clock at night. Marie found this sitting around, only to fulfill a rule, very trying. Not interested in needlework, the usual pastime for girls and women, and prevented from reading as much as she would have liked, she often felt frustrated. She considered these forced family gatherings, with their trivial conversations and desperate attempts to entertain each other, a sad waste of time. Later she vented these frustrations in "Wieder die Alte" where Marie von Meiberg, sullen like her father, utters derogatory remarks about her family life (140). And in "Die arme Kleine" Tante Charlotte can hardly wait to escape the rules of the house order.

> The big grandfather clock at the buttress heaved to strike. "Friend, strike ten!" Charlotte silently called out to it, "announce the hour of liberation." Thus implored it struck—but what? Measly nine strokes plus one. One quarter past nine. Three quarters of an hour had to be sat out and one had to pretend one could do nothing else. Why pretend? Because it is the custom of the house. (624)

Despite the tensions in her family Marie preserved her happy disposition and could at times be exuberant without any apparent reason. She also had a type of humor which sometimes offended people (MK 880). Many protagonists in her work have a vehement temper and may very well spring from Ebner-Eschenbach's own roots. It is very likely that she challenged her governess exactly as Marie von Meiberg of "Wieder die Alte" does, and that she gave her teachers, especially if she did not respect them, an extremely difficult time.

After the departure of Fräulein Karoline, the teacher whom Marie had often defied and driven to despair, Fritzi and Marie were considered old enough to be without a governess. The two girls continued, however, to take music and drawing lessons. In *Meine Kinderjahre* Ebner-Eschenbach recalls an incident where a drawing teacher forgot himself and openly admired Fritzi's eyes which he found "miraculously beautiful" (862). The children considered this little indiscretion pardonable. But the chambermaid, who had been present to watch teacher and children, considered it her duty to report the incident to "higher authorities." Right away a new, much older drawing teacher was hired.[17]

One of Marie's drawing instructors was the painter Franz Alt, who soon became prominent in Austria. Marie was very fond of him. In later years she often visited his studio and bought his famous watercolors which she gave to friends as presents for special occasions. She signed her letters to Alt with "your former student and perpetual friend"(RV I.N.93.117). He must have enjoyed working with a student as gifted at drawing as Marie. He trained her observational skills and taught her to meticulously study the objects she wanted to depict. Her favorite motifs were the horses she liked to ride, the facade and various rooms of the manor house (Gladt, "Skizzenbuch" 4).[18] She further drew portraits of her sister Fritzi and of servants of the household, always trying to present them in as lively a manner as possible.

Marie's favorite pastime and an important outlet for her frustrations was the drawing of caricatures of people she detested. While later voicing her contempt and outrage through the written word, in her teens she expressed her disdain with the help of drawing (Gladt, *Waldfräulein* 32). People whose attitude and notion angered her— and obviously only a few found complete favor in her eyes—invariably ended as caricatures in her notebook. Not surprisingly, therefore also some of her prot- agonists take to drawing as a means of venting their frustrations at their environment. Out of spite Muschi of "Komtesse Muschi" draws a cari- cature of Clara who dares to criticize her. Edith of "Das Schädliche" has "sharp eyes for all human faults, her own not excepted" (599) and a great talent for drawing, which she likewise uses to produce caricatures of acquaintances. Her suitor declares: "She had produced a caricature of me, an ingenious one. It was a likeness which made me scream: my large nose, my broad mouth, my thick mustache. When contemplating this unflattering likeness of mine for some time I noticed the despicable expression which she had given me" (585).

The highlight of Marie's life were the visits to the Burgtheater, then Europe's most prestigious playhouse. When she was twelve and Fritzi thirteen, the two girls were allowed to accompany their parents every other day to the Burg, where the Dubskys had a private box. In *Meine Kinderjahre* she recalls:

> We saw all the classical pieces that were performed in what was then the first German stage. We saw *Das Leben ein Traum* and felt transported into heaven by the elan of its verses, we saw *Wallenstein* with Anschütz in the title-role, *Maria Stuart*, *Hamlet*, we saw the prince in *Emilia Galotti* portrayed by Fichtner in such a moving and lovable way, that we sincerely wished old Edoardo (sic) should give him his blessing for his marriage to Emilia. (834)

Those performances were the great imaginative elements of Marie's childhood and youth. They gave her joy and furthered her aesthetic and moral development. Especially the tragedy with its passions, collisions, and its conflicts between good and evil characters, inspired her and made her want to act as heroically as the protagonists, with whom she deeply empathized. Yet she also immensely enjoyed comedies, among them plays like *Die Stieftochter* and *Der Oheim* by Princess Amalie von Sachsen and *Pauline* by the very popular dramatist Frau von Weissenstein.

Marie's favorite comedian was Louise Neumann. Another of Marie's preferred actors, who had already fascinated her grandmother's generation and who still performed to critical acclaim, was Maximilian Korn, whom she likewise remembers in *Meine Kinderjahre*. One evening, when he asked in his role as Hauptmann Klinger, "And me, nobody wants to marry me?" a young countess courageously replied from a box on the second floor: "I will." This provoked calls of "bravo" while she, shocked about the audience's response, tried to hide behind the back of her embarrassed parents (838-839).

The Burgtheater performances strengthened Marie's desire to become a prominent dramatist and confirmed her conviction that she was destined to become "the Shakespeare of the twentieth century" (MK 276). The productions instilled ideals in her and gave her the endurance to follow her personal goals. She secretly wrote tragedies, comedies, novellas and poems and learned in those years to keep to herself, since there was no one in her family who understood her desire to write. The subject matter that preoccupied her the most was the tragedy of Richelieu's erstwhile favorite and later enemy, Marquis Henri de Cinq-Mars, who had died on the scaffold. In *Meine Kinderjahre* Ebner-Eschenbach reports how moved and excited she had been after she first read the story of this tragic hero: "Everything that was alive in me, deification of the beautiful, contempt and hatred for evil and meanness, and not least of all, an exuberant sense of humor, through which I often provoked and offended, everything could be poured into this as into a golden vessel, shaped for me and for my sake" (880).

Marie also ached to sketch the sovereign, King Louis XIII, with his infidelity and his narrow-mindedness. To delineate characters, to show their triumphs and their sorrows, to look deep into their psychological makeup, was then as later her greatest delight. Especially Cardinal Richelieu provided food for her imagination, fascinating her with his vanity and ambition, with his whole fear-inspiring personality. And finally Cinq-Mars, greatly inspired her (MK 883). For years Marie would labor over this tragedy until she finally burned it. Yet in those days, as a teenager "not the slightest fear of possible failure" (MK 884) overshadowed her confidence in her dramatic talent.

What cast a shadow over her dreams of becoming a professional writer was the fact that her family watched her growing interest in writing with open suspicion. To write verses for entertainment was allowed, to think of writing as a professional career was almost a crime, and, besides, nobody in her circles wanted to believe that she really had potential. As her nephew, Franz Dubsky, observes in his "Erinnerungen" about his aunt's literary struggles: "Her first poetic works were also received by my grandfather with a great deal of distrust. He probably did not really expect anything from them and may not exactly have supported her writing" (*Neue Freie Presse* 17).

For Count Dubsky everything that contravened aristocratic tradition and convention was anathema. He wanted his daughter to grow up like all the other young countesses in his society and fulfill the duties expected of her as a future wife and mother. He thus imposed on Marie a role that was alien to her and forced her more and more to lead a double life. In her sketch to her autobiography she later recalled: "Besides my genuine life I led an imaginary one which was perhaps more intense than the real one. It never occurred to me to tell one of my siblings or someone else about my dream creatures and of the beautiful world in which they moved" (Schmidt 129).

She learned, as many women writers had done before her, to hide her manuscripts "with a swift movement in the drawer" (B II 330) when family members appeared on the scene. Yet she valiantly bore these difficulties, determined to achieve her literary goal and to transcend the restrictions and limitations of her society. The performances at the Burgtheater had shown her the greatness of suffering and of preserving one's integrity. As she remembers in *Meine Kinderjahre*: "I walked like the high personages at solemn processions on stage. Heroic feelings filled my heart. The will to suffer awoke in its full strength and with it the burning desire for a grandiose martyrdom" (836).

She was determined to preserve her self, as later many of her literary figures would try to do. As the narrator says about Levin Bornholm of "Die arme Kleine": "But he had saved something precious, faith im himself, absolute freedom, the strength to wage the war of defense, which makes up the existence of a man, who does not bow to any yoke of convention" (633). Writing was Ebner-Eschenbach's means to escape the oppressive reality in her parents' home. The many artistic children she describes in her work reflect her own situation as a teen-ager. Erich of *Unsühnbar*, vainly craving his mother's love, turns to music for comfort and so does Georg of "Der Vorzugsschüler," when in times of despair he plays his dearly loved flute.

Lacking congenial friends and like-minded classmates with whom she could discuss her work, Marie increasingly withdrew into her inner life. Her day dreams gave her comfort and strength. As she records in the sketch to her autobiography: "At that time I discovered the delight of the inexhaustibly rich, healing, comforting art of dreaming. It remained loyal to me all my life" (Schmidt 133). Yet this did not change the reality that she felt lonely and misunderstood in her family.

It was particularly sad that Marie never had a warm and loving relationship with her second stepmother. Countess Xaverine with her talent for singing and drawing, her taste for a refined life and her aristocratic connections could have become a role model for Marie had she not, in her stepdaughter's eyes, lacked intelligence. At sixteen Marie had developed a very critical mind and a sharp eye for the flaws of those around her. Wherever someone in her circles had shortcomings and idiosyncracies she was the first to mercilessly register them. Various diary entries of the 1860s reveal the contempt she had for her stepmother's alleged intellectual mediocrity.

On February 16, 1866 Ebner-Eschenbach, indignant about Contess Xaverine's interference in Viktor's search for a bride, confided in her diary: "Mother inquired in all seriousness with Hanna E. whether she was inclined to marry V. A more frivolous, tactless, simple-minded woman the earth has never borne" (TB I 80). On September 20, 1866 we read in an entry from Zdislawitz: "What she lacks is a clear sharp mind, her emotions are much richer than I had often thought"(TB I 119). A few days later, seeing how her ailing stepmother suffered, she wrote: "Our poor good mother is suffering and looks ill. I am concerned and I feel that often I had not known how highly she is to be regarded, and I bitterly blame myself" (TB I 119). Yet the entry of April 22, 1867 again shows Marie's disdain for what she believed the countess' want of intellectual capacity: "She has, after all, much less intelligence than one would believe after the first glance, and even after the second" (TB I 171). Marie, from childhood on extremely bright and eager to learn, had soon intellectually surpasssed her stepmother. The gap between the two women widened over the years with Marie beginning to see in Xaverine Dubsky a model she definitely did not want to emulate.

Countess Dubsky-Kolowrat, as the descendant of a renowned Moravian aristocratic family—the Kolowrats having provided the Empire with two prominent politicians[19]—had received the upbringing typical for a girl of her class. She had been trained to move in the highest social circles, to be a hostess and to preside at official functions as a representative of the Austrian elite. Elegance and appearance were extremely important to her. But her stepdaughter did not share these, in her view, artificial and shallow values.

Due to her marital problems the countess became an unhappy and ailing woman. The many quarrels and altercations she had to endure must have made her appear heartless and cold. Her refuge became the Church, her emotional outlet charitable work. Of her own children she preferred Heinrich. She almost despaired when in 1866 as a nineteen-year-old he joined the army and was unable to contact her for a rather long time (TB I 107). Yet with Marie, whom she found too blunt and too critical and whose humor may often have offended her, she never established a close bond.

Therefore those mothers in Ebner-Eschenbach's work who lack deeper feelings and keep an emotional distance from their daughters may very well reflect Marie and Xaverine Dubsky's relationship. Nanette Heissenstein of *Bozena* is confronted with an abrasive stepdaughter who resists all her pedagogical attempts and overtures (82), so that the two never come close. Paula's mother in "Komtesse Paula" prefers her dog to her daughter and is oblivious to a child's psychology (324). The mother of "Poesie des Unbewussten" goes so far as to betray her daughter to her son-in-law. She actually advises him to learn to deceive his young wife in order to remain in control of her (374).

The irony and bitter sarcasm with which these relationships are described reveal Ebner-Eschenbach's grief about her own missing bond with her stepmother. There are only a few mother-daughter connections in her work that may be called intimate. Sorely missing parental love and understanding, Marie Ebner transformed these feelings of loneliness and isolation in her work, expressing them in metaphors of coldness and hardness[20] in her descriptions of parental and marital relationships. In "Das Schädliche" we learn that a "wall of ice" had built up between the parents and their daughter (590), while the suitor, listening to his future in-laws' complaints about their alienated daughter, feels "frozen over" (590). In "Glaubenslos" the estranged husband resents it when his wife, having been deeply offended by him, repeatedly says to him: "I beg you Ambros," because it felt "as if two ice-floes had crashed against each other, and it made him feel frosty and provoked him to an anger in which he poured forth the meanest defamations of his wife and of women in general" (260).

Mrs. Maslan of "Maslans Frau," likewise deeply hurt by her husband, has become hard and unforgiving, her face bearing an expression of "frosty bleakness" (485). The priest, trying to bring about a reconciliation between her and her spouse, notices that "something insuperable stared at him from her stiff features, which looked frozen over" (486).

Countess Xaverine's increasing bigotry, which Marie, much more sceptical and down to earth, tended to ridicule and to consider rather offensive, further led to an inner estrangement. In fact the countess's somewhat simple-minded religious faith may have rendered her even harder and more unforgiving. As Ebner-Eschenbach's narrator would later describe the protagonist of "Das Schädliche": "Maud, so excellent, so dutiful, so loving when she worshiped, was not without that kind of hardness that seems inseparable from great piety" (598). With her alleged penchant for gossip and for disparaging other people (TB I 120) and her persistent efforts to convert Marie to her own understanding of religion, Xaverine aroused her stepdaughter's contempt. After such an argument Marie von Ebner once wrote into her diary: " . . . no faith, I?

What an error, good God. Only one that is adequate for the greatness of Him to whom we both pray. How should I make you understand that, good dear mother?" (TB I 119).

Countess Dubsky-Kolowrat's intolerance in religious matters made a deep impression on Marie's mind. In later years she sometimes spoke derogatively about it to her relatives but found no sympathy for her concerns. In a diary entry of August 9, 1866 she mentioned during a visit with her cousin in Hungary: "Unpleasant controversy with Marie because of mother. She does not accept the fact that I can criticize mother without showing spite toward her" (TB I 112). She also vented her indignation by describing overly pious women in her work.

Paula's mother in "Komtesse Paula," in her eagerness to imbue her daughter with a devotion to Catholicism, decrees that Luther and the age of the Reformation be left out of her syllabus (323). She later dedicates her life to charity, goes to church twice a day and reads only "pious books" (326), yet she does not show the slightest concern for her daughter's well-being. Status and appearance count more than anything else. In "Das tägliche Leben" it is the mother's intolerance which makes life miserable for her talented and philanthropically oriented daughter who, unable to endure life with her uncongenial family any longer, finally commits suicide (632-633).

Marie and Xaverine obviously were no kindred spirits, but their behavior toward each other remained polite, as each was eager to observe the proprieties. They read to each other in the evenings, and Marie always appreciated her stepmother's artistic bent. She also never forgot that she owed Xaverine one of the greatest joys of her childhood, the present of Schiller's complete works. Xaverine also supported her stepdaughter's poetic talent in another important way. Having noticed Marie's love for reading and reciting poetry, having watched her creating verses and prose with remarkable ease, and urged by Mr. Fladung, Marie's teacher, to further her daughter's talent, the countess one day consulted Austria's foremost dramatist about her stepdaughter's work.

When asked by Countess Dubsky-Kolowrat to evaluate some of Marie's poems, Grillparzer did not hesitate to come to the Rabenhaus in order to talk to her personally. Since the family was not at home he wrote the following letter:

Gracious Countess!

Having been previously prevented through my indisposition, I intended yesterday to give myself the honor to personally call on you, but did not find you at home. Since I cannot dispose over my time for the next few days, I do not want to delay expressing in writing my opinion on the poems of your respected daughter.

These poems reveal unmistakable traces of talent, a very felicitous ear for verse, power of expression, a perhaps too profound emotion, insight, and a great gift of observation. Some of the present poems form an endowment which arouses interest and it should not be left to the personal arbitrariness of its owner to neglect its development . . . What is still lacking is that maturity which turns a poet into an artist, that thoroughgoing lucidity which transfers a thought to the listener without hindrance. Compared with young men at the same age, young women are usually several years ahead as far as intelligence and insight is concerned. Yet they are often lacking something which our sometimes humdrum methodical studies provide: order to thought. That is partly lacking in these poems, especially where they try to describe and where emotion blocks the event.

That much in general and in haste. Perhaps I will have the chance orally to add some detail to this.

With great esteem, devotedly, Grillparzer
(RV I.N.6725).

With this letter Marie received the poet's consecration, a blessing which, by vindicating her in the eyes of her suspicious family, gave her the strength to continue writing.[21] The countess perhaps may have hoped Grillparzer's appraisal would be less positive, so as to provide her with authority to discourage Marie from her unfortunate bent for versifying.[22]

When her daughter Julie, the youngest of the Dubksy girls, who had inherited her musicality and talent for singing, grew up, there was never a doubt that she should remain an amateur, using her talent only for entertaining her family. In her story "Die eine Sekunde" Marie Ebner-

Eschenbach has a young woman say to her artistic cousin: "That you have talent, everybody can see." He replies indignantly: "But I should not receive training . . . I should only do it playfully" (559).

Still, Countess Dubsky-Kolowrat appreciated the contact with Grillparzer. A few years later, after a performance of his drama *Esther*, she sent him a bouquet as a token of gratitude for the "pure joy" she had experienced (RV I.N.80250). His acquaintance also meant a great deal to Marie. For years she had enjoyed the performances of his dramas at the Burg—especially *Die Ahnfrau* had held her spellbound and "burned itself into the depths of [her] soul" (RV I.N. 54488)[23]—for years she had read his poems, and now he had deemed her own fledgling verses worthy of his praise. He became her idol, her role model, the hero of her dreams. With a trembling heart she hoped to meet him personally one day.

Finally in the 1860s her long cherished dream came true when she was introduced to him by her friend Josephine Knorr. After the third meeting she wrote to Josef Weil: "How I worship him—what a poor word for the rich emotion which it is meant to express—I cannot tell you. The three times I saw him I shall never forget" (B II 122). By then Grillparzer had retired as Imperial Councillor. He had moved in with Kathi Fröhlich and her sisters and lived in the apartment on the Spiegelgasse, more or less like a recluse, offended and bitter, pondering his thwarted career as a dramatist.

In 1863, due to a fall in a Roman bath, he had lost his hearing (Nadler 338), a fact which made it even more difficult for him to communicate with the people around him, since it increased his suspicion and his irritability. Ebner-Eschenbach knew that Grillparzer was difficult to get along with. He was in many ways as gruff and stubborn as her own father. Yet she felt deeply attracted to him as a man and as an artist. She understood his sarcasm well: did she not herself have a good portion of it? She also sympathized with his desire to be left alone by the public, since she likewise tried to escape from the thraldom of social life. In him she recognized a kindred spirit and ached to adopt him as her mentor in her early years as a young dramatist.

In her essay "Meine Erinnerungen an Grillparzer" Marie von Ebner-Eschenbach, still embarrassed about her naiveté, recalls how she came to Grillparzer's apartment for the first time to read to him a drama of her own. Her heart beat violently, but she plucked up courage and started to recite. He praised her, wanted to hear the whole work, suggested a few changes, but did not pass judgment on the piece.

On the way home she was suddenly attacked by feelings of guilt and anxiety: "I envied every beggar, whom I met, for his good conscience. It would not have occurred to him to read a drama written by himself to the greatest living poet" (887). This first visit was followed by many more, each of them valued as great events in Marie Ebner's life and carefully recorded in her diary. On April 18, 1868 she wrote:

> With Grillparzer. He received me very well. I am proud and happy. "May God reward you," he said, "that you pay a visit to the sick, to the dead." "The Immortal," I answered. That I meet with Grillparzer, that I hear him talk, that I can tell him how great and infinite my admiration for him is, that will remain a treasure for the rest of my life. (TB I 233)

She knew how to handle him because she was extremely fond of him. When he was in a bad mood she was able to cheer him up with her humor. Once, despondent because he felt neglected by his friends and was longing for company, he complained to Marie Ebner: "Nobody is coming to see me any longer; certainly no men, only women—out of charity. I made these verses: 'This similarity I have with Christ—the women are coming to my grave.'" And she replied "And old ogres at that, is it not true, Herr Hofrat?" (EG 903).

During one of Ebner-Eschenbach's visits Grillparzer read to her from a book by his favorite author Lope de Vega. Although she did not understand a single word of Spanish she later considered this hour one of the "most sacred and most beautiful" (EG 991), because she could see how enchanted the old man was while enjoying and recreating a work of art that meant so much to him.

For every birthday she sent flowers to Grillparzer, but for his eightieth she wanted to do something special. Having heard that her beloved friend had expressed a wish for new razors, she asked her husband and her father to buy the best brand to be found in Vienna. When she came to Grillparzer to wish him well and to give him her present he admired the razors, got up and gave her "a long, serious kiss"(EG 905). She recalls in her "Erinnerungen": "I felt as if I had received a consecration, extremely happy and solemn. I really cannot tell whether I walked down the stairs, or whether I ran or floated" (905-906). The next day, however, when Ebner-Eschenbach came to inquire about the razors, she learned that Grillparzer had not approved of them and wanted them to be exchanged. She then felt like a thief because she had accepted a kiss for something her worshiped poet had no use for.

Although she could at times be quite critical of Grillparzer's personal flaws and of his art—she did not like, for instance, his *Jüdin von Toledo*—she generally admired and praised his work. After a performance of *Ein treuer Diener seines Herrn*, which Grillparzer had written for the occasion of Empress Karoline Augusta's coronation as Queen of Hungary, Marie Ebner confided in her diary: "I cried—I do not know a more moving piece; the fifth scene is attracting me irresistibly" (TB I 80). She also adored his *Bruderzwist im Hause Habsburg*: "Excepting Shakespeare, nobody has written a historic tragedy which can compare with the *Bruderzwist*. How can one enter so deeply into the mysteries of a soul? Solve all its riddles? One has to be a god" (TZ 238).

She learned from Grillparzer to place human beings at the center of her work and to focus on the psychology of her characters. With him she was able to freely discuss conceptions of art and through these conversations she gained self-assurance. While her love for him never waned, in later years she thought more highly of him as an artist than as a man. Her diary of September 27, 1889 reveals. "I read Grillparzer again and that is all right. A great poet, but perhaps not a sufficiently great man; sometimes where anger would be required there is only cantankerousness, but one always loves him" (Vesely 238).

Much of Marie Ebner's love and admiration for Franz Grillparzer has filtered into her 1910 story "Ob spät, ob früh," in which she describes the meeting of an Austrian Baroness with Hans Kolberg, a renowned composer and music director. Like Grillparzer, Kolberg gives the appearance of being gruff, unapproachable and averse to compliments paid him by admirers of his art. Those who do not know him consider him a misanthrope (398). Like Grillparzer he regrets a past marked by debauchery (416),[24] and like him he depends emotionally on an artist whose presence as well as absence make him extremely unhappy. As Grillparzer separated from Kathi Fröhlich and later returned to her, so Kolberg is drawn back to his artistic wife, whose "wild love" and "demonic power of heart" (416) hold him firmly in their grip. Both Grillparzer and Kolberg are deeply religious, striving for perfection in their art.[25]

The Baroness directly springs from Marie von Ebner-Eschenbach's own roots. Extremely sensitive and eager to preserve her privacy, she well understands Kolberg's reserve and penchant for avoiding people. Being respectful and congenial she soon gains the artist's confidence and even a kiss on the hand, for which she is envied by other visitors of the spa, where she and the artist take the waters (397). Long before meeting Kolberg personally, she, being likewise a musician and familiar with his art, has played and admired his famous compositions and has acquainted herself with him through his work. Two kindred souls have found each other but have to part again to go their separate ways.

Kolberg has to return to his wife and take care of his daughter (416), the Baroness must resume her life with an obliging but indifferent husband, for whom career and professional achievements count more than his family (370). The tears which the Baroness, usually calm and self-controlled, sheds after Kolberg's farewell visit reveal the depth of her feeling (418). He may have been her first true love.

During the same year in which Countess Dubsky-Kolowrat wrote to Franz Grillparzer requesting him to evaluate her stepdaughter's poems, Marie herself wrote to the well-known poet Betty Paoli to ask her whether she thought she had the talent to become a writer.[26] Through her governess Marie Kittl, a staunch admirer of Paoli, she had become acquainted with the latter's poems, among which she particularly liked "Dunkle Einsamkeit," "Genügen," and "Hinweg" (EBP). Paoli's reply to Marie's quest was much more detailed and much more cautious than Grillparzer's:

> You ask me whether I believe you have poetic talent.
> It seems impossible for me to provide a definite ans-
> wer to this right now. There is no doubt that you
> have a poetic nature . . . There remains the question
> whether you have the ability to give artistic shape to
> everything that is moving within you and to express
> it in a finished form . . . follow the urge that is in
> you; it is the voice through which God speaks to
> humans. . . allow me to give you another piece of
> advice: pay strict attention to form in your poetic
> work, something you seem to have disdained up to
> now . . . even the divine must assume a beautiful

earthly body, if it wishes to reveal itself. (B I 219-220)

In conclusion Betty Paoli expressed the wish to meet Marie personally. Countess Dubsky-Kolowrat therefore invited the poet in February 1848 and thus gave her daughter the opportunity to talk personally to the artist she had so long admired. In later years Betty Paoli became one of Ebner-Eschenbach's staunchest supporters as a novelist and one of her friends in old age.

CHAPTER 4:

"SINCERE LOVE, THAT WAS HER FEELING FOR HIM "

Grillparzer's and Betty Paoli's encouraging remarks did nothing to convince the Dubskys of Marie's talent for professional writing. For them it was more important that she develop her social skills. To write poetry was considered ridiculous in a family where everything had to be geared towards a practical goal. In 1880 Ebner-Eschenbach wrote to Hieronymus Lorm: "Practical, practical, and never poetic! That is our motto. Everything that surrounds us preaches: 'only practical.' It was my cradle-song and even now I still have to take up the cudgels for the view that poetry also has a right to exist in life" (BF 73).

Writing poetry was generally viewed with suspicion in aristocratic circles, seen as a waste of time. To listen to someone reciting his verses was boring in the highest degree to people who lacked literary understanding. In "Nach dem Tode" Marie Ebner later described a countess who finds it an imposition to listen to her husband's poems, even though they are dedicated to her: "He insists on reading all that to me; and, you see, I cannot listen if someone is reading to me, I can't. My thoughts wander as soon as the reading begins, and they do not return until it is ended. Then, of course, I say offhand: 'charming, charming, very beautifully written'— especially the last one"(41).[27]

That Marie enjoyed reading and writing and showed an interest in serious studies was considered an anomaly in the family, and she continued to suffer much because of that.[28] She became more and more painfully aware of the discrepancy between what she dreamed of becoming and what she was expected to be. Forced to deny her true nature she withdrew ever more into herself in order to preserve her identity. Outwardly she fulfilled her duties in the family. She accompanied her stepmother on her social calls, was present when visitors were expected, took lessons in all the subjects fit for a young, nubile girl of her class, but secretly she lived in a different world. Her life with her family was like hiding behind a screen of trivial words. Physically close, her parents were the farthest from Marie's lonely soul.

Count and Countess Dubsky may have hoped that her productive passion would be a passing wave, the impulse toward the poetic only a sign of puberty. Thus they quietly ignored her literary work, offending her deeply in the process. As a septuagenarian Ebner-Eschenbach still had not forgotten the hurt inflicted on her at that time by her family's rejection (MK 809).

Marie's parents not only ignored her literary talent for fear she could turn into a bluestocking and forfeit her chances on the marriage market. They also, like most parents in nineteenth-century Austria, strongly insisted on their authority, demanding strict obedience and the fulfillment of duty. Children had to be grateful for what they received, they were not allowed to make demands and they had to adhere to their parents' values. Young people were generally viewed with suspicion in *Vormärz* Austria, which tried to preserve its *status quo* at all costs. In the words of Stefan Zweig: "Austria was an old state, dominated by an aged Emperor, ruled by old ministers; a state without ambition, which hoped to preserve itself unharmed in the European domain solely by opposing radical changes. Young people, who always instinctively desire rapid and radical changes, were therefore considered a doubtful element that was to be held down or kept inactive for as long a time as possible" (World 33).

Children were strictly brought up to respect the existing conditions without demur. Their opinion counted little, their suggestions for change were ignored. Marie may therefore often have been told that she was not mature enough to discuss problems or questions with her parents and that she simply had to accept what her elders decreed. This attitude and her parents' relentless ways caused her to develop a lack of self-confidence from which she suffered all her life. In her correspondence with Hieronymus Lorm she once confessed: "The insecurity, the anxious hesitancy deriving from it, that is the great sadness of my productivity and the cause of my self-torment" (BF 72).

Especially her father with his unpredictable moods conveyed a repressive attitude and expectations his daughter felt at a loss to fulfill. Like Georg of "Der Vorzugsschüler" Marie may have yearned to please her father and to gain his recognition. Unconsciously she may have cultivated her writing to prove to him that she indeed had talent and was worthy of his praise. Her feelings of marginality and isolation were later to pour out in many novels and tales. In "Die Unverstandene auf dem Dorfe" the narrator says: "And what is one talking about if one feels so strange in front of people, like Marie? The inkling that a creature of her worth would not do well in this evil world clarified into a conviction and constituted her pain but also her elevation" (553).

In "Das Schädliche" we likewise meet a young girl who considers herself a martyr in her family. She is "one of the many young things, whose soul is attuned to a different dominant than that of her environment, and it forms the embodied dissonance in the circle of relations" (586). While her parents were hoping to turn Marie into a young countess like Muschi ("Komtesse Muschi"), superficially educated, fun-loving and submissive to authority, she developed into a girl like Paula ("Komtesse Paula"), who takes a view that is at variance with the norms of her aristocratic environment.

Since Marie hated dancing she did not care for the balls regularly given and attended by her family. Much more serious-minded than other girls her age, she had little desire to mix in the circles to which the family had been introduced through her father's fourth marriage.[29] Countess Xaverine's maiden name gave her the right to move among the highest aristocracy; there was hardly a noble family to whom she was not related. Yet like Paula in "Komtesse Paula" Marie may have eyed social life with some reserve: "I got to know many people and what struck me most was the quantity of sameness of quality. At seventeen one does begin to think and so I thought to myself: If one could release all the souls of these ladies and gentlemen—especially of the gentlemen!—from their bodies and let them wander around freely, I would find it impossible to distinguish one from the other" (Harriman 52).

Observing the young countesses in the ballroom Marie may also have had thoughts like Sarah of *Das Waldfräulein,* who prides herself on speaking her mind and openly voices her disdain in front of a large gathering: "The poor girls! When I see them fly around, dead tired and exhausted, but with a smiling face I have to think of the children of a tight-rope walker who once visited our village" (534). As Marie matured, her observation grew sharper, and she saw the difference between herself and her peers in a much clearer light. She also began to object to the hypocrisy and ostentation of some of the people of her class, to their lack of education or serious interests. She ridiculed their pronounced status awareness and became impatient with their prejudices.

All these objections filtered into those works where female protagonists, like Sarah of *Das Waldfräulein*, Paula of "Komtesse Paula," Maria Dornach of *Unsühnbar*, observe the society around them with misgivings and open indignation. In a society where symbols, appearances and perceptions counted for more than reality, where persons were judged by their attire, where people who did not conform to the standards of elegance were ostracized, Marie Dubsky with her love of nature and her contempt for artificiality had of necessity to become a marginal person. No wonder that she took to the pen as her only weapon to criticize what she considered flaws of her class. In her first published work *Aus Franzensbad* she vented all her frustrations at the shallowness and arrogance of some of her peers. In the works that followed she criticized, although in a somewhat less offensive form, all the shortcomings of society as she had encountered them in her adolescence. Her diary entries from the 1860s onwards abound with critical and censorious references to peers, whose lack of interest in reading Ebner-Eschenbach found particularly annoying. Complaining about people must have been a deeply ingrained habit. Writing about what she considered flaws in her social environment represented the fulfillment of an acutely felt need.

On June 15, 1868 she wrote: "The couple XC. She looks younger than she is, he looks more stupid than he should be. 'I only read when I am bored,' he says. 'I am only bored when I am reading.' she says" (TB I 235). In later years when Marie Ebner had mellowed and had long realized that she would never be able to change the prejudices and habits of her class, she observed her milieu with more humor and less sarcasm. To her friend Fritz Mauthner, who noticed "how delightfully the writer could giggle at these pranks," she told the following anecdote, which likewise points to the aristocracy's aversion to reading: at a hunting party to which she was invited, she became the focus of attention of a young gentleman from the German Embassy, who complimented her on her works. A baroness who sat close by joined the conversation by remarking: "I have also heard of your new book, my dear Ebner. I would have bought it, but what to do with it afterwards?" (*Berliner Tageblatt*, April 2, 1916).

As a teenager Marie was much less tolerant toward those of her peers with whose rigid, conservative values she could not identify. Having a highly developed social consciousness, she deeply resented the ostentation exhibited by some people of her class and the condescension with which they treated their subordinates.

In her childhood she had rebelled against the Burggraf who had brutally beaten a helpless serf (KL 274). As she grew up she became more and more perceptive of the injustices people of the lower strata had to endure from those in power. She noticed poverty and suffering with increased intensity, aching to help. Instead of seeing others suffer she herself wanted to endure pain in order to relieve that of those she pitied. As she recalls in her autobiography, she wanted to suffer, "not because others would benefit by it, but because my suffering was alleviating theirs for me" (792).

A girl whose proclivities and ways of thinking deviated so much from those of her peers was destined to become an outsider in her milieu. Yet she did have one ally in the family, namely her cousin Moritz. He was considered an eccentric like herself, because his intellectual interests also digressed from the aristocratic norm. Moritz von Ebner-Eschenbach was the son of Marie's aunt Helene and her husband, Wenzel von Ebner-Eschenbach. Genealogists are not sure whether, as Moritz would later claim, the Austrian Ebner-Eschenbachs were related to those of Nuremberg, who had settled there in the tenth century (Mitterhofer 4). According to Moritz' memoirs, during the Reformation the family had split into a Protestant and a Catholic branch. The Protestants remained in Nuremberg, retaining the ancient Eschenbach castle, whereas the Catholic branch moved first to Silesia and, after the province's conquest by Prussia, to Moravia which was part of the Austrian Empire. Moritz, who after his retirement indulged in genealogy and decorated his apartment in the Amtshaus in Zdislawitz with ancestral portraits, traced his descent in Austria back to a Wolfgang Ebner in the seventeenth century. An organist under Emperor Ferdinand III, Ebner had excellent connections to the court and was ennobled in 1641. Henceforth he and his two brothers, Mathias and Markus, had a coat of arms which, however, differed from that of the Nuremberg Ebner-Eschenbachs (Mitterhofer 5). Wolfgang Ebner's widow, Susanna Renata, and her sons were accepted into the knighthood in 1694, which allowed them to call themselves "Ritter von Ebner." Their new coat of arms was the same as that of the Ebner-Eschenbachs of Nuremberg (Mitterhofer 5).

Moritz' grandfather, Ferdinand Ritter von Ebner, bought an estate in Auspitz, Moravia, but lost his fortune due to the war, so that the family was left with only a meager income. They had three sons, Johann, who inherited the estate, Ignaz and Wenzel, soon after whose birth in 1743 the father died. The widow, hardly able to make ends meet, sent the two younger boys to Vienna. Ignaz entered the army and was killed at Hochkirch in 1758 during the Seven Years' War. Wenzel, Moritz' father, became an apprentice to a glove maker. Distant relations, to whom his mother had recommended him, secured him a stipend in the Military School of Engineering in Vienna. In 1762 Wenzel Ritter von Ebner entered the Military Engineer corps, became Lieutenant in

1771 and was soon afterwards promoted to Captain. In 1774 he married Josepha von Cunz of Esseg, with whom he moved to Olmütz four years later. The couple had two sons. Karl, born in 1779, was mentally and physically retarded and had to be institutionalized. He died, aged thirty, at the Spital der Barmherzigen Brüder. His younger brother Nikolaus, born in 1782, entered the Military Engineering Academy, was accepted into the Engineer Corps, where his father had served before him, and was killed in 1809 in the battle of Aspern.[30]

Wenzel Ritter von Ebner, a widower since 1787, dedicated his whole life to the military. He served in Smyrna and Slavonia, fought at the Rhine and distinguished himself in 1795 during the occupation of Mannheim, whereupon he received the "Ritterkreuz des Militärischen Maria Theresia Ordens."[31] In 1796 he was promoted to Lieutenant Colonel and elevated to the baronetcy. Emperor Franz II bestowed upon him the predicate "von Eschenbach" and gave him a new coat of arms which differed only slightly from that of the Nuremberg Ebner-Eschenbachs (Mitterhofer 5). After a short service in Mantua Wenzel von Ebner-Eschenbach was transferred to Vienna, where he headed the Engineering Academy as interim director. In 1804 he was promoted to the rank of Major General. One year after his son Nikolaus' death at the battlefront, Baron Wenzel von Ebner-Eschenbach, aged sixty-six, married the latter's fiancée, the twenty-nine year old Helene Dubsky.

After Wenzel's promotion to Fieldmarshal Lieutenant the couple lived very comfortably in their apartment on the Franziskanerplatz in Vienna. In 1815 their son Moritz was born. When he was five his father died, leaving only a small income for his family's support. Fortunately for Helene her brother Franz acquired the Rabenhaus through his marriage and invited her and her son to move in with him and his wife Konradine von Sorgenthal. Later, when Konradine had died and Franz Dubsky remarried in 1827, Zdislawitz castle, Baroness Marie Vockel's inheritance, became Helene's and Moritz' place for the summer.

After his elementary school training at a private school, Pension Kudlig, Moritz, aged twelve, received a scholarship for the exclusive Theresianum, which prepared the sons of the social elite for the civil service. Although an excellent student, he decided in 1834 to exchange the rather monastic Theresianum for the Engineering Academy in order to become an officer in the Austrian Army. In spite of the hard beds, the mediocre food and the shabby sports facilities, he enjoyed life at the academy with its egalitarian spirit and did very well in all the subjects.

His role model became Archduke Johann, the president of the institute, and a man of great military distinction (EME I,4).

In 1837 Moritz became an Engineer Lieutenant. Three years later he was appointed professor of physics and chemistry at the Engineering Academy, the same institute where he had studied for the past six years. In order to improve his knowledge in his subjects he registered as an auditor at the University of Vienna and at the Polytechnic Institute. He attended lectures given by Andreas Ettinghausen, an eminent scholar from whose classes he greatly benefited. In 1842 Moritz started to teach at the Academy, and soon became a well qualified, widely known instructor, making his name through a number of technical inventions and improvements. He later claimed to have been the first to use gun cotton in Austria (EME II,4). He also invented an electric ignition system, which in due time was used by the Austrian army in war. For two years he also gave lectures outside the Engineering Academy. Students from far and wide came to study his experiments. Even Count Theodor Latour occasionally honored him with his presence.

Moritz was a distinguished professor when his little cousin Marie began to take a romantic interest in him. Through Tante Helene, whose heart always swelled with pride when she spoke of her son, she had learned about his childhood, his adventures and achievements at school, and she knew of his promising career at the Engineering Academy. Out of respect for his accomplishments she called him "Onkel Moritz" (MK 815).

For him Marie, his junior by fifteen years, was like a little sister. He had seen her shortly after her birth when he spent the summer holidays in Zdislawitz, he had often carried her around as a baby and had watched her growing up with increasing delight. He enjoyed her boldness, her courage to stand up for her beliefs, he also noticed with pleasure that she was highly intelligent and anxious to learn. As he later recalled in his memoirs: "She grew into a serious, thoughtful girl with no education other than the usual social training, but filled with an ardent desire to do great things" (B II 27). Being a professor, Moritz wanted to educate his cousin and instill in her his own love of academic subjects. Eager to help her fill the gaps in her superficial education, he lent her books on history and science and invited her to watch the stars through his telescope.

Once, after a Sunday dinner, which Moritz regularly shared with Marie and her family in the Rabenhaus, he discovered one of her copybooks containing some of her poems, all of them in French. He read her "Ode à Napoléon" and put it aside, without a word. As Ebner-Eschenbach records it in *Meine Kinderjahre,* he remained "indifferent as if it was a role of thread or some other trivial thing. I did not dare to look at him, even less to ask him 'Did you not like it at all?'" (818). A few days later he sent her a box of delicious sweets, accompanied by a poem from Zedlitz' *Waldfräulein.* He also had added a verse of his own, admonishing his young cousin, since she was German, to only use the German language for her poetry (MK 819).

For Moritz, as for many members of the educated classes in Austria, German culture was superior to the other cultures in the multinational empire. He loved his "magnificent mother tongue" (EME I,3) and always regretted that it had been neglected at the Theresianum, where, in his view, classical studies and grammar had been overemphasized. In the military, however, German was the language of command (Johnston 51). Thus, wherever he was stationed, he could communicate with his fellow soldiers in his mother tongue.

Marie was in raptures about "Onkel Moritz'" verse. He had not blamed or rejected her as Fritzi and Großmutter Vockel had done, but had actually encouraged her to write: "Those verses were meant for me! To me they were directed and I felt highly honored and elevated. And how their content was clear to me and illumined my heart! I could say what I thought if I but said it in German. A very strict man was sanctioning my writing under this condition" (MK 819). From then on she tried to think only in German, and she soon produced a number of German poems, all centering on themes and motifs connected with the "Hymn on the Rhine." She especially enjoyed the verse "Es singen die Sänger zur Harfe laut," which Moritz had taken great pains to copy for her from Zedlitz' epos.

Gradually her mind became preoccupied with one particular "singer," Moritz, to whom she owed her transformation from a French bard into a German poet. Moritz was the only member in the family who understood her love of literature, her interest in academic studies, and he seemed to take her writing seriously. Marie felt that he was a kindred spirit, a person she could trust. He became the man of her dreams. Dark-haired, tall and slim he looked extremely attractive in his colorful Engineer Lieutenant uniform. As a member of the military he was also called on to perform ceremonial functions and had the right to appear at court, a fact which made him all the more admirable in the eyes of his young cousin.

She also adored Moritz for his aplomb, his learning and military know-how. She was proud of him when in 1844 Count Theodor Latour, the Fieldmarshal Lieutenant, invited him to accompany him on a tour of inspection to Dalmatia and the Adriatic coast.[32] She foresaw a promising future for Moritz, yet she also realized that he was, like herself, an outsider in his milieu. He tried to unite two contradicting elements, soldier and scholar, often meeting with suspicion on the part of his peers. While the military service was held in the highest regard among aristocrats, intellectual pursuits were frowned upon and considered degrading.

Count Franz Dubsky, his uncle, for one was not at all pleased that Moritz had adopted the title of professor and embarked on a scholarly career (EME II,4). He often challenged his nephew because of his zest for academic studies. Moritz, however, considered learning "the greatest virtue" and teaching "the greatest honor" (B I 30). Yet both of these ideals were anathema to his uncle who, a dedicated soldier, had nothing but contempt for people who wasted their time with something as impractical as studying.[33] Years earlier Count Dubsky had met the famous philosopher Friedrich Hegel at a German spa and had formed a very low opinion of him, an opinion he henceforth extended to all academics. He objected so much to Moritz' teaching career that the latter had to defend himself fiercely, and the meetings between uncle and nephew frequently threatened to end in quarrels (MK 816).

Moritz, in addition to being a detested intellectual, also angered his uncle on account of his admiration for Admiral Wilhelm von Tegetthoff, the founder of the Austrian navy, and a very distinguished and progressive commander (Kann 273). By sharing Tegetthoff's military and especially his liberal political views he regularly enraged his uncle. Marie always took Moritz' side when controversies between him and her father arose. Much of how she saw her cousin at that time may have filtered into the comedy *Das Waldfräulein*. Count Robert Hochburg, clearly drawn from Moritz, imperturbably bears his peers' suspicion and contempt and gains the love of his young niece on account of his honorable attitude. He is a liberal and sees through the hypocrisy of his class as much as does Baron Benno Schwarzburg of "Komtesse Paula"—another sketch of Moritz—who likewise is ostracized by his peers. They call him a "fool" (338) and ridicule his idealism (361), yet they cannot but feel respect for his expertise and his honorableness (338).

Both these characters resemble Moritz further in their disdain for luxury and pomp. He much preferred the frugal ways of the Engineering Academy to the luxurious style of the Theresianum and later, on his first trip to England, felt embarrassed by being honored in public (EME II,7). Like Marie he enjoyed nature and country life, abhorring glittering social gatherings.

The Dubskys may have had another suitor in mind for their daughter, since after all, Moritz was her cousin, and a marriage between first cousins, although legally permissible, still met with suspicion and social censure in many quarters (Flügel 92). Like most aristocratic parents they sent their nubile daughters to the customary soirées and arranged for their debut when they were eighteen years old. Carneval was usually the time for the big "coming out" event, when the girls, beautifully adorned, went to their first balls. Their parents then began to nurture the hope that soon afterwards an eligible suitor would formally ask for their daughter's hand.

Yet Marie was not the normal young countess who eagerly expected to be introduced to the glitter and amusement of the world. She had no talent and inclination for dancing and therefore tried to avoid the dance floor. She also knew that she was physically not very attractive on account of her somewhat protruding eyes and dented nose.[34] It hurt her deeply to be less beautiful than her older sister who danced with elegance and ease and who never had to sit out a cotillion. How much Marie must have suffered on account of her unattractiveness may be inferred from a passage in "Lotti, die Uhrmacherin." There the narrator mentions that the protagonist avoids looking into the mirror because she fears her own sight: "The time when she had felt her lack of beauty quite painfully and almost like a shame had passed. Now, at age thirty-five, as an honorable spinster, she had long ceased to hate and bewail her appearance" (852). Further on in the story Lotti remembers the glance young men, who met her for the first time, used to give her: "the glance that distinctly asks 'what do you want in the world?' and to which an unattractive girl has to get accustomed" (872).

In 1866, aged thirty-six, Marie Ebner, by now long convinced that beauty alone did not make a woman attractive, commented about a relative: "Beauty, without a valuable background, is not as universally victorious a gift as one believes in one's youth" (TB 116). And further she mused in her diary: "Beauty without nobility of the soul is a sad thing; it is lacking that which makes beauty powerful—if 'I think! I feel!' does not shine forth from beautiful eyes and does not speak from a beautiful face, what is all the splendor for?" (TB I 204). Years later she was even able to joke about her lack of beauty. In reply to Fritz Mauthner's present, a photograph of the poet Annette von Droste-Hülshoff, Marie von Ebner-Eschenbach sent him a picture of herself in younger years and commented teasingly: "True, I no longer look like that! Well, if a countess is being painted, she always turns out beautiful. Even I was a beauty for the painter" (*Berliner Tagblatt*, April 2, 1916). In old age, in her autobiographical story "Der Bildhauer" she referred again to her "old, ugly face" (AW 692). By then she had the comfort of being a highly acclaimed writer, and her physique did not bother her that much any more.

To compensate for her lack of physical attraction Marie read voraciously, wrote poetry and tried to impress the men around her with brilliant talk. With her sharp eye and highly developed observational skills, with her penchant for ridiculing and teasing she must have been quite amusing to listen to. Where wit and biting sarcasm were appreciated Marie surely was in great demand. Yet most young men in her circles were more attracted to girls who excelled on the dance floor than to "bluestockings" flaunting their wisdom. Like Sarah of *Das Waldfräulein* Marie may have more than once been told to hide her knowledge, because a "highly educated girl does not find a husband" (511). Interestingly enough it is the so-called bluestockings in Ebner-Eschenbach's work who find the husband they love. Sarah of *Das Waldfräulein* is happily united with Count Paul, Clara Aarheim of "Comtesse Muschi," considered inelegant and boring on account of her "gaping mouth and everlasting blushes" (Harriman 40) becomes the bride of her adored Count Carl, and Paula of "Komtesse Paula" likewise marries the man of her dreams.

Marie saw Moritz daily. Since his transfer from Olmütz, where he had been involved in building forts and bombproof barracks, he had moved back into his mother's apartment on the third floor of the Rabenhaus (EME II,4). He was extremely dedicated to his work. And further, to live with his mother again in the rooms where he had spent his childhood years was his greatest happiness. It also delighted him to be adored by his cousin, a particularly docile student, who admired his superior knowledge. He shared with her his love of nature, his love of the theater and his political views. Gradually Marie, his "little sister," also became his confidante.

Not long after his return from Dalmatia Moritz proposed to her, and she gladly accepted his hand in marriage. Financially he was not well off, but his prospects in the military looked promising. Like Paula in "Komtesse Paula," whose parents unexpectedly agree to her marriage with Baron Schwarzburg, "the little office clerk" (Harriman 63), Marie had convinced her parents that Moritz was the man of her choice and, like Paula, she may have hoped to "grow wise, clever and better day by day" at his side (Harriman 66). Her feelings for Moritz, whom she had known from childhood on, may have been similar to those of Louise of "Die arme Kleine," of whom the narrator says: "Sincere love, that was her feeling for him, she did not know of powerful passion, she even thought herself incapable of it. But she thought it would be beautiful to go through life loyally united with the dearest person, in joy and in suffering" (760).[35]

Free from the fetters of her parental home, where intellectual occupations had always been disdained, Marie hoped finally to be able to devote herself to her studies. With Moritz' help she thought to develop her literary career, because writing was still her greatest passion.[36] In July 1848 Marie and Moritz von Ebner-Eschenbach were married at Zdislawitz. While the world around them rose in protest against oppression, exploitation, and poverty and demanded the abolition of absolutism in Austria, the newlyweds established their home at the Sternhof on the Jordansplatz in Vienna where they hoped to live in peace and harmony.

At eighteen it was not easy for Marie von Ebner-Eschenbach to adjust to being the wife of a thirty-three-year-old military man, who by then was set in his ways and totally dedicated to his profession. He was used to giving orders and to seeing them followed obediently. He was also accustomed, as a professor, to be considered an authority whom students never dared to contradict. He was used to living with his much loved mother, Marie's aunt Helene, who would henceforth share all the couple's residences until her death in 1864.

Helene Dubsky, by then sixty-seven, was a heavy burden for her daughter-in-law. Constitutionally frail and by nature prone to take things extremely seriously, she had never gotten over her sad, deprived childhood, not to speak of the sufferings she endured in later life. She had lost two brothers in the Napoleonic wars—to one of them she had been particularly deeply attached—where also her fiancé, Nikolaus von Ebner-Eschenbach had been killed in action. Her marriage to the latter's father had lasted only ten years. His death had left her again in financial straits, causing her endless worries about her own and her son's future. She gradually fell into a deep depression leading to a nervous disorder and finally to severe mental and emotional disturbances (EME III,2). Marie had never been very close to her. All her life she remembered that it had been Helene who had asked her as a seven-year-old girl to come to her dying stepmonther's bedside and to suffer the latter's unjust accusations. Helene, fifty-six at the time, must have been quite insensitive and totally oblivious to the feelings of a child. Her mind centered mainly on herself and her soldier son, with whom she seems to have had the most intimate and most beautiful relationship (MK 816). The fact that Helene lived with the couple from the start of their marriage and continued to do so for sixteen years meant that Marie Ebner constantly had to bear with a depressive person and had to nurse her during frequent illnesses. She also had to share Moritz's love with his mother.[37] Since his father had died when Moritz was only five years old, the latter never had a rival for his mother's affection. In his memoirs he lovingly recalls that his mother was everything for him (EME I, 2-3).

Because Helene had never remarried, she gave her undivided attention to her only son, who gratefully returned her attachment. She had watched over his education, securing a scholarship for him at the prestigious Theresianum. She also had taken him to an audience with Emperor Franz, who had encouraged him to follow in his father's footsteps. With a heavy heart she had accepted the fact that indeed Moritz finally did choose his father's career and entered the Engineering Academy. When he was transferred from Olmütz to Vienna after a three-year separation from her he happily welcomed him back to her apartment, and it was only natural for her that she should later stay with him when he was married.

When she died, Moritz was heartbroken and seemingly unable to bear the thought of losing the woman who had been the center of his life (TB I 37).[38] He constantly kept her photograph at his bedside, and as an old man, after an eye operation, he turned his first glance to her (B II 227). In contrast to her husband, Marie von Ebner-Eschenbach was relieved when her aunt and mother-in-law died, wishing her "the long-missed peace" (TB I 37). Nowhere in her diary does she mention that she loved Helene. She only calls her "poor mother" in contrast to her "much loved Großmama Bartenstein" with whom she obviously had a warm and affectionate relationship. After Helene's death Marie Ebner was mainly sorry for the latter's "poor, abandoned room" (TB I 41).

What she really felt for her mother-in-law, who idolized her son, may
be reflected in "Das Schädliche" in which Edith, the protagonist, admits:
"I hate your mother . . . I hate her because you love her more than me.
I always feared that, now I know it" (593).
Marie von Ebner-Eschenbach's work abounds with stories describing
an intimate, tender and loving bond between mother and son. In some
of them, as in "Ob spät, ob früh" and in "Der Erstgeborene," the
relationship even resembles that of two lovers. In her youth she had had
the occasion to observe the deep affection between her piano teacher,
Frau Krähmer, and her violinist son. During a concert she witnessed
how he idolized his mother (MK 790). Living with Moritz and Helene,
Marie had further occasion closely to watch their unique bond. Helene
had a strong hold on him, and even as a husband he continued to be
primarily a son. Therefore there must have been moments of jealousy
and times when Ebner-Eschenbach found it difficult to bear that she
was less important to her husband than his mother. Outwardly calm,
self-composed and reserved, Moritz von Ebner-Eschenbach may often
have given the impression of being indifferent to his young,
demonstrative wife.[39] His work and career preoccupied him greatly, so
much so that he did not mind leaving Marie, less than a year after their
wedding, to spend three months in England as a military reporter (EME
II,6).
　　What she felt toward her serious-minded, career-conscious husband
may have filtered into "Erste Trennung," where a young, recently
married woman—considerably younger than her prominent, awe-
inspiring husband —tests his love for her, because she thinks she is not
important to him. In the end she confesses that he "is everything to me,
to whom I am—something" (554). The story "Ob spät, ob früh" may
likewise reflect some of Ebner-Eschenbach's insights as a newlywed
realizing "that she would only play a side-role in his life. His interests
were outside the family interests. His heart remained back in the office,
his mind, his genius by which he was touched"(379-380).
　　The Ebner-Eschenbach marriage remained childless and probably
intentionally so.[40] They were very close blood-relations as first cousins
and knew that the stock from which they descended was not a healthy
one. On Moritz's side there was his half-brother Karl who had spent all
his life in an asylum because of his physical and mental handicaps
(Mitterhofer 6), and on Marie's side there was Helene, whose nervous
disorder may also have been congenital. Although Marie von Ebner-
Eschenbach's biographer, Anton Bettelheim, claims that she sorely

missed children (B I 41), there is no evidence of that in any available letter or diary entry. At thirty-six, at an age where she still could have borne children, she wrote in her diary: "I awaited the New Year awake, and I greeted it with modest wishes—it need not bring me anything new, it only should not take anything of what I have, away from me" (TB I 135).

Later, after the death of the infant son of Moritz' last Ebner relative she casually commented: "Today at half past eight the little Ebner died . . . They say that the family is destined to die out" (TB I 169). Likewise in her fiction, Elisabeth of "Komtesse Paula" considers it a great blessing not to have children, because she does not love her cool and condescending husband. Habrecht of *Das Gemeindekind* emphatically states: "That is the greatest delusion that one ought to have one's own children—there are enough children in this world!" (120). When her nieces and nephews grew up, Marie von Ebner-Eschenbach became a doting aunt and proudly stated in a poem: "the childless one has the most children" (Reuter 80). Later, as an acclaimed writer, she considered her books her children, emphatically stressing in an aphorism: "There is a relationship which is closer than that between mother and child: that between an artist and his work" (B I 41).

Owing to her husband's long absence and her mother-in-law's depressive state, Ebner-Eschenbach again withdrew into her own world of studying and writing. If Moritz thought she could live vicariously through him, who had his important military tasks and his promising career, he was mistaken.[41] She was ambitious and desired to find her own identity as a professional writer. She also had vowed not to leave this earth "without having imprinted at least a soft track of my steps" (ZT 721). The happiness in their marriage would depend on Moritz von Ebner-Eschenbach's understanding and acceptance of his wife's urge to realize herself.

NOTES

1. As Katherine Dalsimer states in *Female Adolescence*: "While the task of the adolescent is to relinquish the idealization of the parent in order to become free for other attachments, the need of the child or adolescent, whose parent has died, is the opposite: it is to idealize the dead. Enshrined in memory, the lost parent is preserved" (124).

2. See also Viktor Klemperer, a contemporary of Ebner-Eschenbach, who calls her "a most radical personality" (713).

3. This quote may be found in the sketch to Ebner's autobiography. It was later omitted in the published version of *Meine Kinderjahre* (Schmidt 304).

4. See also Jiri Vesely (ESD 91).

5. Piaget observes in *A Child's Conception of the World* : "Just as the child makes his own truth so he makes his own reality" (167).

6. The nineteenth-century German writer Hedwig Dohm adds a significant dimension to the phenomenon of daydreaming when she says: "The reason why my memory had retained so little factual information from my childhood years is probably that I always tried to hide from reality, that my real being was smothered by the rude insensitivity of my surroundings, and it only survived in me in a latent form" (Kössler 88). Likewise George Eliot once remarked: "When I was quite a little girl I could not be satisfied with the things around me; I was constantly living in a world of my own creation and was quite contented to have no companions, so that I might be left to my own musings and imagine scenes in which I was chief actress" (Redinger 52).

7. In the sketch to her autobiography Ebner-Eschenbach says of her characters: "They became real beings for me. I knew how they looked, how they laughed. I invented their daily routine and shared their sadness when they encountered an accident" (Schmidt 128).

8. Compare to Elika of "Die arme Kleine" (652).

9. Marie Ebner's work abounds with sad and unhappy children. See especially "Ein Edelmann," "Komtesse Paula," "Die arme Kleine," where it is explicitly stated that a character has experienced an unhappy childhood. In "Wieder die Alte" the narrator ridicules the countess who speaks of "the sweetness of family life, solidarity that floats like an oasis of oil on the ocean of life" (140).

10. Count Dubsky was made a Privy Councillor in 1869 (TB I 251).

11. Marie von Ebner-Eschenbach was deeply troubled by her parents' unhappy marriage, an emotion she transformed into fiction in order to come to terms with it. While in the 80s and 90s the husband is portrayed as the guilty one, in the 1915 story "Der Herr Hofrat" the author comes to the conclusion that neither husband nor wife is to blame (459).

12. This glove can be seen in the archives of the Vienna City Hall (Rathaus) under the number I.N. 56701.

13. Compare to "Wieder die Alte," where the governess is described as Marie von Meiberg's "confidante of her most holy secrets" (141).

14. Marie Kittl's charge at the Belgian Court was Princess Charlotte, the future wife of Emperor Maximilian of Mexico, Emperor Franz Joseph's hapless brother, who was executed in 1867 (Grun 430).

15. Ebner-Eschenbach's longing for her biological mother increased over the years. Compare to Mrs. Gaskell, who had a similar fate and who wrote, when close to forty: "I think no one but one so unfortunate as to be early motherless can enter into the craving one has after the lost mother" (*Lost Tradition* 104).

16. How deprived Ebner-Eschenbach was by not being able to go to school may be seen from a comparison with Stephan Zweig, who attended a Gymnasium in Vienna. He writes in his autobiography: "But how thankfully I think of that comradeship! How much it helped me! How those fiery discussions, that wild rivalry, that mutual admiration and criticism gave practice to my hand and nerve, how it widened and heightened my view of the intellectual cosmos" (*The World* 56).

17. This incident has been recorded with modifications in "Nach dem Tode," where Thekla's drawing teacher makes advances to her.

18. Marie von Ebner-Eschenbach never considered Zdislawitz a "castle." In her letter of August 5, 1880 to Hieronymus Lorm she calls it a "friendly country house" (BF 72).

19. The Vice-Chancellor of Maria Theresia was Count Leopold Kolowrat-Krakowsky, who was instrumental in helping to abolish the death penalty (Kann 179). In Metternich's cabinet the Minister of the Interior was a Count Kolowrat-Krakowsky who later became the chancellor's fierce opponent (Hantsch 289).

20. In contrast to this, Ebner-Eschenbach describes wrath with metaphors denoting heat, e.g., "Beichte" (483), "Glaubenslos?" (325).

21. It is interesting that in the sketch to her autobiography Ebner-Eschenbach belittles the importance of Grillparzer's letter. She writes, perhaps out of modesty: "What does it prove? That Grillparzer is a polite and noble man" (Schmidt 135).

22. Anton Bettelheim, Ebner-Eschenbach's biographer, alludes to the fact that Countess Dubsky-Kolowrat may have sent Marie's poems to Grillparzer in order to deter her once and for all from writing (B 1 28).

23. Marie von Ebner-Eschenbach wrote this poem in the 1880s after a performance of *Die Ahnfrau* and assured the poet that this drama had already deeply affected her as a child (RV 79177Ja/ I.N. 54488).

24. Grillparzer was once involved with four women at the same time and was living in adultery with his cousin's wife. Heinz Politzer gives a detailed account of Grillparzer's complex relationship with women (101-102)

25. It is interesting that Ebner-Eschenbach entitles Kolberg's masterpiece *Drei Sonaten*. Nadler points out that Grillparzer's work is built around a trilogy. Three times he grouped together three dramatic works, a tragedy, a piece based on a fairy tale, and a psychological drama (Nadler 320).

26. C. M. Schmidt notes how unfortunate it is that we do not know who wrote to Betty Paoli (226). Yet Anton Bettelheim mentions in his first biography that Marie Dubsky turned to the famous poet to ask her advice. He also includes the letter in which Paoli writes: "You ask me whether I believe you have talent" (B I 219). This clearly refers to the young Marie Dubsky.

27. Cf. Ebner-Eschenbach's letter of November 30, 1870 to Hieronymus Lorm, where she quotes her acquaintances judging her novel *Bozena*: "Charming, you know, your Zenoba or Bozena, quite charming, only the characterization I would have liked somewhat sharper, yet all in all charming" (BF 69).

28. In her essay "Komtessen und Stiftsdamen" in *Der Monat* of February 9, 1857 Nora Wydenbruck points out that when she was a young countess everybody was frowned upon who showed an interest in culture, serious literature or philosophy, or who admired modern music or art (39).

29. Ebner-Eschenbach's aversion to glittering social gatherings is reflected in many of her works, e.g., *Unsühnbar*: "They joke, they play, they flirt and carelessly steer towards the same end that awaits the tormented" (469-470). Cf. also in "Das Schädliche," where the narrator criticizes the cliques that have come into existence in Viennese high society (595).

30. In his memoirs Moritz von Ebner-Eschenbach claims that there were five children in his father's first marriage (EME I,1). Yet Bettina Mitterhöfer in her unpublished dissertation mentions only two sons (6).

31. The Maria Theresia Order was a decoration the Empress had established in 1757 as a reward for courage. A soldier received it if he had accomplished a valiant deed "without contravening a direct order" (Johnston 52).

32. Theodor Count Baillet de Latour later became minister of defense. He was brutally murdered during the 1848 Revolution in Vienna. Moritz von Ebner-Eschenbach called this event one of the saddest experiences of his life (EME II,5).

33. Count Franz Dubsky not only had contempt for scholars and for higher learning but also was deeply suspicious of educated people, because they were considered by many aristocrats potential revolutionaries who could deprive the aristocracy of their social and political privileges (Winter 188-189).

34. Eduard Devrient, director of the Karlsruhe theater, confided in his diary, after meeting Marie Ebner in his home in 1863, that he found her "frighteningly ugly" on account of her dented nose (Kabel 423).

35. Critics have remarked on Ebner's inability to describe passion (see A. Bettelheim and G. Gerber in Bittrich 291-292). See also Gabriele Reuter, *Ebner-Eschenbach*, who claims that the author's sole passion was her writing (17). According to J.C. Flügel's theory Marie may not have been able to fully develop her "love instincts in her youth, since she did not transfer them to someone outside the family" (30).

36. In a letter to Marie Kittl she once declared: "I cannot give up writing even if I lost his love" (B I 25).

37. Marie Ebner always saw her husband and his mother as an integrated whole, so much so that several years after Moritz' death she had, according to Bettelheim, his and Helene's casket brought up from the lower crypt to the chapel, where she liked to meditate (B II 292).

38. Carole Klein has observed that "military sons seemed to have enormous difficulty in separating from their mothers or in even wanting to" (228)

39. Moritz may have had a mother fixation. According to J. C. Flügel, "a parent fixation of this kind may make itself felt negatively in an inability to direct love freely and fully upon any other person of the same sex as the loved parent" (57). Flügel also points out that some men with such an abnormal affection may choose to marry only because of "the need to escape from an unconscious incestuous desire" (51-52). Flügel further states that some men with a mother fixation have homosexual inclinations (53).

40. According to Karl Abraham, it was believed at the time that parents' consanguinity led to mental diseases in offspring (110). Abraham also observes that, although sometimes cousins marry for practical reasons, in many cases they are neuropathic individuals, who tend to prefer marriage with a close relative (110-111). He further states that some men with a homosexual inclination tend to marry their cousins. "Since those men are hardly sexually attracted to the opposite sex, they choose a relative out of idleness" (114).

41. Compare to "Das tägliche Leben," where the narrator ironically describes the younger daughter's marriage: "She will sing and be happy about her insignificant life, as if never a shadow had clouded the shine of its monotony — clear and shallow as a mirror" (626). See also "Erste Trennung," where Emmi, the protagonist, sarcastically remarks that her husband considers their relationship "ideal" because she lives vicariously through him (546). He never notices in her eyes the "quiet suffering struggling for release" (547).

PART TWO

ASPIRING DRAMATIST (1849-1873)

Do not consider yourself
poor, because your dreams
have not come true. Only
those are poor who have
never dreamed at all.

CHAPTER 1:

"WHO VENTURES INTO PUBLIC LIFE . . ."

As a consequence of the Revolution of 1848 and in order to forestall further threats, the Engineering Academy, where Moritz von Ebner-Eschenbach taught, was moved from the capital city to the countryside. A former Premonstratensian monastery at Klosterbruck near Znaim in Southern Moravia had been converted into a military institution, which also housed the living quarters of the teachers and officers. Thus in the fall of 1849 Marie, Moritz, and Helene von Ebner-Eschenbach moved to Klosterbruck, where they established themselves quite comfortably. Moritz recalls in his "Erinnerungen": "We moved into a pretty apartment with a view of both the Thaya valley and the garden of the academy. Life in Klosterbruck was far less expensive than in Vienna: we almost considered ourselves rich and we had a carriage and riding horses. Often we received visits from friends and relatives" (III,2).

For Marie von Ebner-Eschenbach's intellectual development the years in Klosterbruck became extremely important. The nearby town of Znaim with its picturesque Renaissance and Baroque houses held many attractions because of the magic of its historic memories. It had been a fortress of the Premysls, the earliest dynasty in Bohemia, until the mid-thirteenth century. Its castle was renowned for its chapel of St. Catherine and for the many precious frescoes of the Premysl princes (EB vol 12, 926). Znaim further had been the meeting place of Archduke Charles and Napoleon Bonaparte after the battle of Wagram. On July 12, 1809 they had concluded an armistice there which considerably diminished Austria's power in Europe (Kann 224).

Except for the theater Marie Ebner did not miss the big city. The closeness of her husband's colleagues provided ample social life and, most importantly, she made the acquaintance of a scholar who taught history and German writing at the academy. Josef Weil became one of her most influential teachers, and she held him in high esteem all her life. In the military environment of Klosterbruck he was the only one with whom she could share her interest in literature and theater. Josef Weil, later ennobled and known as Ritter von Weilen, soon became a regular guest at the Ebner-Eschenbachs' home, inspiring Marie to take up serious study of German language and literature. His lifelong friendship and his stimulating influence cannot be counted highly enough.

Weil was eventually called to become director of the Vienna court library. He also became Imperial Councillor, Ritter der Eisernen Krone, and was appointed editor of *Die österreichische Monarchie in Wort und Bild*, a journal established by Crown Prince Rudolf. In his capacity as president of the Concordia association, he established contact with writers and publishers from abroad. In 1873 he invited Julius Rodenberg to Vienna and introduced him personally to Marie von Ebner-Eschenbach. Weil therefore was one of the first to help launch her career in Austria (B I 37).

Since her husband was often away on extended business trips—some of them occasioned by wars, some by invitations to exhibitions and displays of military novelties—Marie von Ebner-Eschenbach had ample time to herself for reading and writing and for studying her favorite subjects, history, German language and literature. For the first time in her life she was free from the control of a father who had only contempt for the "Gelahrten"(the learned) and who had always objected to Marie's interest in intellectual pursuits.

What a relief she felt from the many social obligations that life in Vienna had imposed upon her as a member of the aristocracy! Now she could finally use her time to educate herself and to build a valid sense of identity. She also availed herself of the opportunity to learn about the military. As the descendant of a family that had provided the country with a number of dedicated and distinguished soldiers she easily fitted into the new milieu. *Bozena* and "Rittmeister Brand" would later show how well acquainted she had become with the military ethos, the jargon and the role of honor, by which all soldiers were bound. As she later confessed to her friend, Dr. Josef Breuer, army life fascinated her so much that she thought she would take a passionate interest in it until her "last breath" (BC 116).

In 1855 she visited Venice. Exactly eleven years earlier her husband had been there during his inspection trip to Dalmatia with Count Theodor Latour (EME II,5), and now she embarked on her first trip abroad. The city with its narrow canals, majestic bridges and buildings in the Byzantine style impressed her so much that years later she still mentioned it in her diary (TB I 7). Even in old age, during her second trip to Venice, she ecstatically commented on it: "For my eye there are no more beautiful buildings than the Venetian ones. So fantastically rich, so gracious and bright" (B II 253).

Back in Klosterbruck she met again with her recently found friend Henriette Tunkler, the wife of one of Moritz' colleagues at the Engineering Academy. Henriette held Marie in high regard and later, when Moritz tried to discourage her from writing, always gave her moral support.

In 1858 Ebner-Eschenbach, yearning to be recognized as a professional writer, secretly and at her own expense published her first prose work. She dedicated it to Henriette, who had shortly before accompanied her to Franzensbad, a famous but, in her view, boring high-class spa in Bohemia. Inspired by George Sand's travelogues and Heinrich Heine's *Reisebilder,* Ebner-Eschenbach had written a satire in which she expressed all her frustrations about the conditions she had encountered at the health resort.

Aus Franzensbad consists of six rather sarcastic letters written by a mischievous young lady who springs from Marie von Ebner-Eschenbach's own roots. She has a very critical eye for the flaws of her surroundings and the shortcomings of her fellow men. She addresses her letters to her pedantic, humorless doctor, on whose advice she is taking the waters at Franzensbad. Not only does she criticize the old-fashioned spa, but she also pours her venom on the Austrian government and its postal services. She further bitterly complains about the Austrian aristocracy, the stratum to which she herself obviously belongs. She is indignant about its arrogance and superficiality, reminding her doctor of how far the aristocracy has strayed from the "mighty aristocratic lion that until a few centuries ago had so vigorously used its paws" (108).

She also ridicules the Jewish visitors, imitating their manner of speaking and reviling their penchant for making money. Finally she expresses her indignation about German critics who ignore Austrian literature and belittle the country's greatest writers. Her doctor is appalled and predicts that she will create many enemies with her "dangerous book" (118). But she remains undeterred, insisting that it be published.

In a nutshell *Aus Franzensbad* contained most of the themes and subjects that would later energize Ebner-Eschenbach's work. She never again wrote anything as cheeky, witty, and devastatingly satirical as this booklet. But she soon regretted having published it. In her youthful exuberance and eagerness to become publicly known as an author she did not realize that *Aus Franzensbad*, written by an unknown woman, would not sell (KL 276). She also did not expect her relatives to so much begrudge the fact that she had dared to run down her peers and to go public with her work. For the first time she became painfully aware how profoundly she had offended against aristocratic conventions that considered professional writing and publication a rejection of the established norms (Bramkamp 28).[1] We can only speculate what she had to endure from her family after the appearance of her satire. Over the years she came to dislike it so much that she finally wrote: "Against the booklet *Aus Franzensbad* I have the same aversion a mother feels against an illegitimate child" (ZT 719). She also may have deeply regretted her mockery of Jews, since she later found her best friends among them.[2] She further knew by that time that, as her fictional doctor had predicted, she indeed had created animosity among her class and that especially a highly placed, socially eminent lady bore her a lifelong grudge. Ebner-Eschenbach therefore later distanced herself from her first work, in order not to estrange more of her peers. She may have felt like Baron Schwarzburg of "Komtesse Paula" who realized that he could not tear himself away from his milieu even though he had many reasons to complain about it. Finally, in the 1890s, at a time when she was widely known and admired as the "poet of kindness" she must have been embarrassed about her uncharitable comments regarding her fellow citizens (Rossbacher 8). Her first venture into the literary world had taught her an important lesson. In an aphorism she would later reflect: "Who ventures into public life can neither expect nor demand indulgence" (Reclam 19).

In 1856, after Moritz' promotion to Major and after his admission to the "Genie-Comité," the Ebner-Eschenbachs moved back to Vienna. With his expertise in explosives he was much in demand in the capital. He helped to demolish the old city wall separating the inner city from the suburbs, which had to be removed in order to allow the development of the famous Ringstraße. Furthermore, his sea mines were used to protect the Austrian fleet during war.

Meanwhile Marie von Ebner-Eschenbach resumed her lessons with Mr. Böhm, her former teacher of German language and literature, who now became her "only confidant and unfortunately a far too lenient critic" (KL 277). In spite of her disappointment over *Aus Franzensbad* and in spite of her family's opposition she did not give up writing. In "Aus meinen Kinder- und Lehrjahren" she recalls: "Henceforth I kept silent about my secret work and devoted only those hours to it to which nobody made the slightest claim. But I was not liberated from my unfortunate love of writing, although there were hours when I was ashamed of it" (277). The motto she had used in *Aus Franzensbad*—"toil on! I have spoken my dearest word, the most magnificent, the most beautiful in life"(73)—became her guiding principle.

At that time she read William Robertson's *History of Scotland* in a German translation. Instantly fascinated by the work, she started doing research in Scottish history. In contrast to Schiller's drama, which presents only the last phase of Maria Stuart's life, she intended to delineate the Scottish Queen's tragic fate during the years she spent in her country before being exiled. When Mr. Böhm joined the Ebner-Eschenbachs for the weekly dinner, Marie secretly gave him her manuscript and then waited with the greatest suspense for his judgment (KL 277). Within a week she hoped to have Mr. Böhm's reply. But he sent his letter the very next day, telling her how pleasantly surprised and how impressed he was and predicting a brilliant success for this drama. As she recalls in her "Kinder- und Lehrjahre": "Now began a time for me—a good time for everyone who has once lived through it! I enjoyed all the bliss, which a beautiful expectation, a firm hope, can give to a human heart. It was perfect, unalloyed happiness, because it remained only in the realm of fantasy. I kept the outside world at bay, it did not throw a shadow, did not allow a dissonance into it" (277).

The manuscript was published and she dispatched it to all the major stages in Austria and Germany. She also sent it to Eduard Devrient, director of the Court Theater at Karlsruhe, requesting him to have it examined with a view to performance. In her covering letter she did everything to hide the fact that she was a woman. Her experience with *Aus Franzensbad* may have alerted her to the difficulties women writers had to face when trying to publish their work. She also knew that drama belonged to the male domain and that only a few women had ever succeeded in having their works performed.

She had seen plays by Johanna Weissenthurn, Amalie Heiter and Charlotte Birch-Pfeiffer on stage, but her work belonged to the field of "high drama," which was still considered the monopoly of men (Gnüg 242). She also knew that Frau von Weissenthurn and Frau Birch-Pfeiffer had long been known as actresses before they ventured to write plays of their own (Bramkamp 49). Ebner-Eschenbach therefore wrote the following lines in her covering letter to Devrient: "By taking the liberty to transmit to you my drama 'Maria Stuart in Schottland' for examination, I submit it to the judgment, the favorable or unfavorable decision of which can become an existential question for the young dramatist . . . Submitted by your most devoted servant M. v. Ebner-Eschenbach" (B II 311).

Once the drama was accepted, she thought proudly to announce to her relatives: "Look, there is something to my talent, I have succeeded after all" (KL 271). Weeks and weeks passed without a reply from the stage directors, and the young author's optimism gradually changed to increasing dejection. Not one positive response arrived (KL 278).

One day, however, while on a visit to Zdislawitz, she was reading Otto Ludwig's *Die Makkabäer* to her stepmother and secretly mused about the author whose talent she thought much superior to her own. At one point she was interrupted by a servant who handed over a bundle of letters to her stepmother. Contrary to her habit Ebner-Eschenbach did not ask whether there was any mail for her. With a wildly beating heart she stared into her book, hardly daring to breathe. Countess Dubsky then handed her a blue envelope from Karlsruhe, addressed to "M. von Eschenbach," the name with which Marie had signed her letter to Eduard Devrient. He warmly praised "Maria Stuart" and promised to study and rehearse the piece "with the same care and love as Otto Ludwigs *Makkabäer*" (KL 278). That coincidence almost overpowered Marie Ebner. A moment earlier she had been reading *Die Makkabäer* and now her own drama would receive the same honor as Otto Ludwig's masterpiece. She was in raptures. Devrient, true to his word, soon performed *Maria Stuart* at his theater in Karlsruhe, where it remained in the repertoire for a full three years (KL 279).

Contrary to Schiller and Ludwig, who both portray Maria Stuart as an accomplice to her husband's assassination, Ebner-Eschenbach saw her heroine as completely innocent. She endowed her with all her own ideals of honesty and fidelity, delineating her as a victim of men's greed for domination and power. Her Maria Stuart is a young, passionate woman, yearning for friendship. Her credulity in men's professions of love becomes her undoing.

The drama starts shortly after Rizzio, Maria Stuart's court musician and confidant, has been murdered. All of Scotland is in an uproar. The queen hurries to Holyrood to preside over the court where the murder charges are brought. She does not know that Darnley, her husband, is the assassin and therefore she innocently convicts people from his entourage. She loves her husband, yet he does not care for her anymore.

All he strives for is power and the long-desired matrimonial crown which his wife has so far withheld from him. He has murdered Rizzio because he knew that the latter possessed the queen's unconditional trust. He also has suspected his wife of an adulterous relationship with the musician.

Maria Stuart, deeply offended by these unfounded accusations, turns to Lord Bothwell, her military adviser. He is a man of bravery and, as she believes, of great honesty. He had once defended her mother, Mary of Guise, against the "Lords of the Congregation" and now he becomes her own stronghold and support. Maria Stuart henceforth neglects her husband, giving herself up to her infatuation with Bothwell. Darnley, upon discovering his wife's affair, threatens to inform all the rulers of Europe and also tries to remove the recently born heir apparent from Maria Stuart's care.

Bothwell does not love the queen but only wants to become King of Scotland. One night he blows up Darnley's castle, in which the latter was spending the night. Now the way seems free for Bothwell to gain Maria Stuart's hand in marriage and to secure the precious Scottish crown. Despite Bothwell's precautions all of Scotland soon knows that he murdered Darnley, and Maria Stuart is accused of having been his accomplice. Yet she defends him against the indictment, firmly believing in his innocence, and finally even marrying him. In the meantime her subjects have become restless. The lords try to kill Bothwell, for the country is faced with a civil war. Only now Maria Stuart realizes that Bothwell assassinated her husband out of desire for the crown. In utter despair she agrees to be taken to England to find shelter at her cousin Elizabeth's court.[3]

Eduard Devrient found "Eschenbach's" portrait of the Scottish Queen intriguing and especially appreciated its "dramatic power and vitality" (B II 316). In his judgment the work was superior to all other dramas submitted to him that year. Unlike the artistic director of the Burg, who had a penchant for French plays and hesitated to employ young actors, Devrient preferred German works and strongly believed in furthering rising talents (Weilen XXXVI). In fact he was so impressed with *Maria Stuart* that he nominated it for the Schillerpreis, which, however, was ultimately awarded to Hebbel's *Nibelungen* (B I 52). Devrient also sent a copy of the work to Otto Ludwig. The latter analyzed it carefully and, although he found a number of flaws, gave the following verdict: "As regards skills, and that which one looks for in technique, the author, without a question, surpasses every other member of his school so far; he also seems to possess the gift of poetry in an unusual fashion. His special forte is rhetorical power" (Bramkamp 4).

Ebner-Eschenbach's course for a successful career as a dramatist seemed to be set. Still, her dearest dream was to see her work performed at the prestigious Burgtheater in Vienna. As Stefan Zweig records: "To have one's play given at the Burgtheater was the greatest dream of every Viennese writer, because it meant a sort of lifelong nobility and brought with it a series of honors such as complimentary tickets for life and invitations to all official functions. One virtually became a guest in the Imperial household" (*The World* 15).

Marie Ebner also knew that by having her work performed on stage she would reach a large part of society. Her favorite genre was the historical drama, her role model was Schiller, after whose work she desired to mould her own. Encouraged by Devrient, in whose judgment she firmly believed, she hoped to conquer the Viennese scene. Since she had signed her letter to Devrient with "M. von Eschenbach" he had assumed her to be a male author. Critics who saw the first performance of *Maria Stuart* in 1860 in Karlsruhe thought likewise and, since the author's name was as yet unknown in theater circles, speculation as to who he would be soon began. One reviewer went as far as to claim that the newly discovered dramatist was living in a monastery (B I 52). Yet Marie Ebner's incognito was all too soon destroyed, causing her to give up hope for fighting her battle "behind a closed visor" (B II 313).

Arnold Hirsch, a former medical doctor turned feuilletonist and dramatist, who knew the Ebner-Eschenbachs, came to visit Devrient in Karlsruhe in the fall of 1861 and revealed the true identity of the author of *Maria Stuart* (Devrient II 393). Marie Ebner therefore had no choice but to make a clear breast of it. She wrote to Devrient: "You are asking me sincerely who I am, highly revered Sir, and thus I have to answer with sincerity. I am really just a poor woman, the wife of the good and brave Lieutenant-Colonel to whom you directed all your letters. Please do not tell anybody, I implore you!" (BII 313). However distressed she was that her identity had been revealed, she insisted on continuing to use a pseudonym. She also knew very well that audiences were prejudiced against women writers (B II 312).[4] But she excused the public's resistance to women dramatists on account of their inner contradictions and struggles of the soul. She obviously did not realize that it was the very society that caused these problems for women. Devrient was highly astonished to learn that "M. von Eschenbach" was a woman. He wrote in his diary on November 3, 1861: "So, a poetess; that is surprising in view of this masculine spirit" (Kabel 391). On November 8, 1861 he remarked: "Letter from Eschenbach: reveals herself as Frau von Ebner but demands to be taken for a man and to be treated without special consideration. She takes criticism of her piece very well, amiably and good-naturedly" (ibid. 393).

Meanwhile Marie Ebner nurtured the hope that, on account of Devrient's positive judgment, her relatives would now also give their blessing to her professional career. In her letter of January 1862 to her mentor in Karlsruhe she sounded quite optimistic: "Now the worst battles are behind me. Your interest in my endeavors ennobles them in the eyes of many who otherwise would not grant them the right to exist. I cannot repeat often enough: I thank you for something ineffable—I thank you for your goodness" (B II 314). She also sent him her photograph as a token of friendship, asking for his picture in return. From then on she kept him informed about all her new projects for the theater.

In July 1863, upon her return from a vacation in Switzerland, Ebner-Eschenbach realized her long-standing desire to meet Eduard Devrient personally and to see a performance of *Maria Stuart* in Karlsruhe. The drama with Helene Lange in the lead had been in the repertoire for three years, but the author had never had a chance to enjoy it on stage. After the many rejections she had received from other stage directors, Devrient's encouraging reports about rehearsals and performances at his theater had been a great support. Now she had a chance to meet the admired director face to face and to share with him all her concerns about her work. The two got along extremely well and Devrient, usually somewhat withdrawn, spoke freely about his problems with his staff and with the critics. He advised Marie von Ebner to take up the battle against malicious reviewers and to fight an honest war with them (TB I 15). In later years the two met again at the health resort Bad Kissingen. Yet, although Devrient kept up his interest in Ebner-Eschenbach's dramatic work, he never performed another of her plays in Karlsruhe. In 1875 she dedicated her first collection of *Erzählungen* to him, thanking him for his support and friendship.

In 1863 she still worked unwaveringly toward her dearest goal of having her dramas performed at the Burg, although she knew that Laube, its director, much preferred comedies. In a letter to Devrient she once voiced her concern: "The present trend of public taste and the great and irresponsible predilection of our directors for French comedy have almost totally excluded serious drama from the Burgtheater; a new poet who enters with a tragedy is courting battle with three powerful adversaries: the directors, the public and the critics" (B II 314-315). Would she ever be able to win the battle against these mighty foes?

She had by then given up hope of seeing *Maria Stuart* staged at the Burg, because she had learned that the "powerful Laube" did not like it (TB I 7). Laube's rejection of *Maria Stuart* did, however, not discourage her from continuing to write dramas. She still firmly believed in her muse which, in her view, needed only "a friendly ray of sunshine in order to remain loyal" to her (B II 315). In the spring of 1861 she had begun reading the biography of Jacobäa of Jülich-Cleve, a fascinating woman who had lived during the time of the Counter Reformation. She was to become the heroine of her next tragedy. Yet, after writing two acts, Ebner-Eschenbach realized that the characters involved were "too gloomy" for her (B II 316). Her next work centered around a strong and single-minded woman, the type of person she admired all her life.

Helene Walter, the heroine of *Die Schauspielerin*, is an actress who defies the prejudices of her family and devotes herself wholeheartedly to her art. When she meets Baron Waldau, a man she deeply respects and ultimately loves, she momentarily thinks of sacrificing her career for him. Yet soon she finds out that he despises the art of acting; she therefore breaks off her relationship with him, realizing that her art and her self-actualization have to come first in her life.

Devrient, although praising *Die Schauspielerin* for its "superb dialogue" (Kabel II 393), considered it a failure as a drama and could not accept it for his stage. Heinrich Laube gave the same reasons for his refusal to stage the play at the Burg. Like Devrient he felt that *Die Schauspielerin* should be published as a book and thus would bring Marie von Ebner honor and satisfaction (B I 65).

Only Julie Rettich, the renowned Burgtheater actress, instantly liked the work and performed it at various stages on her tour through Germany. Yet the sweeping success Ebner-Eschenbach had hoped for failed to materialize. Finally she decided to write a comedy in the hope of gaining the long desired access to the Burg. If that was what Laube wanted, then she would provide it for him. She conceived *Die Veilchen*, a one-act-play, in which a young countess, obsessed with the habit of unconditionally telling the truth, learns that white lies are a necessity to get along in society. Laube immediately liked the play and accepted it for performance at the Burg. Marie Ebner's dream had come true: after all her efforts she would finally see her work performed on Austria's most prestigious stage.

CHAPTER 2:

"THE LEAST FREE PERSON IN THE WHOLE WORLD"

On May 13, 1863, the comedy *Die Veilchen* was performed at the Burgtheater. Shortly before the great event, Heinrich Laube had wanted to cancel it, because he feared the work contained "too much for one act and too little for the clear plasticity the audience needs" (B I 69). Yet the actors, Auguste Baudius, Amalie Haizinger, Therese Pechel and Adolf Sonnenthal, had played so well during the dress rehearsal that the director's doubts had vanished and he had given his consent to the performance. To Marie von Ebner-Eschenbach's great relief the audience received *Die Veilchen* very favorably. But the reviews in the papers the next day were disastrous. *Die Presse* commented: "Pretty idea, but executed without skill" and the author added in her diary: "Quite right. All the other newspapers dreadfully malicious" (TBI 9). She knew that although she had tried to do her best, she had not been able to meet her own standards. Moreover, her social obligations almost overwhelmed her and drove her to despair (TB I 10).

Frequently left alone by her husband, who continued to travel in his capacity as a military engineer, she had to cope with running the household, looking after the servants, attending to her sick mother-in-law, and fulfilling the many duties required of a lady of her class.[5] She had made it a habit to start the day at six o'clock in the morning, to devote the early hours, which no one else claimed, to her literary work. Although this time rightfully belonged to her, she often had a guilty conscience because her husband and her relatives objected to her writing. In a letter to her friend, the poet Hieronymus Lorm, she once complained: "I am the least free person in the whole world. Every day of my life has already been disposed of, my writing and everything that has to do with it are, properly speaking, a thorn in the eye of my dear ones" (BF 69).

It was her much-hated duty to daily receive visitors and pay social calls. After the visiting hours in the morning, when she sometimes attended to up to six or seven guests, who dropped in one after the other to pay their respects, Marie von Ebner had to invite people, many of them quite boring, for lunch, and in the afternoon she herself had to embark on a round of visits. For dinner she often had company as well. Afterwards, at least four times a week, she went to the theater, where she sometimes fell asleep from exhaustion. If she was not invited after a performance she could spend some time with her husband or alone at home, thinking and dreaming about her literary work, before she went to bed, tired and drained after a hectic day.

Her diaries abound with entries in which she complains about her strenuous social life and her relatives' lack of understanding for the importance of her work. On January 25, 1865 we read: "I was hoping to finish the second act. It was impossible. My dearly beloved relatives consider every hour I spend with my work a waste. Dearest! Yet you believe the time well disposed of which I spend, yawning, with the most insignificant people who bore me as well as themselves" (TB I 41). And further we learn: "In the morning not a moment for my work. With parents, then with Papa in the city park. Leo with me. Guido and Alfons at meals. Evening with grandmother" (TB I 90). Again: "Wrote nothing at all—the entire morning not half a minute to myself" (TB 91).

When a family member was ill, "Tante Marie" was invariably expected to help out and to adopt the role of a nurse. Thus she spent several weeks with Fritzi's children who had the whooping cough, and another time, day and night, she looked after her brother Adolph, who had arrived in Vienna with an extremely sore throat. In 1865 her sister-in-law Sophie had the smallpox and had to be separated from her three-month-old daughter in order not to infect her. Having no children of her own, Ebner-Eschenbach was expected to take the baby, the nursemaid and a wet nurse into her home for the time Sophie was ill. From Ebner's diary we know that she enjoyed the baby's presence, but that she was extremly bothered by the jealousy that had erupted between wet nurse and maid (TB I 43). Because of these family problems she often had no time at all for her work, which caused her to be deeply frustrated. Neither her husband nor any of her relatives understood her need to unfold her talent and her impulse to creative production.

Several times a year she was also expected to visit her relatives on their various estates. Her sister Friederike often invited her to Bürgstein, where she lived with her husband Count August Kinsky and their large family. Julie, her youngest sister, married to Duke Eberhard von Waldburg-Wurzach, wanted her to come to Reichenburg castle, and her cousin Marie Zay often asked her to stay some time with her in Bucsan in Hungary. As in her childhood and youth, Ebner-Eschenbach also spent several weeks every summer in Zdislawitz, where her brothers and sisters regularly came to visit with their families. There they rode together, went hunting, called on friends and relatives in the neighborhood and read to each other in the evenings.

On the one hand Ebner-Eschenbach enjoyed these family gatherings, on the other hand she abhorred them, wishing she had more time for her writing. At one occasion she confided to her diary: "In order to be completely happy I would need a few hours of complete solitude every day. Then I would be so happy that I would gladly agree to spend all winter in Zdislawitz" (TB I 122). Another entry ironically states: "What have I done? Nothing! My so-called profession does not rob me of much of my time. You can be pleased with me, my dear ones" (TB I 112).

Unable to discuss her professional goals with her relatives, Marie von Ebner-Eschenbach all the more longed for people who shared her literary interests. What would she have given to belong to a club of young literati where she could have read her works, discussed them and benefited from critical analysis. She greatly missed like-minded friends who could have stimulated her intellectually and artistically.[6]

Shortly after the completion of her drama *Maria Stuart,* she had turned to Grillparzer, her idol, for counsel and judgment. Although he had patiently listened to her reading, commenting on it occasionally, she could nonetheless sense that he had no interest in becoming her mentor. She therefore vowed never to bother him with her work again (EG 887). Grillparzer was already in his seventies at the time and frustrated about his supposedly failed career. Marie Ebner realized that she needed another teacher. For a while she studied alone again, reading Schiller and Shakespeare and also analyzing Tieck's stage works, in order to improve her technique (B II 314).

She kept up her correspondence with Devrient, whom she regularly consulted about her work. He always faithfully responded. Yet being in far-away Karlsruhe and preoccupied with problems of his own, he could give only the most superficial advice. Josephine Knorr, with whom she sometimes met to discuss her poems, could help her polish up her verses but knew next to nothing about dramatic technique. Yet she may have suggested that Marie von Ebner approach a man who by then was a celebrity at the Burg. Baron Eligius Franz Josef Münch-Bellinghausen, in literary circles known as Friedrich Halm, seemed the ideal teacher. Born in Cracow in 1806 he had come to Austria in his youth and ever since devoted himself to the study of literature. At thirty-nine he had become Imperial Councillor and had obtained the coveted position of court librarian. In 1835 his first drama *Griseldis* had been performed at the Burg, where all his subsequent plays were accepted. Especially his

Sohn der Wildnis and *Der Fechter von Ravenna* had brought him great popular and critical acclaim (Nadler 315).

Halm agreed to come to Marie von Ebner's home every Sunday afternoon and to teach her dramatic theory and technique. His models were the great sixteenth and seventeenth-century Spanish dramatists, whose style and theatrical flair he tried to imitate. Like Lope de Vega, an author whom he particularly admired, Halm combined rational and fantastic elements in his work. He knew exactly what his audiences liked and, by appealing to their patriotic emotions, always drew large crowds (Lothar 127). Marie von Ebner-Eschenbach was now particularly happy to have a friend with whom she could discuss her work. She talked to Halm about her projects, and he gave her advice on matters regarding props and setting and as to how the action was to be set up. He recognized Marie's talent, encouraging her after each lesson to develop it. Praise like "you will make a lot of noise in the world" (TB I 165) helped her to build up her confidence in the teeth of her suspicious and prejudiced relatives.

Yet as it turned out, except for the key elements of dramatic art, Marie von Ebner could not learn very much from her new teacher. While she strove for depth of content and originality of interpretation, he stressed structure and theatrical effect, insisting that she emulate his ideas and methods (TB I 30). She soon realized that he was unable to help her develop her own conception of dramatic art. With his dogmatic attitude—"I would do it that way and you should do so too" (TB I 30)—he stifled her artistic creativity, keeping her in the shackles of his own epigonism. Halm firmly believed in the importance of writing one's plays for certain actors (TB I 150) and knew that especially in Vienna the success of a work depended on the performer's personality.

Since Julie Rettich, a renowned Burgtheater actress he adored, was looking for a new leading part, Halm asked Ebner-Eschenbach to write a play for her. Honored, she wrote *Die Heimkehr*, which dealt with the conflict between the hereditary aristocracy and the new moneyed elite. But work on this drama did not proceed well, because she did not like to tailor it to the needs of a specific performer. She also was bothered by Halm's and Rettich's constant suggestions and interferences, with which she did not agree (TB I 7). Frustrated and downcast, she confided in her diary: "I wrote little and the little is bad. I am unwell, moody, unmotivated to the highest degree. I have to change *Die Heimkehr* constantly, but not always with the conviction that it is for the better"

(TB I 6). Another time she sighed: "In the morning with Frau Rettich. We bargained for two hours about *Die Heimkehr*. She is right in everything, she is an excellent woman and artist. I love and admire her, but I shall never again write a part for an actress" (TB I 7). In her thoughts about Frau Rettich she may have been much less polite.

After many changes and revisions Friedrich Halm was finally satisfied, and Julie Rettich performed her role in *Die Heimkehr* in 1863 on her tour to northern Germany. Critics praised her performance but lampooned the author of the play, maliciously pointing out that it came from "the pen of a south German aristocratic lady" (TB I 14). Marie von Ebner was thus faced with two prejudices on the part of the theater critics. In their eyes neither as a woman nor as an aristocrat did she count for much.

Again, at Halm's request, she revised *Die Heimkehr*. By now she was very despondent, though, and seriously doubting her talent (TBI 24). In March 1864 Julie Rettich played her role in Hamburg, again with enormous success, while Marie von Ebner was left empty-handed. Her teacher, who had promised to brief her about the performance, never contacted her, causing her great distress. In her diary she wrote: "Good Friday. One of those days one does not want to endure twice in one's life. I fell asleep in agony and woke up again in agony" (TB I 28). Herr Rettich, the actress's husband, finally broke the bad news: critics in Hamburg had likewise lampooned her play. Ebner-Eschenbach's diary is quiet about how devastated she must have been after this shattering experience; we can only imagine how she suffered on account of this new defeat.

Yet hurt and shaken as she must have been, she single-mindedly went on writing for the stage. Encouraged by Halm, who continued to believe in her talent, she worked on her drama *Das Geständnis,* exploring the theme of adultery. A relative of Countess Xaverine, Zdenko Kolowrat, translated the play into Czech, and to Ebner-Eschenbach's great joy it was accepted by the theater in Prague. This time she had used a pseudonym with a truly bourgeois ring—M. Haller—hoping to win her battle against prejudiced reviewers. But again she was defeated. The Czech daily *Die Politik* wrote: "The heroes are veritable bundles of opposites and exquisite contradictions. The participants did their utmost to keep *Das Geständnis* afloat by good acting, which was to some measure successful" (Vesely 233).

Again Marie von Ebner was deeply disappointed, losing more and more of her self-confidence. Each defeat meant a victory for her husband and her relatives, who now in all seriousness were trying to prevent her from writing for the stage. They resented the fact that a member of their family was panned by the press. They also feared that Moritz' career would be damaged because of his wife's obsession. Repeatedly he tried to persuade her to switch to writing poems or novels, but she could not heed his advice (TBI 76). Instead, she insisted on trying to prove to herself and to her loved ones that she had the talent to achieve success on stage. As she once wrote in her diary to comfort herself in difficult times: "Do not lose heart, I tell myself after each bad experience. I still have a few friends who believe in me and who know: she cannot help it, she cannot give up writing as one gives up a bad habit" (TB I 164).

It took enormous strength and will power to tackle another stage piece, but Marie von Ebner-Eschenbach persisted: she was determined to write a new tragedy. Inspired by a visit to the Burg and by reading Lamartine's *Les Gérondins,* she conceived *Marie Roland,* a drama similar to *Maria Stuart,* with whose heroine she could closely identify. Strong, outstanding women had always fascinated her; describing their lives held a special attraction.

Marie Roland is the beautiful, virtuous and brilliant wife of Jean-Marie Roland, the leader of the Gérondins, a faction of bourgeois revolutionaries during the French Revolution. Her husband, whom she does not love but greatly respects, is much older than she. He knows that she loves Buzat, a leader of the Gérondins, and wants to grant her a divorce, so that she can marry the man of her choice. Although Marie Roland had fought for the right of women to get a divorce independent of the Church, she herself cannot leave her husband and her family, fearing to give the impression that she had only fought for her own cause.[7]

The tragedy starts with a meeting of the Gérondins in the Rolands' home. They are upset, because they have found out that their opponents, the Jacobins, are trying to arouse the people's animosity against them. A decision has to be made. Georges Danton, leader of the Jacobins, has offered a proposal for reconciliation. Should they accept it? Yet Marie Roland, who hates Danton, because he once competed against her husband, persuades the Gérondins not to make peace with their enemies. Meanwhile Lodoïska, the common-law wife of one of the Gérondins, learns that the Jacobins are planning to kill them all the next morning. The Gérondins therefore take the necessary precautions by sending out one of their group to arrest the leaders of their opponents. But their plan is betrayed and fails. Monsieur Roland is arrested. Only now, as a last resort, Marie Roland agrees to meet Danton and to discuss his offer of reconciliation. He immediately agrees to release her husband under the condition that she ally herself with him, Danton. As a woman of integrity she cannot comply with his wishes and thus rejects his proposal.

She foments hatred between the provinces and Paris. She further alienates Danton from the Gérondins and widens the split between the opposing factions. Yet the Jacobins are stronger, and during an insurrection, when all the leading Gérondins are expelled from the Convention, they arrest her. The final act deviates from the historic facts. Instead of having her heroine die as an atheist, Ebner-Eschenbach transforms her into a penitent, longing for God. Marie Roland, having refused an offer to escape unharmed, ruefully stays in prison to await her death and prays for her soul to be freed from delusion.[8]

Marie Ebner's diaries of 1866 and 1867 show how much she was preoccupied with writing this tragedy. On February 26, 1866 she read the first act to her friend Auguste von Littrow, who was deeply impressed. Yet, disappointed because she had expected constructive criticism, the writer later noted in her diary: "If all who come to know the piece are as taken by it as Auguste, then Schiller on his Olympus will be shaking on his throne. A pity that one cannnot get a quiet uninhibited judgment from this intelligent woman" (TBI 82). On March 1, 1866 she wrote: "Suffering a great deal, but very industrious. If my muse kept smiling on me for six more weeks as she does now, *Marie Roland* will be completed and perhaps not too badly. Did not get up all day. O head, keep going" (TB I 83). How much she appreciated being left to do her work is shown by her entry of March 7, 1866: "A good, diligent day. A little early promenade, then home and worked—magnificent!—without interruption!" (TBI 84). On October 22, 1866 she sighed during a visit to Bürgstein: "Spent all morning in the glass and porcelain factories of Haida. Afternoon writing in my room—O Marie Roland" (TB I 124). Four days later she wrote, somewhat more optimistically: "Promenade with Friederl and the children to the Brettsteig. Afternoon a little while to myself. The revision of *Marie Roland* begins to appear to be possible and fruitful, without having to put the whole thing on its head" (TBI 125). In November 1866 she was able to read the revised first act of *Marie Roland* to her sister Fritzi and a guest at Bürgstein. Both were obviously quite moved by it (TBI 127).

Friedrich Halm, still supervising her work at the time, was greatly impressed by the progress his student had made. In a letter to her he wrote: "Who still doubts your talent, after reading *Marie Roland*, must be an idiot or an extremely jealous person," yet he warned that the tragedy was "impractical" because of its revolutionary content (TB I 133). In March 1867 Devrient confirmed Halm's misgivings by stating that *Marie Roland* would not be a success on stage because the "poisonous atmosphere" of the revolution had been presented too realistically (TB I 162). Yet Marie von Ebner still remained hopeful about her work. On March 27, 1867 she sent the last act of *Marie Roland* to the printers, whereupon the manuscript went on its way to various stages in Austria and Germany.

Eduard Devrient, meeting Ebner-Eschenbach that summer in Bad Kissingen, did not want to disappoint her but evasively promised to perform *Marie Roland* in Karlsruhe, once it had been accepted by the Burg. Baron Loën, the stage director in Weimar, however, did not share Devrient's concerns and staged the tragedy in his provincial theater. Critics assumed that the author "M. v. Eschenbach" was a male and a member of the Austrian aristocracy. They pointed out various weaknesses of the work but admitted that "the character of the heroine [was] cogent, and occasionally excellently drawn" (B II 321). Marie von Ebner-Eschenbach, triumphant at this news, was quite overwhelmed when she learned that the Duke of Weimar had asked a friend to convey his compliments to the author of *Marie Roland* (TB I 245). Heinrich Laube also liked the work but suggested changes. He found some scenes too short and not delineated with the necessary empathy. He finally recommended the drama to the board of directors, well aware that it might be rejected by the censor because of its revolutionary implications.

Emperor Joseph II had established censorship at the Burg in order to cleanse performances of inappropriate jokes and vulgarities. Concerned about the decency of the theater he thought to use it as a vehicle for moral and social education. Over the years theater directors had implemented additional rules and restrictions, turning censorship into a "gag that stifled every sound" (Lothar 68). Authors who handed in their pieces at the Burg had to make sure that they did not contain expressions offensive to the court. They were forbidden to verbally attack the Burg directors and the artists, and they were expected to instill high moral standards with their works. Plays containing criticism of current affairs, of the Imperial family or of the Christian religion were rejected. So were pieces that dealt with historical events denouncing the monarchy or describing episodes disgracing the court and the Austrian elite. Dialogues were examined for decency of language. Words derived from the Bible or the catechism had to be eliminated, with the words "holy" or "sin" never being tolerated in a work. Terms like "freedom," "equality" or "enlightenment" were likewise highly suspicious and ran the risk of being deleted by the censor, if he accepted the work at all (Lothar 43).

By the time Laube submitted *Marie Roland,* censorship at the Burg had become intolerably petty. The drama was rejected on the grounds that the French Revolution was "still too recent an event" and that the name of the queen (Marie Antoinette) was mentioned in the piece (Lothar 132). Marie von Ebner knew about the censors' narrow-mindedness and may not have been too astonished about the verdict. She may, however, have suspected a deeper and more far-reaching reason for the rejection. Shortly before submitting *Marie Roland* to Laube she had learned from a friend that the Duchess Auersperg, wife of the theater manager Duke Vincent Auersperg, bore her a severe grudge. The duchess had been deeply offended by Ebner-Eschenbach's ironic description of the aristocracy in her first publication *Aus Franzensbad* (TB I 277). Taking this criticism personally, she had not understood its well-meant intent. Deeply imbued with the conviction of the Austrian aristocracy's superiority she must have resented observations like the following:

> What our aristocracy is today one can see in its women and daughters as well as in its sons, who are destined to carry their old names. Indeed, there are lamentable conclusions to be drawn from its representatives with regard to one of the most noble institutions in the world. In everything it has abandoned substance for appearance and is content to be called what it no longer can be. (103)

Duchess Auersperg further must have been enraged about Ebner-Eschenbach's view that aristocratic daughters had "never learned to think and to suffer" (106) and that their emotions, judgments and conversations were pitiably shallow (103). Offended in her vanity, pride and deepest convictions about her aristocratic origins, the duchess never forgave Marie von Ebner these satirical observations. And what better way to take revenge than to try to thwart the latter's career as a dramatist? As far as the duchess' influence reached, Ebner-Eschenbach would certainly be doomed to fail. Not only may the duchess have asked her husband as the highest authority at the Burg to reject her works,[9] she also had the power to influence the press.[10] Some of those critics who reviled Marie von Ebner's plays may have been strong supporters of the aristocracy, and each of their negative reviews may have been a "ticket granting entry to a soirée" (Benesch 95). Thus the duchess did not even have to bribe the censors to reject a work, nor did she need to ask the critics to write disparaging reviews; a regular invitation to her parties sufficed to secure their unflinching loyalty.

Marie von Ebner was concerned about Duchess Auersperg's resentment and referred to it twice in her diary that year. She knew that as far as the powerful lady's influence reached, the doors at the Burg would be closed for her. More than once she regretted having published *Aus Franzensbad*. Now she began to take a profound dislike to it, knowing it to be the cause of active animosity. Unfortunately, Laube, who, on account of his position and authority, could have tried to intervene for Marie Ebner at the Burg, at that time resigned from his directorship. Duke Auersperg had appointed Friedrich Halm as superintendent, and the latter soon tried to undermine the artistic director's responsibilities. So far it had been Laube's unrestricted right to decide on the repertoire and to look after the casting. Now Friedrich Halm curtailed this purview and Laube, interpreting this as an act of intentional humiliation, decided to abdicate (Lothar 119).[12]

Laube's resignation was a great disappointment for Marie von Ebner-Eschenbach. She much appreciated him as artistic director and valued his judgment of her work, although she never quite knew if he believed in her talent. Halm's appointment as superintendent did not please her at all, because she had an inkling that, although he was now in a position to perform *Marie Roland* at the Burg, he did not have the courage to intercede for her. On July 11, 1867, upon learning of Halm's appointment as superintendent, she sadly noted in her diary: "Farewell

Marie Roland!—Another one of my children has died before it was actually born" (TB I 193). But she swore not to lose heart and to continue the painful struggle for a successful dramatic career.

Yet the Halm-Laube controversy affected her deeply. She was convinced that her teacher had done Laube a great wrong, although he professed his innocence and hoped to effect a reconciliation with his opponent (TB I 212). Henceforth she could not respect Halm anymore, and her relationship with him soured. After his death in 1871 she wrote in her diary: "I shall never get over the fact that our so amicable relationship had to be clouded during the last few years because of the unfortunate conflict with Laube" (TB II 38).

Marie Roland, Ebner-Eschenbach's last historical drama, is still considered her best work for the stage (Rocek 581). After his resignation Heinrich Laube praised it in the *Neue Freie Presse* as a work of "entirely pure high-mindedness" and blamed the Burg for rejecting it out of "court-theater prejudice against certain historic periods" (B II 319). Yet other stages as well refused to perform the play, perhaps because of its unconventional conclusion (Necker 27).

In 1869 Marie von Ebner-Eschenbach was asked to write a one-act play about Friedrich Schiller for the Schiller Memorial Fund. She felt very flattered and intrigued by this task, especially since Schiller had been her idol since childhood. At first she wanted to call the play *Ein Tag aus Schillers Leben* (A Day in Schiller's Life), but then changed the title to *Doktor Ritter*, the pseudonym Schiller had adopted during his stay in Thuringia (TB I 239). The play presents Schiller's stay at Henriette von Wolzogen's estate in Bauernbach. He falls in love with Charlotte, his hostess's daughter who, however, does not reciprocate his feelings for her. In his passion for the girl Schiller even thinks of renouncing his art but finally realizes that he can never give up his vocation.[13]

Marie von Ebner started writing the play on January 7, 1869 and completed it on January 22. During these two weeks she was able to work without interruption. At the same time Sigmund Schlesinger, a journalist who wrote occasional pieces for the theater, had been asked to contribute a piece for the Schiller Fund. Since he was unable to complete his play *Die Schwestern von Rudolstadt* in time, Ebner-Eschenbach's piece was accepted by the committee. Her anonymity was preserved. Only her husband, her brother Adolph, and his wife Sophie, her brother Viktor and a few very close friends knew that she was the author.

Both theaters, the Kärntnertheater and the Burg, staged *Doctor Ritter*. After the rehearsal at the Burg a relieved Marie von Ebner wrote in her diary: "I begin to hope and cease to be afraid" (TB I 246). The performance on February 21, 1869 surpassed all her expectations. The actors, encouraged by an audience which became more and more supportive, gave their best and in the end applauded enthusiastically (TB I 246). Two days later Marie von Ebner was called to the stage, an event that must have given her deep satisfaction. Finally she was able to prove her talent to her ever doubting relatives and friends.

Moritz von Ebner-Eschenbach, impressed by her achievement, had sent her a bust of Schiller the day she had completed the piece (TB I 241). Adolph and Viktor sent her a bouquet of flowers after the premiere as a token of their admiration. Her father had enjoyed the performance without knowing that the drama came from the pen of his own daughter. As Franz von Dubsky, Marie von Ebner-Eschenbach's nephew, recalls:

> The play was performed without anyone excepting the few who shared the secret being able to guess that she was the author. It pleased, amongst others, my grandfather, who had attended the performance, being left in ignorance, as the rest. Having returned home, he expressed his satisfaction with the piece and added in Aunt Marie's presence: "Here she is always writing, our Marie. If she had accomplished something like this I would not mind her writing!" He was not exactly sentimental, my grandfather. But when Aunt Marie confessed that she actually was the author, he could not hide his joy and embraced her. ("Erinnerungen" 17)

Doctor Ritter was performed five times at the Burgtheater between February and March 1869 and was also staged in Leipzig and Prague later that year. It then disappeared from the repertoire only to be performed again during Ebner-Eschenbach's seventieth-birthday celebrations.

As much as the audience enjoyed the play, the review in the papers in 1869 was again far from flattering. Ludwig Speidel, a very prominent theater critic, revealed the author as "Frau Baronin Ebner, in the literary field known under the nom-de-guerre of Eschenbach" and continued: "She did well to hide behind the effective name of Schiller, because by dint of her own she could hardly make it work" (B I 131). Was Speidel, "the actual preserver of the Burgtheater tradition" (Lothar 109), a friend of the Duchess Auersperg and did he try to please her with this devastating review, or was he otherwise annoyed? Frau Gabillon, one of the performers of *Dr. Ritter*, for reasons best known to herself, had persuaded the committee of the Schiller Memorial Fund not to send free tickets to the editor of the *Sonntagszeitung*. Marie von Ebner therefore expected negative repercussions (TB I 245). The editor of that paper may have thought her behind the scheme and used Speidel to take revenge.[14] Still another reason for the malicious write-up may have been that Sigmund Schlesinger felt offended because Ebner-Eschenbach's work had been preferred to his own and had asked Speidel to write a negative review.

In her diary Ebner-Eschenbach notes that henceforth Schlesinger bore the ladies' committee of the Schiller Fund a grudge. He may have cherished illwill against her as well (TB I 243). She was, however, not upset about Speidel's invective—the success at the premiere had uplifted her—and therefore she could comment in her diary: "It would be a pity if the man did not allow himself that innocent pleasure" (TB I 248). She was proud of her accomplishment and for once did not take too seriously what the critics had to say. In her reminiscences of Grillparzer she later recalled the performance of *Dr. Ritter*: "The audience was warm and responded in a friendly way. Critics ridiculed and nagged. I had done everything wrong. Completely different—that would have been the right thing to do" (898). She then went to see Grillparzer, who assured her that he had long wanted to tell her how happy he was about the success of her play. To hear that Grillparzer took an interest in her work was compensation enough for all the vicious reviews.

Soon afterwards family problems cast a dark shadow over Marie von Ebner's life, so that her literary work had to be set aside. In August her stepmother, having been unwell and suffering from nerve and heart problems for a long time, became seriously ill. Her relationship with Count Dubsky had deteriorated over the years to such a degree that family members dreaded to visit the couple. In February 1869 Ebner-

Eschenbach mentioned having been to dinner with her parents, who were at odds again. She blamed her father alone for the sad situation (TB I 248). Countess Xaverine Dubsky-Kolowrat died on Sept 4, 1869, leaving the family to look after her husband and to endure his cantankerous moods. How much this affected Marie von Ebner is shown by her diary entries, which deal exclusively with her father and the problems he caused the family during their stay in Zdislawitz, where the countess was buried. On September 22 she wrote: "Perhaps the worst day we have lived through since the death of our good mother" (TB I 278). September 23: "A day worse than yesterday. I am very tired, very discouraged". September 24: "Papa is slightly better today and in a softer mood. May God preserve it! The whole day Papa remained good and friendly with us, not a single relapse into the almost hostile way in which he has treated us thus far" (TB I 279).

By that time Count Dubsky had demanded that the Ebner-Eschenbachs move back into the Rabenhaus with him and take care of his needs. The couple contemplated such a prospect with horror. Marie von Ebner consequently went through a severe crisis. For a long time she felt that she should refuse her father's request, because she did not have the strength to be constantly around him (TB I 277). On September 27 she confided to her diary: "Again a magnificent sunny summer day, if one had a joyful heart to enjoy it. I am looking into the future as into a hopeless void. What good can come out of it? At any rate my existence will be called: joylessness, dependence, deepest loneliness" (TB I 279). Moritz likewise felt that moving into his father-in-law's house and giving up his privacy went beyond his strength. On October 30, 1869 Marie von Ebner-Eschenbach entered in her diary: "The whole day at home. It was snowing and raining. Moriz quite miserable . . . we talk a lot about the sad future before us. No green twig can be seen that would allow us to catch a ray of hope" (TB I 284). She was particularly apprehensive because she knew that her husband and her father did not get along. When they were together tempers always ran high and she had to settle their quarrels. Yet Marie and Moritz finally realized that it was their duty to care for Count Dubsky and that everyone in the family expected it of them.

On November 4 Marie von Ebner moved back into her father's house, while her husband departed for a trip to Egypt. In her diary she noted with resignation. "Packed up. Our last dinner at our own table. We parted with difficulty. A new existence begins. The old life was not always pure happiness, but we were used to it" (TBI 285). She suddenly found herself again under the supervision of her autocratic and authoritarian father, who tried to control her life as he had done in her youth. Moritz von Ebner-Eschenbach avoided the old man as well as he could, going on extended trips whenever the opportunity arose. How much his wife chafed under these conditions is revealed by the following diary entry: "Early Dr. Schmidt, later Count Paar. We struggled through to mealtime. In the evening a party of tarok and Adolph's good humor were helpful . . . Thus it would be tolerable—but how does my inner life look! My soul is crying for my work, for my activities" (TB I 289).

It took weeks to reorganize her father's sloppily run household. For now at least he had a lady who came every morning to read the papers to him and to keep him company until lunchtime. She was a great help, yet for obvious reasons she did not want to accept a permanent position (TB I 291). Then a housekeeper had to be found, someone who was efficient and willing to bear Count Dubsky's fluctuating moods. How would his daughter be able to cope with all these new responsibilities and still find time and composure to concentrate on her writing?

CHAPTER 3:

"GOALS SET TOO HIGH"

Since 1867 Marie von Ebner-Eschenbach had thought about a comedy she wanted to call *Das Waldfräulein* after Zedlitz' epic poem, from which Moritz had once copied some verses for her. Having had many disappointments with her dramas, she hoped to be more successful with another comedy, the genre that was still the most popular at the Burg. In November that year she had started her work, but was often prevented from writing because of severe headaches, ear problems and worries about her parents, whose life together was turning more and more into a nightmare. On December 6, 1867 she dejectedly wrote in her diary:

> Very unwell, slept very badly. I may be wrong but according to my feelings I am no better off than any patient. And on top of it that heavy atmosphere in my parents' home! I am supposed to help, dear God! and am beaten sore with a hundred thousand cudgels. The only solace, the only remedy to gain courage would be to be able to work, or even better, to be allowed to work. (TB I 216)

She also felt that her dark room, giving on to a gloomy inner courtyard, was not conducive to writing a cheerful comedy. In her diary she sighed on November 17: "I got up late and all day long felt sick and very weak. In my gloomy backyard room it is hardly possible to write. That spoils my mood and that, I fear, will influence my work. *Das Waldfräulein* should be composed in a room flooded with sunshine, warm and bright it should be therein and in the heart of the one who writes it" (TB I 231). She regularly read individual acts to friends who all seemed to enjoy them, but she herself was not pleased (TB I 231). Yet in spite of her own forebodings and Halm's criticism of the play, she did not give up hope that the comedy would one day be a success on stage. In 1869 she sent the manuscript to various friends, among them Hieronymus Lorm and Betty Paoli, whose judgment she valued and who encouraged her to continue her work. More than two years later she finally completed the comedy for publication.

The manuscript, which is preserved in the Stadtbibliothek in Vienna, shows Ebner-Eschenbach's dedication to this work. Even the last version—neatly handwritten and bound—shows crossed out passages and major changes. A whole act is rewritten. She also wrote down suggestions as to which actors should play which parts. In both Zedlitz' and Ebner-Eschenbach's version the heroine is a young, nubile aristocratic girl who has been brought up in the countryside and is transferred to the city to find a suitable husband. Having grown up in the country, she feels very close to nature, often being at odds with the conventions and customs practiced in the urban salons. But despite her lack of elegance and despite her interest in learning, an interest frowned upon by her peers, she ultimately finds a suitor and, after some comic misunderstandings, gives her hand to the man she loves.

Heinrich Laube enthusiastically accepted the comedy for his newly established stage. After his resignation from the Burg he had first gone to Leipzig, but was soon called back to Vienna to found the Stadttheater, a theater meant to be a rival for the Burg. The first performance of *Das Waldfräulein* turned out to be a social event. Rumor preceding the performance had it that the play portrayed and caricatured a number of highly placed personalities and that the name Eschenbach was a pseudonym behind which a well-known Viennese socialite was hiding. The house was filling fast. Mounted police tried in vain to bring order into the chaos of carriages and buggies. Archduke Wilhelm, a member of the Imperial family, was present, besides a great number of the aristocratic elite. The suspense in the place was almost intolerable. Due to the audience's lack of response the performers did not give their best, so that the whole production was stiff, leaving a lot to be desired. Marie von Ebner, who watched the performance partly in her brother Adolph's box, later joining the Laubes in theirs, felt utterly mortified, since in the end she heard more hissing than applause.

The next day critics of various dailies showered their ridicule and malice upon the performance and the author. They found fault with the structure of the comedy, objected to the protagonist's affection for a servant and missed the "clerical element as the most modern of character traits " (Gladt 47). One critic confirmed that he "had seen worse," while another pondered: "Where people laugh like mad, one asks oneself: 'Why did I laugh'? If I reflect on the characters and scenes of the *Waldfräulein* I ask the reverse question: 'Why did I not laugh at this or that?' Then I discover by hindsight that there is real comedy in these figures and scenes" (Gladt 48).

As once before, Ebner-Eschenbach was also maligned for being an aristocrat, her intentions being viciously distorted. She was jeered as a woman writer who advocated the "noble guild of learned women." Her protagonist was blamed for behaving like a "boor" with "a bold, even insolent appearance" and for having a penchant for becoming a bluestocking[15] (Gladt 47). The critic further remarked that the species of bluestocking was more common among women of the aristocracy than among the bourgeoisie because the latter were not bored enough to aspire to a writing career (ibid.). Another, particularly malicious, comment read: "Do these mean little family quarrels in the way in which they are presented here—detailed as is the wont of women and repeated from one act to the next—not give the petty impression of family gossip which is being brought to dramatic publicity?" (B I 89). Yet there were also a few positive reviews, which gave the author credit for her brilliant and realistic characterization and for her witty dialogues (Tyrolt 31). Heinrich Laube also commented positively in his history of the Wiener Stadttheater, highlighting "the piquant, intelligently developed theme and the talented dialogue" (95-96). He further asserted: "The author's name Eschenbach indeed hides a lady of the world of the aristocracy, who with talent and taste is writing for the stage" (96). Laube clearly had good intentions toward Ebner-Eschenbach. He tried to encourage her to write for the theater, but he was powerless against the malice of the press. Instead of offering constructive advice about the plays, critics invariably attacked the author. If the Duchess Auersperg was behind the critics' viciousness, she certainly had done a thorough job.

Meanwhile, in spite of the corrupt and spiteful press, *Das Waldfräulein* was performed eleven times, a sign that it was capable of drawing an audience.[16] After the seventh performance the actress Katharina Schratt, later mistress of Emperor Franz Joseph, played the protagonist's part and delighted the crowd (Gladt 48). Her personality and popularity ultimately contributed to the popular success of the comedy. Yet the disparaging reviews had hurt Ebner-Eschenbach to the quick. How deeply she suffered at that time may be inferred from her 1875 story "Ein Spätgeborener," into which she admittedly poured her grief and frustration about the critics' panning of her play (Schmidt 305). Like her hero, she realized that the audience was eager for sensationalism and vulgarity and that she could not cater to the modern taste. Like her hero she also knew that she was "born too late" (668).

In a letter to Devrient she wrote: "Like my poor hero I should have come fifty years earlier into the world, if I was to achieve in it more than my own maturing, a coping with my self, or, to say it in a few words, resignation, which has nothing to do with pessimistic lassitude" (B I 95).

Andreas Muth, the protagonist of this story, is a simple office clerk, who in his free time dedicates himself to writing dramas. His artistic talent has developed in isolation. Nobody but a very close friend knows about his secret aspirations. All of Muth's dramas, diligently written and regularly submitted to the theater office, have been turned down. Yet one day the unbelievable happens: his play *Marc Aurel* is accepted by the stage-director, due to a misunderstanding. Rumor has it that Count Auwald, a well-known controversial statesman, is hiding behind Muth's pseudonym "Karl Stein." The play is performed but does not please and the review, actually geared to insulting Count Auwald, devastates Andreas Muth so much that he begins to doubt his talent. He realizes that he has been born too late and that the audience does not appreciate his conception of art any more. Yet he refuses to become a hack writer. Lampooned by a vindictive critic, Andreas Muth in his desperation runs for hours through a cold winter night, contracts a severe fever and dies in a delirium.

Like her hapless hero, far too sensitive for the harsh reality of the theater and unable to cope with the craftiness of vicious critics, Marie von Ebner was too easily affected by negative criticism. When she had written a piece in her youth and someone saw a flaw in it, she destroyed it immediately and started another work (KL 276). In 1867, having learned about Otto Ludwig's analysis of her *Maria Stuart*, she called his comment "cruel criticism" and totally overlooked his compliments (TB 212). Since she knew how much her husband and her relatives objected to her writing professionally, she saw every negative review as a victory for them and as a painful defeat for herself.

Yet unlike Andreas Muth, who never wrote a line again after his tragic experience with theater critics, Ebner-Eschenbach did not give up. In spite of her disappointment with *Das Waldfräulein* she submitted another play, called *Untröstlich*, to Laube's Wiener Stadttheater.[17] The play dealt with the theme of the widow of Ephesus and was announced as an "Original Comedy by Meier," a new pseudonym she had chosen to hide her aristocratic background and her gender (Gladt 48). Yet despite these precautions the performance, on March 16, 1874, was likewise less than a success.

Nor did *Männertreue*, Marie von Ebner's second comedy of 1874, succeed on stage. Although she had by now given up her dream of reforming the German theater and becoming "the Shakespeare of the nineteenth century," she continued writing plays. Some were performed by her relatives on the occasion of special family events, others on small, provincial stages. After completing a farce for the Bürgsteiner Residenztheater she entered with satisfaction in her diary: "I finished *Abgesagt* this morning. It is nonsense, but it pleases me that I have been able to complete a presentable piece in five days. And yet I had, at the most, only one hour per day for writing. Therefore, if it had to be, I could earn my living quite well" (TB II 290). Between 1880 and 1903 she wrote several dialogue novellas, some of which were successfully performed. In 1881 she conceived the farce *Es wandelt niemand ungestraft unter Palmen.* It was first published in *Die Dioskuren*, and later staged at the Freie Bühne in Berlin (Gladt 25).

The one-act play *Ohne Liebe*, which initially appeared in *Westermanns Monatshefte*, was also performed on various stages in Berlin and was later accepted at the Burg in Vienna. There it remained in the repertoire for two years and was finally presented on the occasion of Marie von Ebner-Eschenbach's seventieth birthday. The other one-act plays, *Ein Sportsmann, Genesen, Zwei Schwestern,* and *Am Ende,* likewise show that until the last years of her life Marie Ebner conceived works with the stage in mind. Yet by the time *Das Waldfräulein* was lampooned by the press, she had begun to realize that too many obstacles prevented her from achieving her goal as a dramatist.[18]

The hectic double life she had to lead also took its toll on her health. She very frequently suffered from severe headaches and often had to take to her bed, especially after she had worked intensely on a play. Apart from having a problem with her right ear, which was gradually going deaf, she also suffered from excruciating back pain at the time she was composing *Das Waldfräulein* (TB I 212). Writing was not only a physical strain on her but also a heavy psychological burden. She trembled before each performance of her plays and often spent sleepless nights, because she worried so much about how they would be received by audience and critics. After the great event she apprehensively awaited the reviews, being regularly in despair due to the malice and spite of the reviewers, who did not understand or did not want to understand her message and intent. She gradually realized that she was temperamentally unsuited to be a dramatist. Overly sensitive, a real "worry wart," she not only fretted about her "paper children" but also to a very great extent about the people she knew, especially her relatives. When Claudius, a cousin, committed suicide on Christmas Day, ending a long and painful battle with cancer, Ebner-Eschenbach was devastated and for a long time could not think about her literary work. Shortly afterwards her dearly loved grandmother Bartenstein died, an incident which again undermined the writer's strength for her art.

A particularly upsetting time had been the war between Austria and Prussia in 1866, the time when she had tried to work on *Marie Roland*. The political events had interfered in her private life, especially since her husband and her two brothers Viktor and Heinrich were directly affected by the war. In her diary of March 15, 1866, Ebner-Eschenbach had mentioned: "We keep thoughtlessly living our small lives, while in the outside world great happenings are shaping up. The war with Prussia is sure to come" (TB I 86). On May 2, 1866 she noted: "Worked quite well without really being in a good mood. The events which are spreading in the world are depressing" (TB I 94).

Apart from worrying about her relatives who were fighting in the war—her brother Adolph, for example, had joined as a volunteer under Archduke Albrecht — Marie Ebner was personally incommodated. On July 12, 1866 she was visiting her relatives at their Hungarian estate in Bucsan and wrote in her diary that she could no longer return to Moravia. In Gänserndorf they were told that the Prussians had already arrived in Brünn (TB I 108). In August Prussian soldiers were quartered in Zdislawitz: "Artillery, infantry, a hundred and seventy men in the village, in the office three officers, twelve men, twenty-two horses" (TB I 113). Shortly afterwards cholera broke out. Ebner-Eschenbach was greatly worried, not least because her father caught it, although in a mild form. Further, because of the deadly disease, her brother Adolph and his wife Sophie were prevented from joining their family at home in Löschna.

All these events in her family and around Zdislawitz affected her deeply and were not conducive to progress in her literary work. Yet she continued to write. On September 28, 1866 she noted in her diary: "In the morning I read and thought about the prologue to *Roland*; difficult, but could turn out well. In the afternoon a drive; a dear long letter from Marie. Cholera had broken out already in Bucsan and even now had claimed some victims before she departed" (TB I 120). Highly sensitive, Marie von Ebner-Eschenbach was again profoundly affected by the suffering of those around her. She knew, however, another reason why she had not achieved the desired success in the theater world. Marie Ebner strongly believed that she had never been able to find her own voice.

After Halm's death in 1871 she turned to his friend Faust Pachler, court librarian and aspiring dramatist, who took great pains to read her manuscripts. But since he himself was not particularly talented in the field, his advice was of no great value to her. He had written about twenty-five theater pieces, none of which was ever performed. Once he gave Marie von Ebner the manuscript of his drama *Begum Somru* with the dedication: "The jubilee of this piece, never accepted by any stage, may consist in the enjoyment of the good luck to have come into the hands of a dear friend" (B II 154). Despite the numerous disappointments with his own stage works, he was a very lenient judge of other people's dramatic achievements. Having read Ebner-Eschenbach's play *Männertreue* in 1874, he wrote her enthusiastically: "You have accomplished in it—almost—what I always wanted to see: the liberation from Halm, without sacrificing the good points of his method" (RV I.N.60687).

While Pachler tried to flatter her and failed to give constructive advice, Heinrich Laube regularly offered suggestions as to how to change her plays. He often felt they were too long, too novelistic and not effective enough on stage. Yet he did not tell her exactly how to improve her work. As much as she respected him as artistic director of the Burg she did not think of him as highly as a dramatist. Once, after Laube had suggested changes in *Marie Roland*, Ebner-Eschenbach wrote in her diary: "Not all the changes he suggests please me—I would have liked to leave my piece as it is, with all its mistakes and merits. Thus it would at least be—my own" (TB I 170). She also did not like Laube's 1868 comedy *Böse Zungen*, which had been rejected by Halm at the Burg and was then performed with little success at the Theater an der Wien and later in Prague (TB 232). Indeed, Laube's forte was not so much creating but directing plays (Lothar 105). Marie von Ebner thus never had a teacher who, besides giving her a solid formal training, could have helped her to develop her own conception of drama and to assert her own artistic ideas.

With all these disadvantages, together with her powerful enemies in the highest circles, she could not hope to ever succeed in a career as a dramatist. The more disparaging the reviews in the press became, the less did her relatives believe in her talent, and the more they urged her to give up an occupation they had always considered an embarrassment for the family. As long as she had studied philosophy and literature and had written plays to be performed at home, her interest in these fields was treated as a whim and as a tolerable hobby. Yet as soon as she insisted that she wanted to be taken seriously as an artist and declared writing her avowed profession, her relatives began to feel uneasy and blamed her for neglecting her duties toward them. Her husband began to make life very difficult for her.

Angrily she noted how zealously he worked on his war projects, while denying her the satisfaction of achieving her own goals:

> I told him today: It is easy for you to work. In your, that is, in our family, nobody finds anything wrong with you wanting to deploy sea-mines, while you would like best to explode my poor theater pieces. That I find incomprehensible: how my people can believe that my interest for my writing would damage my love for them. Dear God! The moment one of them is lacking even the smallest thing, all my thoughts are with him and I have no thoughts anymore for my work. (TB I 93)

After the devastating reviews of *Das Waldfräulein* her relatives were determined to discourage her from following her literary career. On July 5, 1873 she wrote in her diary that both of her brothers urged her to give up her writing (Vesely 216). But at that time she was still not ready to relinquish her long-cherished dream. If *Untröstlich* and *Männertreue* had succeeded, her husband and her relatives would have had to admit that she was gifted and that writing was indeed her vocation. But the comedies also failed to capture the audience's interest. Disappointed, Marie von Ebner for a while felt like Andreas Muth of "Ein Spätgeborener," whose "creative urge was gone because the belief in his talent had left him" (663). She was fully aware of the vicious circle in which she found herself. First her "dear ones" hardly left her a minute to herself, so that she had no time to concentrate on her work, and then they distrusted her talent. She also knew that being a woman was a great obstacle to her career. The theater was a male domain and basically rejected women dramatists. Not only were women faced with many moral restrictions and limitations, but they also were intellectually and emotionally little conditioned for the harsh reality of the theater world.

Men, on account of their psycho-physical make-up, their education and worldly experience had all the advantages to succeed in the field.[19] As Ebner-Eschenbach has her hero of "Ein Spätgeborener" say: "Yes, you are a man! You have grown up in the real world, you are entitled to carry your head high in the crowd. You have lived, you have fought, you have experienced storms and have been victorious, you have been wounded and you have recovered . . . I am not strong like you. The strokes which hardly grazed your skin have cost me the blood of my heart" (686).

A further obstacle was her aristocratic background. Bourgeois critics vilified her plays, criticizing her for not being able to overcome her class prejudices. Reviewers in the service of the aristocracy maligned her for soiling the nest. Gradually she also became convinced that she did not have enough talent to become a successful dramatist (Schmidt 305).

When, in 1900, Anton Bettelheim wanted to persuade Paul Schlenther, then stage director of the Burg, to perform her comedy *Die Egoisten*, she discouraged him from pursuing this plan (B II 140). She feared that this work, written in 1871 and never accepted by any stage, would not be a success. She also knew that her works *Am Ende, Dr. Ritter* and *Ohne Liebe* were staged at the Burg only as a tribute on the occasion of her seventieth birthday. In her own view her best dramatic works were *Maria Stuart, Marie Roland*, and *Dr. Ritter* (Schmidt 305). Thus in 1874 Marie von Ebner-Eschenbach finally relinquished her dearest wish to become a dramatist. Yet she did not give up writing.

Supported by friends like Louise Neumann, the Weils, Tunklers and Zimmermanns, who believed in her gift and thought she was right to devote her free time to her literary interests, she found the strength to go on. She wrote the story "Ein Spätgeborener," sublimating her personal conflicts in fictional depiction, which helped her to liberate herself from her many complexes and pent-up fears. While her hero had to die in despair over his alleged failure, she would continue to fight for the realization of her talent. As she recalls in "Aus meinen Kinder- und

Lehrjahren": "The life-struggle of someone who seriously and intensely aims at goals set too high is very difficult indeed. What he would need most for his salvation he achieves last: humility. It takes a long time before the dreamer, having thought he could breathe freely only at the mountain top, builds a little hut at its foot and finds his peace" (279).

So far Schiller and the classical tradition had been the model to which she had subordinated her own conception of art. She had imitated and striven to follow the masters she had most admired. She now realized that she had to try to liberate herself in order to find her own voice.[20] She would not have to be the mouthpiece of her mentors anymore—she would be an artist in her own right. Little did she know at that time that she was not "at the end of her career," as she wrote to Devrient, but that she was entering the path to literary fame.[21]

NOTES

1. Some people in Marie von Ebner's circles were impressed with her book. Bertha Suttner writes in her memoirs that Ebner-Eschenbach's "star was then beginning to rise" (44) and that her cousin Elvira therefore also consulted the writer on her literary future. Ebner-Eschenbach, like Grillparzer, then came to the young dramatist's home and encouraged her to keep writing (Suttner 44-45).

2. K.H. Rossbacher in his Introduction to *Aus Franzensbad* also holds this view (128).

3. *Maria Stuart* is available at the Deutsche Staatsbibliothek, Berlin.

4. This view is confirmed by Sylvia Bovenschen in *Die imaginierte Weiblichkeit* (218-219).

5. See I. Winter, who writes in *Der Adel* about the social obligations of the aristocracy: "The social net is more closely knit than that of a welfare state, unwritten laws are more effective than the most progressive legislation of government" (243).

6. Paul Heyse and Theodor Fontane were members of the "Tunnel an der Spree" (Krausnick 43); Anastasius Grün regularly met with Eduard Bauernfeld, Josef von Hammer and Nikolaus Lenau (Schlossar 38), and Stefan Zweig had his classmates with whom he could discuss art and literature (*The World*, 39).

7. *Marie Roland* is available at the Österreichische Nationalbibliothek in Vienna.

8. Necker speculates that this fifth act with its sentimental conclusion may have deterred stage directors from accepting the tragedy (27).

9. Heinrich Laube mentions in his letter of September 1867, in which he states the reasons for his resignation, that Duke Auersperg, shortly after his appointment as Generalintendant, demanded a greater right to interfere in Laube's purview (Lothar 120). William Johnston points out in *The Austrian Mind* that the opera and the Burgtheater "suffered

constant interference" by the aristocracy and the Imperial family. In 1900 Schnitzler's *Der grüne Kakadu* was removed from the Burgtheater; officially, because the director had lost his taste for it; in reality it was "because an archduchess had objected to its praise of the French Revolution" (43).

10. Karl Kraus, editor of *Die Fackel*, repeatedly pointed out the corruption of the press (See Bramkamp 55).

12. Laube later claimed that his resignation had been granted because he had staged pieces that attacked some ministers in the government (Lothar 124).

13. *Dr. Ritter* can be found at the Deutsche Staatsbibliothek, Berlin.

14. Maria Grundner in her dissertation "Marie von Ebner-Eschenbach. Wechselbeziehung zwischen Leben, Werk und Umwelt der Dichterin" claims that Speidel objected to the work because it was written by a woman. She also points out that Speidel may have inspired other colleagues to condemn Ebner-Eschenbach's work (Bramkamp 55). According to Karl Kraus, Speidel never had anything positive to say about any performance at the Burg (Bramkamp 55). See also Saar —Ebner-Eschenbach correspondence (Kindermann 50).

15. To be called a "bluestocking" was almost a swear word for women. Women who wrote were often maligned with this term, which implied that they neglected their households and their husbands (Fuchs 479-480).

16. Alexander Weilen states in *Der Spielplan des neuen Burgtheaters* that works performed more than ten times were considered successful (XIX).

17. In 1884 Marie Ebner wrote an essay for the *Besucherhefte des Schillertheaters* in which she stated that the failure of *Das Waldfräulein* cured her forever from the desire to write for the stage (Schmidt 305). Critics therefore assumed for a long time that the above named comedy was her last theater piece. Karl Gladt was the first to point out that Ebner-Eschenbach wrote pieces for the stage until the beginning of the

twentieth century (*Waldfräulein* 15). She was in the habit of regularly writing comedies for birthday celebrations in her family (B II 164).

18. It is interesting to note that in 1878, in a letter to "die Herren Hohenhausen," Marie Ebner explains her lack of success as a dramatist by referring to the social prejudice against women who face too many "difficulties and obstacles" as dramatists (Schmidt 304). Yet in 1884 in her above mentioned essay she states that she had "insufficient talent" (Schmidt 305).

19. Renate Möhrmann points out in "Die lesende Vormärzautorin" that boys at high schools had classes in drama and epic writing (319).

20. See Otto Rank, who aptly states that young artists "must ultimately, so to say, carve their own individuality out of the collective ideology that prevails and that they themselves have accepted, like the sculptor who carves his figures out of the sawstone" (187).

21. Critics unanimously agree that Ebner-Eschenbach's epic talent surpassed her dramatic skills. Gabriele Reuter in her 1904 monograph on Ebner-Eschenbach observed that the latter did not have the sense of passion needed for dramatic productions and that she also lacked the insight "into the dark and wild beauty of guilt" (28). Johannes Klein points out that Ebner-Eschenbach was very insecure when writing her dramas. "The historical themes and persons she dealt with were too far removed from her sphere of experience, and she was unable to really identify with them" (I 965). Roman Rocek, although considering *Marie Roland* "a masterpiece of dramatic literature written by a woman," recognizes the predominantly epic tenor of the work. Karl Gladt reflects on Marie von Ebner's inability to put herself into the shoes of an unethical character and stresses that due to her husband's position and her membership in the aristocracy she was prevented from advocating truly revolutionary ideas. She was further impeded, one might add, by her authoritarian upbringing and the rigidity of the conventions of her milieu. As Gladt rightly points out, she did not have the frivolous attitude needed for the then popular burlesque, but rather confronted the audience with uncomfortable moral demands. "She considered the stage—like Joseph II—as a means for social and moral reform. But the Viennese theatergoers did not go to the Burgtheater to be reformed or

morally awakened, they wanted to be entertained" (45). Summing up Ebner-Eschenbach's career as a dramatist, Karl Gladt observes: "If one surveys the scope of the dramatic work of Marie von Ebner-Eschenbach, which, over half a century, reaches from the classicist epigonic attempts, *Cinq Mars* and *Maria Stuart*, to the last one-act plays which are close to naturalism, one will have to consider it a great loss for Austrian literature that this line of development did not unfold harmoniously, although it is moot today to speculate whether and how a more welcoming critique and greater appreciation by the public would have affected her dramatic work. There remains the fact that through these failures Marie von Ebner-Eschenbach was more and more pushed into a field in which she achieved something lasting" (26-27).

PART III

STRUGGLING NOVELIST (1874-1883)

> If there is a faith that can move mountains, it is the faith in one's own strength.

CHAPTER 1:

"THE FRUITS OF RESIGNATION"

At the end of 1873 Marie von Ebner-Eschenbach's father died, an event that left her with a sense of relief. In her diary she wrote: "Goodbye, my beloved father. You are taking much with you that has filled my life—sometimes joyfully, sometimes sadly, but always importantly and convincingly" (TB II 176). Four long years she had been at his beck and call, had trembled in apprehension of his regular and unfounded fits of anger and had endured his subsequent spells of self-pity. For the first half year after her stepmother's death she even had to live in her father's apartment and run his household until, after a long and painful search, a housekeeper was found. Count Dubsky was and remained until the end an extremely difficult man. Ebner-Eschenbach had taken on her new duty with a heavy heart, knowing that she would have to give up the little privacy she had and devote herself totally to her father's care.

Her diary entries of November and December of 1869 give substantive evidence of how hard it was for her to live again in her father's house. He was sullen and quarrelsome, always holding the people around him responsible for his depressive moods. His daughter, formerly glad when nobody visited her, now clamored for guests to entertain her father and to distract him from his moaning and grumbling. To be alone with him was a nightmare, because invariably he would try to pick a fight. Every day she had to take him with her on her round of social calls. If she went out alone she had to report when she would be back, and when she came home later than originally planned, she had to fear a row. After a visit with friends she once wrote in her diary: "We chatted so long that it was a quarter to twelve, when I remembered that Papa had wanted to send the carriage for me to the theater. With a beating heart I came home—for the second time at twelve-thirty. Papa was very good and friendly and did not reproach me at all" (TB I 290). But Count Dubsky was not always that tolerant and sometimes kept his daughter, thirty-nine at the time, in fear and trembling like a child.

His death therefore meant release. Marie von Ebner was finally able to live her own life again. Something of how she and the whole family felt at the time may echo through her story "Die Reisegefährten," where the narrator describes the servant and the family of a man who had tyrannized his whole household: "They all sat together around the table of the large reception room, not as before, everyone to himself in a different corner. The light of the ceiling lamp, covered with a red silk shade, fell on cheerful, peaceful faces. Everything seemed to call out to me: we are free" (Harriman 115). And about his beloved, who had had to nurse the tyrant and be at his beck and call until his last breath, the narrator says: "You lived as if in a grave, now the stone is raised. The cellar vault where you, a living corpse, vegetated, has been opened" (Harriman 114).

Although physically released from her father, psychologically she remained tied to him. His nagging, fear-inspiring presence loomed over her for many years to come. The reasons for her fear of him had changed, yet the anxiety as such had remained. In her childhood dreams she had created a loving father to compensate for the harshness of reality. Now, as she started to write her prose works, she portrayed him as the despot he really had been. No longer did she have to repress her uneasiness and pain about her father's behavior, but could bring it into the open in fictionalized form.[1]

She may up to then have considered prose writing inferior to creating dramas,[2] but she soon became aware that it meant therapy, a means to help her come to terms with her conflicts and fears. By living and identifying with her literary figures—closely drawn after people she knew—she could explore their psyches and, by trying to understand their feelings and reasonings, she could analyze her own. She realized that in order to cope with her situation in the present she had to come to terms with the problems of the past. Like one of her heroes she may have felt that "from a past which I thought buried, a ghost's hand reaches into the present and appropriates one piece of my consciousness after the other" ("Chlodwig" 67).

Once she had finished "Ein Spätgeborener," the story into which she had poured all her grief about her failure as a dramatist, she resumed work on "Ein Edelmann." She had started this story in 1869, the year when her brother Adolph had been elected to the board of the Union Bank of Vienna.[3] Like her relatives she was deeply concerned about his involvement in the business world. In her view the life style of an aristocrat and that of an industrialist were irreconcilable. She therefore had her protagonist, a former count, who had relinquished his title, warn his son:

> As Count Tannberg, do not be an industrialist; do not call yourself Count Tannberg if you are an industrialist. The one excludes the other. The

honorable businessman pursues material values, the
nobleman—according to the meaning of the
word—ideal values. The moment the latter forgets
that he owes to them and to them alone his power, he
has given up on himself as a nobleman. (DS 64)

As she worked on this story, the theme of the threatening,
oppressive father surfaced again. She then described her protagonist's
father as a stern, unyielding autocrat, who disinherits his son, because
he wants to marry a girl of inferior social status. Since Adolph's
unconventional choice of a profession had inspired the story, it is
possible that Marie von Ebner also thought of Adolph's problems with
his father regarding his inheritance. On December 7, 1866 she had
entered in her diary: "Later Adolf came, returned from Brünn where he
has gone to make arrangements regarding the property. Unfortunately
the matter won't be settled, Papa makes demands, which Adolf cannot
fulfill" (TB I 130). Instead of bequeathing his estate Löschna to his
oldest son, Count Dubsky insisted that he buy it, and the rift between
father and son began. Then suddenly, later in 1866, Count Dubsky
decided to give all his children their inheritance. However, at the last
minute he changed his mind, causing much uneasiness among the
family members (TB I 130).

Ebner-Eschenbach's next story was "Die Großmutter," written in
August 1874 in the Swiss holiday resort of Seelisberg, where she spent
her vacation with Ida von Fleischl-Marxow. This time she used a
friend's account and transformed it into a piece of art. Dr. Ernst Fleischl
was assistant at the Anatomical Institute in Vienna. He told her about
a poor old woman whose grandson had drowned and who had come to
inspect the corpse. Instead of crying over the loss of the boy the
grandmother seemed only concerned about his clothes, which she
wanted to sell. While the doctor could not understand such callousness,
Marie von Ebner saw deeper. With keen psychological insight she
portrayed the old woman's quiet greatness and the stoicism with which
she faced her life: "There she sat, a picture of sorrow, of poverty and
need. Yet not of such need that submits to misery, but of a need that
valiantly battles it, that looks it into the eye and defeats it, that does not
enervate itself by self-pity and is not cowed down by care about the
future" (Paetel, 1920, 160). Ebner-Eschenbach had met many a woman
in her childhood who bore her fate with admirable dignity and quiet
determination. With this story she also was able in a way to pay tribute

to her grandmother Vockel, whom people had mistakenly considered indifferent and cold.

That same month she started a new story, entitled "Die erste Beichte." She finished it in eleven days, but revised it a few times until in March of 1875 she was ready to submit it for publication. This story was admittedly autobiographical. Ebner-Eschenbach now regressed further into the past, trying to come to terms with her own childhood relationship with her father. The work became her personal catharsis: for the first time she could openly say how she had suffered from her father's rigid authoritarianism. Because he had insisted that she make her First Confession as an immature child she had almost committed suicide. It is doubtful whether Count Dubsky ever learned of his daughter's attempt to take her own life, for the people around him were far too afraid of him to bring such an incident to his attention. He certainly would have as severely arraigned the priest, as the count does in the story: "'That is madness! What did you suggest to the child?' His powerful voice rolled like thunder in the small room. 'What did you inflame her head with and create this confusion of concepts? . . . It is your fault . . .'" (483). Yet she wanted her story to end happily and thus, as formerly in her childish fantasies, in the end she portrayed a loving father who showers his little daughter with an affection she may never have experienced in real life (485).

"Chlodwig," Ebner-Eschenbach's last story begun in 1874, again dealt with the theme of the autocratic, uncomprehending father, this time a father who ruins his daughter's and her prospective suitor's happiness. Chlodwig, the eponymous protagonist, had a very unhappy childhood: "It was a cursed thing, my life. That father! . . . And this poor, crushed mother who did not dare to take my side and, much less, to show me affection" (Paetel, 1920, 70). Now he falls in love with a girl beyond his station, whose father likewise thinks only of increasing his own status and completely controls her life. He has already made two of his daughters desperately unhappy by marrying them off to highly-placed but uncongenial suitors. Now he is also about to force his youngest daughter, Hedwig, into a marriage with an unloved man: "Because I love my children I demand obedience, and I know how to force them, if necessary, to obey me, when their happiness is at stake" (ibid. 102). Hedwig indeed obeys her despotic father and marries the man of his choice, causing Chlodwig, who deeply loves her and thus loses her forever, to go insane.

Looking at "Chlodwig" and the previously written stories, Marie von Ebner realized what "a chain of dismal impressions" (TB II 303) they projected. Yet they had helped her to come to terms with her rejection as a dramatist and with her sorrow over her father's character. As she resigned herself to becoming a writer of prose she also gradually began to see with greater leniency the man who had made life miserable for her and for his family. But henceforth the motif of the wrathful, unbalanced, despotic husband and father would be an integral part of her work.

In February 1875 she sent her stories to her sister Julie, Duchess von Waldburg-Wurzach, asking her help to get them published. Julie, with her love for music and the arts, was a kindred spirit. Marie von Ebner regularly visited her and her husband at castle Reichenburg and always fondly remembered their family, consisting now of six "angelic" girls (TB I 173). During one of her visits at Wurzbach she noted in her diary that, should she intend to stay longer, she would be given time to write, because Julie had respect for her work (TB II 277).

Eager to help her sister find recognition, Julie wrote to Baron Reischach at the Cotta publishers, asking him to print Marie von Ebner-Eschenbach's five stories. He replied: "If your sister's novel is found even remotely suitable for Cotta, you may rest assured that it will begin its journey into the world under the protection of the Cotta firm." (B II 158-159). It was, on balance, a clever move to have Julie write, because she was socially superior to Baron Reischach. Titles were important in those days. They were used to climb up the social ladder and to manipulate influence. On February 19, 1875 Marie von Ebner received a telegram from her sister with the message: "Baron Reischach has accepted your manuscript—overjoyed" (B II 159). On February 21, the writer learned from Cotta that 1025 copies of her *Erzählungen* were going to be printed and that she would receive a 400 Mark honorarium and twenty-five free copies. She was glad and relieved. For the first time in her life she had the satisfaction of real accomplishment. And instead of malicious, disparaging reviews she now received admiration and praise. Heinrich Laube warmly commended her for her story "Ein Spätgeborener," which he had read "with the best impressions, at the end with great emotion" (RV I.N. 56145). Josef Weilen, her friend and former teacher from Klosterbruck, wrote to her: "I must tell you that the story "Ein Spätgeborener" has gripped me in the depth of my soul. That is not imagination, that is life; drops of blood lie between the lines" (B II 149).

Ferdinand von Saar, who had read "Ein Spätgeborener" before it was published, was likewise deeply impressed. He was one of the first of her friends to appreciate the "incomparable, epic kind of representation which from now on would characterize all of Ebner-Eschenbach's creations in a special way" (Saar, *Gartenlaube* 504). In a letter he also praised "Chlodwig" and "Die erste Beichte," pieces which both had "overwhelmed him." He further referred to her originality, her power of characterization, the purity and precision of form (Kindermann 40). In conclusion he predicted: "You can be proud of your book! It breathes the spirit of honesty and will force the critics to be honest" (ibid.).

What united Ebner-Eschenbach and Saar, apart from discussing their own literary achievements, was their common dislike of critics and the press. After the publication of Ebner-Eschenbach's *Bozena* Saar complained: "I wish that a major paper took an interest in us; otherwise we can, all in all, read our books for ourselves. Sooner a camel will go through a needle's eye than a Speidel or someone like him would write something about an author who is honestly struggling" (Kindermann 50). Always concerned about Saar's precarious financial situation, Marie von Ebner was constantly on the lookout for a possibility of providing some income for him. In 1885 Franz Lipperheide, the editor of a woman's journal in Berlin, requested a biographical sketch of her. She instantly suggested that Saar write it. Although reluctant to comply, he finally wrote the essay, but had to admit how difficult it was for him to give a "striking and exhaustive description of a writer and his works" (Kindermann 74). He was, however, grateful for the "decent honorarium" (Kindermann 75). Thus Ferdinand von Saar became Marie von Ebner's first biographer, writing an essay which immensely pleased her: "You have done excellent work and surpassed my wildest hopes a thousand times. There is not the slightest word I would have changed. You are doing me great honor, dear friend, and it would be vulgar hypocrisy if I denied that I am extremely happy about it" (Kindermann 74). To honor Ebner-Eschenbach on her seventieth birthday Ferdinand von Saar wrote an essay in *Die Gartenlaube* about his first meeting with the writer, who was later to become his confidante (504). Saar also wrote a prologue for her seventieth-birthday celebrations at the Burgtheater, but owing to illness he could not recite it personally. In gratitude for his encomium, which she considered "far too beautiful," she sent him a bottle of wine from Moravia, accompanied by a poem expressing her deeply felt joy.

Shortly before his death Saar sent Marie von Ebner his photograph, signed "A poet's greetings," and she probably understood it as his farewell. After his death she wrote into her notebook:

> Saar dead. The last fellow-fighter. How long did it take us to grow to our modest hill-size height. We both dreamed of reaching fame as dramatic playwrights, he with much more justification than I. Then we achieved success with a first novel, he with *Innocens* I with the *Spätgeborner*. He progressed, step by step, and finally his art culminated in a volume of lyrical poetry and mine in a volume of aphorisms. (B II 278-279)

It had, however, taken many years before Marie von Ebner's aphorisms, each "the ring of a long chain of thoughts" (Reclam 3) found recognition.[4] In 1857, at twenty-seven, she had begun to set down short maxims expressing her insights on life.[5] It was a valuable exercise for writing in a precise and succinct manner. At that time she had come to the conclusion that "Love is the only positive entity that doubles when being shared" and firmly believed: "If there is a faith that can move mountains it is the faith in one's own power" (B II 35-36).

In 1875 she published her first collection of aphorisms in the *Jahrbuch des österreichischen Beamtenvereins* and simply signed "M.E" (B II 322). In 1877-1878 a small selection was published in the journal *Die Dioskuren*. One of the maxims said prophetically: "Only what is too good for the present is good for the future" (B II 202). In 1879 she privately published three hundred of her aphorisms at Ebhardt in Berlin. The production was beautiful—too expensive in Marie von Ebner's eyes—but it gradually caught on and slowly found a readership. It is impossible to date most of the aphorisms exactly, but collectively they reveal some of the stages of development through which she had gone. Many are born out of frustration and disappointment and, far from reflecting her much publicized "sunlike soul" (B II 202), they exhibit biting sarcasm and bitter irony.[6]

Many of Ebner-Eschenbach's colleagues were deeply impressed by her aphorisms. Fanny Lewald considered them superior to the famous maxims of La Rochefoucauld (B II 9). Louise von François termed them in a letter to the critic Erich Schmidt as coming from "a child's heart under a man's skull" (B II 9), and the critic Moritz Necker recognized in them "the striving of a human soul to reach harmony with herself" (*Neue Freie Presse* 1895). Anton Bettelheim's rather eulogistic appraisal stated: "Wit and wisdom of her thoroughly independent thoughts about the course of the world are rooted in her unconditional truthfulness, and all the rainbow colors in which she displays her moods lead to the one pure source of light of her 'sunlike soul'" (B II 202).[7]

Marie von Ebner's aphorisms express her ethics and her aesthetic views. They were partly born out of her loneliness and suffering in an aristocratic milieu that did not understand and appreciate her work. Many of these maxims also reflect her personal experiences in her family and her social circle. Her saying "Patience with the aggressiveness of the simple-minded! It is not easy to understand that someone does not understand" (Reclam 4) reminds one of her diary entry of July 18, 1869, where she vowed not to quarrel anymore with her relatives about politics, and where she reminded herself to be patient with people of lesser intelligence: "To be lenient with error, to be patient with limitation is impossible for me. To someone who errs and is limited, what I consider to be truth and wisdom appears again only as error and limitation. He believes he is defending the good cause against me, and he lacks the power to examine the nature of his own belief" (TB I 269).

The aphorism "Nothing else can make the coming of some people bearable, but the hope of their departing"(Reclam 16) expresses the frustration she regularly experienced when beleaguered by relatives and so-called friends. Finding their meaningless gossip unbearable at times, she vented her feelings of disgust in her diary. Her entries abound with laments about being interrupted in her writing by visitors. On March 4, 1866 she wrote: "I could have achieved much, had Leo not interrupted me. Day after day the same comedy" (TB I 85). And a few weeks later she sighed: "Sefine and I were just busy polishing up our poems when Leo appeared with her insufferable Bello, who spoiled my whole lunch with his intrusive voracity" (TB 88). On March 19, 1867 she complained: "Oh, if I could only stay with my work and were not constantly interrupted" (TB 164). The saying "The sensation of loneliness is painful if it hits us in the midst of a crowd, intolerable if it overcomes us in the midst of our family" (Reclam 56) reminds of the following entry: "It pains me that I am outgrowing the circle of my relations. If I cannot make myself understood to those who show me such good will to understand me, the fault must be mine" (TB 269). And also: "Did I move ahead, have my dear ones—regressed, or is perhaps the opposite the case? We no longer find anything really in common. As soon as the conversation reaches some kind of depth and leaves the most shallow ranges of superficiality, abysses of misunderstandings open up" (TB I 269-270).

The aphorism "Do not call yourself poor because your dreams did not come true; he alone is truly poor who has never dreamed at all" (Reclam 45) may have been born out of Ebner-Eschenbach's sad experience with the stage in the sixties and early seventies. Likewise, sayings such as "Get up after each fall from the heights! Either the fall will kill you or you grow wings!" (Reclam 47) or "A proudly born defeat is also a victory" (Reclam 51) and "Nobody writes like a god who has not suffered like a dog" (Reclam 51) reflect her own determination not to admit defeat. Further, her later experiences with the reading world may be reflected in the sayings: "For the great public a book is not easily too bad but very easily too good" (Reclam 53) or "The wives of mediocre artists are the most merciless judges of others' artistic achievements" (Reclam 33).

After the first edition of her aphorisms, which did not sell well, she still continued writing a hundred more, published in 1884. By 1888 she had written six hundred maxims, which had become so popular that they appeared in a sixth edition. In 1889 she mentioned in her diary that a simple peasant had taken such a liking to her short statements that he took them along to his work in the fields (Vesely 226). Yet not all of her readers were aware of how much talent and time it took to write these brief statements. In "Aus einem zeitlosen Tagebuche" Marie von Ebner recounts the following anecdote about a woman who obviously underestimated her achievement: "I received the first verdict of my booklet from a twenty-year old fellow tenant: 'O, Frau Ebner,' she said, 'if I sat down—in an hour I could put such a book together.' She was truly convinced that it took nothing but the ability to sit still" (726). Fortunately the writer found other readers and critics who thought more highly of her talent and accomplishment.

At the time of the first publication of her *Erzählungen* and *Aphorismen* Marie von Ebner, by now appoaching fifty, felt rather desperate about the sluggish sale of her books. In an age that did not have the professional advertising machinery we are used to nowadays, it took time for a new author to become known. Even now, with advertising blitzes and promotions, instant recognition of a serious writer is rare. Ebner-Eschenbach's topics were neither sensational nor avant-garde and therefore did not instantly draw a large readership. She also had made the mistake of criticizing and satirizing the critics in "Ein Spätgeborener," the opening story of her first collection of *Erzählungen*. By the time Saar pointed this out to her it was already too late. The book had been published (Kindermann 41).

When she embarked on her career as a novelist she also had to compete with a number of highly acclaimed Austrian writers like Robert Hamerling, Ludwig Anzengruber, Karl Emil Franzos and Peter Rosegger (Necker 47). She not only had to battle with the public's and critics' prejudice against aristocrats who were seen as dilettantes and as antagonists of higher learning and serious art. But she also was a woman and therefore had to fight all the harder to be taken seriously in the male dominated field of serious literature,[8] where women had to compromise in order to receive recognition (Bramkamp 79). Yet Marie von Ebner, from childhood on used to moving in the male sphere,[9] was ready for the battle. She was determined to make headway as a novelist and willing to confront her male colleagues. Would they ever accept her into their ranks?

CHAPTER 2:

"DISAPPOINTMENT AFTER DISAPPOINTMENT"

In July 1875 Marie visited her sister Friederike at her Bohemian castle Trpist, where she started her story *Bozena*, another work in which she tried to come to terms with her past. On the one hand, she wanted to create a work of art, but on the other hand there was her urge to deal with her repressed emotions and to resolve the conflicts that went along with them.[10] She still had to verbalize her unhappiness in her family, caused by her father's remarriage and his authoritarian ways. At first she wanted to call her novel "Das weiße Haus" (The White House), presumably as a camouflage for the name of her parental home, the "Drei-Raben-Haus" (Three-Raven-House), which denotes the color black. Later, on the advice of her friends Ida Fleischl and Josephine Knorr, she settled for the title "Bozena" (Binneberg 105).

The story is set in Western Moravia, then part of the Austrian Empire, during the period from 1830 to 1860. Geographically in the backwaters of world politics, the lives of the protagonists are nevertheless touched by major events transforming Europe at this time: the beginning of the Industrial Revolution with its impact on the fortunes of the traditional upper class, the Revolution of 1848, which mobilized the lower classes in an effort to deprive hereditary nobility of its influence and property, and the unrest in the multinational Habsburg Empire, which finally disintegrated in World War I.

The focus is on two families: the Heissensteins, a bourgeois family, and the Rondspergs, members of the Austrian hereditary aristocracy. Bozena, the eponymous heroine, is a trusted servant of the Heissensteins, playing a key role in linking the two families. Leopold Heissenstein is a wealthy wine merchant and a respected citizen of the provincial town of Weinberg.[11] His greatest hope and pride lies in his young son, destined to become his successor and heir. But the boy dies at a boarding school in Vienna, where his father had placed him. Heissenstein sees the purpose of his life's work destroyed. Shortly afterwards his wife, who did not attract much attention during her life, dies, leaving him with his young daughter, Rosa. In his hope to obtain a male heir to his family business, Heissenstein marries Nanette, a former governess, who, instead of stabilizing the family, antagonizes the maid and causes a rift with her stepdaughter.

After Nanette, to her husband's profoundest disappointment, has given birth to a daughter, her whole endeavor is geared towards securing for her own child, Regula, the position of her father's favorite and heir. Rosa, leading a marginal existence in the family and denied permisssion to marry a lieutenant in the Austrian Army, elopes with him. Bozena, instead of guarding her ward, has spent the night with an unworthy lover and now tries to atone for her guilt by following Rosa and by supporting the young couple emotionally and financially. She stays with them as their servant in Vienna and later in Hungary. Things do not go well for Rosa. She gives birth to a daughter, then to a son, who lives only for a few days. Shortly afterwards she dies of exhaustion. Her husband falls in a military action in Hungary. Long before her death Rosa had tried to reestablish connections with her father, who had disinherited her in his rage over her elopement, but Nanette, acting like the proverbial wicked stepmother, had intercepted the letter which might have changed Heissenstein's mind.

Bozena takes care of Röschen, Rosa's little daughter, and returns to the Heissenstein house in the hope that the old man will provide for his grandchild. The maid arrives shortly before her master's death. He has repented his harshness toward his daughter Rosa, but is by now too ill and too much under the control of his wife to make legal provisions for Röschen. After her parents' death Regula becomes sole heiress to the family fortune. The firm is dissolved according to the father's wish, due to the lack of a male heir. The suitor whom Leopold Heissenstein had had in mind, first for Rosa, and later for his second daughter, has fled because of Regula's unattractiveness.

Regula, now extremely wealthy, has a host of admirers who would like to marry her for her money. But she has an eye on Ronald Rondsperg, the only son of the aristocratic family in whose house her mother had been governess. The Rondspergs, lacking business acumen, have come close to bankruptcy. Regula has been approached to buy their estate, and she expects Ronald to marry her. Thus her mother's fondest dreams would be fulfilled. Instead, Ronald falls in love with Röschen, who is penniless. In the most dramatic move of the story, Bozena saves the situation by threatening to disclose her well-kept secret, that Regula's mother was a legacy hunter. Under pressure, Regula yields to Bozena's demand and gives her niece, Röschen, the newly acquired Rondsperg estate as a dowry for her wedding. The story ends with two blissfully married couples. Regula consents to become the wife of Ludwig Bauer, a high-school teacher and long-time admirer, and Röschen can stay in Rondsperg at the side of the man she loves.

Bozena will have the privilege of taking care of the next generation of Rondspergs.

Writing this story made Marie von Ebner confront and articulate her inner self again and reexperience emotionally what she had endured in the past. Rosa, Leopold Heissenstein's unhappy daughter, became a vehicle for her to air her own grievances about her isolation and marginality in her family and about her less than satisfactory relationship with her stepmother. As the narrator states: "What a hiatus there was between him and her, how alone she was in the midst of her family, how lonely in her father's house" (111).

Ebner-Eschenbach further used her fictional work to deal again with her hurt over her despotic, obstinate father, who never even tried to understand her. At one point Rosa implores her father and enunciates views that must have been close to the writer's own: "Please, think like a father now—forgive me—think that if I have done injustice to you it was half your own fault. Forgive me, father, and let me go. You know I have been a headstrong creature all my life" (113). By ridiculing Regula, Heissenstein's second daughter, who "grew in ugliness and wealth" (88) and who was endowed with a great thirst for knowledge, Marie von Ebner could express her own associations with the term bluestocking.[12]

The description of the two patriarchal, fear-inspiring fathers, Leopold Heissenstein and the old Count Rondsperg, gave her the opportunity to characterize her own father again. Heissenstein is "the hard, rough master—the relentless lord, before whom they all tremble, whom they all call merciless, who punishes the tiniest inadvertence like an unforgivable mistake" (118). His wife, trained in subservience, lives like a shadow in his house (76).[13] Count Rondsperg represents some other aspects of Count Dubsky: his arrogance, impatience and penchant for deriding his family members. He challenges his son by mocking him in front of his guests and is ready at any time to pick a fight. His wife has moped away her life at his side: "She reflected how in the end she had been able to endure everything, since he had always trusted in her love, although he himself had often been unloving and unkind" (234).

In her letter of 13 October 1876, Ebner-Eschenbach admitted to Hieronymus Lorm that she had drawn Count and Countess Rondsperg and their son, their servants and the hunter Bernhard exactly after people in her environment. The other figures, she stated, had "only traits" of personages she personally knew (BF 68). Yet about her eponymous heroine she said: "Bozena has lived only in my soul" (BF

68). With this heroine she wanted to portray a woman "so honest and truthful" that she would be able to bring about the solution to the conflict (ibid.).

By conceiving the tall, strong and honest maid, Marie von Ebner consciously or subconsciously created a counterforce to the image of the despotic, patriarchal father who had haunted her for years. Bozena, the matriarch, is equal to Heissenstein in her wrath and in her strength: "Straight and with her head thrown back, her arms akimbo, she stood there like a rock. She challenged her master with her gaze. His solid figure looked almost puny beside her giant frame" (84). She is morally and ethically infinitely superior to her master and also financially independent, since she has saved enough money to leave his service when she sees fit (84).

Yet her real strength is service, nurture and protection. She endures humiliation, is able to forgive and is willing to make good whatever she may have failed. While Heissenstein, stubborn and imbued with the patriarchal notion of male superiority, brings about his family's and his firm's decline, Bozena restores a shattered family and enhances life for all involved. Love and altruism are her motivating forces. They give her the courage to assert herself and to fight for her convictions. At the end of the story she stands "surrounded by a wonderful, calm and proud majesty; her towering figure still seemed to grow, her whole being breathed power and her voice sounded like metal when she said: 'I cannot prove it, but I shall tell the truth and people will believe me'" (245). She successfully accomplishes what she has set out to do. Endowed with all of Ebner-Eschenbach's ideals of strong, self-sufficient womanhood, Bozena also becomes the symbol of the motherly love for which her author had always yearned.[14]

As she portrayed her heroine and rendered her victorious over her tyrannical master, Marie von Ebner herself emerged as a winner. Liberated from the repressed feelings of anger over her father's obstinate ways, she could henceforth deal with them much more objectively. She was now on the path to finding her identity. While working on *Bozena* she received some very encouraging news. Her *Erzählungen*, though not yet widely known, had brought her some positive critical acclaim. Julius Rodenberg, editor of the renowned journal *Deutsche Rundschau* in Berlin, had read the reviews and, always on the lookout for novelistic contributions, invited her to send him her next work (B II 172). Honored and happy about Rodenberg's overtures, she replied shortly afterwards: "I shall be delighted to follow your kind request . . . If only it were given to me to come up to your high opinion and soon to send you a work which you will find worthy of your support" (B II 172). At that time she was still plagued by self-doubts and by insecurity about her writing and knew how much she depended on the good will of critics and publishers.

Work on *Bozena* progressed slowly—after forty days only forty pages were written—causing the writer to be often depressed and doubtful about its success. She therefore began to rely more and more on her friend Ida Fleischl, whose judgment she trusted implicitly and whose advice she gladly followed. Her diary of November 23, 1875 reveals: "Afternoon: Ida, to whom I read the scene between Barbara and Bernhard and who rejected it with complete justification" (Binneberg 197). Desperate about her work, she later wrote in her diary that she certainly could earn her upkeep better with a wheelbarrow than with a pen and that her work was "good only for the stove" (qtd. in Binneberg 199). Yet, with Ida Fleischl's and Betty Paoli's advice and moral support she finally accomplished her task. Less than a year after starting *Bozena* she was now able to send her manuscript to Rodenberg who had promised: " . . . for gifts from a pen like yours, most gracious lady, there has to be and will always be space" (qtd. in Binneberg 200). Consequently it came as a great shock and disappointment when he did not accept the story, believing it to be too long for serialization. Two other editors likewise rejected the work because it was split into too many scenes and, in their view, did not move along fast enough (Binneberg 208). It was therefore a great comfort to her when she could sign a contract with Cotta, who the year before had published her first collection of stories. Elated and relieved, she noted that in her joy she had bought a pencil for the occasion which cost her sixteen guilders, but was absolutely useless for writing (Binneberg 202). Cotta would print 1020 copies, she would receive 500 marks and twenty complimentary copies. The book would be sold for 4.20 marks in Germany.

Soon after its publication Marie von Ebner sent copies of *Bozena* to her friends, and from most of them she received very positive reactions. Betty Paoli, with whom in the meantime she had become quite friendly, wrote a very positive review in the *Allgemeine Zeitung*, stressing her talent for characterization and her narrative skills. The writer Hieronymus Lorm likewise took notice of *Bozena* and gave a very favorable account of it in the *Abendpost*. He stressed the writer's empathy and psychological insight and especially appreciated her humor which, he thought, contributed greatly to the book's effect (Binneberg 212).

In May 1877 Ebner-Eschenbach met Lorm personally for the first time at Ida Fleischl's home. After this meeting she no longer addressed him with "Verehrtester Herr" (Most Revered Sir) in her letters, but called him "Verehrter, lieber Freund" (Revered, dear friend). Yet she never accepted his invitation to visit him in Dresden, excusing herself with pressing family obligations which forced her to stay at home. At the end of her letter, in which she tried to make Lorm understand the reasons for not visiting him, she wrote: "I am in bondage, but voluntarily so, and therefore I should not complain about it" (BF 70). She preferred to correspond with Lorm and especially welcomed the opportunity to discuss her literary plans with him. She also valued him as a critic of her work. In 1869 she had sent him her manuscript of *Das Waldfräulein*, and from then on had kept him informed about every new project. When he offered to write a review of *Bozena* in the *Abendpost* she was honored and overjoyed. Since her devastating experience with theater critics she was horrified of write-ups in the press, but she trusted Lorm and knew that he would be fair. Having read his very positive account in the paper she immediately wrote to thank him (BF 69).

After reading the historian Adam Wolf's positive discussion of *Bozena* in the *Neue Freie Presse*, Ebner-Eschenbach remarked to Saar how very grateful she was, because the approval of the highly respected historian protected her from being made fun of "in the worst of all big papers" (Kindermann 47-48). This time she was spared embarrassment, as literary critics largely ignored her work.[15] The public was not yet ready to recognize her as a great writer. The average reader may not have been attracted to *Bozena* because the trend of the day was toward suspense novels with fast-paced action (Binneberg 208). Another reason may have been the public's prejudice against women writers. Women were thought to belong in the home and were to deploy their talents within the domestic sphere. If they ventured into public life they were highly suspect (Necker XIII).

At the end of 1877 Cotta still had 620 unsold copies,[16] which led Baron Cotta, the owner of the firm, to solemnly vow that he would never publish anything written by a "South German woman aristocrat" (B II 160). He was obviously aware of the fact that some aristocrats as well as commoners tended to react negatively to aristocratic writers.[17]

Yet in December 1877 he asked Ebner-Eschenbach for permission to include her stories "Ein Spätgeborener," "Chlodwig" and "Die Großmutter" in a new series of the "Volksbibliothek," a sign that readers had begun to take an interest in them (B II 164). Shortly afterwards the house of Cotta was overtaken by tragedy: the business was close to bankruptcy, rumors about financial and other wrongdoings were flying. Cotta's seventeen-year-old son hanged himself, Baron Reischach, Cotta's companion, shot himself dead—and Baron Cotta, aged seventy, died soon afterwards (B II 160). The new management, disappointed with the lack of reader interest in *Bozena*, did not accept any more of Marie von Ebner's works, a decision it was later to regret. Only in 1895, to her great surprise, Cotta decided to bring out a second edition of *Bozena*. The writer was just then in St. Gilgen on a holiday, when she learned the news and wrote to the critic Moritz Necker about the "resurrection" of her book: "It came to nobody more unexpectedly than to me. I considered *Bozena* dead and buried: it makes me profoundly happy that she is now accepted by the people and that especially housemaids are asking for her in the lending libraries" (qtd. in Binneberg 215).

She had to wait nineteen years to see *Bozena* revived. Enthusiastically she began to revise the rather sloppy and inconsistent orthography of her first edition. She also tried to simplify her vocabulary and her sentences, thus achieving a precision of style which was thought to be more appealing to readers and critics alike. After four months the second edition of *Bozena* was sold out. Cotta then decided to have a third edition. In 1908, when an eighth edition was planned, Marie von Ebner-Eschenbach triumphantly wrote in her diary that "all those who did not see from the story that the author had some talent, were not very incisive" (qtd. in Binneberg 224).

As early as 1877 she had been asked by the editor of the Bohemian journal *Pokrok* to give permission for translation and publication of *Bozena*. She was very keen on it, even offering to pay the fee Cotta demanded for translation rights. Unfortunately the deal came to nothing. However, Helene Tafel, a friend since the 1880s, rendered the novel into Italian (Binneberg 227). Finally, when *Bozena* was translated into French, a happy Marie von Ebner wrote to Cotta: "May my favorite child, my old Bozena, find a reception even approximately as friendly as it has found it in Germany, largely thanks to your good offices" (qtd. in Binneberg 227).

Yet in 1876, after *Bozena's* first publication, prospects looked rather bleak. Ebner-Eschenbach worried about the slow sales of her book and seriously considered giving up writing altogether (TZ 729-730). She had, however, an additional, much deeper worry at that time. Sophie, her dearly beloved sister-in-law was suffering from a severe heart problem. Countess Sophie Dubsky, née Stockau, was the widow of Count Josip Jelacic de Buzim, a Croatian politician and soldier. She and Marie von Ebner's brother Adolph had been married on May 10, 1863 at Castle Reichenburg, the home of Julie, Duchess of Waldburg-Wurzach. The writer's first favorable impressions of Sophie had been correct. The two women became close friends and always had a very warm regard for each other. Marie von Ebner sympathized with Sophie after a miscarriage and rejoiced with her when her first daughter, Maria Gisela Eugenie Sophie, called Stutzi, was born in 1864. This was an event of great importance for Ebner-Eschenbach. In her diary she wrote: "For nothing in the world would I miss the moment when the little one arrived" (TB I 36). She always prided herself that she had known Stutzi longer even than her own father, who had been away hunting and who saw his daughter only four hours after her birth.

Adolph von Dubsky, by then a very prominent man, was elected to the Moravian Parliament in 1865 and lived at Skalitzka castle in the Weisskirchen area. Marie von Ebner often stayed there with Sophie when Adolph was away on business. In 1867 the Dubskys moved to Castle Löschna, an estate Adolph had bought from his father and renovated with great care. The other Dubskys, the Kinskys and the Ebner-Eschenbachs regularly visited there and kept close contact.

Adolph and Sophie von Dubsky had two more children. Viktor, and Eugen, to all of whom Marie von Ebner became a doting aunt. She watched them grow up, told them stories and fairy tales and s
uffered with them when they were ill. When, in 1876, Sophie began to suffer from a heart condition the family was devastated. Ebner-Eschenbach worried so much that she could not think about her writing anymore. Sophie was finally released from her suffering on January 17, 1877. All her life Marie von Ebner would remember her sincerity, loyalty and her generosity of spirit, and would be proud to notice in her nieces and nephews their late mother's admirable qualities. Sophie was the type of woman she adored. She had the love, compassion and strength of character many of her female protagonists display.

Ebner-Eschenbach was grief-stricken by the loss of her sister-in-law, and her heart overflowed with pity for the three motherless children. They now became her first concern. To Hieronymus Lorm she once wrote that the three little ones took much of her time but that she truly enjoyed looking after them. About herself and her husband she said: "It is immensely good for both of us old, childless folks to have suddenly gained great importance in the life of three little persons, who are themselves so important to us" (BF 70). And she continued, claiming that writing her fictional work was not a priority for her. "If I write a few novels less because of these children, it will be a very small misfortune; but if I succeed in contributing something to their becoming good, helpful and loving human beings, it will be a very great accomplishment" (BF 70).

She watched over the children's education, regularly invited them to her home with their tutors and governesses, and also took them to outings during the summer in Zdislawitz. With Stutzi, the oldest of the Dubsky children, she had forged a particularly strong bond, that lasted all her life. When the little girl was sick, Marie von Ebner noted it in her diary, where she also collected her niece's funny utterances (TB I 282). When the children were older she wrote stage plays for them to be performed at family celebrations, and Stutzi always excelled in them (B II 163).

Yet in spite of her preoccupation with the children, who remained her first priority until her brother Adolph married again, she still found time to think about her literary work. She knew that she had to write in order to relieve her suffering. In the fall of 1876, under the influence of Sophie's impending death, she had started the story "Nach dem Tode," in which she described a nobleman who begins to love and appreciate his wife only after her death. She may have thought of Adolph, who sometimes had been in a bad mood and at odds with his wife (TB I 107), often making her unhappy because of his many absences (TB I 282). Business had always been more important to him than his family. Adolph, the "revolutionary and democrat" (TB I 82-83), may again have been on Ebner-Eschenbach's mind, when she conceived *Die Freiherren von Gemperlein* in Zdislawitz.

At that time she also must have thought of Viktor, her second brother, who in 1865 and 1866 had been turned down by several ladies he had envisaged as marriage partners. At one time Marie von Ebner-Eschenbach herself had attempted to become matchmaker, at another time his stepmother Xaverine Dubsky had tried to be of help. In her diary the writer noted in February 1866: "Mama told me little Julie Erdödy had declared she could not understand how one could marry 'a Dubsky,' and that Victor was an 'old baldpate.' With her he would not stand a chance" (TB I 79). Viktor, having searched quite a while for a suitable bride, later married Rosine, Countess Thun-Hohenstein. He became Austrian ambassador to Teheran and Athens and later lived on his estate at Ziadlowitz. He may have lent some features to the more traditional brother of the two Gemperleins.

On September 14, 1867 Ebner-Eschenbach had written in her diary: "Early in the morning Adolf and Viktor went to Löschna. Viktor has marriage plans and intends to pay a visit to the people at Krasna. Before and during breakfast there was a lively discussion of these marriage plans—the "asses" were flying back and forth, one had to watch out not to be hit on one's head" (TB I 203). A week later she had entered: "In the afternoon my dear, pugnacious brothers came back from Löschna" (TB I 204). She then wrote the story about the two Gemperlein brothers, whose prevalent character trait was that very pugnaciousness (275). While her relatives went on outings, she spent days in the company of these two eccentric gentlemen (TB II 521).[18]

Friedrich, the royalist, and Ludwig, the republican, are the descendants of the ancient and noble dynasty of Gemperlein. They both have left public life and reside together on their inherited, dearly beloved country estate Wlastowitz, "the essence of everything good and beautiful" (276). True to temperament they quarrel much about social, political, and religious problems, but they are both highly esteemed by the people in their neighborhood. Shortly after taking up residence in Wlastowitz, the two brothers had decided to marry. As befited his station, Friedrich had selected his bride from the hereditary aristocracy. He had consulted the genealogical almanac, instead of personally going courting. Ludwig, in accordance with his republican ideals, had decided on a commoner. Yet soon their hopes were shattered. Friedrich's distant love, registered in the almanac as Josephine, turns out to be Joseph, a man, and Ludwig's Lina Apfelblüh is already married to a notary.

One day they visit their neighbor, an old widowed baroness, who is very fond of them and enjoys setting them up against each other. Since their hunter has recently shot one of her deer, she has vowed to play a trick on them and to make them both fall in love with her visiting niece, Klara Siebert. Her plan succeeds. Ludwig and Friedrich are immediately taken by Klara, a descendant of an old Saxonian aristocratic family, and they both want to marry her. Yet after an accident each of the brothers generously makes up his mind to renounce the admired lady and to leave her to the other as a sign of brotherly love. As it turns out, Klara is already married, and the Gemperleins learn from the baroness that they have fallen into her snare. They never marry, causing the Gemperlein dynasty to die out.

By October 1877 the novella was completed, but the writer wanted it to rest for a while before giving it a final revision. In December she sent the manuscript to Cotta in Stuttgart but received a rejection. The publisher thought he had run too great a risk with her *Erzählungen* and *Bozena* and did not want to embark on another futile adventure. Julius Rodenberg also declined publication and so did other editors (TB II 567). Baron Falke, the editor of *Die Dioskuren*, finally accepted the novella for his journal. Later, in 1881, the publisher Ebhard in Berlin included the "Gemperlein" in the collection *Neue Erzählungen*. Hofrat Hemsen, librarian at the court of Württemberg, was much taken with it and recommended it to Paul Heyse for his collection *Neuer Deutscher Novellenschatz* of 1883. Heyse, who enjoyed its humor and high spirits, immediately accepted the work (Heyse 9).[19] Ferdinand von Saar also liked the "Gemperlein." Thanking him for his compliments, Marie von Ebner wrote: "Honestly speaking, I love my silly old bachelors and what one does to them one has done to me" (Kindermann 53). During World War I she received a postcard from an acquaintance, who was likewise very fond of her "Gemperlein" and had read the story at the battlefront (B II 298).

In 1879 Marie von Ebner-Eschenbach realized a wish she had entertained for a long time. Ever since her youth she had been greatly interested in clocks and watches, and now with Adolph's gift of a Nürnberger Ei—one of the earliest, egg-shaped pocket watches from Nuremberg—she started a collection of her own. She bought a work desk and tools, starting soon afterwards lessons with a former watchmaker, who now sold watches in his shop. She learned how to repair damaged clockworks and entered deeply into the work and jargon of the craft. At first she bought old clockworks in order to study them, take them apart and put them together again. Often she paid horrendous prices, as sellers cheated her, but gradually she learned to recognize valuable watches and became familiar with the most famous clockmakers.

In 1896 she was asked to write an article for *Westermanns Monatshefte* about her watches. Since she had read widely on the history of watches, she could make her essay interesting through a wealth of anecdotal detail. She stated that she considered herself quite knowledgeable but that she also was occasionally cheated in a deal. Thus she admitted that on December 28, 1879 she thought she had acquired a much coveted *Kalenderuhr* (calendar watch) made by the famous Breguet. Later her master-watchmaker enlightened her that she had erred, but comforted her by assuring that it was still a very beautiful and useful timepiece. On another occasion she bought a watch under the impression that it was a creation of the famous Renaissance watchmaker Peter Hele. When she came home she discovered that it had the shape of a snail and could not possibly have been made by the famous craftsman. She put it into a corner of her clock cabinet and forgot about it. Next morning, while all other clocks stayed silent "there sounded the quick and merrily energetic *pulsare* of the Nuremberg girl. She gave a sign of life, she wanted to be noted. Thus I took her again into my hand—I had to admire her. It may not have been Peter Hele who made her—but it was still a master craftsman" (536). From that moment on the "pseudo-Hele" received a special place in Ebner-Eschenbach's clock-cabinet. By the end of her life she owned two hundred watches. Each of them was an individual—each one had its peculiarities of mechanism, its own history and its own character.

She later bequeathed her watch collection to the City of Vienna. It suffered greatly during World-War II when many of the most precious pieces were lost to bombing and looting. But the "Uhrenmuseum" in Schulhof 2 still keeps a room with the "Sammlung Marie Freiin Ebner von Eschenbach," housing over a hundred watches from her collection together with her handwritten inventory. She meticulously entered the period, the locale, the watchmaker, the species, the price, the year the watch was purchased by her or given to her, and commented about the state of repair. The room also contains some paintings. One, by Marie Müller, represents the writer at age seventy-one, the other shows her study at Spiegelgasse 1, painted by Alois Hänisch, commissioned by the Magistrate of Vienna.

Marie von Ebner's expertise in watches became so well known that she was occasionally consulted by colleagues. Thus Jacob Minor asked her advice in connection with the verse in Goethe's *Faust* "The clock stands still, the hand is falling," and she explained the phrase to him with great professional insight (B II 337). All her friends admired her skill with watches and her delicate, ivory-like hands with which she so affectionately handled them. How much she empathized with watches is revealed in her indignant reply to the poet Erdmann Edler who told her about his own fifty-year-old neglected clock: "Cruel man! Do you not know that the whole life of the clock from the first to the last tick is nothing but suffering, and it cannot even cry out or crawl into hiding as we do?" (B II 287). She compared the escapement and the balance spring of a clock to suffering humankind that is prevented from moving forward by a cog. Her deep attachment to her watches can also be seen from a statement she made in old age when talking to Alexander Gross, a connoisseur: "My dear watches make dying hard for me. Who will treat them as well as I did after I have gone?" (B II 287).[20] In 1914, however, she decided to part with her treasured collection in order to fund a "model kindergarten" in Zdislawitz. She had greatly benefited from her watches not only from an aesthetic and scholarly point of view, but also for psychological and emotional reasons. They gave her the opportunity to lovingly care for them and by doing so, to avoid a total surrender to her strenuous literary work.[21]

CHAPTER 3:

"THE MOST BEAUTIFUL THING THERE IS"

It may be a coincidence that the time of Marie von Ebner-Eschenbach's apprenticeship as a watchmaker was also the time when she wrote her first instantly successful work. Possibly there is a deeper connection. Watchmaking and repairing gave her the satisfaction of seeing her efforts succeed in a visible and demonstrable way. It helped her to broaden her personal horizon and to gain a sense of accomplishment through active involvement. It gave her self-confidence, took her mind away from personal problems and provided a new purpose to her existence. She loved her watches, conscientiously cared for them and, like Lotti, the heroine of her new story, gained "daily new joy . . . peace, cheerfulness and independence" (862) through them.

Her diary entries reveal that *Lotti, die Uhrmacherin* was begun in May 1879 and completed in November the same year. On May 26, 1879 she observed: "Fräulein Lotti begins to occupy a larger space in my soul. I am giving her all the watches I would like to possess" (B II 170). Not only did she put her heroine in possession of the watches she would have liked to own, she also endowed her with a father she herself would have wanted to possess. By writing *Bozena* she had sublimated the fear of her bullying father and had become her own therapist. As she has her narrator say about Lotti, the watchmaker: "Her sufferings had to be fully lived through before they could die. There was no use of slinking away, or of talking them away, they demanded their right and ceded only after justice had been done to them" (888). Now she was free to create a father in whom she could invest all her ideals.

Johannes Fessler is a deeply caring man whose goal in life is to live harmoniously with his children and to train them to continue his beloved craft of watchmaking. He treats them as equals, calling them "my journeymen . . . and later with pride, my helpers" (860). As they become more accomplished in their art, he even considers them his partners who, hopefully, will one day surpass him (860). He does not discriminate against his daughter, does not believe her to be inferior to his son. Eagerly he furthers her talent and praises each of her accomplishments.

Accepted by her loving father and by her dedicated, adopted brother, Lotti has spent a happy childhood and has grown into an integrated personality. Having "a rich source of serenity" in her soul (852) she is at one with life. With such a background she possesses the strength to face and solve the problems that invariably will come her way. Her peaceful existence is interrupted by a short and rather stormy engagement to Hermann Halwig, an exuberant young clerk, who writes novellas on the side. Yet Lotti soon realizes that he is not the man she can marry. The more convinced he becomes of his talent and the more vehemently he insists that his bride admire his trashy work, the less highly she thinks of his accomplishments. As Halwig reveals his true character and his lack of self-control by throwing temper tantrums, Lotti calmly dissolves the engagement. She still loves him but knows that she would never be happy with him. Trained by her idealistic father to demand the highest standard of a work of art, she has contempt for those who throw their talent away for material benefit.

After several years during which she does not hear from Halwig, Lotti learns that he has married an aristocrat. She also finds out that he has turned into a hack writer in order to provide for his beautiful, elegant and high-living wife. Hearing that he is close to bankruptcy, Lotti in a moment of great pity decides to sell the precious watch collection she has inherited from her father. Halwig never learns that Lotti is his benefactress. Free to buy a country estate from his parents-in-law, he can give up writing for the purpose of simply making a living. He now has the opportunity to develop into a true artist (937). Yet his peaceful life in the country is nothing but an interlude. His wife misses social life and he, addicted to writing trash, likewise returns to the city to again produce cheap sensational works. It looks as if Lotti's sacrifice was in vain. Yet she is convinced of having made the right decision by selling her watch collection "to save the soul of a man" (929) who once was dear to her. She knows that her father would have done the same (931). His altruism is the guiding principle of her life, an altruism which ultimately leads to her own and her brother's happiness.

Writing *Lotti* was an emotional outlet for Marie von Ebner, a means to employ her newly gained knowledge about watches, their origins and creators. It also gave her the opportunity to relieve her frustration about the increasing number of writers who, in order to make money, catered to the public's desire for sensationalism, sacrificing the aesthetic standards of genuine art. After a theater performance in 1866 she had written in her diary: "It hurts, this art which has obviously been created for material reasons" (TB I 105). Now in *Lotti* she had invented a mercenary writer who succumbed to vulgar public taste. While accusing

Halwig of degrading art, she simultaneously voiced her criticism of the reading public. It demanded and generously rewarded writers of worthless literature and often had no appreciation of aesthetic excellence.

When the story was completed, Ebner-Eschenbach admitted in her diary: "Of all my children, this is the one born with the greatest pain. If it is viable, then mind has won a victory over matter, since the latter has mightily resisted its coming into existence" (B II 171). In spite of her fear that she would never be able to live up to Julius Rodenberg's standards she sent him the manuscript with the following words: "Here it is—may it come up to your expectations. I leave it to you to decide whether to call it *Lotti, die Uhrmacherin* instead of *Kunst und Handwerk* (Art and Craft). I cannot tell you how happy I would be if you were satisfied with my work—because there is no expression for it!" (B II 175). Rodenberg not only accepted the work but praised it enthusiastically: "I spent a whole day with your *Lotti* and it felt so good, as if I was really close to a kind, pure, noble human being" (B II 175). He wholeheartedly agreed with Marie von Ebner's moral and artistic message, confident that his readers would likewise approve of it. He further enjoyed the work's clarity and simplicity "in this time of exaggerations and incongruities" (B II 182).

Like many members of the educated classes, Rodenberg was aware of the cultural decline that had taken place in his country since the foundation of the German Empire in 1871 (Sagarra 342). As a writer and editor he knew that in recent years aesthetic worth had been sacrificed more and more to sensationalism and showy glorification of the state. Spiritual life was deteriorating,[22] idealism, dignity and integrity were vanishing; many writers tailored their work to popular demand, thus lowering aesthetic standards. Rodenberg therefore truly appreciated Ebner-Eschenbach's conception of art and her concern with the preservation of the highest artistic criteria. Imbued with neoclassical ideals, she considered a poet a priest "who has been entrusted with a sacred office here on earth" (*Lotti* 921).[23] Her story also advocated a work ethic, which greatly appealed to Rodenberg. He knew that all the bourgeois values described in *Lotti, die Uhrmacherin*, like modesty, loyalty, conscientiousness, adaptability to reality and humanitarian service, would find resonance with his readers who liked to see themselves reflected in the works they read. After promising to publish *Lotti* soon in the *Rundschau* he expressed the hope that Marie von

Ebner would "create many such works and give the *Rundschau* the opportunity to repay her loyalty" (B II 176). He also thanked her for her willingness to keep her promise to write something for his periodical in spite of his refusal not only of *Bozena*, but also of *Gemperlein* and the *Aphorisms,* which she had offered him in previous years.

If Rodenberg was happy to have a masterwork from the hand of Marie von Ebner-Eschenbach, confident that it met the standards which the readers of the *Rundschau* had come to expect, she was even happier to have finally arrived where she always wanted to be. Enthusiastically she wrote: "My most daring and ambitious wishes are now fulfilled. For me it is more than I would ever have dared to dream, that you not only send me "greetings" but also give me hope that I can come again. I have reached a goal which I have pursued for a long time—that is the most beautiful thing there is, even if it happens at an age which is no longer beautiful, as you can see from the attached photograph" (Brandt 1004). In the years to come she sent all her new works to Rodenberg. He published many of them, including "Novelle in Korrespondenz-karten," "Die Unverstandene auf dem Dorfe," "Das Gemeindekind," "Unsühnbar," "Oversberg," "Verschollen" and "Meine Kinderjahre," enhancing the author's reputation and the standing of his journal.

Over the years a close relationship developed. Rodenberg was very fond of Vienna, a city where he felt at home (Kindheit 212), and he became a personal friend of the Ebner-Eschenbachs. The friendship lasted almost forty years. Marie von Ebner dedicated her collection of stories, "Alte Schule," to him and gave him one of her most cherished watches as a present. She never forgot that she owed her recognition as a writer to the editor of the *Deutsche Rundschau* in Berlin. All her life she remembered that he had drawn her out of her anonymity and had helped her to assert herself as a novelist. Soon she would be acknowledged not only in Germany but in her home country as well.

CHAPTER 4:

"THE SPIRIT THAT IS BLOWING"

Marie von Ebner-Eschenbach's fighting instinct and her determination had so far helped her to brave all adversaries on her path to literary recognition. She had pitted her will against relatives who tried to prevent her from writing, she had defied critics whose rancorous reviews would have defeated a less determined soul. She had continued to write in spite of the sluggish sales of her books and despite rejections from editors of various journals. She had finally won a place as contributor to Rodenberg's *Deutsche Rundschau*, but she had yet to face another adversary. Her health, precarious since her infancy, caused her serious worries.

A look at her diaries of the 1860s and 1870s shows how often she suffered from migraine caused by heat, by too many social commitments, and by exhaustion following strenuous literary work. In May 1866 she complained: "Many people, great heat. I came home with such severe headaches that I could not write at all and had to spend all day being idle" (TB I 94). On April 6, 1867, shortly after she had sent her manuscript of *Marie Roland* to the printers, she entered in her diary: "Suffering a great deal, under very great strain. My head has to be given rest for a good while" (TB I 168). The next day she still complained about "wicked headaches all day long" (ibid.). Whenever she managed to steal a few hours from her busy schedule and to wholly concentrate on her writing she later had to pay with "dreadful headaches" (TB I 240). On January 13, 1872 she complained of having for three days had unbearable pains in the head that made her unable to think (TB II 85).

We have no medical report about the injuries Ebner-Eschenbach suffered when she tried to jump out of the window as a seven-year-old girl and hit her head against the windowframe. It is possible that she suffered a severe concussion which could have caused chronic headaches in later years. In *Meine Kinderjahre* she states that especially the heat in the city caused her unbearable discomfort: "A May day with summer temperatures, blissful in the country, in the city for me a breeder of headaches. They came violently, and when my parents wanted to go out in the forenoon, I asked to be left at home" (871). And in "Die arme Kleine" she has the narrator say about the protagonist: "She had reached her eighth year, grew in height but remained disquietingly tender and slim. There were not many days, when she was not affected by headaches, but when it happened, she felt remunerated for a long time of suffering" (661).

Throughout her youth Marie von Ebner had lived under reprimand for her writing. Her headaches, therefore, may have been a psychosomatic symptom of suppressed anger against those relatives who considered her creative impulse a sin (Horney 56). Later she was torn between a convention which demanded that she devote herself wholly to caring for relatives and friends, and a vocation that needed time and concentration. She therefore may have developed a high state of tension, causing her headaches and many of the ailments that made life difficult for her. Trying to cope with her double life by rising early and working late must have brought her to a state of permanent near-exhaustion, which in turn may have caused her headaches. Something of how she felt under these conditions may have gone into the description of Bertram Vogel, the protagonist of *Bertram Vogelweid*: "Sudddenly it felt as if an iron band was strangling his neck or as if a dagger pierced his ears, and then a roaring and humming started in his head, which made thinking a hellish torture" (4). Time and again Ebner-Eschenbach complained about feeling extremely unwell and plagued by severe migraines after the completion of a stage play. It is obvious that each of her works at that time and in later years had been accomplished under great stress and a nagging guilt feeling on account of her relatives' discontent about her writing.[24] Her headaches were essentially an expression of the conflict within her personality.

She also suffered from her demon, her urge to create. She knew that life would be easier in many ways if she did not write, yet she had to give in to her literary passion. Her poem *So ist es* vividly expresses how much she felt enslaved by this "demon," in whose service she saw her whole being entrapped, deprived of the possibility to determine herself how she wanted to live: "The demon takes possession of your heart, steals your soul, fills your whole thinking. You have only him, indeed your very own life, your human erring, every emotion, your burning compassion, hate, wrath and pain, your most quiet longing, your most secret dream . . . everything bears the coinage of one's service to him" (Paetel,1901, vol.1, 179-180).

In April 1864, due to a chronic infection in three places on her back, she had to undergo a hated water cure. She noted in her diary: "Moriz accompanies me to the Zoo, because I am supposed to promenade during my cure, which up to now has had no other effect than making me worse and insufferable" (TB I 32). Around this time she was also plagued by an ear problem that caused her great concern. In her diary we only read: "Dr.Pollitzer treats my right ear, which is going deaf" (TB I 37). But this entry belongs to those she revised in old age. Originally it most probably revealed her profound unhappiness about this tragic fact. As a young woman of thirty-four she must have been desperate on learning that she was about to lose her hearing in one ear. Three years later, resigned to her fate, she wrote in her diary: "I am suffering, my cure with Gruber is embarrassing; I am losing my hearing in the right ear. There is nothing to be done" (TB I 217). For a long time this caused her great discomfort, especially since she was afflicted by a constant buzzing that distracted her from her work (TB I 43).

Another great source of worry were her eyes. She often suffered from eye infections, preventing her from reading and writing, which seriously depressed her. To her friend Ferdinand von Saar she wrote: "I am in a bad mood and morose, because my eyes are worse again. May you fare better! A poet should never be ill. He has already a hard enough life in this world" (Kindermann 77). Because of her eye problem she was sometimes prevented from attending theater performances. She was once particularly upset when she had to miss Paul Heyse's tragedy *Don Juan* (HC 272). Often she had to rely on friends to read to her. When Heyse sent her a collection of his latest novellas, she had them read to her by Friedrich Halm's niece. In her letter to Heyse she later wrote that the young lady read extremely well, but "then I read for myself, I read and reread, and if it was not good for the bodily eyes, to whom reading had been interdicted, it benefited the mental eyes, sharpening, delighting and consoling them" (HC 279).

In another letter to Heyse she mentioned that the windows of her room had to be curtained in order to prevent light from entering the room and from damaging her weak eyes. Using an apt metaphor, she let Heyse know that "a brave heart always finds ways through ever so much suffering to break a path for a ray of sunshine, filled with pure joy" (HC 280)—the ray of sunshine being Heyse's book, which she had just read.

Since she could not see well she had to dictate her letters to friends, relatives and, in later years, to her secretary. But she was always unhappy about not being able to write herself. To her friend, Natalie von Milde, she once confided having dictated a letter addressed to her which had turned out so badly that she could not send it off. She sadly

continued: "Lately that happens to almost all of my letters; those that
have been dictated in the evening cause me horror when I read them the
next morning" (RV I.N. 129013). The more she suffered from her
ailments, the more she appreciated her ability to daydream and to create
an imaginary world of her own. As she once observed:

> Since the bad condition of my health restricts the
> possibility of serious and sustained occupation more
> and more, the joy one finds in the exercise of
> intellectual occupation appears to me in a wonderful
> light. I ask myself, what can the worst adversities do
> to us if we possess the magic wand that enables us to
> transport ourselves at any time from this earthly
> misery into a world created by ourselves, in which we
> may rule according to just and beautiful laws (B II
> 108-109).

She often suffered from coughs and catarrhs, yet continued to smoke,
not only cigarettes, but also strong cigars. She did not know at that time
that smoking reduces immune responses and increases the possibility of
viral infections (Dunlop 81). When she traveled by train she always
enjoyed sitting alone, smoking a cigar, and meditating (TB I 274). She
never saw a connection between smoking and her throat problems.

At fifty-nine she suffered from exophthalmic goiter, which may
have been caused by emotional stress, leading to nervous and
intrapsychic disturbances (Wageman 501). In her diary of March 3,
1889 the patient noted: "I have Basedow's disease; Moriz told me today.
Now I am supposed to seriously determine to lead the life of a patient
and I promise to do it as soon as my work is completed" (Vesely 232).
In spite of her illness, which caused her extreme fatigue, jumpiness and
restlessness, she only thought of her literary commitments.

Her most persistent ailment, however, was a very painful trigeminal
neuralgia (*tic douloureux*), which doctors attributed to a long-standing
anemia (B II 156).[25] Yet it may also have been of psychosomatic origin.
Marie von Ebner had mentioned "facial pains" for the first time in her
diary of 1866 in connection with a cold she had caught during a visit
to Swoika, where her sister Friederike's in-laws lived. She found this
family gathering particularly strenuous and afterwards confided in her
diary: "From 3 to 10 at Swoika. Say seven hours. This surpasses the

strength of my talent for being agreeable" (TB I 126). Stress and the fear of constant intrusions on her work may have affected Ebner-Eschenbach's nervous system to produce the infamous trigeminal neuralgia which would plague her for twenty-four years, causing her many sleepless nights and workless days. There were times when she could hardly speak (TB II 343).

Trigeminal neuralgia appears in involuntary, regularly repeated spasmodic contractions of a muscle, generally of neurotic origin, caused by anxiety, depression and phobias. It is characterized by a shooting, stabbing excruciating pain along the branches of the trigeminal nerve on the skull in front of the ears. The disease is known to occur mainly in women in middle-age. Attacks are brief in the beginning, but as the illness progresses, the intervals between them decrease. Patients find it difficult to eat, drink or talk, since the areas around the mouth and nose are very sensitive and, when moved, may trigger a painful spasm. The cause of the disease is unknown, the only cure available today being surgery of the nerve in the vicinity of the ganglion (Wagman 673).

During times of physical suffering the writer had to curtail her social commitments, in fact she hardly received any visitors at all. As Ferdinand von Saar writes in *Die Gartenlaube*: "During one of the few and short visits I was able to put in with her during many years, I was witness to the fortitude with which she mastered a severe bodily ailment she finally overcame mostly by unflinching will power" (504). Visits to spas like Bad Reichenhall, Bad Nauheim, Bad Kissingen and Königswart did not bring her relief from her pain, and doctors were helpless against her "rebellious nerves" (B I 129). What ultimately helped her were strict rest, relief from those strenuous and nerve-racking social commitments, and her determination to free herself from her painful condition.

In a sense Ebner-Eschenbach's ailments were her body's rebellion against the relentless demands of her social environment. They were a blessing in disguise, providing her with the long-desired, desperately needed time to channel her energies into the field where she could develop herself: writing. She had paid too high a price for constantly being available to others. Now she had a valid excuse to give up some of her irksome obligations. In a roundabout way her ailments helped her towards self-realization. They allowed her legitimately to keep interruptions of her literary work at bay, and they even compelled her to exercise her talent as the only worthwhile thing to do.[26] Her relatives thought her hypersensitive and fastidious and often criticized her for feeling sorry for herself (TB II 490). They did not realize that she used her ailments partly as an excuse to be left alone. Thus on November 29, 1874 she wrote in her diary: "All day in bed. Very diligent and so happy about this diligence" (TB II 302). Around her sixtieth birthday, she was finally able to write to her friend Louise that she felt better and that she might even be completely cured from her *tic douloureux* (B II 223).

Louise von François, a fellow writer, had a very special place in her life. After years of exchanging letters and publications, in June 1880 the two friends at last personally met in Bad Nauheim and found confirmed what they had so far only assumed: that they were kindred souls. From the beginning of her correspondence Marie von Ebner knew that she had met a person of great honesty and integrity, since Louise had frankly admitted in her first letter that she had never heard of her. And her Austrian correspondent much appreciated that sincerity. When she met von François, Marie von Ebner-Eschenbach was impressed by her tall, noble appearance and elegance, in spite of her simple clothes, and felt awe and compassion for the woman who bore her life of deprivation with such composure and dignity. Louise von Francois, likewise taken with her newly found friend, observed Marie von Ebner's "wavy, silvery hair, her esprit, her eyes full of kindness and her native wit" (B I 123). From her correspondence with her she knew that the Austrian writer was different from many others who had written to her earlier, praising her literary accomplishments.

During those days in Bad Nauheim, while taking the waters at the famous spa, the two friends had ample opportunity to exchange ideas, to discover their common historical interests, to express their likes and dislikes. Marie von Ebner-Eschenbach soon discovered that Louise had eyes that not only looked but saw, eyes "whose glance examined heart and mind, that seemed to possess their own light and that lit up when the vivacious genial woman waxed enthusiastic, whenever something provoked her admiration or her outrage" (ELF 20). She learned from her friend that unwittingly she had described Louise's life story in *Lotti, die Uhrmacherin*, since she, too, liked to collect, if not watches, then pearls and gold nuggets. Ebner-Eschenbach for her part recognized the similarity between Louise von François and Hardine, the protagonist of her work *Die letzte Reckenburgerin*, who both exemplified the strength of character and the spirit of generosity she so greatly admired.

To Marie von Ebner's great delight von François was full of entertaining stories about people who had made a name for themselves in the literary world. About Fanny Lewald she said: "She is tall, tall, tall, but never forgets her umbrella" (B II 207). About Louise Brachmann she knew that "she had a number of love affairs, which were almost always one-sided, like the poor poet herself. Out of shame and despair over her unhappy, passionate nature she once threw herself out of the window and made many an attempt at suicide" (ibid.). The two friends spent many an hour discussing their own and other writers' works, and Louise von François always showed a clear and informed judgment. Toward her own works she was so rigorously critical, that Marie von Ebner called her "an enhanced Brutus, because he only judged his children, whereas she defamed hers" (ELF 20).

The two vacationers so much enjoyed their stay in Bad Reichenhall that they promised each other to meet there again the following year. This time Marie von Ebner had also invited her brother Viktor and his wife Rosine, who both were happy to meet the author of *Die letzte Reckenburgerin*. Louise von François again spoke freely about her work and also encouraged Ebner-Eschenbach to continue writing. She persuaded her to send the manuscript of *Margarethe* to Rodenberg for his *Deutsche Rundschau*, where some of her own works had been published, and wrote a warm recommendation (B II 209).

Marie von Ebner in her way also tried to further her friend's career. She discussed plans with her for the performance of her historical comedy *Der Posten der Frau*, adapted from her 1886 novella of the same name. Eventually she also managed to provide a prize for Louise von François from the Schillerstiftung for that very comedy (B II 265). During this stay in Bad Reichenhall Louise von François' two novellas *Phosphorus Hollunder* and *Zu Füssen des Monarchen* appeared, and almost daily she received letters from fans and admiring colleagues. One day she proudly showed her friend a letter by the Swiss writer Conrad Ferdinand Meyer, who called himself "your colleague in the *Rundschau*," wishing he also were her "colleague in talent" (ELF 27). From then on C. F. Meyer became Louise von François' friend and a regular correspondent, whose letters enriched the last years of her life. He likewise treasured his acquaintance with her, highly valuing her judgment in literary questions. On a trip to Switzerland she once made a stopover in Zürich and spent some time with him at his estate in Kilchberg on Lake Zürich (ELF 27). She also told him about Marie von Ebner-Eschenbach, but the Swiss writer never contacted his Austrian colleague, probably because he realized that in temperament and Weltanschauung they stood too far apart.

Marie von Ebner and Louise von François again made the most of their vacation in Bad Reichenhall. They both greatly enjoyed the beautiful, mountainous scenery and daily went on outings, which sometimes took them as far as Berchtesgaden, another famous tourist spot. They also participated in the social life of the town. Once they were invited to attend a piano recital and a choir concert at the convent. In the end a priest had to give a speech, which obviously was somewhat problematic for him. Marie Ebner found the event so amusing that she recorded it in her diary: "At first [the priest] praised the administrators of the institution, then he turned to the students of the convent saying: `But you also have to look upon this year (pause) as a receptacle, which you are supposed to fill up (pause) with the works of your diligence.'" And she continued: "It was an embarrassing moment for me, I fought with an almost insurmountable urge to laugh. I am often deaf, why did my ear not let me down during this speech ?" (B II 210).[27]

On another outing it happened that a big cat crossed the tourists' path and quickly vanished again. Marie von Ebner later reported in her diary: "Louise was totally beside herself. She clasped her hands and ran ahead of us into the house. We heard her wail and cry loudly" (B II 209). Nobody understood her better than Ebner-Eschenbach, who likewise since her childhood suffered from an indescribable fear of cats. In her autobiography she later reported how much, as a child, she detested those "murderers of birds, with the inaudible step, the repulsively soft movements, the false phosphorescent eyes. I shuddered when I saw them, hands and feet turned into icicles, my whole body was shaking when my brothers and sisters brought a kitten into the house" (MK 795). Yet she also recalls that, driven by her conscience and vanity, she once saved a cat from drowning in a tub filled with water, a feat that left her trembling with fright (MK 796). And in a letter to Hieronymus Lorm she once wrote: "The only one of God's creatures which I hate, the cat, tortures the poor mouse to death with its most delicate and most graceful movements" (BF 68).

Fear of cats may have been part of a larger psychoneurosis. It could be attributed to the frustration of infantile sexual drives or to a general insecurity in childhood. Louise von François as well as Marie von

Ebner-Eschenbach had both experienced many losses and worries during their formative years. Both of them may, however, also have heard gruesome stories about cats from their nursemaids and nannies. As Marie von Ebner mentions in *Meine Kinderjahre,* cats were generally not tolerated in the yard and were even sometimes killed by the gardener because they caused harm to birds (797). Due to her great love for birds she considered cats as natural enemies and in several stories she describes them as that. Thus in "Der Fink" the cat is portrayed moving about "like a velvet snake," approaching Pia, the protagonist, "on its elastic paws." Holding a young finch in her hands she takes great care to protect it from the vicious beast of prey, which looks at her "again and again as if to say: 'I still don't have the right victim, you are keeping it from me. Just wait, I'll get it, I'm strong, I have claws'" (Harriman 99).

In her family her fear of cats must have been proverbial, so much so that her husband teased her about it by having the narrator in his story *Hypnosis perennis* mention that he knows a lady who once came to Paris and could not sleep all night because she suspected there was a cat in the adjacent room (30). He was clearly referring to his wife, who had visited him in Paris during the World Exposition in 1867 (TB I 174).

Their common fear of cats must have been a regular topic of conversation between Louise von François and her Austrian friend. For both it most likely was an endearing sign of eccentricity. In a letter to Enrica von Handel-Mazzetti Marie von Ebner years later nostalgically wrote: "O, Louise was precious! She always made fun of herself, and when I told her: 'Your eloquent, your genial eyes'—she retorted: 'My cat eyes'" (Mumbauer 35). The friendship between these two cat-haters lasted for thirteen years, until von François' death.

Marie von Ebner-Eschenbach, aware of her friend's precarious financial state, went out of her way to help her without hurting her pride. Every Christmas she sent Hungarian wine to Weissenfels where Louise von François spent her last years almost as a recluse. She had a need, like Marie von Ebner, for being alone and for being left undisturbed. Marie von Ebner-Eschenbach was also instrumental in procuring a pension for Louise from the "Schillerfund," which her friend, instead of using for herself, put aside for her young officer nephew, to whom she wanted to leave an inheritance. Once Marie von Ebner asked Paul von Szczepanski to visit Louise in her garret in

Weissenfels under the pretext of asking for a literary contribution from her for *Velhagen und Klasings Monatshefte*. She had read in the papers an exaggerated essay about Louise von François' impoverished life and wanted to find out through Szczepanski how much truth was in the report. He returned with the conviction that von François, however simple her life, did not suffer poverty but rather was by nature a frugal person (Szczepanski 642). Like her friend she had the talent to escape from the narrowness of her surroundings by creating her own imaginary world. Instead of traveling to Italy, her lifelong, unfulfilled dream, she read for a whole winter about the history of Rome and found the greatest pleasure in it.

Ebner-Eschenbach could not but admire her friend's ability to cope with life and to preserve her humor and optimism. In her diary of July 9, 1881 she had already written: "I often think Louise von François has been hammered into ore by the hand of fate, whereas I have crumbled in it" (B II 209). For her this friendship with the German author was invaluable. To discuss her work with Louise and to listen to her well-meant critique helped her to grow as a writer. In 1883 the two friends met for the third and last time in Bad Reichenhall. Henceforth they kept in touch by correspondence. In 1887, on the occasion of Louise von François' seventieth birthday, her friend collected hundred signatures from the most prominent Austrian authors and patrons of art for an album she sent to her as a special token of appreciation (B II 210).

Meanwhile Marie von Ebner-Eschenbach herself had become quite renowned in her country. In 1881, Ebhardt in Berlin had published a volume called *Neue Erzählungen*, containing her works "Ein kleiner Roman," "Die Freiherren von Gemperlein," "Lotti, die Uhrmacherin" and "Nach dem Tode." The last novella, completed in 1877, was first accepted for serialization by Blumenthal, who considered it her best story since "Ein Spätgeborener" (B II 162). Hieronymus Lorm, likewise an admirer of the work, enthusiastically wrote: "I bow in reverence before the glimmer of the eternal that fell into your soul" (ibid.). Laube, too, contacted her on June 18, 1877, expressing his delight with "Nach dem Tode" and complimenting her for the detailed description and the excellent character sketching (B I 153). In 1883 the publishing house of Gebrüder Paetel eagerly accepted Marie von Ebner-Eschenbach's stories "Der Kreisphysikus," "Krambambuli," "Jakob Szela," "Die Poesie des Unbewussten" and "Die Resel," publishing them under the title *Dorf- und Schloßgeschichten*. A year later she finally achieved the desired breakthrough in Austria. Her story "Komtesse Muschi," published in the *Wiener Illustrierte Zeitung* became a great favorite with her compatriots (Necker 48). The "little tree of [her] talent" was beginning to bear fruit.

NOTES:

1. Ernst Kris points out in *Psychoanalytic Explorations in Art* that writing is problem-solving for an author. He also holds that no artist can "divest his work of the personal component." Yet the artist has to refashion the problems of his own life, in order to create a work that can stand separate from him (253-254). Doris Lessing alludes to writing as therapy in *The Golden Notebook*, where her protagonist says: "I had to 'name' the frightening things . . . making past events harmless by naming them, but making sure they were still there" (616).

2. In her letter of May 28, 1878 to the "Herren Hohenhausen" Marie von Ebner mentioned that the accomplishments she had achieved with her stories were "the fruits of resignation" (Schmidt 304). Grillparzer did not share Ebner-Eschenbach's notion that the novel was inferior to drama. In a diary entry of 1839 he maintained: "Every good novel can be transposed into verses; it really is an undeveloped poetical subject . . ." He also articulated the difference between drama and novella in a very poignant way: "This is the essential difference between novella and drama: the novella is a thought-out possibility, the drama is a thought-out reality".

3. It is possible that Ebner-Eschenbach wrote "Ein Edelmann" in order to teach her brother a lesson, since later she conceived the fairy tale *Hirzepinzchen* for her nephew Franz Dubsky for the same reason (Franz Dubksy, "Erinnerungen" 17). According to I. Winter (*Der Adel*) it was considered vulgar to deal with money, and aristocrats never carried cash with them (228).

4. Bettelheim calls them the "diary of the soul" (B II 36).

5. Ebner-Eschenbach incorporated some of these maxims in her first prose work *Aus Franzensbad* and would later regularly use them in her works.

6. Johannes Klein aptly remarks about Ebner-Eschenbach's aphorisms: "Only someone who has seen abysses can formulate like this, someone who has himself gone through such abysses, and on those paths, which he has left behind long ago, he was alone" (Winkler edition,

Gemeindekind, Novellen, Aphorismen, 970).

7. Dr. Eduard Hanslick, to whom Marie von Ebner had sent a copy of her aphorisms, called the book "a gold mine of wisdom, goodness and insight into human beings, on which one draws again and again with pleasure" (RV I.N. 56472). Ebner-Eschenbach also sent a copy to Elisabeth, Princess of Saxony, who had visited her in Vienna (RV I.N. 61235).

8. It is interesting to note that Marie von Ebner claims in her letter of June 5, 1878 to Hieronymus Lorm, that "thank goodness only in Germany" works by women writers are treated with disdain (BF 71).

9. She raced with the boys, liked to play being a priest and preferred male roles when performing her own stage works.

10. See Ernst Kris, *Psychoanalytic Explorations in Art,* in which he discusses "aesthetic creation" as "a type of problem-solving behavior" (40).

11. Note that the name of Marie von Ebner's maternal ancestors was Kaschnitz von Weinberg.

12. That Ebner-Eschenbach was preoccupied with the implications of the term "bluestocking" may be seen from the fact that she applied it several times to herself. In her letter of 3 March 1875 to Devrient she refers to herself as "a dangerous bluestocking" (B II 318), and in her letter of 27 January 1894 she calls herself "an old bluestocking" (Kindermann 93). She further uses the term in several of her works to ridicule girls who enjoy writing ("Muschi" 310) and have an interest in learning ("Paula" 333). Finally, she wrote a poem *Saint Peter and the Bluestocking,* in which a woman, who calls herself a "bluestocking," finds entry into heaven despite Saint Peter's initial reservations (Paetel, 1901, vol.1, 173-174).

13. Compare to Marie von Ebner's description of her father: "What was missing was balance and the delicate understanding for the happenings in the souls of those who were closest to him" (MK 770).

14. Heidi Beutin interprets Bozena as a symbol of the matriarchate (252).

15. There was one negative review in the *Neue Preussische Kreuzzeitung* which objected to Ebner-Eschenbach's alluding to biblical phrases. The writer also blamed her for caricaturing some of her characters (RV folder 77243).

16. As Marie von Ebner wrote to Lorm (BF 72).

17. Many aristocrats therefore used pseudonyms. Thus Freiherr von Hardenberg wrote under the name "Novalis," Graf von Auersperg under the pseudonym "Anastasius Grün," Nikolaus Edler von Strehlenau used the pen name "Nikolaus Lenau." This custom is continued even today. The person behind "Barbara Ritter" is Gräfin Waltraud von Einsiedel, "Elisabeth Plessen" in real life is a Gräfin von Holstein (Winter, *Der Adel*, 190).

18. The Gemperlein dynasty much resembles the ancestors of the Dubsky family (275). Ebner-Eschenbach's brother Viktor as a young boy gave early proof of his pugnaciousness by smacking his teacher during a lesson, and Marie, as a true Dubsky, envied him for having performed "the deed of which I was dreaming" (KL 274-275).

19. Critics in Marie von Ebner-Eschenbach's time first and foremost saw the humorous aspects of the work, envisioning it as a comedy performed on stage (B II 7). Modern critics, while still able to appreciate Ebner's humor, have focused more on the fact that the author portrays the two "Gemperlein" as symbols of an aristocracy doomed to lose its power. Elisabeth Endres rightly points out that Ebner-Eschenbach's novella really deals with the same theme as Grillparzer's *Ein Bruderzwist im Hause Habsburg*. Yet, whereas in Grillparzer's work the end is bloody, in Marie von Ebner's story humor mitigates "the half-heartedness of a life which was already ripe for its demise when it began" (124). Danuta Lloyd points out the two noblemen's "humiliating condescension," their "cruelty to animals" and observes that Ebner-Eschenbach does not see the aristocracy fit to continue the feudal tradition (37). Johannes Klein also sees the two brothers as representatives of the old, feudal Austria" which was unable to solve its

problems (I, 382). Finally, Agatha Bramkamp, in her feminist interpretation, points toward the Gemperleins' self-delusion. "The whole
story revolves around the male psyche with its distorted sense of
reality—symbolized in the brothers' misuse of time and their disrespect
for space—and their imagined world where women are invented and
oblite-rated freely" (108).

20. Compare to *Lotti, die Uhrmacherin*, where Lotti thinks: "Yes, my
watches—they will make dying hard for me" (866).

21. According to Otto Rank "one means of salvation from this total
absorption in creation is . . . the division of attention among two or
more simultaneous activities" (*Myth* 204).

22. As the Prussian diplomat Varnhagen von Ense noted, the young
generation is hostile to all idealistic endeavor and "rushes headlong
toward brutal reality and . . . will soon accept nothing that is not
concerned with material needs and pleasures" (Mann 122).

23. Compare to the ninth letter of Schiller's *Aesthetical Essays*, where
he claims that art has saved humankind that has lost its dignity (57).

24. Even in later years Ebner-Eschenbach was not free of this guilt
feeling. To Rodenberg she once wrote: "The way I write one does not
continue for any length of time. Imagine that it almost always happens
with a heartbreaking fear of an interruption, very often also with qualms
of conscience, because this or that obligation is being neglected (B II
193).

25. Her anemia seems to have been so bad that she once fainted in the
train on her trip to Trpist (TB I 268).

26. In "Aus einem zeitlosen Tagebuch" Marie von Ebner writes from
experience when she says: "As so many a woman writer who has done
good and even lasting work can say about herself: 'I could only work
when I had nothing else to do' " (731).

27. In German "to fill a receptacle" is ambiguous. Marie von Ebner obviously interpreted it as relating to a chamber-pot.

PART FOUR

SUCCESS AT LAST (1884-1898)

Shared intellectual activity
unites more than the bond
of marriage.

CHAPTER 1:

"A BRAVE, STRONG, DEEPLY FEELING NATURE"

One of the most significant people in Marie von Ebner-Eschen-bach's life and career was Ida von Fleischl-Marxow, a woman with rich gifts of heart and mind. The writer met her for the first time in 1866, after the performance of her comedy *Die Veilchen*. Ida Fleischl took an immediate interest in her newly found friend's stage play, discussing the performance with honesty and understanding. Marie von Ebner was so impressed by Frau von Fleischl's appreciation of art and literature that shortly afterwards she asked her for an opinion on her work in progress and sent her the manuscript of *Maria Stuart* as a token of friendship. Her diary entries of the 1860s show how much she was taken with Ida von Fleischl, in whom she instantly recognized a woman of great sophistication, superior intelligence and warmth, dry humor and simplic-ity of manner (TB 97/98). Never before had she met someone with whom she immediately felt so much at ease and with whom she could so openly and honestly discuss her work. Ida Fleischl listened, empa-thized, and understood. To be with her meant being emotionally and intellectually enriched.

Soon Marie von Ebner adopted the habit of reading all her stage works to Frau von Fleischl, whose judgment she gladly accepted. After a session with her new mentor she once wrote in her diary: "At 3 p.m. Ida Fleischl came and I read the *Roland* to her in one sitting. She must be a brave, strong, deeply feeling nature, to be capable of absorbing and surveying someone else's work with such sympathy and such energetic interest" (TB I 97). In 1867, after one of Ida Fleischl's visits, she noted enthusiastically: "In the morning Frau von Fleischl paid me a visit. I believe there is much in this woman: straightforwardness, simplicity, intelligence to find the truth, character to tell it" (TB I 213).

Von Fleischl's love of literature and art, nourished by her associa-tion with artists from Austria and abroad, was a great blessing for Marie von Ebner, who became a regular guest at the Fleischl soirées. Finally she had found a circle of like-minded friends in whose midst she felt totally at ease. These people did not consider her strange because she wrote, they did not judge her by her appearance but honestly valued her accomplishments. They considered it an honor when she read her works to them before submitting them to the publisher, and they inspired and stimulated her with their questions and fair criticism. Moreover, because they fully accepted her and strongly believed in her talent, they gave her self-confidence.

Having hardly ever met dignitaries from abroad, she now came into contact with writers and artists from various parts of the monarchy, from Germany and even from France. One day she met the poet Siegfried Lippiner at Ida von Fleischl's place. He had come from Galicia to Vienna and had made a name for himself with his epic *Der entfesselte Prometheus*. He later had a great influence on the workers' movement run by Victor Adler and Engelbert Pernersdorfer, who both worked indefatigably for the political union of the workers and for their cultural education. She had the pleasure of getting to know Levin Schücking, a close friend of the German writer Annette von Droste-Hülshoff, with his daughter Theo, who would remain a lifelong friend. She also met the internationally renowned dancer Fanny Elssler who performed mainly in London and Paris and who also had connections in America. She was an artist Ebner-Eschenbach was particularly proud to know.[1]

By the end of 1869 Marie Ebner and Ida Fleischl were intimate friends. When Marie had to move back into her father's home Ida came visiting to help dispel Count Dubsky's bad moods. When Marie needed a break from looking after her father Ida invited her to her home. There was not a day when the two friends did not meet or write to each other and share their mutual joys and concerns. In 1871 Ida's oldest son, Dr. Ernst Fleischl, aged twenty-five, caught an infection from a corpse at the Institute of Pathological Anatomy. For twenty-five years, until his death, he suffered excruciating pain while his mother could only helplessly look on (Fleischl-Marxow 2). In those trying years it was a blessing for her to have a friend like Marie von Ebner-Eschenbach, on whose sympathy she could always count and with whom she could share her deepest worries.

She always considered it a special privilege to be the writer's literary advisor and to have the opportunity to collaborate with her on her work. She, for her part, rendered her friend an invaluable service by helping her with her rather faulty grammar. As Anton Bettelheim says: "She recognized the genuine talent of Marie Ebner; however, she did not conceal in her manly straightforwardness to the born Comtesse Dubsky that her education which, according to the custom of the nobility of the time, was basically French, was not sufficient for a woman aiming for the laurels of a German poet" ("Ida" 2). As a member of the Austrian hereditary aristocracy Marie von Ebner had never learned to speak grammatically correct German. The dialect, called "Kutscherton" or "Schönbrunner Dialekt," spoken by the Austrian nobility, was full of grammatical flaws and mixed with English and French idioms.[2] Ebner-Eschenbach always felt insecure with her German. Therefore she came to rely more and more on Ida Fleischl's excellent knowledge of the language and subordinated herself to the latter's authority.

Every morning the writer got up at six o'clock in order to work, a habit she had started in the 1860s as a playwright. Hermine Villinger, who later met her in 1886, became a witness to her friend's daily routine: "While all her dear ones and those who crowd around her are still lying asleep she has long been working at the task she has set herself. She works for several hours and then, before the visiting hour has come, she hurries with her manuscript tucked under her arm first through a doorway, then through the Graben into Habsburgergasse No. 5, because there lives Frau Ida von Fleischl, Marie von Ebner-Eschenbach's best friend, her 'Supreme Court'" (Villinger 63).

Only after von Fleischl had been consulted and had approved of a work, did her friend send it to a publisher. In 1886 after Rodenberg had accepted *Das Gemeindekind* for publication in the *Deutsche Rundschau* Marie von Ebner entered in her diary:

> Rodenberg acknowledges in an overly generous letter the receipt of the last part of "Gemeindekind," and now I have to say: In this entire story there is not a single chapter for which I did not draw on Ida's advice, there is not a line which was not approved by her. How much and how often did I introduce changes. But when she said: "Let it be, it is good," then I was relieved of all my anxiety. (B II 220)

During these years of intense collaboration with her friend Marie von Ebner-Eschenbach reached the apex of her career. The greater her success, the more Ida rejoiced with her, like a mother with her child. Ida, as only a few of Ebner-Eschenbach's friends, understood her need to write and wholeheartedly encouraged her in all her endeavors. Through her part in her achievement she also helped her to find emotional stability. By providing a close relationship of personal trust, by sharing her friend's interests and values, she helped Ebner to define herself and to find her identity as a writer. A reliable ally and an able judge, Ida reassured her of her worth and tried to promote her self-esteem. As Marie Ebner once wrote to Hieronymus Lorm, Ida also attempted to cure her from her habit of disparaging and tormenting herself (BF 72).

Ida von Fleischl's philosophical interests also inspired her and induced her to read works like Gustav Fechner's *Zend -Avesta*, Henry Drummond's *Natural Law in the Spiritual World* and W. Salter's *Die Religion der Moral*. Books like these made her reflect on her own religion, providing many an idea for her later works.

From 1879 until the late 1880s the two friends spent their summer vacation—at first a few weeks, later several months—in St. Gilgen on the Abersee. Friends of Ida's sons, the physiologist Sigmund Exner and the renowned surgeon Theodor Billroth with their families, had settled close by, so that they never lacked social life. Although officially on vacation, Marie von Ebner kept her strict routine. As Hermine Villinger, who sometimes came to visit her, recalls: "In the morning here too one could see Marie von Ebner-Eschenbach hurry with her manuscript across the street to her friend. And, when the work was done, the rest of the time belonged to friends who gathered in the afternoon at Marie von Ebner-Eschenbach's place and in the evenings at Ida Fleischl's" (Villinger 64). When von Fleischl was satisfied with Ebner's literary work the latter read it to a circle of friends who considered it a special treat to hear her. Emilie Exner, who often came to visit from nearby Brunnwinkl, the summer residence of the Exner family,[3] likewise reminisces about these readings: "One could virtually see how every word came from the heart as part of her soul, poured into crystal clear moulds" (B I 191).

Memorable were also the walks the two friends undertook every day after five o'clock in the evening. According to Emilie Exner's, alias Felicie Ewart's report, Marie von Ebner-Eschenbach was still walking in a sprightly way and was able to race with the young girls, whereas Ida Fleischl had difficulty walking and was later given a corset to ease her pain. Marie von Ebner gladly adapted her pace to that of her friend on their daily promenades (B I 186). Gradually Ida von Fleischl and Marie von Ebner extended their stay in St.Gilgen. Finally they remained all summer and became quiet but active members of the community. Ebner-Eschenbach took a great interest in the villagers, looking after the poor and the sick, as she had always done in Zdislawitz. She also supported the local school and local artistic groups. Once she invited all her friends to a play called "Kaiser Joseph und die Schusterstochter" (Emperor Joseph and the Cobbler's Daughter) which, as it turned out, was not suitable for young girls. When she realized, after an "end of an act with disarming directness," that all the young girls had disappeared from the audience, she felt extremely embarrassed and vowed never again to sponsor such a play. Yet she continued to support the local actors and their stage (B I 189).

Ida von Fleischl was always at Marie von Ebner's side, taking a motherly interest in everything she did. Yet the two also had their little squabbles. As Felicie Ewart observes: "Although the two friends were one heart and one soul, their natures were far apart, and it was sometimes an amusing scene to witness" (B I 191). Marie von Ebner-Eschenbach and her friend became virtually inseparable. When the former was ill and could not write her customary letters, Ida would write them for her, and she received this solicitude with deepest gratitude. In 1892 she dedicated her collection *Parabeln, Märchen und Gedichte* to Ida, always aware that she was her mentor, her sounding board, her editor, and her stern critic, on whom she could unconditionally rely. Through von Fleischl she also found a third friend: Betty Paoli, on account of whom she met her future biographer, Anton Bettelheim, and also her later family doctor, friend and correspondent, Josef Breuer.

For more than ten years the three ladies, Marie von Ebner, Ida von Fleischl and Betty Paoli, played tarok together and, though sometimes criticized for doing so, derived inspiration and stimulation from these gatherings. A friend of the von Fleischls, the artist and critic Friedrich Pecht, once "grew quite angry and asked in irritation whether three intelligent women really had nothing better to do than to play tarok at their get-togethers" (EBP 2). Hermine Villinger sometimes was a witness to these parties and recalls: "The playing itself was a side-affair. What clever speech did I hear there! And how heartily these three women could laugh! At the same time they were indescribably modest and unassuming in their behavior. But every one of them was, in her own way, a well-rounded and mature personality" (Villinger 63).

After Betty Paoli's death Marie von Ebner and Ida von Fleischl continued to play tarok in memory of their revered friend. Even in St. Gilgen they did not part from their tradition. Anton Bettelheim remembers in his essay on Ida von Fleischl-Marxow: "In St.Gilgen, too, one could, as eyewitness to the rustic domicile of Ida Fleischl, participate in a tarok party; when the hostess' favorite parrot began to squeak ever more loudly, and when the risks of the game became ever greater, Frau Ida was humming suddenly in her alto voice a tune unknown to all of us, of which only her good son, Dr. Otto von Fleischl, who spent his winters in Rome, could tell that his mother was attempting to sing the Austrian national anthem" (2). Bettelheim also repeatedly points out how intimately the two friends understood each other, "in every wink, every word, so too in deeply shared silence, that summit of understanding" (2). Most of all, the two women gave each other a strong feeling of camaraderie and solidarity. And this feeling of fellowship, this personal affection is reflected in many of Marie von Ebner-Eschenbach's works where, as in "Wieder die Alte" or "Ein kleiner Roman," two congenial women enjoy a friendship that comes close to a mother-daughter relationship. Ida Fleischl, therefore, may have been the principal model for the baroness of "Wieder die Alte":

> The deep furrows on that woman's brows had been
> dug by assiduous thoughts—thoughts that did not give
> in to rest, thoughts that asked for ultimate reasons.
> The astringent line around the narrow mouth indicates
> a strength which is unbending, a courage which
> knows no limits. And if the capability to think and to
> have a will determines our rank among humans, yours
> is as high as only few people can aspire to. (117)

Like von Fleischl, the baroness is interested in Buddhism, like her she is possessed of wisdom and of a clear judgment, and like her she has learned to practice self-control. Just as Claire, the protagonist of "Wieder die Alte," looks up to the baroness as her role model, so Marie von Ebner deeply admired her friend and gratefully accepted her counsel.

Ida von Fleischl also introduced her to the works of great writers, like Ivan Turgenev, whose novellas she henceforth read with growing fascination. She admired in the Russian master the skilled painter of sceneries, the advocate of the oppressed, the writer who had a deep psychological understanding for humans and whose aim was to reveal the goodness in humankind. Reading his work stimulated her to observe her milieu more closely and to focus especially on the inner life of her literary characters. She found much that she had in common with

Turgenev, who thereafter became a model for her. His *Faust* deeply impressed her and so did his *Poems in Prose*, yet sometimes she had reservations and noted in her diary: "Read 'Helene' by Turgenev. The weakest piece I know by him. That the hero dies of pneumonia is even worse for the novel than for him" (Vesely 218). Yet, when her friend Joseph von Weilen explained to her that she had not really understood Turgenev's intent she decided to immerse herself again in this novella (Vesely 218). In 1877 she sent Turgenev one of her own works, and he replied from Paris with a friendly note (RV I.N. 56309).

It is therefore no wonder that several of Marie von Ebner-Eschen-bach's works were inspired by the great Russian writer. Turgenev's dog-story "Mumu" may have been a model for her "Kram-bambuli" (Gese-rick 61). His story "The Brigadier" may have inspired the tragic tale "Er laßt die Hand küsssen" and his 1883 collected poems *Senilia* are reflected in Ebner-Eschenbach's 1892 collection *Parabeln, Märchen und Gedichte* (B I 194). In her novella "Ob spät, ob früh" she modeled her plot on Turgenev's *First Love*, using the sixteen-year-old Vladimir Pe-trovich's first love experience as an analogy for Harald's encounter with an Austrian countess at the spa Bad Reichenhall. As Harald of "Ob spät, ob früh" ecstatically states of Turgenev's *First Love*: "it is ravishing, it is divine! . . . It is life and also poetry . . . it is a revelation" (382), so his creator, Marie von Ebner, must have felt about the work of her Russian idol. In her 1916 collection "Aus einem zeitlosen Tagebuch" she describes a fictitious dialogue between the Russian writer Gorki and herself, predicting that Turgenev, whom Gorki calls a "soft and pleasant writer," and whose work he considers outdated, will outlast Gorki's achievement: "O Gorki! Your name will have disappeared like smoke, while the name of Turgenev will shine like a star" (724). Her own star had just begun to rise, and it was due to Turgenev's influence and to Ida von Fleischl's friendship and collaboration that she was able to create her greatest "Dorfgeschichte" (village story), *Das Gemeindekind*.

CHAPTER 2:

"YOU HAVE CREATED A MASTERPIECE"

1886 was a very productive year for Marie von Ebner-Eschenbach. Since 1879 she had been thinking about writing the story of some children whose parents were incarcerated and who, as charges of the parish, largely had to fend for themselves in order to survive. What had inspired her to choose this subject matter was a visit from the mayor and some people from the village council in Zdislawitz.[4] She just happened to be in the courtyard when they came with two boys aged six and four and a three-year-old girl, to ask for her brother Adolph's financial support for these children. Since their parents were both in prison, the parish had to look after the youngsters, but money was scarce and it was hoped that Count Adolph Dubsky would agree to help. The sight of these poor, neglected children deeply affected Ebner-Eschenbach. As she later wrote to Anton Bettelheim: "The oldest is cross-eyed, looks miserable and so sad, as if he knew what to expect from life. The little boy and the girl are lively and trusting. The little one proudly showed her new shoes and her hat, which she lifted from her head in order to have it properly admired. Good people gave these things to them while they were on their way" (B II 171).

Marie von Ebner saw poverty in Zdislawitz. She also was more than familiar with some villagers' slovenliness and their penchant for stealing and drinking. In July that same year nineteen homes of the poorest of the villagers of Zdislawitz had burned down. When the writer and her niece, Marie, came to see the fire site they met a blind woman who tried to get bread from the village inn, while her husband, drunk and bursting with health, was dozing in front of his burned-down shack (B II 170).

In April 1875 she had been approached by a thirteen-year-old begging child with a dying baby in his arms (Vesely 229), and in June that same year she had another experience with an impoverished boy who desperately tried to sell some tin dishes (Rieder *Weisheit* 109-110). All these incidents, and especially the one with the three neglected youngsters, whose fate as wards of the parish she could foresee in the bleakest colors, preoccupied her for a long time. Seven years later she conceived the story of Pavel Holub, the protagonist of *Das Gemeindekind*. The young boy's fate may have particularly touched her, becaus eit reminded her of her own "poor, motherless childhood ("Schattenleben") ttad of the sense of helplessness and forlornness she had so often experienced among people who seeemed antagonistic to her.

Pavel Holub's story begins in 1860 in Soleschau, a fictitious village in the vicinity of Brünn, the capital of Moravia. He is thirteen years old. His father is an itinerant brick-maker, who takes his family with him from job to job to assist him in his unskilled labor. An alcoholic, he is eventually sentenced to death for the murder of the curate of Kunovic, a village where he had worked and from which he had been expelled at the instigation of the very same priest. Barbara Holub, his wife, an unwilling accomplice to the deed, too terrified to tell the truth and too loyal to give her husband away, is condemned to ten years in prison. Their two children, Pavel and his ten-year-old sister Milada, become wards of the community in which they originally had their home. Although living with an alcoholic, wife- and child-abusing husband and father was far from ideal, it still appeared to the children as "home" over against the homelessness of their new situation.

The father's crime and the mother's assumed complicity cause the children, especially Pavel, to be ineradicably stigmatized. Milada has the good fortune to favorably impress the baroness of the nearby castle by her personality and her manners. She agrees to accept the girl into her household. Pavel, however, offends her sense of decorum and is therefore left to the mercy of the villagers. The customary arrangement in such cases was that each peasant family in turn would provide food and lodging for one day, but even that was unacceptable to the peasants. "Not one of them was willing to have the son of a murderer in the company of his own children, even for a day in every five or six weeks" (20).[5] Pavel is treated like an outcast because his parents belong to a social group unacceptable to society. He shares his father's crime, coerced into a situation in which he cannot win.

The villagers discharge their responsibilities toward him by making sure that he is given no chance to improve his fate. Pavel is assigned as an aid to Virgil, the parish herdsman. The latter is known as a drunkard, his wife Virgilova has a reputation as a dangerous quack and a thief. Even this stratum, itself marginal to the village society, has its own ranking system: in the herdsman's cottage Pavel is given the worst place to sleep, the herdsman's daughter, Vinska, treats him as her subordinated servant. The enticement of "four pecks of grain," which the community offers the herdsman to reimburse him for his expenses, is enhanced by the offer to use Pavel as an assistant, freeing Virgil effectively from all work. The villagers' obligation to look after Pavel's education is accommodated in the provision to send him to church on Sundays and to school "as often as possible." This arrangement is considered appropriate, because he "won't see anything bad while with them that he had not seen a hundred times at home" (21).

For the community Pavel, the person, does not count; the "Pavel case" has been solved beyond legal reproof. His fate appears to be sealed. He has been assigned a status and a role which he plays as expected. For the next three years the herdsman's family becomes the group which exerts decisive influence over him, socializing him into a subculture with its own anti-social norms and values. Virgil's cottage becomes Pavel's microworld. He is pushed around and exploited. Instead of being sent to school—education is not valued in these circles—he is sent to work in a factory. The money he earns is taken away by his warden, who needs it for alcohol.

In order to satisfy his hunger Pavel has to steal. Separated from his mother who had loved him in her own undemonstrative way, and his sister, to whom he is deeply attached, Pavel focuses his emotions on Vinska, the herdsman's daughter, "like an ill-natured dog who, dissatisfied with his master, is always ready for rebellion and yet submits again and again" (43). Vinska unscrupulously uses and abuses Pavel's attachment. "Whatever she wished was done: he went on her errands, he stole wood from the forest for her, as well as eggs from the barns of the peasants; he fell more and more under the subjection to her" (43).

But Pavel's love for his sister eventually prevails. He dreams of rescuing her from the baroness' castle and of starting a new life with her. "He would penetrate into the castle, carry off his sister, go with her over the mountains into foreign countries, hire himself out as a laborer and never again hear the reproach that he was the son of his parents" (26). The plan he devises to carry out his dream fails, and his intentions are misconstrued. The society which denied him basic human rights and stigmatized him for the crime of his father, exerts its "paternal rights" and condemns him to public flogging at the school. Pavel is well on the way to playing the very role which the community expects him to assume, namely that of a deviant.

But gradually, with the schoolteacher's help, Pavel is integrated into his village community. Habrecht is in his own way an outsider, since he was once taken for dead, and superstitious people now believe him to be a wizard. Having suffered himself under social prejudice and persecution, he knows about the resources that can prevent an individual from succumbing to social stereotyping. The teacher is the voice of reason that speaks out against the chorus of social prejudice. He does not simply take Pavel's side against the village but also tries to change his mind and ways. There is considerable resistance. When impressing upon Pavel the need for an education, he is up against the prejudice of the "underprivileged," for whom cleverness is more important than schooling.

Ebner-Eschenbach shows consummate skill as a story writer in the way she prepares for Pavel's inner and outer progress toward moral rehabilitation and integration into society. She gives the reader glimpses of her protagonist's innate goodness by describing his attachment to his sister, his loyalty toward his comrades and his saving of a partridge mother and her young from the clutches of a cat. She also prepares the reader for the role which Habrecht, the teacher, is going to play in the process of Pavel's re-socialization which, like his deviance, requires the coming together of both inner and outer motives. Pavel's fate begins to turn just at the moment when everything seems to be lost. In order to oblige his faithless friend Vinska, Pavel ventures to rob the baroness' peacock of his last few feathers. Unhappily he kills the bird in an effort to ward off its attacks. He is caught and brought before the baroness.

Now everything seems lost. Pavel cannot even excuse himself by pretending that he committed the crime in order to satisfy his hunger. His viciousness and his perversity seem to be beyond excuse. However, Habrecht succeeds in extricating him from his predicament. He even wins for him the opportunity to see his beloved sister at the convent school, where she is being educated to become its future Superior. Milada is horrified when she hears that Pavel steals and implores him to lead a respectable life for their parents' sake: "You ought to be the best boy in the whole village, so that God will pardon our parents, so that their souls may be saved " (99).

Milada's words of admonition and encouragement reach Pavel's heart, and he leaves her with the firm determination to change his ways. His life, which seemed so useless and directionless, is given a new aim and purpose by his sister. She entrusts him with her monthly allowance from the baroness, begging him to work and save money in order to buy a plot and to build a house for their mother, so that she may have a home after her release from prison. Although rather alienated from Christianity, Pavel accepts his sister's Christian norms and values, striving to become worthy of her respect and love. Milada is his best friend whom he cherishes and trusts. Her attitude decisively influences his development and his concept of himself.

Pavel is now determined to change his life. "And as he walked along slowly the dreams he wove shaped themselves more and more distinctly into the conviction that he was drawing near to a great change in his destiny, the mysterious beginning of a fairer, better life" (116). He instinctively perceives that his change of inner direction needs a change of social environment. He approaches Habrecht, begging him to give him a new home. From then on the teacher becomes his role model. Through interaction with him Pavel's view of society changes. He is given a place to hide his money, he is given shelter and food, and he no longer has to suffer exploitation. He accepts the teacher's notion of right and wrong and to that extent also the basic values of society. He begins to understand the need to learn in school and to work for one's sustenance. The new environment has its effect.

Pavel—like any other human being—wants to be an accepted member of his own society. He wants to belong and to participate, and his dream to buy land and build a house reflects the criteria of belonging to a village society. He also knows that he needs help in order to accomplish his goal. While formerly his thoughts had centered on his own well-being and on how to outsmart others for his benefit, he now shows an interest in becoming socially and economically productive: he offers to transform the field adjoining the school into a garden.

Through involvement in a close relationship with the teacher, who stands at his side even when he is accused of having poisoned the mayor, Pavel learns to respect himself and to believe in his own capabilities. He internalizes the positive view reflected by the teacher's estimation of his intrinsic value. Habrecht thus assumes the role of father for Pavel, who has never known a real father in his life, and educates him according to his own ethical values. The trustful relationship between student and teacher removes the barrier that prevented the youngster from corresponding with his mother and sister. He is no longer ashamed of himself and his circumstances. If Milada's piously Christian outlook, her trust and financial support, provided the initial impetus for Pavel's resolve to begin a new life, Habrecht's more liberal and humanistic orientation gives it a goal which he can realize in the less than perfect world of the village. Habrecht reveals to Pavel the tragedy of his own life, in order both to prove his trust in him and also to teach him to be leery of public opinion.

Marie von Ebner-Eschenbach places two important symbols of her protagonist's successful re-socialization closely together: his being declared of age and his buying property from the parish. When he comes of age, Pavel's status changes from child to adult, and when he purchases property he moves from being an outcast to being a reputable member of society. In a sense confirming Pavel's social maturity and also advancing it, Habrecht's rather sudden transfer from the village marks one of the major stages in the development of the novel. By making a gift of his modest furniture and of some of his books to his student, Habrecht acknowledges his fully responsible personality and also again antagonizes public opinion.

With the teacher's departure Pavel loses his most trusted friend and supporter, but gains self-confidence and self-reliance in the process. He can now hold his own against those whom a happier fate had spared the bitter experiences of his own life. Through hard work and discipline he has risen from the ranks of the disreputable poor to the status of a respected worker and owner of modest property. He has internalized society's precepts. He identifies with them, rising morally above his community. In the end Pavel is still a day-laborer, but he is strong, eager to work, and willing to save his money. If he continues to invest his capital in land he will perhaps one day be a farmer. He has proven leadership ability for good and for bad. He is loyal, and he has never betrayed his friends, even when at personal risk. Normally the mayor in the village is a well-to-do peasant with good judgment and acknowledged authority among his peers. Pavel has acquired reputable standing in the village, therefore Habrecht's ambitions for Pavel to become mayor are not implausible. The young man has also impressed the baroness favorably by his development. Partly in order to make good for what the village has failed to do for him, partly in order to express her appreciation of what—against almost overwhelming odds—he has become, she makes him a gift of several acres of land.

There is a little irony in the scene: Pavel, who apparently has also acquired a fair sense of farming, thinks the plot the baroness wants to give him would be good for cherry-trees, and the baroness agrees. Was it not stolen cherries which had brought him first to the baroness' rather unfavorable attention? Far from having to steal her cherries, as he had done only a few years ago, he can now grow his own on land given him by the baroness in recognition of his respectability! When confronted by criticism—typically the steward and the curate think it too generous a gift—the lady counters that her present was "exactly suitable to a youth hitherto neglected by fate" (297). The material goods Pavel has acquired from the baroness become visible symbols of his inner worth and confer honor upon him.

Pavel's final worry is now the return of his mother from the penitentiary. The re-awakened memory of the past could ruin what he has so carefully built up. He himself has doubts about his mother's innocence, but for the village she is a murderess. Some people in the community make snide remarks. Pavel even considers leaving the village in order to avoid the unpleasantness of having to face his mother and to confront the village together with her. But eventually the bond between mother and son proves stronger than everything else. Once Pavel learns that his mother is innocent and was wrongly convicted, he is determined to share his life with her.

Thus, in a sense, Pavel's life has come full circle: if his misery as "child of the parish" began with his mother's conviction and imprisonment, his status as a full member of the parish—and possibly its future leader—is reached when she returns from prison. It is Pavel who offers a home and security to her: he has become what his father never was, a protector and provider. Against all the odds that fate as well as malice have put in his way, he has succeeded with the help of a few friends who dared to follow their own judgment and who believed in him.

Work on the social novel—Ebner preferred to call it a "story"—proceeded relatively fast.[6] In spite of a troublesome winter in Vienna, where she always felt like "a horse in a pond filled with leeches" (B II 40) because of her many social commitments, she had been able to write and was especially looking forward to her stay in Zdislawitz. There she hoped to regain, in the quiet of the long-missed country life, "first of all creative zest and then a little confidence in the created work" (Baasner 188). In August she finished the sixteenth chapter and promised Rodenberg the complete manuscript by October 1886. After reading the first chapter he sent her a most encouraging reply:"Dear friend, that is the most beautiful thing you have ever written and it is one of the most beautiful things that has been written for a long time . . . You have created a masterpiece that will endure in German literature, and it will be a great distinction for the *Rundschau* to have been the first to publish it" (B II 186).

After completion of the seventeenth chapter she noted in her diary: "Now the moment comes where one puts one's hand on the shoulder of the child who is eager to run away and asks: 'Are you really ready to go? Do you really not miss anything you might need while on your way? Or do you carry something superfluous in your knapsack which is an unnecessary burden to you? Let me have another look! '" (B II 219-220). Each book was Ebner-Eschenbach's "child," born in long and painful labor, nursed with love and great care. When Rodenberg approved of her latest offspring, she was so elated and relieved that she feared she would not sleep all night (Vesely 211).

How emotionally involved she was in her work can also be gathered from her next letter to Rodenberg which accompanied the final chapters of *Das Gemeindekind*: "Dear friend, it is not a book that comes to you, but a soul; everything that is in my heart is coming, everything that I would wish to entrust to good people" (Baasner 190). Rodenberg eagerly accepted the work for serialization in the *Rundschau* and after the first issue received an enthusiastic response from his readers, who could hardly wait to learn more about Pavel Holub's fate (Baasner 192). When the Paetel publishing house, which also published the *Rundschau*, brought out *Das Gemeindekind* in 1887, the book immediately became its best drawing card (Bittrich 240).

The reaction among Ebner-Eschenbach's friends was mixed. Hermine Villinger, always ecstatic about her revered mentor's work, could hardly wait until she held the book in her hands and especially appreciated the last scene, the reunion between Pavel and his mother (Baasner 193). Another acquaintance, Marie von Naymayer, did not like the novel at all, mocking the writer for having conceived a peasant story like Turgenev and Tolstoi (Baasner 194). All the more the writer appreciated Gottfried Keller's opinion. She thought of him particularly highly and had vowed to learn from his literary technique (B II 158). When he enthusiastically praised *Das Gemeindekind* she was extremely proud and felt reassured (Vesely 226). Conrad Ferdinand Meyer was less impressed. He could not understand that Ebner-Eschenbach had chosen a protagonist from the agricultural proletariat, a class he considered as low "as animals" (Vesely 226). The German writer Paul Heyse enjoyed the novel, but wished Marie von Ebner had provided a happier ending to Pavel's sorrowful story (HC 303), a notion also expressed by Anton Bettelheim in his review in *Die Nation* (Baasner 198). Ferdinand von Saar found the work too didactic (Baasner 228). All literary critics, including the formidable Erich Schmidt, whose reviews Ebner-Eschenbach always anticipated with fear and trembling, were impressed by her observational skills, her realistic concept of rural life and her insight into the character and the inner state of her literary figures. During her lifetime *Das Gemeindekind* experienced sixteen editions, a sign of how popular she had become by now. In due course the work was translated into Dutch, English, and Czech (Baasner 215).

As Marie von Ebner-Eschenbach's fame spread in Germany and Austria, more and more reviews of the story were written. Whenever she was celebrated as a great writer, *Das Gemeindekind*, by now acknowledged as her masterpiece, was praised as well (Baasner 233). The name of the author became identified with this achievement. She must have read all these positive discussions with deep satisfaction. The "tree of her talent" had finally born fruit, she was now recognized as an outstanding author and her relatives had to admit that "there [was] something to her talent." Her portrait was published in calendars that hung in public buildings, the name Marie von Ebner-Eschenbach had become a household word (Necker 49).

Still, there were some critics who eyed her work with skepticism, if not with outright hostility. Karl Kraus, notorious for his pungent essays in his journal *Die Fackel*, accused Ebner-Eschenbach of siding with the very "press mafia," that had once panned her as a dramatist, and that had created "an oligarchy of mediocrity," which she had initially condemned in her story "Ein Spätgeborener." He maliciously observed: "Age makes one farsighted. The writer who, a quarter of a century ago, saw through the clique, today overlooks what has managed to press too close to her" (qtd. in Baasner 224).

More annoying for Marie von Ebner was the criticism coming from authorities close to the Catholic Church. They objected to the fact that she had dared to criticize priests and institutionalized religion in her work. They pointed out that she had propagated ideas that contradicted Christian dogma and morals, and they therefore tried to prevent her works from being placed in public libraries (Reinke 780). By describing narrow-minded, inexorable and hard-hearted nuns and by exposing the pettiness and opportunism of a priest in her latest story, she had deeply offended some Catholic readers.

Indeed, *Das Gemeindekind* may be seen as a satire on what she perceived as the artificiality of convent life, a life regulated according to the rules of an institution that sacrificed humanity in order to keep its anachronistic and abstract organization intact. When Pavel's mother tries to contact her daughter Milada at the convent by writing to her from prison, the nuns do not even pass on the letter to her child and tell the mother it would be best if her daughter never heard from her. When Pavel pleads with a nun to find a place for him where he can live and work, he only meets with indifference: "She looked down in front of herself, infinitely pious, infinitely indifferent. Her entire entourage did likewise and the thick-skulled Pavel finally understood that he had asked in vain" (67). The story further shows, and some people may have resented it, that Ebner-Eschenbach, like Habrecht of *Das Gemeindekind*, had found a substitute for the Christian faith in Salter's concept of morality that elevated humanitarianism to the status of religion. In 1885 William Mackintire Salter's lectures on ethical religion at the Society for Moral Culture in Chicago were translated by Georg von Gizycki[7] under the title *Die Religion der Moral*. Marie von Ebner was instantly fascinated by this work, soon calling herself Salter's "most humble disciple" (FMC 199). Like Salter she believed in those years that the only valid religion was the religion of morality.

As she matured she increasingly realized to what extent religion was a means for patriarchy to subordinate, oppress, and marginalize women, and she began to rebel against it. In her story "Komtesse Paula" she has Elisabeth, trapped in an unhappy marriage, indignantly say: "Who causes a scandal? Who goes into the water? Only ordinary people, who have no religion, do such things" (352). Ebner-Eschenbach saw religion as a means to force women to obediently succumb to the "sacred yoke" (ibid.) and to tolerate husbands who were given authority by the Church to treat them like their chattels. She further realized that religion taught women to accept without demur whatever difficulties they encountered in their lives. As she points out in *Meine Kinderjahre*, all the women she knew in her childhood and youth bore their suffering stoically, imbued with Church teachings and promises of a better hereafter. The two stepgrandmothers, as well as Tante Helene, and the piano teacher Frau Krähmer, all heroically bore their burden—caused by financial insecurity and the double standards of society—nourished by the dubious comforts of their religion. Fräulein Karoline, one of young Marie Dubsky's governesses and later a highly accomplished teacher at a girls' school, was forced by the authorities to retire prematurely, being thus prevented fom enjoying the full pension which would have been her due. Perhaps with a tinge of sarcasm Ebner remarks: "Her deep piety taught her to forgive and instead of a fortune she gained peace of soul" (MK 847).

Ebner-Eschenbach also assumed as early as her teenage years that the Church preached obscurantism and purposely kept its priests in ignorance. Father Borek, an "image of longsuffering" (MK 802) and a man of the kindest disposition, sacrificed himself for his parishioners and taught their children catechism but totally lacked a higher education. His hobby was to create animal figures out of paper maché; to read a scientific book would have seemed a scandal to him.

He was no help at a time when Marie Dubsky went through a very serious crisis of faith which caused her painful dreams and innumerable sleepless nights. For him God had created the world as the Church catechism taught it, books on astronomy did not count as authority: "P. Borek only read the title, smiled and said that this book had been written by a human: it was better to trust divine wisdom instead of human knowledge" (MK 855). Any other doubts Marie had regarding the teachings of the Church, like the doctrine of original sin or the ubiquity of Christ, the priest tried to dispel by repeating: "My child, we should worship the mystery, believe in the mystery, but not ask: How can that be? Were it a mystery if it could be explained?" (MK 857). Yet Marie was not satisfied with the priest's parroting of the catechism. At that time she had already intellectually outgrown her spiritual advisor, and over the years her misgivings about the Church and its representatives increased. In "Komtesse Paula" Marie von Ebner has her young protagonist say about her confessor: "He held views in learned matters which no one shared save maybe Madame Duphot and myself— and even we did only for a while" (Harriman 47).

From these religious conflicts, incurred in her youth, her later doubts and scepticism regarding institutionalized religion developed, doubts that removed her further and further from the deep piety she had experienced as a child. As a teenager she had already rebelled against what she considered hypocrisy and chauvinism in Christianity. In a fierce debate with her governess during a history lesson she called Widukind and Albion, the Saxon leaders converted to Christianity by Charlemagne, cowards and hypocrites: "What could they think of a religion which condoned the crimes of its adherents, as Emperor Charles had committed against the Saxons?" (MK 846). Such arguments were too much for the pious governess who, frightened by a young girl that dared take sides against her religion, tried to find refuge in prayer.

As a young woman, under the influence of her science-oriented, progressive, and liberal-minded husband, Marie von Ebner-Eschenbach became more and more estranged from Church dogma. Yet her diary entries of the 1860s still reveal her as a churchgoing Catholic. She regularly attended mass when visiting her relatives in Bucsan, Bürgstein, Reichenburg, and Zdislawitz and had masses read for the deceased of the family (TB I 121). Eduard Devrient, meeting her in Karlsruhe in 1863, remarked in his diary that he found her "very Catholic" (Kabel 393). Churches as artistic monuments were always of great interest to her, and wherever she went on her trips, to Germany, Switzerland, or to different spas in Austria, she always took great pleasure in visiting them. In her beliefs, though, she deviated more and more from the notions of her relatives who did not feel the need to question their faith. As she sensed that she had outgrown her loved ones intellectually she also was aware of a discrepancy between their faith and her own (TB I 272). She prayed regularly, thanking God for all the blessings she had received. At the end of 1865 she noted in her diary: "Thus I thank you from the fullness of my heart, you who order the greatest and the smallest in the universe; bless all whom I love—all who are being loved and who love" (TB I 69).[8]

Her faith in God was, however, not identical with Church teachings and led her stepmother, in whose view she always had been too liberal-minded, to make some "conversion efforts" (TB I 119). In her tragedy *Marie Roland* she later had her heroine say: "I am returning to God, not to the Church" (Vesely 213). In her view God revealed himself first and foremost in the human heart.[9] In 1867 she alluded in her diary to the fact that she was against the agreement between the Vatican and Austria: "It is said that the camarilla around the emperor has gathered in Ischl, urging him to maintain the Concordat. If he gives in, we are going to hell by special delivery" (TB I 206).

The Concordat of 1855 had given the Church vast powers, not only in ecclesiastical matters but also in politics and education, where it had become the "powerful arm of the state" (Kann 321). The Church was given access to income from government funds and, apart from control over religious education, it also had a say in the instruction of history, languages and science. What must have bothered Ebner-Eschenbach the most was the fact that the Church now also had the right to censor literature it considered unfit for the faithful (Kann 322). Like her husband, Ida von Fleischl, and other Jewish friends, who were all proponents of liberalism, she must have rejoiced when the Concordat was abolished in 1870 during the government of Counts Karl and Adolf

Auersperg. The influence of the Church was again confined to the religious sphere, and state supremacy was re-established (Kann 357).

Personal experiences regarding her stepmother's and some other relatives' bigotry and superstition may further have helped to estrange her from institutional faith. In 1884 she indignantly noted in her diary that a priest had been threatening a dying child with the punishments of hell (Vesely 213). In the 1880s Karl Freiherr von Vogelsang with his anti-capitalist, anti-Jewish, anti-liberal doctrine gained considerable influence in Viennese Catholic circles (Geehr 75). His militant Catholicism may have increased Ebner-Eschenbach's disaffection with the Church. When in 1895 Pope Leo XIII endorsed Karl Lueger in spite of his demagoguery, slander, and anti-Semitism, in his bid for the mayoralty in Vienna, she must have been infuriated.

Many of her works in the 1880s and 1890s reflect her disappointment with the clergy and the Church as an institution. In her 1883 story "Die Resel" she points out that the deacon considers Church principles more important than a dying human being (227). In *Unsühnbar* of 1889 Maria Dornach, the protagonist, no longer finds comfort and help in her religion, which is like a "shimmering star," "only a reflection of the longing for consolation, of the hope—in [her] own heart" (470). Her aunt, Countess Dolph, even suggests that God only imitated Satan's creation (476). Maria Dornach's mother writes in her diary: "If God were good and just at all, he would have listened to me. But there is no God in the heavens, only a devil, and he is punishing me"[10] (408).

Father Leo Klinger, the protagonist of her 1893 story "Glaubenslos?," likewise echoes the writer's scepticism toward the Church. He is unable to fulfill the tasks set by his authorities and seriously thinks of leaving the priesthood. His superior, sent to investigate the situation in the parish, demonstrates, like the priest in *Das Gemeindekind*, the inhumanity of the bureaucratic attitude in the Church. Until 1910 in stories like "Unverbesserlich," "Ob spät, ob früh" and "Das tägliche Leben," Ebner-Eschenbach portrays the cruelty of an institution that demands of its followers the strictest observance of dogma without showing much regard for their humanity. Although a diary entry of 1887 reveals that Marie von Ebner still attended church at that time (Vesely 213), mentally she was far removed from its teachings. Salter, whose philosophy she had eagerly embraced, denied the existence of a personal God, accusing Christian theology of creating a deity who was nothing but a reflection of the possibilities inherent in human beings (8). Whether it was Salter's influence or some personal disappointments in her life that led to Ebner-Eschenbach's loss of faith in a personal God we do not know. We only have her letter to Natalie von Milde, in which she sadly confesses: "The warm faith in God which every one of your lines bespeaks has moved me deeply. I would like to share it, but regrettably I have for a long time not been able to do so. This great gift, once lost, can never be regained" (RV I.N. 129 272).[11]

CHAPTER 3:

THE "GREAT MOTHER"

Raised by female relations who bravely and stoically bore their often most difficult and trying fates, Marie von Ebner-Eschenbach had a lifelong admiration for heroic women. As a child she had composed fervent poems to the Virgin Mary, the symbol of suffering motherhood, and in later years she tried to immortalize great historic women in her dramas. The fate of Mary Stuart, the unhappy Queen of Scots, had moved her greatly; so much did she empathize with her that she drew a more innocent portrait of the monarch than any other playwright had ever done before. Marie Roland, another heroine whose life story had fascinated the writer, was likewise idealized and drawn with a rare compassion. Having to struggle herself to find her identity Marie von Ebner saw in these women—Jakobäa of Jülich may also be mentioned—a role model of courage, determination and integrity.[12] Further plays like *Die Schauspielerin, Die Heimkehr, Das Waldfräulein* show how much she was concerned with women's personalities and their quest for fulfillment in a patriarchal society that denied them equal rights.

She was always intrigued by women who escaped the straitjacket society tried to force on them. In her diary of January 5, 1867 she mentioned how fascinating it would be to write the biography of the actress Anna Marie Adamberger née Jaquet, who, against her father's demand that she play tragic roles, had chosen the part of the ingenue, which was in accord with her actual personality (TB I 150). There was nothing Ebner-Eschenbach admired more than a woman who followed her convictions in the teeth of the greatest obstacles. Thus, she was in awe when in the 1860s she learned about an Austrian duchess who admitted after her husband's death that her son, destined to inherit the large family estate, was not the legitimate heir but the fruit of adultery. This "heroic decision of a noble and generally revered woman . . . who for truth's sake sacrificed her unsullied reputation" (qtd. in Bittrich 235) impressed her so much that she used this motif in several of her works. In 1863 she wrote *Das Geständnis*, in which a Baroness Werner confesses to Thekla, her daughter-in-law, that she is guilty of adultery, thus preventing the latter from committing the same wrong. Four years later, in her novel *Bozena*, Ebner-Eschenbach again used the theme of a woman's couragous confession of a sexual transgression to emphasize her greatness.

In 1886 she read Tolstoi's *Anna Karenina*, which deeply moved her. She also may have read Ossip Schubin's novel *Gloria victis!*, which turned her thoughts toward the social novel she had promised Paul Heyse to write (Bittrich 348).[13] She began *Unsühnbar* in May 1888 and worked incessantly on it for fourteen months, in spite of being ill during the winter with Basedow's disease (Vesely 232),[14] heart problems and difficulties with breathing (Bittrich 237). Writing was, as always, therapy for her, distracting her from thinking about her ailments. Yet she found it particularly strenuous at this time and thought this novel would be her last major work (Bittrich 238).

Maria Wolfsberg, the heroine, is being forced into marriage by her arrogant, status-conscious father. The man he has chosen for her is Hermann Dornach, the only, idolized son of Countess Dornach, and heir to the family fortune. Yet Maria's heart belongs to Duke Felix Tessin, a man of doubtful reputation, who has managed to charm her with his elegance, wit, and impeccable manners. He wants to marry her. When rejected by her father, he schemes to take revenge. Not long after Maria's wedding to Count Dornach, Tessin, with the help of Maria's bastard brother Wolfi, effects a meeting with Maria and manages to seduce her. Nine months later she bears a son who is considered the offspring of her marriage until Hermann Dornach and his oldest son are killed in a tragic accident. Out of her need to do penance, to be truthful to her relatives, and most of all, to herself, Maria confesses her adultery, leaves Castle Dornach with her illegitimate son and spends the remaining years of her short life in exile at one of her father's country estates.

Once the first draft was finished, Marie von Ebner revised it diligently, aware that "[W]hen the dilettante says 'now my work is complete,' the artist says 'now the work begins'" (qtd. in Bittrich 237). She took the final two chapters to St. Gilgen in June 1889, where she had the necessary peace and quiet to write. By July Rodenberg had the almost completed manuscript and she, as always, eagerly and apprehensively awaited his verdict. He did not keep her on tenterhooks for long. His reply came swiftly. Relieved and elated she noted in her diary of June 6, 1889: "Vivat! Vivat! Letter from Rodenberg. And what a letter! Now I am happy" (qtd. in Bittrich 238). Once he had received the finished work, Rodenberg, full of praise, replied: "I think it is the highest that can be said about any work, that the world is mirrored in it, the world as it is, and that it nevertheless provides an inkling, an expectancy for a better one, which we all desire, for which we all hope" (B II 190). *Unsühnbar* was serialized in the *Deutsche Rundschau* in October and December 1889 and was then published in 1890 by Gebrüder Paetel, who paid Marie Ebner 10,000 marks for it, a very large sum at that time.

Reaction to the novel was mixed. Her sister Julie took offense that Marie had chosen the theme of adultery (Bittrich 242). Yet while shrugging off Julie's prudish concerns, Ebner-Eschenbach was deeply hurt that Paul Heyse, her longtime friend and correspondent, was indignant about her choice of subject matter (Bittrich 242), especially since he himself had not been prim in conceiving his own works (HC 280-281).

Louise von François, always trying to do justice to her friend's creations, admired the last chapter of *Unsühnbar* with its deeply moving description of Maria Dornach's mental anguish, comparing it to the gloomiest works of Shakespeare, "the father of pessimism" (qtd. in Bittrich 242-243). She wrote a rather negative review about the novel as a whole, however, and was worried afterwards that her friend might be offended by her generally low opinion of the work (Szczepanski 643). The critic Friedrich Pecht declared the novel one of Ebner-Eschenbach's "most accomplished creations" (qtd. in Bittrich 249), but many later reviewers expressed serious doubts about the psychological credibility of the protagonist's character and her adultery.[15] Fritz Mauthner found Maria Dornach's *faux pas* more incomprehensible than unatonable (Bittrich 253), and his view was shared by a number of critics, the most prominent among them the formidable Erich Schmidt. Before reading his comments Ebner-Eschenbach wrote to Natalie von Milde: "I am much afraid of Professor Schmidt's review of *Unsühnbar*. I believe I know in advance what he will have to say" (qtd. in Bittrich 257). When Schmidt confirmed the other critics' conviction that Maria Dornach's "fall" was not convincingly portrayed, she took his judgment very seriously and began to revise the novel. She even informed Moritz Necker, a regular reviewer of her work, about her revision.

Unsühnbar sold well in spite, or perhaps because, of the critics' mixed reaction, and in 1891 a third edition appeared. Ebner-Eschenbach had by now endowed the seducer Tessin with qualities "beyond good and evil" and given him an irresistible "Manfred beauty" to make Maria Dornach much more a victim of his demonic attraction and love. She had also tried to furnish the heroine with more passionate feelings, but she nevertheless remained a rather innocent and saintly figure. Eager to please Erich Schmidt, she sent him a copy of the third edition with the timid question:"Is it somewhat better now?" (qtd. in Bittrich 268), which the critic answered in the affirmative. Yet even after these revisions later reviewers could not accept Maria Dornach's indiscretion, since in their view it was not in keeping with her character (Bittrich 275).[16]

Preoccupied with the possibility and impossibility of the protagonist's capability of adultery, most critics overlooked Marie von Ebner-Eschenbach's intent. Her main concern had been to delineate Maria Dornach's development from a status symbol and a commodity of her class to a mature woman, able to assert herself in the face of social prejudice and narrow-mindedness. In her diary entry of December 1889, where she mentions her sister Julie's aversion to *Unsühnbar*, Ebner-Eschenbach wrote: "They do not see that Maria develops only through remorse into what she is before her death" (qtd. in Bittrich 242). Thus the author ultimately intended to make a statement about a woman's quest for identity and about a woman's idea of womanhood in a world dominated by male concepts and stereotypes.

A careful reading of *Unsühnbar* shows that women's inequality in a patriarchal society is a major theme next to the criticism of the Austrian aristocracy, whose decline the author foresaw with great clarity.[17] Not only in her dramas but increasingly in her prose work, Marie von Ebner became the advocate of women. Bozena defeats her employer and gains power on account of her truthfulness and strength of character. The governess of "Ein kleiner Roman," Lotti, the title figure of "Lotti, die Uhrmacherin," Countess Neumark of "Nach dem Tode," and Anna of "Totenwacht," are all women who show independence and judgment by rejecting suitors they recognize as incompatible. In "Komtesse Paula" Ebner-Eschenbach pleads for respect for women as human beings, voicing her concern about the still commonly accepted marriage of convenience which condemned many innocent girls to often lifelong suffering at the side of unworthy men (Harriman 70). In *Ohne Liebe* she has her protagonist demand that she become Marko's socially equal marriage partner (509). In "Komtesse Paula" and "Komtesse Muschi" she directly and implicitly deplores the insufficiency of female education, a theme she had already discussed in *Aus Franzensbad,* referring to it again in *Meine Kinderjahre:* "I was only a girl. How many things are considered inappropriate, unbecoming for a girl! The walls before me grew sky-high, walls between which my thinking and longing had to move, walls which—pacified me" (MK 878). The walls that "pacified" the young Marie Dubsky reminded her of the walls of a cemetery; they protected her from the outside world but also prevented her from getting in touch with life and reality. At a time when Otto Weininger published his infamous work *Geschlecht und Charakter*, stamping woman as evil, imbecile, and lacking any vestige of creativity (145),[18] Marie von Ebner-Eschenbach emphasized in *Meine Kinderjahre* that a woman can indeed have creative talent and ultimately find self-fulfillment through her art.

She had always admired women who asserted themselves and voiced their feminist concerns. In her youth she had read Fanny Lewald's works, admiring her courageous commitment to the women's cause (Schmidt 227). In 1878 she had read with great fascination Malvida von Meysenbug's memoirs, ever since harboring a great respect for the woman, who had indefatigably worked for women's emancipation (TB II 571). The writer considered herself extremely fortunate when she later met the admired feminist in Rome, where she had the chance to regularly visit her.

Marie von Ebner-Eschenbach, like her feminist friend, supported artistically inclined women, especially writers. She became a member of the Association of Women Writers and Artists in Vienna and later even named the association as beneficiary in her will (Harriman, *Stories* XVIII). She kept close contact with Helene von Druskowitz,[19] the author of a work on Shelley, with Marie von Najmajer and Bruno Walden, two young authors, who were likewise trying to earn their literary spurs. As Fritz Mauthner recalls in his "Erinnerungen," Ebner-Eschenbach was always ready to help deserving colleagues. Once, in order to make a young, seriously ill female novelist happy, she pretended to Rodenberg that her own work was not ready yet, in order to make him publish the younger writer's story. When in 1877 a woman author won a comedy competition sponsored by Laube, Marie von Ebner rejoiced, entering in her diary: "She defeated four hundred and fifty competitors. This makes me as happy as if I myself had won the prize" (TB II 531).

A woman writer of whom Ebner-Eschenbach was envious was Selma Lagerlöf. Speaking to Mauthner about the acclaimed author she said: "I admire her very much, but I still have to learn to be completely happy in this admiration" (Mauthner, "Erinnerungen"). She also kept in close touch with Emilie Exner, alias Felicie Ewart, a staunch feminist, who was president of the "Frauenverein" (association for professional women) and regularly wrote feminist essays.[20] How much Ebner-Eschenbach admired her is expressed in the obituary she wrote after her friend's death: "Someone who saw her in her home, in her family, whose heart and center she had been, could not but abandon his prejudice against learned women, even if it had been deeply ingrained in him" (Bettelheim, "Emilie" 53). In a sense Ewart had been a role model for her, a fellow fighter for the cause of women's rights to break out of the restricting domestic sphere.

Marie von Ebner also kept in touch with Natalie von Milde, a writer twenty years her junior and heavily involved in the women's movement.[21] She corresponded with von Milde for almost twenty-five years and must have been influenced by and in agreement with the feminist's ideas regarding the equality of women in nineteenth-century society. Natalie von Milde especially advocated a better education for girls and the opportunity for women to work. In her 1901 essay "Von den Männern und Frauen" in the *Hamburgischer Correspondent*, she reported that a Mr. Otto Ernst had once called George Eliot, George Sand, and Marie von Ebner-Eschenbach "freaks of nature" because they had been able to overcome social prejudice through their art (25). Von Milde mocked all those who believed that women lacked esprit or that they were dangerous when they possessed it. She passionately worked for the social equality of women.

In her letters to Natalie, Marie von Ebner regularly discussed the progress of her work and also informed her about its reception by critics. On April 10, 1890, having read a negative review of *Unsühnbar*, she wrote to her from St.Gilgen: "Have you read the essay about the book in the *Münchner Allgemeine Zeitung*? It came from Vienna. This is how I am appreciated at home. If the 'foreigners' weren't there, who would make good for Austria's 'thanks'?" (qtd. in Bittrich 252). She also warned her younger friend about the stress of writing: "O my dear child, you are just about to embark on this terrible profession. May God protect your nerves, mine are gone" (RV 129 255). Natalie revered her friend and colleague, basking in the bliss of knowing a person like her: "For me you are born anew every day and there is not an hour in which I do not think it a blessing that your soul thinks and feels for all our highest goods. This feeling is stronger than myself, it is stronger than *anything* else in me" (RV 129.788).

Von Milde especially appreciated that her friend voiced feminist concerns in her work. In her essay on Ebner-Eschenbach's importance

for the women's cause she pointed out: "It is the unmatched
achievement of Marie von Ebner-Eschenbach for the women's
movement to have placed the highest values, happiness, and freedom in
the right perspective, to have given appropriate ethical value to the
strength to live" (*Centralblatt* 3). She commended her on the heroine of
"Die Totenwacht": "Happiness is not her portion, but a higher one: the
consciousness that one must fulfill one's duty . . . The woman's
movement with its solemn, moral, ethical goals will accept this
consciousness on behalf of all our sex" (Harriman, *Stories* XXXII).

Like Natalie von Milde, Ebner-Eschenbach became indignant if
women and women writers were not taken as seriously as they
deserved. In a letter she mentioned to her friend that Hermann Bahr had
made a particularly derogatory remark about women who wrote: "Have
you ever read a line of H. Bahr (from Linz, where the best tarts and the
worst critics come from), for whom woman is a fishy monster and who
naturally thinks 'that none of them has a word' but only 'finds joy in
cunning ruses' etc."[22] (RV 129.380). Whenever a tactless remark was
made about a woman writer she took it personally. Hieronymus Lorm,
obviously not thinking very highly of women who wrote, once called
her an exception, and she became quite cross (BF 71). She insisted that
only the creation of works of art mattered and not who created them,
men or women, stating that, because of Lorm's negative attitude to
women authors, she no longer felt like informing him about her work
(ibid.). Her letter shows how deeply she had been hurt, how
passionately she could defend a case. She later sublimated her anger
about critics' negative opinion of women's writings and had the narrator
of her story "Die Visite" ironically state: "But if no woman had ever
achieved anything in literature, Denker may serve as that exception,
which appears to be necessary to prove the rule. Her book was almost
as good as if a man had written it" (Paetel, 1901, vol 2, 306).

She further had a special aversion toward critics who showed
astonishment that a woman writer could think clearly and write with
precision. She therefore mentioned with contempt in her essay on
Louise von François that a reviewer had observed how amazed he was
about the latter's "manly" style (ELF 26).[23] In 1879 she had complained
to Emmerich du Mont, author of the book *Das Weib,* that while the
French and the English were proud of their great women writers, "here
a newly found history of nature has made the discovery that woman by

and of herself is nothing, that she can become something only with the help of man" (Harriman "Feminist Perspective" 30).[24]

Yet, although an advocate of women's intellectual and economic emancipation, Marie von Ebner-Eschenbach never publicly voiced her opinion on feminist issues outside her works. In the above mentioned letter to Emmerich du Mont, she declined to write an article on what a woman thinks about women. Politely she replied: "I myself am of the opinion that we should keep silent and defeat many a mistaken notion about us, not by a hue and a cry, but by our work" (B II 276). According to her vignette "Eine dumme Geschichte" she must have been convinced that with intelligence, love, and charm women would one day succeed in achieving social equality.[25]

Feminists around the turn of the century truly appreciated Marie von Ebner-Eschenbach in spite of the fact that she had never volunteered to become the mouthpiece of the Austrian women's movement.[26] Still, its leaders knew that the by now famous author stood behind them in their efforts to gain emancipation for women. It is understandable that feminists hailed her as a model, when one considers that in 1910 a general agreement about equal education for women and men did not yet exist. One Professor Max Gruber had just then published a book entitled *Mädchenerziehung und Rassenhygiene* in which he had postulated: "Properly speaking, young girls, like young cows and heifers, should be led to the pasture. If thereby their feelings, their character and their common sense can be cultivated and developed, they may well be spared all the learned rubbish" (Gerhard 8)

Not only had Marie von Ebner voiced feminist concerns in her work,[27] she also was a living example of a woman who had successfully battled against societal prejudice, defeating the notion of her husband and her class that a woman should not become a professional writer. She had shown stamina by continuing to write after her failure as a dramatist, she had further exhibited remarkable strength in overcoming her severe ailments. In spite of seemingly insurmountable obstacles she had reached her literary goal.

On the occasion of Marie von Ebner-Eschenbach's seventieth birthday ten thousand Viennese women from all levels of society thanked her for her work and her moral support in an address consisting of one hundred and twenty pages, decorated by women painters from the art school in Vienna. Marie Eugenie delle Grazie wrote a glowing dedication "to the great poet, the noble woman, to the profound connoisseur of the female heart . . . to the wise woman who sees and gives meaning to things, to the mother in love and understanding . . ." (qtd. in Harriman, "Perspective" 27-28). When, during the same year, the septuagenarian was honored for her work by the philosophical faculty of the University of Vienna, feminists were ecstatic. Henceforth all the obstacles would be removed which had prevented outstanding women from being granted such a distinction. In 1878 women had for the first time been admitted to the University of Vienna.[28] This was a major step in their battle against discrimination and the still widely held notion that academic studies were detrimental to the female sex.

Considering the fact that in the eighteenth century women had hardly received any education beyond religious and household instructions, feminists could be proud of the achievement of their movement (Möhrmann 12). Women's emancipation in Austria proceeded on three social levels: aristocratic, middle-class and proletariat. While middle and lower-class women were working toward professional equality, aristocratic women, financially secure, were striving for emotional and intellectual equality. Marie von Ebner-Eschenbach, the descendant of an aristocratic family, was therefore mainly concerned with women's intellectual progress and did not focus much on their desire to enter the workplace. But in a notebook she once stated that an upper-class woman, having lived most of her life within the narrow confines of the domestic sphere, should be given the opportunity to develop her intellectual faculties and to engage in serious work outside the family. She bemoaned the fact that "in spite of the energy that is in the best women, the most noble of all human rights, the right to work, is not being exercised by the female members of the so-called upper classes" (RV 81233 Ja/I.N. 60448). Yet, her women protagonists remain closely tied to the domestic sphere, most of them opting for marriage and motherhood. Widows and spinsters have socially acceptable occupations like governess, seamstress, servant and watchmaker, and only two female figures realize their artistic ambitions: Helene Walter of *Die Schauspielerin* devotes her life to acting, and Cäsarine Denker of "Die Visite" achieves recognition as a writer. All other artists in Ebner-Eschenbach's work are male.[29]

She never wanted to be labeled a propagandist,[30] since she saw herself first and foremost as an artist expressing her concerns and trying to find the truth through her literary work. Instead of writing ephemeral slogans for the women's movement, she wrote aphorisms that remain of

lasting value. "An intelligent woman has millions of born enemies —
all stupid men" (Harriman "Talent" 18). "A man who feels himself
worsted in an argument with his wife begins at once to drown her voice
by his. He wants, and is able, to prove that even when he sings false,
the first voice always belongs to him" (Needler 39). "When a woman
says 'everyone' she means everyone. When a man says 'everyone' he
means every man" (Needler 101). "Let us not look for truthfulness in
women as long as they are reared in the belief that their chief end in
life is . . . to please (Needler 22). "When a woman learned to read, the
woman question entered the world" (Harriman "Talent" 18).

She not only read but also wrote and thus intensified the "woman
question" (Endres 126). She considered herself the mother of her works,
those "paper children," about whose well-being she worried until she
could send them on their voyage into the world. In *Meine Kinderjahre*
she writes that early on she felt "a motherly love" for her verses and
prose (808), and to Louise Schönfeld she once wrote: "What one writes
down one has felt, what one has born one loves and views with the eyes
of the heart" (B I 89-90). Readers likewise considered her "a great
mother" to whose work they could relate and in whom they saw an ally
for their cause (Necker 50). Especially female readers were strongly
attracted to her writing.[31] In her diary of 1890 she mentions that a
young woman, profoundly affected by her latest novel had written the
following letter: "In spite of my twenty-three years I have so far little
concerned myself with novels. Yet I trusted you, and thus *Unsühnbar*
was the first novel into which I really immersed myself, because I had
the impression that it deepened me" (qtd. in Bittrich 262). Without
voicing feminist slogans and becoming a mouthpiece of the women's
movement, Marie Ebner guided her readers' imagination, leading them
to sympathize with the women's cause. Just as she had realized herself
through her writing, so she also helped other women who immersed
themselves in her work to come to a better understanding of their lives
and to find their true identity.[32]

CHAPTER 4:

"THERE ARE MANY MUCH WORSE MARRIAGES"

By the time Marie von Ebner-Eschenbach turned sixty, she had become one of the monarchy's foremost writers. On her birthday she received over two hundred letters, dozens of telegrams, flowers, and poems from people from all over Austria and Germany. She was particularly delighted to receive a Black Forest Clock with a note from some Swabian fans, telling her that she was no stranger in their parts (B II 223). The City of Vienna now considered her worthy of being painted for the municipal archives. Essays were written in various journals in praise of her literary achievements. Walter Paetow, in his article in the *Vossische Zeitung* of September 14, 1890, called her a "favorite of the readership" and claimed: "However sceptical one has to be toward public opinion, especially in literary matters, here one can agree with it, even if one makes great demands on a writer" (qtd. in Bittrich 261).

Moritz Necker praised her in the *Deutsche Rundschau* as one of the most important literary talents who did not need to emulate contemporaries like Turgenev, Heyse or Storm. He maintained that the author stood within her time, yet was also beyond it. Her most important works were, in his view, *Bozena, Lotti,* "Nach dem Tode," "Kreisphysikus," "Unverstandene," *Das Gemeindekind* and *Unsühnbar* (Bittrich 261). Deeply moved by such praise she thanked the critic for his friendly words, assuring him that he had made her immensely happy. To celebrate the memorable day her nieces and nephews performed a play in her honor, as was the custom in the family, and the veterans of Zdislawitz serenaded her, showing their great admiration for their "flag mother." Her brother Adolph, since his father's death the owner of Zdislawitz, treated the villagers to a meal in the courtyard and invited young and old to amuse themselves at a huge garden party.

For the first time in many years she felt physically better and hoped to recover completely from her ailments. On the last day of 1890 she thankfully commented about the year: "You have brought me the celebrations of September 13 and with it the proof that I am not living in vain" (B II 223). By now she was so famous, her work in such demand, that her publishers, Gebrüder Paetel, planned to bring out her collected works in six volumes. Yet she anxiously persuaded them to publish only what she considered her best. Thus she did not want to include her 1872 fairy tale "Die Prinzessin von Banalien" and her novella "Ein kleiner Roman," nor did she allow her dramas to be republished (B I 196). While her star was still ascending and her work, in spite of her various discomforts, was progressing, her husband's life was ebbing away. He gradually lost his eyesight. Repeated cataract operations brought temporary relief but no real cure. He bore his tribulation stoically, trying to keep occupied by composing songs and working on his four-volume memoirs "Denkwürdigkeiten eines Veteranen," which he dictated to his secretary, who also entertained him by reading to him his favorite works.

In 1897 Moritz von Ebner-Eschenbach, having so far written only scholarly articles for military purposes, conceived a work of fiction, *Zwei Wiener Geschichten*, consisting of the stories "Das Wunder des Heiligen Sebastian" and "Hypnosis Perennis," which he dedicated to his wife. In the last-named work, the eighty-two-year-old author, who admittedly was not demonstrative and had always had an aversion to his wife's literary career (Vesely 217), finally eulogized her by having his narrator state about a prominent aristocratic writer: "I am happy to be personally acquainted with her. She is a woman full of grace, who knows what only very few people understand, because one can only receive and possess it as a free gift from heaven" (46). Further, in the same story, the shoemaker's sister, a former countess with a great understanding for music and art, likewise refers to this great writer by saying: "I only hope that commentators and interpreters do not cling to the works of this woman, because they do more harm than good" (46). Ultimately the narrator, Count Hollenstein, confesses about the woman he loves that "instead of being happy about her new and glorious flowering, I was insane and arrogant enough to have wanted to pluck it for myself" (19 20). In his memoirs the octogenarian alluded to the same theme when observing: "The cousin, who did advanced studies, wanted to enhance the as yet small knowledge of his little cousin, whose fantasy threw a golden bridge across the abyss. He did so in a highly inappropriate and clumsy way" (MK 850). Less restricted than in his memoirs and with much greater honesty, he could express in his fiction his admiration for his wife and his regret for having been unable to understand and further her talent. When he died in 1898, she had the consolation that in old age her husband finally seemed to have begun to understand and to appreciate her urge to write.

Marie and Moritz von Ebner-Eschenbach had not been as happily married as they had made it appear. The fact that Moritz objected for a long time to his wife's writing put a strain on their marriage which made them practically lead separate lives. Viktor Klemperer, who met Marie von Ebner in her eighties, was amazed how indignant she still became when thinking how her husband had tried to thwart her career: "The serene and highly acclaimed matron, while remembering it, still made a fist when she told me some months ago that her husband had ordered her then: 'I forbid you to write, I do not want my name to be dishonored in that fashion'" ("Frauengestalten" 712). Idolized by a doting widowed mother who considered him the only purpose of her life, Moritz von Ebner-Eschenbach had never learned to share love. He therefore was jealous upon finding out that he was not the center of his wife's existence. Like the husband in her story "Erste Trennung" he probably would have liked his wife to say: "I love you more than you love me, and that is in order. You have got the world, your great task, you have the future; I have you, you are my world" (546).[33] She, however, was no Emmi but an aspiring writer, and therefore their relationship suffered. Something of Moritz's jealousy may have filtered into Ebner-Eschenbach's 1905 story "Ihr Beruf," where Count Staudenheim confesses: "My jealousy was fiercer than any jealousy toward a man could ever have been" (Paetel 1920, vol 6, 172).[34] And Staudenheim further states about his wife: "Not that she made me feel 'you take second place.' Never! She forgave . . . ! She respected my foolish moods. She interrupted every sacred hour of work for the sake of something trivial, when she saw me valuing it ever so much. It was in vain. My neurotic pain could not be healed" (ibid. 173).

Moritz von Ebner-Eschenbach, in his time internationally renowned for his important military inventions and considered one of the most progressive and far-sighted officers of the Austrian army, was extremely dedicated to his work. From their first year of marriage on he regularly left his young wife for weeks and months to follow his professional and personal interests. Instead of totally immersing herself in social commitments, as befitted her station, and lovingly devoting herself to the care of her by then increasingly depressive aunt and mother-in-law, she used as much time as possible to improve herself as a writer. Although her husband tried to further her education, she soon realized that he was averse to her becoming a professional writer. Thus she wrote secretly, disappointed that the man she had worshiped for his intellect and erudition failed to understand her deepest longings. Something of how she felt may be expressed in "Bettelbriefe," where she has Countess Beate say about her husband: "Up to then Hochfeldt she has Countess Beate say about her husband: "Up to then Hochfeldt appeared to me like a great and high person to whom I happened to belong, but whom I did not know. I thought there must be a bridge from my understanding to his, and I searched for it. In that hour it suddenly dawned on me . . . that I would never find it" (648). Baron Max, trying to hide his gloating, is astonished that with this "lost bridge" she could continue to exist. But Countess Beate interrupts him, assuring him that "there are many much worse marriages" than hers (648).

While Moritz indefatigably worked at his technical inventions, his wife battled with her muse, nursing her old ambition to become a published author. In 1858 she had, without her husband's knowledge, published her first prose work *Aus Franzensbad*, and in 1860 she had sent her drama *Maria Stuart*, approved only by her teacher, to the printer. Her husband, retired by then from his professorship at the Engineering Academy in Klosterbruck, was in the meantime promoted to the rank of Major and had become a member of the "Genie Comité" in Vienna.

In 1859 he was able to use his newly constructed floodlight in the defense of the harbor of Venice (EME II 4). During the second World Exhibition in 1862 he traveled again to London as a military reporter, leaving his wife to her strenuous social commitments and to care for his by now mentally deranged mother, about whom he states in his "Erinnerungen": "Her seventieth year became tragic for her; a heart and nerve-disease clouded the mind of the dear woman . . . what a cruel test for my wife and me, to helplessly face the suffering of the beloved" (III,2).

No wonder that the thirty-two-year-old Marie von Ebner wrote in her diary at the end of 1861: "I congratulate myself that another year has passed; I express my sympathies to myself that another year begins! 1862" (TB I 1). Four years later—her mother-in-law was dead by now—she was still very pessimistic and mentioned in her diary: "Thirty-six years ago to the day I committed a great stupidity, namely: to have been born. The punishment followed instantly" (TB I 118). And soon afterwards she confided: "I find my life often so sad; however, how many joys were already given to me, which I did not know how to relish" (TB I 119).

Writing had by now become a desperately needed escape from the suffering around her and from the emotional isolation she experienced,

Marie had learned to accept the fact that for Moritz his mother and his work came first. Therefore she created a dream world for herself.

Whenever Moritz was away the couple faithfully corresponded, informing each other about daily events and family concerns. They never ceased to care for each other as cousins and friends, but it is difficult to imagine them as ever having been lovers. When Moritz von Ebner-Eschenbach was at home he read new books to his wife, familiarized her with the natural sciences and introduced her to Schopenhauer, his favorite philosopher. As long as she devoted her time and interests totally to him, life went smoothly.

In 1860 she had been full of hope that her dream of becoming a recognized dramatist would be fulfilled, especially since Eduard Devrient in Karlsruhe had been much impressed by her talent. Things also looked up for her husband. In May 1863 he was elected Corresponding Member of the Academy of Sciences in Vienna for his contributions to the field of military sciences (EME III,5). Founded in 1847, the Academy counted among its members scholars of various areas in philosophy and the sciences, membership in it being "the loftiest honor to which a Viennese intellectual could aspire" (May 52). In June Moritz was promoted to Colonel and granted an extended vacation in recognition of his services in the army. Thus, for the first time, the couple was able to go on a long holiday together. Via picturesque Salzburg, where they visited many famous monuments and churches, they traveled to Bad Gastein, one of the most famous health resorts in west central Austria. Situated in the Gastein valley on a slope of the Hohe Tauern mountains and crossed by the Gastein River, the town offered a rare scenic beauty, heightened by its two magnificent waterfalls.

The Ebner-Eschenbachs then spent a month taking the waters at the thermal springs and going on regular hiking tours, sometimes for more than ten hours. The writer's diary reveals the happiness she experienced when seeing the majestic cascades, "Kesselfall," "Schleierfall," "Bärenfall," grandiose phenomena of nature she could never admire enough. On their hiking tours the couple visited many famous tourist spots like the Windischgrätz Höhe and the Götschach Tal. There they once came into a torrential downpour, but were lucky that the maid at the Rudolphshütte lent Marie von Ebner her shoes, her own being soaking wet (TB I 14).

From Bad Gastein the couple traveled—"not only washed but also purified"—as the diary states (TB I 14) via Salzburg to Munich, where

From Bad Gastein the couple traveled—"not only washed but also purified"—as the diary states (TB I 14) via Salzburg to Munich, where they spent three days sight-seeing and attending the theater in the evening. The Neue Pinakothek with its magnificent collection of paintings particularly impressed Marie. In July the couple arrived in Karlsruhe and paid a visit to Eduard Devrient. After a short stay in Baden-Baden, where they met with Marie's brother Adolph and his wife Sophie, with her sister Friederike and her husband August Kinsky, they traveled to Switzerland to visit Zürich, Luzern, Küssnacht and Rigi, Andermath, and Interlaken. On their way back they stayed at Nuremberg, the beautiful town on the uplands of Franconia, surrounded by a medieval wall and famous for its many Gothic and Renaissance monuments. In September they celebrated Marie's birthday together in Zdislawitz—quite optimistic about their future.

In 1866 Marie von Ebner regularly mentioned in her diary that her husband strongly objected to her writing. He obviously minded her writing out of concern that she did not have enough time for him and her social commitments. He may also by then have realized that he was shut out from the most meaningful part of her life and thus became deeply jealous. Further, he had read quite a few devastating reviews of her plays, causing him to become more and more concerned for two reasons. First of all, critics could assume him to be the untalented author because she had the same initials as he. Second, he did not like his name to be dragged through the press in a disparaging way. As an aristocrat he not only felt responsible for his own honor and reputation but also for that of his family members and ancestors, whose honorable name it was his duty to preserve.[35] His wife ran the risk of being ridiculed in their circles, but he also feared becoming the laughing stock at his office. Besides, when at home in the 1860s and early 70s, he experienced at first hand how apprehensive and nervous she was before every performance of her plays, and how little she could bear criticism after they had been staged. Writing also affected her health, as each play was written with severe headaches and ailing conditions. He knew how exhausted she often was when, after a long day with innumerable social calls, she still tried to finish an act of a piece late at night and rose very early in the morning to put on the final touch. On January 18, 1874 she commented in her diary that she had excruciating facial pains and that her husband had to bear with her: "My poor Moriz needs much, very much patience with me and has it. But—I should give up writing, the reason for all my suffering" (TB II 240). He watched and that her talent was insufficient. If she could at least prove that her work was a success!

And that was exactly what Marie von Ebner-Eschenbach intended to do. In November that same year she entered in her diary: "How little is missing for a most intimate understanding! I only would have to give an indisputable, complete proof that I am not writing out of pigheadedness or vanity. It would be a matter of achievement. It would have to be appropriate" (TB I 128). Although obviously still optimistic at that time that he would one day understand and respect her creative urge, she gradually must have realized that "the little" that was missing for a deeper understanding would forever remain missing, and that she had to live "with the lost bridge."

In March 1867 she was still hopeful when writing about Moritz and herself in her diary: "We did not make life easy for each other lately—it will improve." As an afterthought she added: "Will I be able to leave writing alone? And if not, then what? O *could* I leave it" (TB I 163). As much as she may have wished, for the sake of her marriage, to be able to give up writing, she could not renounce a fulfilling activity that had by now become a necessary emotional outlet. When, after the very negative reviews of *Das Geständnis*, her husband became extremely indignant, seriously threatening to forbid her to write, she conceded that he had every reason to be angry—yet she remained all the more determined to proceed with her work (TB I 213). Having once asserted herself against her uncomprehending relatives, she was now all the more convinced that she had to remain true to her nature.[36] By now she was certain that she could not count on her husband's sympathy for her literary occupation, especially since she desired to make writing her profession.

Already in 1867 after her six-week stay in Paris, where Moritz von Ebner-Eschenbach was head of the military show during the World Exposition, she realized how beneficial her living alone was for her work. Her husband had gone out of his way to show her the exhibition. He had taken her on sight-seeing tours to the most famous churches, castles, and galleries. He had invited her to various restaurants and theaters in the evenings, and she was truly grateful for these experiences. Yet later that summer, in Bad Kissingen, where she took the waters alone, she observed in her diary: "Now I have lived for three weeks at my own expense and found out that I am not missing weeks at my own expense and found out that I am not missing anything: I discovered that I could live that way also for three months, even for three years" (TB I 193-194).

As long as she could write daily letters to her husband she was content. His presence only caused her guilt feelings because she realized that writing was indeed most important in her life. She created her literary figures in order to enter into a dialogue with them, as truly kindred spirits to whom she could relate. As she once remarked in an aphorism: "The exchange with persons whom he himself has created is often the only source of strength for a writer, enabling him to endure the people God has created" (Rieder, *Weisheit* 87). At that time she considered herself "bruised by a hundred thousands cudgels" and knew that her only consolation was "to be able to work. But also—to be allowed to work" (TB I 216). When her husband, after the success of her play *Dr. Ritter*, anonymously sent her the bust of Schiller, she may have hoped that he would gradually adjust to her having a professional career. But she knew that he would always feel short-changed and ultimately also be jealous in the event of her gaining fame.

It was, however, not only her ambition and urge to write, which caused problems in her marriage. Her husband came from an impoverished family and since his father's death had always lived very modestly, depending on imperial scholarships during his formative years. Although advancing in his career and honored with various medals he never earned a large income as a public servant.[37] In December 1867 Marie von Ebner dejectedly noted in her diary: "All evening we were doing our accounts and found out again that we did not have enough money" (TB I 215). In 1869 their financial situation still had not improved, since she mentioned that her brother Adolph was trying to help them out: "Adolf again wants to send 800 guilders for the trip to the baths. I am excited and depressed about it. The mere thought that Moriz did not roundly reject the gift makes me angry" (TB I 270). It obviously hurt her pride to accept money from her brother, but her husband realized that they needed the latter's support in order to keep up the life style she had been used to during her childhood and youth. Admittedly she was not good at calculating, accounting, and keeping order in her budget (TB I 167). In the appendix to her diary of 1869 she gives proof of her missing arithmetical skills.

So, I should possess on the twelfth, by which day I
had spent 18.99, a grand total of 245 guilders and 96
kreuzer. Instead, diligently as I may search and
calculate, there are only 212 guilders here. From this
it follows that either through my own or through
someone else's fault I suffered a loss of 52 guilders
95 kreuzer. May God forgive me or them! Amen. (TB
I 302)

Marie von Ebner-Eschenbach also repeatedly admitted that people
could easily cheat her, because she thought too highly of them. She
loved good food, good cigars and liked to live in style. She dressed
simply but elegantly and also furnished her apartment with exquisite
taste. Her books she liked to be tastefully bound, a fact that caused
some protests from her publishers who had to make sure that people of
lesser income could also afford to buy her works (Schmidt 188).

She also had great compassion with the poor, often being overly
generous towards them. How her family felt about this may have
filtered into *Margarete*, where the narrator observes about Countess
Priska: "Since there is nothing as wrong as the judgments of a family
about its members, she was considered weak and uncommonly
impractical by her family.[38] This reputation she had acquired mainly
through her invincible urge to do good, an urge that was out of line
with the meager income of her maternal home" (Cotta, 1906, 19). In
"Der Muff" she records how the general's wife, a sketch of herself, left
her purse in a muff she had generously given to a poor woman (177).
While the old general in this story graciously resigns himself to his
spouse's charity, the count of "Bettelbriefe" is not at all happy with his
young wife's magnanimity and warns her to further refrain from her
"subtle feelings" (648). Henceforth she knows that the gap between her
own and her husband's thinking is unbridgeable.

How much Marie von Ebner valued money and the opportunity to
help the poor may be seen from the following statement: "How should
I not love money, since it provides me with the pleasure of giving it
away ?" (Rieder, *Weisheit* 73). The couple's financial situation slightly
improved after Count Dubsky's death, when all his children received
their inheritance. Yet after Moritz' retirement they again had to
economize (TB II 297).

In 1869 a new problem beset them. Moritz von Ebner-Eschenbach began to encounter serious difficulties at work. A man by the name of Bylandt, whom he disliked, had become his superior. Moritz at first considered leaving the Genie Comité and asking for a transfer to Bruck. Ultimately he stayed on, but during this year his situation at the office became more and more unpleasant. One reason for some of the unfair treatment he received may have been his quarrels with Captain von Tunkler, a colleague and collaborator at the Engineer-Academy in Klosterbruck. The two men had worked together on the employment of electric and optic telegraphs for war purposes (EME III 3) and ever since had been good friends. But when Tunkler embraced spiritism, Moritz von Ebner-Eschenbach became so upset that he began to engage in fierce debates with him. Marie von Ebner, a close friend of Tunkler's wife Henriette, was caught in the middle between her husband and his colleague. On January 22, 1869 she noted in her diary after a visit with "Jetty" Tunkler: "Found Tunkler still cross with Moriz. I hope I can get him round. But Tunkler says: `You are partisan' and Moriz says `You are siding with my enemies'. Never mind" (TB I 240-241). On December 26, 1871 she observed: "New disagreements between Moriz and Tunkler. T is very bitter. M's arrogance fills him with indignation—he may be a thousand times right, he won't change T, but will always only harden him" (TB II 73).

Although she thought it trivial at first, Ebner-Eschenbach suffered from the additional strain that the controversy between her husband and Tunkler imposed upon her marriage. On February 5, 1869 she mentioned in her diary that Moritz' colleague Neuhauser, with whom he had likewise worked on the construction of his war devices, had come to see her and had said that Moritz was quite wrong to deal so spitefully with T(unkler) in the Comité affair (TB I 243). Instead of talking to Moritz, Neuhauser burdened Marie von Ebner with these problems. She had to bear the brunt and in addition was accused by her relatives, who claimed that her "romantic-liberal views" were the cause of Moritz' professional problems (TB I 245). From Ebner's diaries we know that her husband could be rather stubborn and undiplomatic. He was "very unfriendly, even impertinent against Tunkler" (TB I 252), so that she became annoyed, and although he had known since 1866 that Tunkler had shown signs of a deep depression (TB I 122) he regularly quarreled with him. In order to take revenge Tunkler may have blackened Moritz' name with his bosses.

Moritz von Ebner-Eschenbach further made the mistake of criticizing the conditions in the Austrian army. He insisted on enlightening his superiors on the corruption and the inefficiency in their midst, things they certainly did not want to hear. Thus he created many enemies in his circles. In 1866, after the war with Prusssia, he would have deserved an award for his services to the army, yet the newspapers published only a short imperial statement: "The highest satisfaction for Colonel Ebner and Captain Coczycka for inventing and positioning of sea-mines" (TB I 122). Marie von Ebner was incensed, called the superior's attitude an "infamous dirty business" (TB I 122) and in the appendix to her diary that year even blamed the emperor for having behaved stingily (TB I 146). In July 1869 Moritz was made an "extraordinary member" of the military technical committee, whereupon his wife sarcastically noted in her diary: "Do you know what that means? We have no use for you, but we do not want to dismiss you" (TB I 268). She was very upset about the situation but could not even find sympathy from her relations, who did not see eye to eye with her views.

In the fall of 1869 her stepmother passed away, which cast a new shadow over the Ebner-Eschenbach's marriage. Franz Dubsky, by now in his eighties, bullied all his family members and forced especially Marie and Moritz to put aside all thoughts of themselves. Tempers flared. At one point a depressed Marie von Ebner wrote about Moritz in her diary: "I am afraid he is going too far. P(apa) all day in tears, asking me ten times to promise him not to leave him alone, to move into his house in Vienna. One does not know whether one suffers more on such days or on stormy ones" (TB I 283). Moving into Count Dubsky's house meant a new life and new responsibilities for the couple. As Ebner-Eschenbach had predicted in her diary, an existence began for her which was marked by profound solitude.

Promoted to the rank of general in the fall of 1869, Moritz von Ebner-Eschenbach was invited by the Khedive of Egypt to attend the opening of the Suez Canal and left shortly before his wife dissolved their household. A new life began not only because she had to take care of her father, making sure his household ran smoothly and he was pleasantly entertained, but also because from then on her husband increasingly went his own way.

She gradually adjusted to her new situation, whenever possible immersing herself in her work. Finally her father's death freed her from a heavy burden but did nothing to improve her marital relations. Moritz, by now Genie-Chef at the General Command, was very busy as a member of the international jury at the Vienna World Exposition and extremely concerned about his reputation. His resentment against his wife's writing was kindled again by the vicious write-up she received for her play *Das Waldfräulein*. In her diary of April 4, 1873 she noted: "Moritz talked to me, not angrily, not outraged. But he said nevertheless: 'If my warnings and my requests do not prevent you from writing for the stage, I shall forbid you to do it.' Will I be able to obey?" (Vesely 216).

In nineteenth-century Austria a husband had full responsibility for his wife, and she was legally obliged to subordinate herself to him. Yet Marie von Ebner, by now forty-three, was far too independent-minded to be intimidated by her spouse. She regularly observed in her diaries that he would prefer her to give up writing, but she never for a moment seriously considered complying with his wishes. Like the protagonist of "Das tägliche Leben" she single-mindedly followed her goal: "She held fast to the activity which gave rich meaning to her life and also a noble purpose. But what must have been the price for the victory, which she so bravely won every day?" (633).

Writing against her husband's wishes caused renewed tensions in her marriage, and Ebner-Eschenbach often resented his lack of understanding for her art. On November 13, 1874 she confided to her diary: "In the evening Moriz returned from Lissitz. A lot could be said about him. That he has not enough understanding for a writer who wants to accomplish something nowadays is an old story. Now, however, many new stories may be added" (TB II 299). And on January 30, 1878 she sighed about her husband: "Whenever M gets to know a work of mine in manuscript form, each time there is a disaster" (TB II 546). How much she yearned for a kindred spirit may be gauged from the following aphorism: "A congenial soul who understands something—that is what one is longing for" (Rieder, *Weisheit* 72). But although the emotional gap between the couple deepened, Marie von Ebner always remained loyal to her husband, and he could rely on her.

As Moritz von Ebner-Eschenbach's problems at work increased, his wife suffered and sympathized with him. In 1874 things came to a head at the General Command when Moritz, somewhat undiplomatically, submitted a paper in which he criticized military logistics, again offending many of his superiors, especially Baron Beck, the emperor's closest military advisor.[39] Afraid that his subordinate would try to reorganize the army and discover more corruption, Beck declared him a traitor, doing his utmost to effect his dismissal from his post.

Marie von Ebner-Eschenbach took the situation very hard. In her 1874 correspondence with Saar she mentioned being "extremely miserable and thus extremely grumpy" and suffering from severe headaches (Kindermann 30-33) which may have been related to her husband's professional problems. On April 30, 1874 she noted in her diary: "The consequences of the limitless misunderstanding caused by Moriz' paper become most painful and most outrageous. People are always even worse and more ridiculous than one would have thought possible" (TB II 261). In June she again complained to Saar of being unwell and suffering from facial pain (Kindermann 37), a sign of how deeply the injustice had affected her. Moritz von Ebner-Eschenbach had taught science for two years to the emperor's youngest brother, Archduke Ludwig Viktor. With his explosive devices he had helped Austria to win many victories against her enemies and had distinguished himself as a soldier and scholar. However, the emperor did not come to his aid. Having offended the camarilla, consisting of the emperor's mother and her entourage, he was dismissed in a very brutal way.

During the summer, on an inspection tour in Salzburg, he learned through his sister-in-law, Duchess Julie von Waldburg-Wurzach, that he had been pensioned off. Before even telling him about his dismissal, his superiors announced it in the paper *Bohemia*, where his wife learned of his forced retirement. It came as a severe blow to the whole family. Downhearted, Marie von Ebner wrote in her diary: "This news, conveyed in such unexpectedly rude fashion, has hurt me unspeakably in a personal way. I wonder how Moriz is taking it. It is a turning point, and in old age one finds it difficult to change" (TB II 293). For thirty-eight years he had served the Austrian army, had always put his work first and had devoted himself totally to whatever task had been demanded of him. He was extremely bitter, though doing his best not to show it.

From now on he tried to find comfort for this almost unbearable injustice by embarking on extended trips to Iran, Italy, Sweden, Norway, Iceland, Turkey, Russia, and Greece (EME III,5). His wife would have been condemned to lead a Penelope-like existence, waiting for her Ulysses who roamed the world, had she not had her writing. Her relationship turned more and more into a marriage of convenience, where both partners went their own ways, pursuing their own interests.

In June she usually traveled to a spa for a month—Bad Reichenhall, Bad Kissingen, or Königswart—then spent some time with Ida Fleischl and her family at a holiday resort. Later she visited her relatives in Bürgstein or Wurzach for a few weeks, and afterwards traveled to Zdislawitz, where she stayed until late fall. Her husband liked to take the waters at Marienbad, then met her for a few days at their relatives', and when she returned to Vienna to spend the winter there, he moved into the Amtshaus in Zdislawitz. For Christmas, during the 1870s he sent his wife a postcard, whereas she sometimes mailed him a parcel.

While regularly mentioning her relatives' and friends' birth- and namedays, she never entered her husband's feast days or her wedding anniversaries in her diaries of the 1870s. On November 27, 1877, Moritz' sixty-second birthday, she stayed in Vienna, while he spent the day with his relatives in Zdislawitz. She knew he was well taken care of, and that sufficed for her (TB II 535). Due to her ailments—her facial pains developed into a persistent *tic douloureux* during these years—she was unable to go on long journeys and also did not enjoy traveling as much as her husband did. In "Ein kleiner Roman" she has the narrator derogatively say about Anka's desire to see different places: "Up to the end she is said to have had a penchant for traveling, something which many people have, in whose souls nothing happens. Unconsciously they feel impelled to replace the lack of inner movement by outer motion" (67).

She had her dream world about which she longed to write. Socially and emotionally she had found a substitute for her husband in Ida von Fleischl-Marxow. Since their stay in Switzerland in 1872, the two women and members of Ida's family regularly spent some time in Switzerland together. She was content that her husband was in Vienna during that time, although she sympathized with him when he complained about the heat. In 1875 Moritz traveled to Teheran to spend eight months there with his brother-in-law Viktor Dubsky, then Austrian ambassador to Persia. Marie von Ebner understood that Moritz needed a change of scenery in order to find peace of mind. She also knew by now that she and her husband got better along by correspondence than by being around each other. "Loneliness is not happiness, but togetherness is often unhappiness" (Reclam 56) says one aphorism, and another motto reveals: "Nothing can more estrange two people, who are related to each other, than living together" (Reclam 46).

Due to their moderate income the Ebner-Eschenbachs always lived in small and rather uncomfortable apartments. Since Moritz liked to play the piano and his wife needed quiet to concentrate on her writing, the couple must have often got on each other's nerves. On February 22, 1875 she noted in her diary: "A beautiful warm spring day. I left already at 11:30, driven away from my work on account of M's piano playing" (TB II 550). In 1873 the couple, having lived for a while in a house in the suburbs of Vienna, moved back into a very small apartment in the Rabenhaus. Moritz liked it because he had lived in the very same rooms with his mother when he was a little boy. Marie, however, detested her new dwelling, dejectedly observing in her diary how small, sad and bare it looked and how difficult she found it to make it look like a home (TB II 169).

Because both were of a rather fiery temperament—the Gemperlein's pugnaciousness ran in their veins as well—they may have had some serious rows. Since Moritz von Ebner-Eschenbach had quarreled vehemently with Count Dubsky and with Captain von Tunkler, he may likewise not have shied away from giving his wife a piece of his mind. The fact that she noticed once that he had talked to her "not angrily, not outraged" (Vesely 216) leads one to suspect that at times he spoke to her otherwise and could indeed become very angry and incensed. On March 2, 1875, shortly before he left for Teheran, she observed in her diary: "Major dispute with Moriz because of Ofenheim and the Free Press. I am seriously determined not to touch this topic anymore. Seriously! Do you listen, Marie? Ass, do you listen?" (TB II 328-329). In 1877 she once entered in her diary that he had enlightened her in a restaurant in Vienna "in a loud voice about the duties a woman of my station has toward—herself" (TB II 506). As in the case of his conversion efforts with his friend Tunkler, Moritz also here achieved only greater resistance and possibly even bitterness.

Ebner-Eschenbach, for her part, could likewise fly into a violent rage (MK 791). She was not shy in voicing her indignation. One time she mentioned in her diary that some friends, the Colloredos, were deeply upset about her, because she had been "very vehement" (TB I 153). Shortly afterwards she revealed that her husband thought she had appeared at a party "like the thunder among the pots" (TB I 159). Therefore, when provoked, she may have defended her case quite vociferously. She also was often quite morose when ill (Kindermann 77) and not easy to get along with. Moritz therefore had many reasons for traveling. Having no children of their own, the couple never had to subordinate their interests to that of a growing family, and each could look to his or her own devices. Lacking a deep bond with her husband, Marie concentrated all the more on her work. When Saar once mentioned being lonely, she told him about her husband's absence and remarked: "As far as I am concerned, I am living in Vienna not less lonely than you do in the countryside; of course I am busy again with a story, which gives me joy and worry, as it is and as it has to be" (Kindermann 42).

By now she was resigned to being separated from her husband for many months and to spending Christmas and other feast days without him. Her feelings may have been ambivalent; on the one hand she may have felt the burden of having to carry all the household responsibilities and social commitments alone, on the other hand she was relieved, because now she had more time for her art. In fact, her career as a prose writer began in those years when, plagued by many ailments and freed from her husband's presence, she finally found the time to write and to pour her soul into her work.

In 1877 Moritz von Ebner-Eschenbach and his cousin Emmo Dubsky embarked on a visit to Italy. Marie always kept in touch with her husband through correspondence. Nowhere in her diary does she mention that she missed him. As long as she regularly heard from him by mail and knew he was well, she was content. At home the couple very likely would have had some serious quarrels. Increasingly preoccupied by now with her writing, Ebner-Eschenbach certainly was not easy to live with. In 1876, while conceiving *Bozena*, she confessed in her diary: "The strenuous work makes one *feroce*. Whatever is not related to the book passes me by. Does it deserve that much love?" (qtd. in Binneberg 196). Writing affected her so deeply that she cried with and about her protagonists, pouring into their lives all her own sorrows, frustrations and joys. Often she was desperate while working on her stories and novellas. In 1889, when laboring on *Unsühnbar*, she noted in her diary: "In despair about my work," and in March she still sighed over her "nerve-racking nineteenth chapter" (qtd. in Bittrich 238). To Natalie von Milde she once confessed: "Because my nerves are already bad I am always mortally afraid after one of my little books has started its trip to the readers" (RV I.N. 129.188). In her diary she observed that her brother Viktor had blamed her for her, in his view, "forbidden, morbid, boundless fastidiousness." And she added: "He is right, but this cannot be changed anymore; it is impossible, the worn-out nerves cannot become strong and healthy anymore. By the way, V. has no idea what I have swallowed already without making a sound" (TB II 490).

When she was ill she worried about not being able to finish her work, and once it was finished she felt desolate about parting with the literary figures she had created. In July 1889 she wrote to Rodenberg about *Unsühnbar*: "In the beginning I will feel quite orphaned. Through fourteen months my Maria has preoccupied me, exclusively and solely, not one day excepted" (qtd. in Bittrich 239). When Ebner-Eschenbach did not have to hold her breath anymore about whether the manuscript had been accepted by the publisher and her work approved, the strenuous task of correcting the galley proofs began, which she often did late at night (Bittrich 243). Even after the publication of her works she still had worries and problems with her publisher. On April 10, 1889 she observed in her diary: "The complimentary copies of *Unsühnbar* have arrived: some ass and ignoramus corrected into the text on p.130: 'We liberate ourselves from our passions by thinking *of* them.' Cheers! And in the rescue-scene they left out that Hermann has got hold of the child" (qtd. in Bittrich 263).

Even though his wife had become a prominent writer and his name was now honored far and wide, Moritz still had reservations about her literary career. Her diary of 1889 proves that he had a positive aversion to her writing and indeed was very jealous of it: "Talked to Moriz about the miserable writing career. It is still antipathetic to him, but he admits that I cannot help it. My dear ones, just do not believe that you are getting short-changed on account of my paper children" (Vesely 217). Moritz von Ebner-Eschenbach may also have been envious of his wife's fame. Ambitious like her and as much dedicated to his own work, he had not been properly recognized for his accomplishments and was now living in his wife's shadow. His name, about which he had always been concerned, was famous by now, yet not on his but on his wife's account. In a sense the couple may have found themselves in a vicious circle: Ebner-Eschenbach partly wrote because her husband left her alone for so long, and he in turn left her partly for the reason that she spent too much time writing.

By now they had found a routine allowing them only a short time together each year. Since 1879 Marie von Ebner had made it a habit to spend her summer in St. Gilgen with Ida, putting her time to good use by composing, revising and correcting her works. After her vacation in St. Gilgen she usually traveled to Zdislawitz, her domicile until the fall.

She and her maid stayed in the new rooms her brother Adolph had furnished for her in the new addition to the castle. Moritz always occupied the Amtshaus which she had decorated for him, and where he was settled comfortably. When not traveling abroad, he used his time either for hunting and for his studies in science, history and philosophy, or for writing his memoirs and for conducting physical experiments in his laboratory at Zdislawitz.

In the park he had a weather station constructed in the form of the famous Ahmed fountain, built by Sultan Ahmed III near the Hagia Sophia in Constantinople. There he conducted his metereological experiments. From Marie von Ebner's correpondence with Saar we know that, while she was in Vienna "disgruntled, preoccupied and restless" (Kindermann 63), her husband was "still in the country" even during the winter. Long gone were those cozy evenings of the sixties, when he had invited friends thrice weekly to accompany him on the piano or on the violin. Past were the dinners, where one of the musicians, Mr. Becs, a favorite of Marie von Ebner, dug into his teeth with the fork and then right away helped himself with it from the bowl on the table (TB I 66). The couple hardly saw each other anymore. Only later, in the 1880s, when Moritz's eye problems increased, was he forced to stay at home more often.

It may be no coincidence that Marie von Ebner wrote her play "Am Ende" in 1885 at the very time when her husband, now a septuagenarian, turned half-blind and had to curtail his travels. Count Erwein and Countess Klothilde Seinsburg, the protagonists, had been separated for twenty-six years, when he, half deaf and disappointed after many adventures with women, returns home to his wife. She remembers how hard it had been for her to realize that her husband, whom she had adored, was a big disappointment: "The inner break between us had happened, years ago—finally it showed outwardly" (Hafis edition, vol. 12, 411). When Count Erwein, deeply moved and repentant, apologizes to his wife for what he has done to her, she comforts him by confessing that right after their separation she had hoped they still would have a future together: "Let him breeze through his life, I said to myself. At the end we will find each other again" (412). In her 1901 story "Maslans Frau," Ebner-Eschenbach likewise portrays a couple that quite often was separated because the husband felt the need to travel."At the last farewell he had merrily called out to her: 'See you again next spring!'" (464-465).

During his last years Moritz von Ebner-Eschenbach, now an invalid and largely dependent on his wife, may have overcome his jealousy and better understood her, especially since he himself had begun to dabble in fiction writing. But the years of estrangement and aversion toward her literary career could not be blotted out. As for her, the experience of her marriage had profoundly influenced her views on matrimony, so that the reader will hardly find truly happily married spouses in her writings. Husbands usually treat their wives like children, being totally oblivious to the fact that they have interests, talents, and desires of their own. Young wives soon realize that they are less important to their husbands than their work and that they love their husbands more than they are loved in return ("Ob spät," "Erste Trennung," "Bettelbriefe," "Nach dem Tode").

Sometimes husbands realize only after their wife's death that they have loved them and that their wives have been suffering while at their side ("Nach dem Tode," "Ich warte") (ZT 743-744). Where there is outward harmony between a couple there are, as Herr von Rothenburg of "Nach dem Tode" confirms, "inner conflicts" (921). Passion does not exist between couples in Ebner-Eschenbach's fiction; in good marriages there is cooperation and true friendship at best. In fact there are many more unhappy marriages than happy ones, as for instance in "Glaubenslos?," "Das tägliche Leben," "Paula," *Gemeindekind, Bozena*—to mention but a few. While good marriages are never described in detail, unhappy marriages, with the spouses' quarrels and mutual reproaches, are extensively discussed. Once married, women usually do not want to risk another such relationship. In "Die Poesie des Unbewußten" matrimony is described as a battle that needs strong weapons (396). In "Komtesse Paula" the author has Elisabeth, the victim of an unhappy marriage, wryly say about her sister: "See, how clever, how prudent she is. Three years of probation are too few, she prefers ten. Ah, she knows dying is nothing, but marrying is a risky undertaking" (Harriman 80). In "Unverbesserlich" she repeats Elisabeth's statement with a slight modification: "dying is nothing—marrying is something" (187) and has Fräulein Monika warn her maid: "Death, you see, is the end of all fighting, whereas with the entering into marriage fighting begins" (187). When Baron Max of "Bettelbriefe" declares his intention to marry, Countess Hochfeldt sarcastically retorts: "You could not say in a different tone 'I shall take poison'" (636). And finally, in an an aphorism, we learn: "Marriages are made in heaven, but nobody pays any attention there whether they turn out well" (Reclam 56).

A close analysis of Ebner-Eschenbach's description of the marital state shows her cynicism about it. Her parents' unhappy marriage and her own rather unsatisfactory married life must have led to this negative notion. Like her stepmother she tried to hide the fact that she was not happy in her marriage, since it was considered a shame for a woman not to be on good terms with her husband. In "Die Reisegefährten" she has the narrator confirm: "It is a matter of honor for a wife at least to appear happy in her marriage. She degrades herself when she confesses that she is not. In this the world demands heroic hypocrisy, perhaps a good idea. But that is beside the point" (Harriman 107). When life was difficult in her marriage and otherwise, Marie von Ebner may have told herself, as in her childhood years: "It must be borne, it will pass" (MK 781). She was a strong-willed, determined personality, declaring in old age: "Blessed be my will to suffer! To it I owe my inner peace, my courage in the battle of life, my strength and my vigor" (Vesely 217). All her life Moritz remained her cousin, her "Onkel," her friend. Passionate love was missing in their relationship, and thus critics were right in pointing out that Ebner-Eschenbach was unable to describe this feeling in her fiction. The one passion with which she was extremely familiar was wrath, which consequently features prominently in all her writings.

People who had briefly met Moritz von Ebner-Eschenbach had found him a "good husband for a writer" (Kabel 495). Faust Pachler even advised her to heed her husband's excellent judgment of her work (RV I.N. 172.148). From Marie von Ebner's diaries we know that Moritz read her work. He liked her drama *Marie Roland* (TB I 155), but he criticized *Bozena* as not passionate enough, advising her to create more conflicts for the characters (Binneberg 205). He further objected to her story *Margarete*, pointing out that she had not been able to come to terms with the subject matter (B II 165). Yet, although conceding that her husband was right in his criticism, she never chose him as her mentor. Rather, she turned to Ida von Fleischl, whose judgment she valued much more highly than his. In fact, Ida's company meant for her "really the only one in life" (Kindermann 48).

It was therefore again Ida Fleischl to whom Ebner-Eschenbach turned during her first months of widowhood. Ida had lost her son Ernst in 1891, her husband Karl in 1893 and her friend of forty years, Betty

Paoli, in 1894. Physically and mentally exhausted, she was grateful
when Marie von Ebner's brother Adolph suggested that the two friends
travel together to Rome in the fall and visit Ida's son Otto, who still
practiced medicine at the Austro-Hungarian Embassy. Von Fleischl had
been in Rome before but for Ebner-Eschenbach this first trip to Rome
was like a revelation. On February 28, 1899 she enthusiastically wrote
to Dr. Josef Breuer: "This sojourn stands out like a fairy island from the
mole-like life which I have led so far. Until today I have not yet
overcome the wonderment that I can see Rome with my own eyes" (BC
34). And in her essay "Aus Rom—an meine Freunde" she further
ecstatically described her impressions of the magnificent city that had
such a lasting impact on her.

   While in Rome she experienced a great honor. She learned that
Emperor Francis Joseph had bestowed upon her, as the first woman, the
"Ehrenzeichen für Kunst und Wissenschaft" (medal for arts and
sciences). She was invited to dinner with three other medalists who
lived in Rome at the time: Theodor von Sickel, a renowned medievalist
and director of the Austrian Historical Institute in Rome (Kann 555),
Monsignore Fraknoi, secretary of the Hungarian Academy of Sciences,
(BC 177) and Father Denifle, a renowned medievalist from Tyrol. Into
the album, where all the recipients of the medal entered their name,
Marie von Ebner-Eschenbach wrote the following lines: "Today a
worldling was admitted to the table of the prophets. She felt very poor
and small, yet was in raptures to have been accepted" (B II 231). She
genuinely savored the token of appreciation, which furthermore gave her
the opportunity to make contact with other distinguished members of the
Austrian community in Rome.

NOTES:

1. Ebner-Eschenbach mentions Fanny Elssler in her story "Novellenstoffe" (689).

2. As Alexander Lernet-Holenia states about the "Kutscherton": "The loose driver- and aristocrat slang originally belonged only to the aristocrats. Drivers used it only when they thought they would amuse the aristocrats to whom they talked. Among each other they used completely normal language" (40).

3. Emilie Exner was the daughter-in-law of the philosopher and pedagogue Franz Exner. She wrote under the pseudonym Felicie Ewart—reminiscent of her maiden name Winiwater—and was married to the physiologist Sigmund Exner. Brunnwinkl was the home of Professor von Frisch and his wife Marianne, née Exner, who incidentally were close friends of the Swiss writer Gottfried Keller. Every summer all the members of the Exner family gathered at Brunnwinkl and also regularly came to St. Gilgen to visit the two vacationers, Ida von Fleischl and Marie von Ebner-Eschenbach (Bettelheim "Exner").

4. Rainer Baasner stresses the similarity of *Das Gemeindekind* to Schiller's *Verbrecher aus verlorener Ehre*, George Sand's *François le Champi* and Ludwig Anzengruber's *Sternsteinhof* (352-359). During Ebner-Eschenbach's life critics regularly pointed out resemblances between her work and that of other writers and she became rather upset, calling these critics "Ähnlichkeitsjäger" (similarity hunters) In her "Notizen" we find the following entry: "That someone would draw his inspiration from life and not from printed matter, a similiarity hunter will never admit" (Rieder, *Weisheit des Herzens* 117). She also felt that "similarity hunting" was "the most appalling daughter of excessive reading" (ibid.). In a diary entry of 1893 she declares in regard to her story "Glaubenslos?": "I have never been inspired by a book to write a story, but always only by a human being" (B II 12).

5. Quotes are taken from Marie von Ebner-Eschenbach, *The Child of the Parish*, translated by Mary A. Robinson. Robert Benner's Sons: New York, 1893.

6. Rainer Baasner calls the work a "social novel" (350) and an "Entwicklungsroman" (351) but admits that it is not easy to classify (352).

7. Ebner-Eschenbach personally contacted Georg von Gizycki, a moral philosopher, and later sent him her novel *Unsühnbar*, a work he praised for its beauty and depth (Bittrich 26).

8. This is an entry classified as "B" by K.K. Polheim, an entry Ebner-Eschenbach revised in her seventies before handing her diary to her biographer Anton Bettelheim (Polheim, Introduction to *Marie von Ebner-Eschenbach Tagebücher I* 1862-1869, XII).

9. See her poem "Sankt Peter und der Blaustrumpf," Paetel edition Bd.1, 1901, 173-174.

10. If the novella *Margarete* is an indicator, then Ebner-Eschenbach may already in 1878 have been in doubt about God's love for His creation. Her protagonist states: "This God—I speak now as if I still believed in him, but—and that is dreadful— I doubt . . . It sometimes seems to me that I am finished with Him, with hope, with everything . . ." (54).

11. Enrica von Handel Mazzetti confirms that Marie Ebner had been estranged from God and Church. In a letter to Johannes Mumbauer she writes: "Since Marie was so modest she found her way to her God in later years so easily, so marvelously fast, after, in her mature years, she had been not exactly hostile to him--for that she had been too noble--but estranged from him. What I know about her spiritual transformation I do not like to reveal publicly" (Mumbauer 33-34).

12. Katherine Goodman draws attention to the fact that, according to *Meine Kinderjahre*, a major reason for writing her drama *Richelieu* was her fascination with queen Anna (179-180).

13. Burkhard Bittrich sees a close similarity between Schubin's (alias Aloysia Kirchner) *Gloria victis!* and *Unsühnbar* (348).

14. Basedow's disease is called Graves' disease in English.

15. Some reviewers considered the novel a total failure (Bunsen 32).

16. Modern critics still debate the probability or impossibility of Maria Dornach's adultery. In her 1945 dissertation Gertrud Gerber called the work "the totally wrong *Unsühnbar*," arguing, like some of Ebner-Eschenbach's contemporary critics, that Maria Dornach's adultery is not sufficiently motivated (Bittrich 292). Burkhard Bittrich, however, in his very thorough and perceptive 1978 analysis of Maria Dornach's character, comes to the conclusion that her adultery is psychologically credible (303).

17. See Roman Rocek, who contends that the social inequality of men and women is one of the most important themes in Ebner-Eschenbach's oeuvre (586). See also H. Harriman who convincingly argues: "Whether on the highest or lowest rungs of the social ladder, a self-reliant woman with a clear vision of her duty appears regularly in Ebner-Eschenbach's fiction. Characters similar to Anna ("Totenwacht") include the title character of *Bozena*, Maria Dornach in *Unsühnbar* and Claire Dubois in "Wieder die Alte." Without uttering feminist rhetoric in strident tones, these figures are emancipated in the deepest meaning of the word" ("Perspective" 31).

18. See also E. Fuchs 1906 *Sozialgeschichte der Frau*, in which he emphasizes man's creative superiority (464-465). In fact Ebner-Eschenbach's autobiography may be interpreted as a reaction against her times' scepticism toward women's creative talent.

19. Helene von Druskowitz struggled for years to be recognized as a dramatist. She became insane in the 1890s and died in an asylum in Vienna in 1918 (B II 324-325).

20. Two of her essays are "Die Emanzipation in der Ehe" (1895) and "Eine Abrechnung in der Frauenfrage" (1906) (Bettelheim "Exner" 59).

21. Her essays include "Frauenfrage und Männerbedenken. Ein Beitrag zur Verständigung" (1890) and "Der Richter zwischen Mann und Weib" (1899). She also gave a lecture on the topic "Ist die Frauenbewegung natürlich?" (*NDB* 1080).

22. See also Bahr's essay "Die Epigonen des Marxismus," in which he discusses the "woman question" and enlightens his readers on the hatred between the sexes (Wunberg 472). Ebner-Eschenbach may also have disliked Bahr because of his avowed anti-Semitism. In 1883 when the "Union of German Students" invited Bahr to honor the composer Richard Wagner who had died a few months earlier, Bahr eulogized Wagner, the anti-Semite, and turned the whole gathering into an anti-Semitic riot. Only much later did Bahr repudiate his anti-Semitism (Berkley 73).

23. She may have referred to Helmut Motekat, editor of *Die Akte Louise von François*, who wrote about *Die letzte Reckenburgerin*: "I have read that charming book and must admit that—peculiarly original in its presentation—it does not betray a woman's hand in either structure or characterisation" (qtd. in Bramkamp 89).

24. In this letter Ebner-Eschenbach also blames critics for not reading, much less analyzing, books by women (B II 278).

25. See Necker 256-261.

26. Marie von Ebner may have felt like the Canadian writer Margaret Laurence, who explains her reticence to take an active part in the women's movement: "I have not taken an active or direct part in the women's movement, just as I have not taken an active or direct part in any politics, simply because my work resides in my fiction which must always feel easy with paradox and accommodate contradictions, and which must, if anything, proclaim the human individual, unique and irreplaceable, and the human spirit, amazingly strong and yet in need of strength and grace. But in making this statement of my own belief, I do not mean that I have been unaware of the women's movement. I have been aware and, I hope, supportive in my own way, and I have felt the warmth and support of many of my sisters, both those who are my contemporaries and those who are very much younger than my half century (Daymond/Monkman 258).

27. H. Harriman points out that Ebner-Eschenbach worked for the dignity of the female sex in an understated yet impressive way. Indeed, the feminine ideal she forged in her life and in her work can still serve

as an inspiration to those who seek a better world for women ("Perspective" 35). Katherine Goodman, emphasizing the remarkable strength and intelligence of Marie Ebner's woman protagonists, alludes to the fact that she must have been influenced by Mme. de Staël and George Sand. Agatha Bramkamp states that in all of the author's work "female appraisal of the female experience in a male-dominated world is more or less consciously at work" (74) and she, like Harriman, is of the opinion that Ebner-Eschenbach's writing still has an important message for women today.

28. Arthur J. May states that in 1878 women were "grudgingly admitted to study in the philosophical faculty, though few actually matriculated" (51). George E. Berkley claims that although women were legally accepted at the University of Vienna, they faced "many practical impediments," like resistance from their families and lack of tutoring for the entrance examinations. If they managed to enroll, they often were given a hard time by professors and male students (20).

29. As Jürgen Serke indicates, Annette von Droste-Hülshoff never realized her feminine "I" in poetry, but had herself addressed as "Herr" (26-27). Like Marie von Ebner she had been accused of sinning by following her vocation and therefore always felt guilty about it (40).

30. H. Harriman attributes Ebner-Eschenbach's "lack of militancy for the women's cause" to her "essentially unpolitical nature" ("Perspective" 34).

31. Judith Kegan Gardiner convincingly argues that "recent women's novels portray the growth of women's self-awareness in the characters' minds and also work to create that awareness. Through the relationship between the narrator and the reader, such fictions re-create the ambivalent experiences of ego violation and mutual identification that occur between mother and daughter. The woman writer allies herself intimately with her female reader through this identification" (358).

32. Marie von Ebner was well aware of how much a text manipulates a reader's thoughts (See ZT 738).

33. Compare also to "Das tägliche Leben," which describes the ideal officer's wife as a woman who "is completely absorbed in the

admiration of her smart-looking husband and who finds everything trivial that does not concern him and his regiment" (629).

34. Compare to Jacques Necker, Mme. de Staël's father, who once said about his wife: "Imagine . . . how worried I was; I didn't dare go into her room for fear of tearing her away from an occupation that was more pleasant to her than my presence. I watched her, in my arms, still pursuing an idea" (Hogsett 16).

35. See I. Winter, who convincingly remarks about the aristocracy: "Every single one of them is tied into his ancestry, to which he feels responsible. He feels the power of his ancestors. The blood of his forebears is obligation and solace at the same time. He understands himself as a member of a long chain of ancestors" (62-63).

36. See *Lotti,* where Ebner-Eschenbach calls that crime the greatest that is committed against man's innate nature (927).

37. Wilhelm Treue rightly observes: "If one disregards the `dotations,' the 'salaries' were often very modest, because the civil servant nobleman, who was a landlord, considered service for the state as a *nobile officium*, not as the basis of his existence" (Winter 161).

38. Compare to her diary entry of February 2, 1893: "My loved ones consider my opinion on practical matters with greatest disdain. Of these, they think, I cannot understand a thing. In their eyes my writing has robbed me of my common sense. They have no idea how much of it one needs especially for writing" (B II 224).

39. Berkley confirms the inefficiency of the Austrian army, pointing out that the commanders often received their positions solely on account of their connections to the imperial family (14-15).

PART FIVE

THE PUBLIC HAS A NOTION (1899-1909)

No reputation is more painful to maintain than the one of being kind.

CHAPTER 1:

A SPLENDID FIGHTER SPIRIT

Shortly after Marie von Ebner-Eschenbach and Ida von Fleischl had returned from their trip to Rome, Ida experienced a very bad fall in her house and fractured her thighbone. It was on May 27, exactly one day before the two friends were to leave for their by now customary summer holiday in St. Gilgen. Instead of recuperating quickly as hoped, von Fleischl caught pneumonia and died on June 4, 1899. Before she passed away she told her confidante of over thirty years: "It was the good fortune of my life that I was sometimes allowed to help you with your work. Actually it was by chance, because four eyes can see more than two eyes do" (B II 238).

Her friend's death totally devastated Marie von Ebner. She had lost many people who had been close to her, many of whom had been dear friends. With Ida it seemed as if part of herself had gone, and she thought that with the latter's departure her creativity and her ability to write had also come to an end. For months she did not produce a line. She kept an oil-painting of her friend, given to her by the painter Marie Müller, on her desk, in order to be as close to her as possible. She never again went to St. Gilgen, the place fraught with memories of Ida. In a letter to her friend and family doctor Josef Breuer, who also had been a friend of Ida von Fleischl, she wrote: "One who was used to being with Ida would feel nostalgia even in heaven. Nobody is as magnanimous, as wise, as sincere to the bottom of the heart" (BC 36). In a letter to Julius Rodenberg she sadly remarked: "Since I began writing I have never published a line that she did not examine in a most conscientious, severe, and loving manner. . . I believe that I will never again decide to face the public with one of my works" (qtd. in Binneberg 196-197). Therefore, when asked to contribute a prologue for a Goethe celebration at the Burgtheater, Marie von Ebner-Eschenbach declined with the comment: "If Ida were alive, if we were at St. Gilgen—what a pleasure would it have given me to oblige!" (B II 239).

Gradually, however, she recovered from her shock and from the depression her friend's death had caused her. She now gave her love for Ida to the latter's family, especially to her son Otto, whom she was soon to meet in Rome again. He much appreciated the affection she showered on him. In a letter on the occasion of her eightieth birthday he wrote: "From all my heart I thank you for the love you have shown me during all these years I had the privilege of knowing you. You have transferred some of your love for Mama to me and for this I can never thank you enough" (RV I.N. 61029). To Paul Heyse she admitted that the people with whom she loved to socialize most in Rome were Otto von Fleischl and his wife Mina (HC 389).

In spite of her initial feeling that she would never again have the courage to publish, Marie Ebner resumed her writing. As in so many instances before, her work was therapy for her, giving her consolation in her darkest hours. Hermine Villinger remembers her during that time and quotes her as finally saying: "I am working again and my writing has helped me to get over bad days; I am grateful to it" (Villinger 64).

Without von Fleischl's support she felt helpless in the beginning, but her "demon" carried her along, inspiring her with stories her publisher brought out in 1901 under the title *Spätherbsttage*. Ida had stimulated her when she conceived these tales. She was also on her mind when correcting the second edition of the volume. To Dr. Breuer she later wrote: "I am half killing myself reading the proofs for the second edition of *Spätherbsttage* in order to bring its spelling up to date. What would Ida have said about our most recent pamphlet on orthography?" (Baasner 210). Due to Konrad Alexander Duden's indefatigable efforts to unify German orthography according to phonetic rules, in 1901 new spelling regulations were established in Germany, Austria and Switzerland, based on Duden's 1880 dictionary *Das vollständige orthographische Wörterbuch der deutschen Sprache* (NDB, vol.4, 153). This "orthography revolution" (qtd. in Baasner 210) caused her many problems.

Every year she remembered the anniversary of Ida's death, remarking on it in her diary and expressing how sorely she missed her. She also commemorated the day on which she had first met her best friend. In 1916 she published a collection of sketches and anecdotes called "Aus einem zeitlosen Tagebuch," in which she immortalized in a little anecdote Ida's often used and in various situations differently pronounced "so" (711). Until the end of her days she would cherish Ida von Fleischl's friendship.

Life went on, and Marie von Ebner-Eschenbach could not remain idle. She had discussed an artist novel with Ida during their stay together in Rome the previous year, and she now wanted to work on the piece in memory of her friend. During a promenade in the Villa Mattei that year she had seen a beautiful tropical plant which was identified to her as an agave, a plant that flowers only at long intervals. Earlier, at the painters' academy in Vienna, she had seen a group of young, self-

assured students and, as she later told Jacob Minor, she could not help
thinking:

> How many of you young people will achieve the
> success you are all so confidently hoping for? I had
> heard that there were some among them who had
> raised the highest expectations, and I imagined how
> it would be if one of them came up to these
> expectations but only for a short while, exhausting
> everything that was given to him by way of talent,
> and would soon be unable to achieve anything great
> anymore. (B II 241)

She then conceived the story of Antonio Venesco, a potter's son from
Ariccia and a favorite student of the famous fifteenth-century painter,
Masaccio. Like the agave that brings forth but one flower and then dies,
Antonio Venesco was to produce one great work of art, after which he
ended in resignation.

The story, significantly entitled *Agave*, was to be set in Florence.
For that reason Marie von Ebner and Ida von Fleischl had spent two
weeks there on their return trip from Rome to experience the ambience
of the city and to study Masaccio's celebrated frescoes in the Brancacci
Chapel of the church of Santa Maria del Carmine. In order to present
her literary figures convincingly, Ebner-Eschenbach knew that she had
to visit Florence again, especially since she wanted to give an authentic
topographical background. Seeing how much she had suffered on
account of Ida's death, her family encouraged her to travel again to
Italy, in order to gain new strength and energy. Her brother Adolph
accompanied her to Florence, where she met with Helene Tafel, a
Swabian friend, who, two years earlier, had already tried to persuade
her to visit Italy. She had a reputation as an excellent translator and had
first approached Marie von Ebner in 1876 after the publication of
Bozena, with the request to be allowed to render the story into Italian.
She later translated more of Ebner-Eschenbach's works and also
provided Italian versions for Heyse's, Voss' and Sudermann's novellas
(B II 328-329).

At Helene Tafel's Marie Ebner also met Theo Schücking again, who
had been introduced to her by Ida in Vienna several years earlier. The
three ladies then eagerly explored Florence with Helene Tafel as their

guide. To her friend Louise Schönfeld-Neumann Marie von Ebner wrote
enthusiastically:

> As far as landscape goes, Florence is more beautiful
> than Rome. The view from Fiesole over the city, the
> surroundings, dotted with villas, the hills of Ferrara,
> over the Appenine mountains, appearing blue in the
> remote distance, is one of the most lovely pictures
> which the creator has made. I understand well why
> Hildebrandt, Boecklin and other great artists made
> their home here. If I did not have my dear ones at
> home, I too would settle in Florence in order to die
> there. (NBV 9078/48-1)

The three friends spent hours in the Uffici, the chapel of the Medici, the
Palazzo Pitti, and also visited the Museo Nazionale. So eager was
Ebner-Eschenbach to familiarize herself with life in fifteenth-century
Florence that later she even consulted Professor Pogartscher, a specialist
in the field (B II 242). Always deeply stirred by great art, Marie von
Ebner wrote to Dr. Breuer: "What I have enjoyed most so far is the
view of the Madonna au Chardonneret. Simply perfect! Those who
accomplish something perfect are our greatest benefactors" (BC 35).
Faultless, in her view, were also Masaccio's frescoes in the Brancacci
chapel, the place she later described in *Agave* where Antonio Venesco
admires his master's accomplishment (427-428).

She traveled a third time to Florence in order to be able to create
an authentic social and cultural setting for her novel. Yet, in spite of her
great desire to recreate the quattrocento, critics did not find it
convincingly enough described. After the novel's publication in 1903
they claimed that her best works were those that had grown on Austrian
soil. Ferdinand von Saar also noticed that she had not been able to
express her usual "peculiar power of the heart" or her "incomparable
humor." Yet he admired the work's artistry, believing that future
generations might better understand it (Kindermann 126).

She would have had to stay much longer in Florence and to
socialize more with its inhabitants in order to better capture their
mentality and the local color in her work. All in all she had spent only
nine days in the city before moving to Rome. There she rented the same
apartment on the Piazza di Spagna where she had stayed the previous

year. Rome, having deeply impressed her the year before, had not lost its attraction. Indefatigably she visited churches, galleries and museums, trying to take in as much of Roman history and culture as possible. Unfortunately she did not learn Italian as she had intended. Therefore, when she had to see an American dentist who neither spoke German nor French but was fluent in Italian, she had to communicate in sign language with him (BC 36).

All the more easily she moved among the people of the German-speaking colony. Earlier she had been introduced to Emanuel Loewy, a professor at the Sapienza, one of the Roman universities, who was also the founder of the local Plaster Museum. He became her tourist guide in the Vatican Museum and, grateful for her interest and enthusiasm for his field, he dedicated his book on the history of Greek sculpture to her. He also acquainted her with Zaccagnini, a famous sculptor, who later made a bust of Ebner-Eschenbach and her sister-in-law (B II 331).[1] Professor Christian Hülsen likewise often accompanied her to the Forum Romanum where an excavation was underway which brought forth many artifacts from ancient times. He much appreciated Marie von Ebner's enthusiasm for the Holy City and her interest in the daily progress of the excavations. In return for the book on the Forum Romanum which he dedicated to her, she gave him a watch, put together by herself and bearing the inscription: "Chr. Hülsen, learned—venerated—full of compassion with those who are poor in learning—Marie Ebner-Eschenbach 1904" (qtd. in B II 328).

She often invited the two professors and Baron von Sickel, the historian, who like her, had once received the Austrian Medal for Arts and Sciences. In her apartment they held discussions and regularly met for social gatherings. She also celebrated Christmas with her new friends, giving them presents embellished with her own poems and mottos.

The time in Rome was extremely fruitful for her. She made rapid progress with her novel *Agave*, she wrote many aphorisms, a parable called "Der Engel," as well as a poem about an ancient vestal virgin whose bust, found in the 1880s at the Atrium Vestae, she had admired in the National Museum (B II 236). Professor Hülsen had published a picture of this vestal virgin in his book *Das Forum Romanum*, and Ebner-Eschenbach wrote a story about the latter's sense of duty and compassion which saved a gladiator's life. Marie Ebner liked the bust of this virgin so much that she bought a reproduction of it and kept it on her desk in Vienna. Like the vestal virgin she herself always deeply empathized with the suffering.

In the spring of 1900 she returned to Vienna. The Drei-Raben-Haus had been demolished for the purpose of enlarging the street, so that she had to establish a new home on the Haarmarkt.

During this summer she experienced one of the greatest triumphs of her life upon learning that she was to be the recipient of the first honorary doctorate ever to be bestowed on a woman by the University of Vienna. As Anton Bettelheim in his 1900 biography aptly remarks: "In that hour she must have felt that her name had been a blessing for her family" (B I 240). In the fall, on the eve of her seventieth birthday, a delegation from the university, consisting of the Rector Dr. v. Schrutka-Rechtenstamm, Dr. Mueller, the Dean of the philosophical faculty, and Dr. Minor, Professor of German Language and Literature, met her in Count Adolph Dubsky's city-apartment and presented the parchment to her. The document described Ebner-Eschenbach as *matrona illustrissima* and praised her "divine gift for narrative" (B I 248). She was also called "the greatest among living Austrian authors" (ibid.). The move had been initiated by Jacob Minor, professor of the history of literature, and was approved unanimously by the entire Senate of the University. Minor had emphasized that recognition and fame had come to her only after "hard battles and through tireless discipline" (B I 246). He singled out *Das Gemeindekind* as the basis of her fame, calling her message a "gospel of humanity." He also called the author a "true child of the new time," even though she had refused to follow any of the trendy literary fashions of the age (ibid.). He expressed the conviction that she was the only writer after Fontane who appealed to young and old alike. In his presentation Professor Minor again stressed her assiduity and discipline, the respect her personality had instilled, and the ethical wisdom she had articulated in her aphorisms.

Professor Müller, the Dean of the Philosophical Faculty, focused on the appropriateness of Marie von Ebner-Eschenbach's promotion to a *Doctor philosophiae*:

> A master of language, you had become a *magister artium* of your art. A subtle observer of life and explorer of the human heart, you have entered the fields of philosophy and psychology. Your descriptions of nature show a deep insight into the world and

> make the forces of nature come to life . . . All are
> seen with a loving eye; humans with tender and
> discerning love, nature with reverence. (B I 238)

Ebner-Eschenbach was overwhelmed by so much praise. Eye witnesses report that, moved to tears, she was unable to speak (B I 239). Still, later she confided to Paul Heyse: "You know, my dear and highly revered friend, the 'doctor' has, after all, curiously enough, greatly delighted me" (HC 382). She also must have been proud that the University of Vienna had a votive plaque designed on the occasion of her honorary doctorate award.

Although she would have preferred to celebrate her seventieth birthday quietly, it became a national event. Telegrams and greetings arrived from members of the nobility, as well as from all other levels of society. Peter Rosegger, Hieronymus Lorm, Paul Heyse, Count Wickenburg—to name but a few—sent congratulatory poems, and numerous articles were written in the papers on the occasion of her anniversary. Many German and Austrian journals, such as *Die Arbeiterzeitung*, *Die Frau*, *Die Jugend*, published lengthy essays honoring her life and work. Moritz Necker in his essay in *Die Neue Freie Presse* praised her for presenting to her readers positive values at a time when Nietzsche's "radical individualism" had many admirers. He also stated that she had created "more than great art—namely, a new culture" (3).

In his write-up in *Velhagen und Klasings Monatshefte* Dr. Richard Meyer pointed out how difficult it had been for the septuagenarian to establish herself as a writer in the years after the 1848 Revolution when the country was plagued by "cynical scepticism and embittered tiredness." He highlighted her "splendid fighter spirit" and her "invincible idealism" (57). After a discussion of several of her works he stated that her life had been "an example of victorious self-discipline" (60). The Burgtheater arranged an "Ebner-evening" where the performance of three of her own dramas (*Dr. Ritter, Ohne Liebe, Am Ende*) was prefaced with a prologue by Ferdinand von Saar, who wrote that Ebner-Eschenbach had had to fight against "the dull sense of this world" until she became Germany's greatest poet, whose humanity shines even brighter than her literary powers" (Kindermann 116).

So universal was the joy and the expression of gratitude, that she could no longer doubt having reached the pinnacle of fame, arrived on

Parnassus. It was by a different route than she had dreamed as a fourteen-year-old, but arrived she had. Behind the superlatives occasioned by the festive event there was genuine appreciation of her personality and her work by a broad spectrum of the population. A group of eminent people in Munich sent an address, articulating what many felt: "The ancient art of storytelling has found a new master in you. Plainly and simply you tell the truth as it appears to you. . . In the face of such achievements the controversy about the legitimacy of women in literature must cease; these are works which carry the stamp of necessity; and about the necessary there is no quarrel" (B I 231-32). Among the undersigned were the writers Paul Heyse, Ludwig Ganghofer and the painter Eduard Ille, who had once illustrated Ebner-Eschenbach's fairy tale "Die Prinzessin von Banalien."

Friends in Austria sent an Ebner-medal made of silver, accompanied by a panegyric by Paul Heyse (B I 230). On the day after her birthday she thanked Heyse, deeply moved by his "royal generosity" and begged him to convey her thanks to the other contributors to the album from Munich (HC 382). She also experienced the joy of being made an honorary member of the Viennese watchmaker cooperative. As a special surprise Archduke Ludwig Victor, a former student of Moritz von Ebner-Eschenbach, visited her and presented her with a watch, set in a Maria-Theresia-Thaler. She further received diplomas from Concordia, the Viennese association of writers and journalists, bestowing upon her an honorary membership.

The leaders of the labor movement, Victor Adler and Engelbert Pernerstorfer, congratulated her, and so did the Mayor of Vienna. Among the younger writers who wished her well were Arthur Schnitzler and Gerhard Hauptmann. Aldermen from Zdislawitz, Homietitz and Hostitz came to congratulate her, followed by teachers and students who recited poems and brought flowers. As usual on her birthdays the veterans serenaded her, this year even organizing a nocturnal procession with Chinese lanterns. The villagers were again entertained in the park. All members of Ebner-Eschenbach's family wanted to show their affection for the septuagenarian and joined in establishing a fund for the Children's Hospital in Brünn in memory of her seventieth birthday. The day after, a special mass was celebrated at the chapel in Zdislawitz.

Donations for an album had been collected in an ivory box. On September 14 it was presented to Ebner-Eschenbach, filled with copper coins donated by women of the poorest district of Vienna (*Neue Freie*

Presse September 14, 1900, 5). To her great joy the Ebner prize for women writers was established, which gave her the opportunity to further the career of deserving younger colleagues.[2] Marie von Ebner was overwhelmed by all these signs of affection and at the same time a little doubtful whether she really deserved them (Kindermann 82).

In November she embarked on her third trip to Rome. Due to the negligence of a train conductor—he had torn out a section of her ticket booklet which contained the connection between Bologna and Florence—she and her secretary had to leave the train in Bologna instead of continuing to Florence as planned. Angela, her secretary, went away with the porter to check their luggage, and Marie von Ebner was suddenly left alone in the dark train station. She walked slowly in the same direction as she thought Angela had gone. It was so dark that she hardly saw anything. Suddenly she felt pushed by a silently advancing locomotive, but before she really became aware of the danger she was in, someone quietly took hold of her and saved her life. Afterwards, when she thought of her near fatal accident, she was stunned how mysteriously and noiselessly the train had moved. About the person, who appeared just in time to prevent her brush with death, she remembered: "Equally soundlessly someone grabbed me at that moment and pushed me aside and went his way without further ado. I neither saw nor heard my lifesaver" (B II 241).

Rome this year also inspired her to write. In the spring of 1901 she started work on "Der Erstgeborene," the first part of a work initially called "Mutterherz" and later entitled *Die unbesiegbare Macht.* "Der Erstgeborene" became one of Ebner-Eschenbach's most beautiful stories about the emotional gratification of the mother-son relationship. Like Hieronymus Lorm, with whose 1882 novel *Ein Schatten aus vergangenen Tagen* Ebner's story has some similarity,[3] she believed the love of a mother for her son to be one of the purest and most gratifying sentiments.

Ilona, the poor Csarda-girl, initially rejects Akos, the child forced upon her by a Hungarian count in an act of rape. Yet the mother-child bond is so strong that Ilona not only finally accepts her son but achieves a salvation-like state of bliss through this relationship. In Ebner-Eschenbach's view the bond between mother and son is not only "invincible," it is redemptive. A son complements a mother, he is closer to her than a lover, because he is part of her flesh.[4]

Ilona's and her son Akos' relationship is the culmination of what she had described in earlier works as the love between mother and son. Pavel of *Das Gemeindekind*, when reunited with his mother after many years of separation, realizes "that he now held in his arms his best treasure, his most valuable and dearest possession" (417). In "Der Vorzugsschüler" mother and son ally themselves against a tyrannical father, behind whose back the loving mother sells handicrafts in order to be able to sufficiently nourish her son. He, in turn, cherishes and worships her: "For his mother he felt an adoring love and he was the one and all for the joyless, prematurely aged woman" (515). Harald of "Ob früh, ob spät" considers his mother his precious property, the light of his life. She has brought him up with love and tender care, for which he pays her back with equally tender affection.

In the second story, entitled "Ihr Beruf," likewise part of *Die unbesiegbare Macht*, she described a woman who, although drawn to the life of a nun, renounces her vocation in order to care for a little semi-orphan whose father once had been close to her. Again, woman's motherly instinct is "invincible," woman's nature is, in the author's view, defined by her mothering activities.

In the fall of 1902 Ebner-Eschenbach came again to Rome, where she renewed her friendship with the people she had formerly encountered there. She received a visit from Isolde Kurz, a younger colleague, whom she had met before in Florence. With her she shared her love of poetry and of the Italian Renaissance.[5] Well known for her *Florentiner Novellen*, Isolde Kurz still greatly admired Marie von Ebner, about whom she had once confessed to Paul Heyse: "I hardly know the feeling of envy, but when I read a novel by Frau von Ebner, my joy and my admiration are not entirely free of this feeling" (HC 289).

Again Marie von Ebner explored the city's culture and its historic treasures, undertook promenades to the Forum with Professor Hülsen, visited the Passegiata Margherita, the Villa Borghese and the tomb of Cecilia Metella. The city never lost its appeal, and the climate refreshed and strengthened her. In her letters to her friends from Rome she hardly ever complained about poor health.

Back in Vienna in the summer of 1903, she started to order her correspondence, edited her diaries and burned manuscripts she did not think worth preserving. Her thoughts turned more and more to her childhood. In "Die arme Kleine," published in 1903, she had been preoccupied with the formative years of a protagonist whom she had endowed with many of her own traits and ideals. Having finished this story she may have begun to wonder whether she should write her autobiography, especially since Louise von François had already suggested it to her several years earlier (B I 15). Rodenberg, whom she had told about her plan, encouraged her, stating that "she could offer nothing dearer to him and her countless admirers than a 'life portrait'; to encounter her personally, the creator who has looked so deeply into the souls and fortunes of others—what a thought!" (B II 39). And so she started *Meine Kinderjahre*, the first eight chapters of which came easily. Afterwards work proceeded slowly, partly because of many social commitments. She had decided not to spend that winter in Rome but to stay closer to her relatives—a pleasure she had to pay for with the price of not being able to write as much as she would have liked. She had also resolved to describe her life only up to her fourteenth year because, as she explained in a letter to Rodenberg, "the whole future, my whole life, poor in external events, was already outlined there. I had decided that I would marry my dear cousin and that I would also become a writer" (B II 40).

Evidently she believed that the foundations of a personality were laid during the early years of life and that the following years only revealed the directions manifested in childhood. She may also have stopped short of dealing with her whole life because she did not think much of confessional writing.[6] As she would later say in "Novellenstoffe," the public, that "moloch," has no right to a person's "private, intellectual property" (698). She may further have felt that she would have to evoke too many unpleasant memories by delineating her whole life. In "Schattenleben" she says that she had *many* sad experiences and *some* happy ones, making it clear that she still has not forgotten the most painful incidents: "There are some (memories) that are deeply rooted. They threaten, they want to hurt, even in death" (464). She would have had to say uncomplimentary things about too many people — something she obviously wanted to avoid. She also had her doubts whether people would be interested in a life she herself considered "uneventful" in its outer course. Further, she may have been concerned with preserving the public image critics and friends had propagated (Baasner 230).[7] People who venerated her as an exemplary personality would have been shocked and disillusioned had she dared to be anything but generous, kind and compassionate in the description of her contemporaries. As Paetel, her publisher, pointed out, readers saw her as a "personal friend and advisor" (Schmidt 185), a role she gladly accepted to play.

It was therefore of the essence that she preserve this façade and avoid everything that could be considered offensive to the public as well as to her own family members. The many changes, corrections, and excisions she undertook in her manuscript in preparation for her *Kinderjahre* show that she had to safeguard many concerns, besides and beyond telling what had really happened.

A typical minor episode: Ebner-Eschenbach had written in the first edition of her autobiography about Frau Krähmer, her piano teacher, and had mentioned her "narrow, yellow face." When Frau Krähmer's grandson wrote to her, thanking her for mentioning his grandmother in her work, the author changed Frau Krähmer's face into a "narrow" and "noble" one in the second edition of her autobiography (Schmidt 184). Similarly Frau Krähmer appeared in the first edition as "a poor woman in a threadbare black dress." In the second edition she became an "ingenious artist in a simple gown" (Schmidt 195). While noting in her sketchbook that as a child she learned French poems, some of which contained "highly inappropriate matters" but that "such things did no harm," she did not publish anything of that sort in the final version of *Meine Kinderjahre* (Schmidt 135). This shows how conscious she was of her role as educator.

Overall her revisions prove her eagerness to avoid judgments which might have been perceived as harsh, and her endeavor to be conciliatory and understanding. She was a genuinely thoughtful person who did not wish to purposely hurt anyone. She also had to beware of possible reflections on the family. While the original sketch of *Kinderjahre* shows spontaneous feelings, the published version exhibits a very high degree of circumspection. Her first impulsive memories about some of her relatives were probably not always "kind"—but considering that she needed the family's approval, she changed a great many things, as the extensive revisions and excisions in the notebook show.

The *Kinderjahre* quite clearly are not the recorded impressions of a child but the memories of a wise old woman who could dispassionately look back at her beginnings. She is a skillful writer who thinks of publication and of fitting the work into the total opus. One feels reminded of the countess of "Er laßt die Hand küssen," who has some reservations about her friend's memory and sarcastically calls it "a one-sided slavish muse! She only remembers things that are to your advantage!"(230). Writing her autobiography was part of the process of "putting her literary house in order" (Schmidt 171), of coming to terms with her past, of reassuring herself that the problems she had encountered had been solved, that her suffering had not been in vain.

As social criticism *Meine Kinderjahre* is invaluable, but it should be read with reservations regarding Ebner-Eschenbach's personal life, especially her relationship with some of her family members.[8] It was a tool to provide her first biographer Anton Bettelheim with material to propagate the public self she wanted to project. It was further a means to prevent the biographer from drawing his own conclusions of her less than idyllic childhood. It was moreover an opportunity for her to hide her private self.

While correcting the galley proofs of her autobiography in Rome in 1905, she was often assailed by doubts as to the worth of the account of her life. Under the impression of Rome's grandiose past she wrote on January 13, 1905 to Julius Rodenberg:

> Today I had an attack of despair. I came down from
> the Pincio, and the illumination was exceptionally
> beautiful; even the clouds, which towered over the
> city, had a monumental appearance. Immeasurable
> was the greatness of that impression, and now I went
> home and began to read my proofs. It was impossible.
> My miserable children's stories simply nauseated me.
> It was as if the shrill chirping of a cricket had struck
> my ear after having heard a lion's roar. (B I 244-245)

Rome gave her much food for thought. She had loved and admired the city from early childhood, devouring Louis Richard a.k.a. Bressel's *Histoire universelle*, which ended with the decline of the Roman Empire, and which she "followed whether suffering, full of pain or hatred, whether jubilantly admiring, always with burning intensity" (MK 785). Rome, in 1905 the capital of the restored Kingdom of Italy, had none of the industrial and financial power of London, none of the glitter of modernity of Paris, none of the display of world diplomacy of Vienna. But for her it was "the true and actual capital of the world" (Bucher 71), a city she loved and praised more than any other. It was in Rome that she belatedly found access to the literary and artistic circles which many other artists had enjoyed in their early careers. Rome had on her the effect of a revelation; new worlds of insight opened up to her.

There was, indeed, a close relationship between Marie von Ebner and the Eternal City, a deep inner bond. Like no other place on earth it lived in and by its art. Rome was, as it had been for centuries, the world's greatest cultural and religious center, an immeasurably rich storehouse of the art of millennia. Roman values and Roman virtues had helped shape the Europe of which Marie von Ebner-Eschenbach was part. She may have recognized Rome as the source of her own values, seeing much of her life's struggle as a parallel to the history of Rome. As Rome saw its mission in civilizing the world of the barbarians, so she believed that she had to remind her age—an age she felt was sliding into a new barbarism—of its moral destiny and its humanistic inheritance. Tradition was important to Rome and the Romans; it also was a major factor in her own thought and work.

That winter Ebner-Eschenbach was to see Rome for the last time. In the fall of 1907 she visited Venice instead, accompanied by her niece, Countess Marianne Kinsky, Dr. Otto von Fleischl, and Count Viktor Dubsky. Plagued by a chronic cold she wanted to avoid the inclement weather of Vienna and was looking forward to the refreshingly beautiful Venetian scenery.

CHAPTER 2:

"LET ME GET AWAY FROM VIENNA"

Italy had had a salubrious effect on Marie von Ebner's constitution. Her stay there had enriched her intellectually and emotionally by letting her find new friends. It also had helped her in another important way: it had given her spiritual comfort and had reconciled her with the Catholic Church. In her 1893 novel "Glaubenslos?" she had already shown a much more positive attitude toward the Church and the priesthood than in *Das Gemeindekind* and in *Unsühnbar*. In fact, in "Glaubenslos?" she had solved the very religious problems she had encountered as a young girl when confronted with a work on astronomy, which contradicted the teachings of her catechism.

In *Meine Kinderjahre* she describes how painful it was for her when she realized after reading this astronomical work how insignificant she was in God's creation. Her ensuing doubt in her long-cherished concept of a loving Father God could not be removed by P. Borek, who advised the thirteen-year-old girl that it was better to rely on sacred wisdom than on human knowledge (856-857). Ebner-Eschenbach further recalls how much she suffered when she began to doubt her faith: "During daytime I could master my heavy thoughts, too heavy for a child's head. But when I woke up at night and they came, I became their prey. Often I could not help myself and then I cried loud due to the pain of my doubts" (855).

Kogler, the rich farmer of "Glaubenslos?," does not have to endure such agony. He asks the same questions the writer had asked as a young girl: "If the earth means only as much to God as a speck of dust on my field means to me, why should he care for it?" (329). And Leo Klinger, the young priest, admitting that he himself once had the same doubts, comforts the farmer by making him aware of the love that permeates all creation (330). The priest, although unhappy with church dogma and with the hypocrisy in the Church, professes his faith by saying: "Believing is more than knowing, and to be able to believe is ultimate bliss" (364). From now on priests in Ebner-Eschenbach's work again care for the people entrusted to them and these, in turn, respect them for their kindness and self-sacrifice.

This change in her attitude toward the Catholic Church came about partly through her reading in Gustav Fechner's transcendental mysticism, which resembled her former Catholic beliefs. Between 1890 and 1900 she had lost many loved ones, among them her old friends Josef

Weilen, Louise von François, Betty Paoli, her favorite sister "Fritzi," her husband, and above all Ida von Fleischl. The fact that the latter had no faith to cling to in her last years may have persuaded Ebner-Eschenbach to find a new spiritual anchor by reading religious works. In her diary she once wrote about her friend: "Poor Ida! I am often frightened by her being so immersed in deep thoughts, by her absent-mindedness and by the expression of hopelessness her eyes have assumed" (B II 225).

Von Fleischl had introduced her to Fechner's teachings as expressed in his works *Zend-Avesta* and *Die Elemente der Psychophysik*. The philosopher believed that the physical and the psychical realm were two facets of one and the same reality, and he therefore claimed that even plants have a psychic life. Using this principle of analogy, Fechner believed in psychophysical parallels between human beings and objects and between all things and the whole universe. He was also convinced of personal immortality, as well as of the capability of the dead to communicate with the living. Inspired by Johann Friedrich Herbart, Fechner saw the universe in animistic terms with God as its soul. His greatest accomplishment was the study of exact relationships in aesthetics and psychology (Copleston 376).

Marie von Ebner-Eschenbach especially admired Fechner's work *Zend-Avesta*, subtitled "On the Things of Heaven and the Hereafter," where he expounded his concept of a universal consciousness. So much was she taken by his theory of panpsychism that she later wrote the story "Vielleicht," in which she described a young man, an admirer of Fechner's *Zend-Avesta*, who visits graves at night in order to discover the deepest secrets of the dead. Under Fechner's influence she had explored the problem of suffering and guilt (*Unsühnbar*, "Die Reise-gefährten"), of evil ("Das Schädliche," "Ein kleiner Roman," "Oversberg") and the phenomenon of conscience ("Das Schädliche," "Die Reisegefährten"), which she defined like him as something innate, something divine (Alkemade 241).

In Rome, then, in 1899, Marie von Ebner, having lost her friend Ida and longing for spiritual comfort, turned to Father Denifle, whom she had met at a dinner given in her honor by the Austrian Embassy. Contrary to Father Borek, the priest who had watched over her religious instruction in her childhood, P. Denifle was a cleric and scholar who could intelligently respond to her religious quest. A scholar in the field of Church history and mysticism (EF vol.I, 1479), he helped her to find her way back to the Church. After many years of doubt about the Catholic faith, she was finally ready to go to confession again.

Her changed attitude toward religion is reflected in her 1903 novella "Die arme Kleine," where she has Elika say: "I am not a strong mind who could do without faith" (704). It likewise shows in her *Kinderjahre*, which she concludes with the conviction that, although she is only a "passing breath on a speck of dust," she is enveloped in God's love: "In order to understand this I needed the grace of the Infinite, a ray of light from His spirit. He has given it to me, his creature, and I may now say 'My Father' to him" (885). To be able to relate to a personal God became a great necessity for her during these final years. In her diary of October 1909 she wrote: "I have to have a God to whom I can give thanks for the fresh air which I breathe, for the sun, the moon, the stars, for the trees, the grass, the mountains, the snow" (Vesely 212). Later, in Vienna, when her niece, Countess Marianne Kinsky, a very devout Catholic, moved into her apartment to take care of her, Ebner-Eschenbach regularly attended church, and a Fr. Rossmiller became her confessor, in her view a model of caring and self-sacrificing priesthood (Rieder, *Weisheit* 125).

She needed an emotional outlet and found it in Catholicism. Gone was her scepticism toward Church doctrine and dogma, gone her discontent with what she had formerly perceived as its propagation of obscurantism and servility. She now clung to her faith with childlike simplicity, grateful for the niche she had been able to find in the Church. Consequently she felt so secure as a writer and as a Catholic that she was not disquieted when a young chaplain, having read some of her works in which she had pointed out the inhumanity of the Church, called her a "poisoner of souls" (Vesely 232). Nor did it upset her when she was denounced as an "atheist poet" in an article of the Catholic journal *Vaterland* (ibid.). Unperturbed, she retorted: "Someone who can consider my writings irreligious is not open to and not worthy of a counterargument" (qtd. in Vesely 232).

She had long known about Karl Freiherr von Vogelsang, the editor of *Das Vaterland*, and his coterie of publicist priests, who tried to propagate a very aggressive Catholicism (Geehr 75). She also was aware that these journalists were anti-Semites and objected to her friendship with Jews. While personal accusations regarding her faith did not overly worry her, the growing anti-Semitism in Vienna did. It made her feel more and more uneasy in her native city.

She had never been a great admirer of Vienna. Therefore she had never described the city in the enthusiastic terms used by writers who occasionally visited it and who were deeply impressed and enchanted by its splendor. Rodenberg, coming to the Austrian capital in the mid-1870s, had been charmed by Viennese hospitality, by the city's richness in musical and artistic culture and tradition, and by its ability to blend harmoniously the old and the new (*Wiener Sommertage* 75). Gottfried Keller, arriving from Switzerland, had immediately felt at home there, calling it "a city of joy, of melody, that happy proud Vienna" (May 102). That "gay Vienna" with its long tradition as the musical capital of the world, with its exciting creativity, its alleged hedonism, its refined taste in sculpture, architecture, and painting does not feature in Ebner-Eschenbach's work. Nor does she allude to the city's "Heurige" wines, its delicious food or its cozy cafés, where one could sit all day with a cup of coffee, topped with "Schlagober" (whipping cream) and read newspapers from around the world.

Yet in 1885 she wrote to Paul Heyse after the brilliant performance of his *Don Juans Ende*: "I finally am pleased again with my old Vienna. Fewer craftsmen and more poetic works—and we remember again that, once upon a time, we showed love and understanding, not only to the deceased, but also to the living poets" (HC 273). Most of the time, however, she criticized the Danubian metropolis, pointing out how much she suffered from its climate and from the hectic life she had to lead there.[9] Even as a child she had preferred the country to the city. In old age she still tried to spend as little time as possible in her apartment in Vienna. In a letter to Dr. Breuer she wrote from Löschna: "Can one live well in the city? No, one cannot live well, and one cannot die well. And here both are so easy" (BC 46). And in another letter she remarked: "In three weeks I shall return home. It will not be as agreeable in the city as it is in the country. If my friends could visit me from time to time in Löschna, three locomotives could not drag me to Vienna" (BC 102).

After 1907, when traveling to Italy had become too strenuous, Marie von Ebner continued to attend theater performances at the Burgtheater during the winter and thus took part in at least one of the cultural offerings of the city. Still, the political atmosphere in fin-de-siècle Vienna repelled her. By nature and upbringing rather tradition-conscious and cosmopolitan, she watched with horror the development of the new political movements, Czech nationalism, Pan-Germanism, Christian Socialism, Social Democracy and Zionism, which caused aggression and hatred among the various nations in the Habsburg Monarchy and poisoned the atmosphere in the capital. Especially the growing hatred against the Jewish population deeply troubled her. For centuries people in Austria had harbored anti-Semitic sentiments. Hatred against the Jews as a religious group had often flared up in times of wars and economic crises. The seventeenth-century Capuchin monk, Abraham a Santa Clara, had denounced the Jews as "the scum of the godless and faithless" (Kann 77-78), and Maria Theresia had hated all unconverted Jews as enemies of Christianity. Yet, anti-Semitism as a political mass-movement and as a viable political force was new in nineteenth-century Austria. At its base were the emancipation of the Jews and the emancipation of the masses (Fraenkel 431).

Due to Emperor Joseph's II Tolerance Patent of October 1781, which allowed them to live outside the ghetto, to open a business and to send their children to state-run schools, Jews were free to assimilate into Austrian society. In 1849 they were given the right to vote and to possess land, and in 1867 they were totally emancipated by receiving the same civil, political and religious rights as other Austrian citizens. The ghetto was dissolved. Jewish people from various parts of the monarchy—Hungary, Bohemia, Moravia and later from Galicia —flocked to the capital to find job opportunities and to take part in Vienna's stimulating cultural and intellectual life. While Jewish life style and tradition had often irritated the gentile population, rising nationalism and disillusionment with industrial capitalism now aroused the anger and suspicion of the masses. People wrongly identified anti-capitalism with anti-Semitism, since they had witnessed the growing economic and political influence of Jewish entrepreneurs. Railways, banks, joint stock companies, and newspapers were in the hands of wealthy Jews, who thus were able to exert great influence on public life. An angry Freiherr Karl von Vogelsang wrote in his journal *Das Vaterland*: "The Christian social order is increasingly dissolved by Jewry . . . a few more years of such 'progress' and Vienna will be called Jerusalem and old Austria—Palestine" (qtd. in Fraenkel 430-431).

Not only had some Jews stimulated Austrian industrialization and amassed wealth to the great consternation of peasants, craftsmen, and shopkeepers who could not compete against their lower prices, they also had antagonized the Catholic Church by joining the Liberal Party and by pledging their allegiance to Pan-Germanism. Because of the bank crash of 1873, the Jews became the scapegoats for all social problems in Austrian society.[10] After the war against Prussia Austria had some extremely good harvests. In contrast to the rest of Europe it could increase its exports, thus achieving industrial growth and renewed optimism in the economy. People of all levels of society took part in a "speculation orgy" (Berkley 11), and the promising economy collapsed, leading to a severe depression which affected the whole world, but first and foremost the Habsburg Monarchy. A cholera epidemic and extremely poor subsequent harvests further contributed to the country's plight. Many businesses went bankrupt. The government had to step in to prevent further damage. It nationalized the railroads, took control of imports, and imposed price regulations in various trades. The population began to mistrust politicians, blaming industrialists, many of them Jews, for the country's disastrous condition. Since many Jews had not taken part in the unwise speculations, they were therefore thought to have profited by the crash—a fact that further aroused hatred against their race (Berkley 71).

Anti-Semitism had further been fanned by Theodor Billroth's 1876 work *The Teaching and Learning of Medical Science*. The famous surgeon, a friend of Ebner-Eschenbach, had been irritated by the fact that many of the Jewish medical students who had come from Galicia to study at the university sold firewood in the streets in their spare time. He inferred from this that Jews were addicted to money-grubbing. Little did he know that these poor students were forced into this sideline in order to pay their tuition fees at the medical school. As much as Billroth later regretted his disparaging remarks and became a friend of the Jews, his book propagated anti-Semitism at the University of Vienna (Berkley 72). After the middle of the nineteenth century many Jews had left the traditional occupations of their forebears and entered the professions—especially law and medicine—where they often outshone the gentiles. This further antagonized many anti-Semites, who saw in them a threat to their own career aspirations. Since many Jews had repudiated their faith and converted to Christianity, they themselves had actually contributed to the notion that to be Jewish was disgraceful. Jews were accused of performing ritual murders, their Scriptures were said to present Christians as animals (Berkley 78).

Georg von Schönerer, leader of the Pan-German movement, did his utmost to bait the Jews and to spread hate propaganda against them in mass rallies and in his journal *Unverfälschte deutsche Worte* (Geehr 80). An anti-Semitic paper, *Deutsches Volksblatt* had been founded in the early 80s. In 1889 a socio-political society was established by Karl Freiherr von Vogelsang and by prelate Franz Schindler. This society met regularly at the hotel "Zur goldenen Ente" in Vienna, attracting clergy, members of parliament and anti-Semites of all stripes. Anti-Semitic agitation was still under control as long as Crown Prince Rudolf lived. He was a great friend of the Jews—one of his collaborators was Moritz Szeps, the founder and editor of the *Wiener Tagblatt*— and did not tolerate any anti-Semitic agitation in his circles. After Rudolf's suicide, his cousin, Archduke Franz Ferdinand, chosen to become the new successor to the throne, gave anti-Semitism free reign and did nothing to curb the hate propaganda, which increased from year to year. By 1890 anti-Semitism had become an election issue in the Landtag. Jews were seen by many as a great danger to be defeated only by a unified mass movement. Christian Socialists and Pan-Germans therefore united to demand the expulsion of Jews from law, medicine, city government, and various other professions and occupations (Geehr 83).

Marie von Ebner-Eschenbach watched these events with growing alarm. Long past was the time when she had ridiculed the Jews in her work. In her 1883 novella "Der Kreisphysikus" she lovingly portrayed a Jewish doctor, delineating his conversion from a materialistic, pleasure-loving man to a friend of the poor. Her friendship with Ida von Fleischl and with some of Vienna's most prominent Jews had made her appreciate Jewish traditions and values, sensitizing her to the atrocities spread about members of the Jewish race. She therefore heartily welcomed Baron Arthur Gundaccar von Suttner's endeavors to initiate the establishment of the Vienna branch of the "Verein zur Abwehr des Anti-Semitismus" (Association for the Rejection of anti-Semitism). In an article in *Die Neue Freie Presse* von Suttner described his Association as a "rescue society . . . namely for the purpose of rescuing the good old Austrian spirit of patience, of justice, of brotherly love" (Suttner II, 72). Yet he also realized that opportunism in the highest ranks of the government had so far prevented him from succeeding in crushing anti-Semitism, which he considered "dangerous to society, deeply injurious to the existence and the fundamental laws of the state" (Suttner II, 74).

In 1891 Marie von Ebner and her husband had joined the association, which included, among many others, the composer Johann Strauss, the surgeon Theodor Billroth and his colleague Carl W.H. Nothnagel, a professor of pathology and therapy. The latter had been a long-time target of the Christian Socialists because of his strict stance against anti-Semitism. In his address on the occasion of the association's first general meeting, Nothnagel described anti-Semitism as "rooted in the murky and hateful qualities of human nature" (Berkley 89). Disappointed with the lack of support they received from government circles for their crusade against anti-Semitism, Baron von Suttner and his wife Bertha turned their energies more to the peace movement, for which they recruited Alfred B. Nobel who, under Bertha von Suttner's influence, established the famous Nobel peace prize and, after his death, left a generous fund for the promotion of the peace movement (Suttner II, 142). The "Verein" was thus without leadership and did not fulfill its members' expectations (Berkley 89). Bertha von Suttner,[11] however, kept in contact with Marie von Ebner-Eschenbach by correspondence. Both women had become the target of the *Vaterland* journalists and von Suttner once informed her friend that she had the honor of being mentioned next to her as "typical of 'Kultur-Weibertum,' estranged from God" (Vesely 232).

In spite of having many like-minded friends in the city, Marie von Ebner felt an increasing aversion to Vienna. It bothered her that the Christian Socialists had succeeded in taking over the municipal council from the liberals. Their leader, a born polemicist and a staunch anti-Semite, had been elected as mayor. In May 1899 she wrote in her diary:

> Let me get away from Vienna! Away from that city
> which has been infected by an anti-Semitic eczema;
> which tears down its palaces and puts in their stead
> garish market stands; in whose churches they preach
> hatred and which has a crook as a mayor and dull
> boors as school inspectors. (Vesely 214)

This "crook as a mayor" was Karl Lueger, a man she sometimes called "the brutal con man," "the bad man Lueger," and "the canaille Lueger" (qtd. in Vesely 214). Contrary to some of his contemporaries, even members of the Jewish population who claimed that he, especially after winning the mayoralty, did not pursue an active anti-Semitic policy, Marie von Ebner knew about his pronounced hatred of the Jews.[12] Lueger had used anti-Semitism to further his political career and, once in power as mayor of Vienna, he not only continued to make anti-

Semitic statements, but he also actively supported violence against Jews (Geehr 178).

Although considered by some as Vienna's "greatest mayor" (Hantsch 442), who established excellent social programs and enjoyed the confidence of the underprivileged, Lueger was by many believed to be responsible for the increase of political anti-Semitism in Vienna during his rule. He influenced not only municipal but also regional and national politics. Under his regime the Jew remained a constant scapegoat and the exclusive target of hate. Whenever the mayor spoke at mass rallies, gatherings of the Church (Katholikentage), and other public occasions, he alluded to the Jews as "the destructive element in every country" (Geehr 181).

While writing her story *Bertram Vogelweid*—published in 1897, the same year Lueger's appoinment was ratified—Ebner-Eschenbach may well have thought of the aspirant to the mayoralty when conceiving the figure of Meisenmann, the village teacher. Bertram Vogelweid hates him because he spreads anti-Semitic propaganda among the rural population. When the countess excuses Meisenmann as a "good man" who, although denouncing the Jews, "would never harm a hair on anybody's head" (Paetel, vol. 8, 174), the count counters with a statement that may be seen as a warning against Lueger, who was also considered by many as a harmless rhetorician: "Will the people whom he incites have an equally platonic hatred? . . . I believe that they are quite in the mood to use clubs and hatchets" (ibid.).

Marie von Ebner's assessment was correct. Once in office, Lueger made sure that anti-Semitism was not only continued but intensified. When he appeared in public the "Lueger-march" was played and people would sing "Lueger will live and the Jews will croak" (Fraenkel 316). Under his rule Jewish teachers were fired, blatant discrimination against Jewish municipal employees and Jewish doctors abounded. Wherever Karl Lueger, often called "der schöne Karl" because of his well-groomed, stylish appearance, went, he voiced his anti-Semitic propaganda, which by now had become an acknowledged agitational weapon.

Political anti-Semitism under Lueger had progressed so far that even members of the higher clergy, like the Archbishop of Olmütz, made anti-Semitic statements from the pulpit, and special government agents watched people who patronized Jewish stores. From Rome a defiant Ebner-Eschenbach wrote to Dr. Breuer in 1899: "Were I in Vienna, I would only shop in Jewish stores, and I would purposely attract the watchman's attention" (BC 36).

Ebner was determined to show her loyalty to her Jewish friends. They did not bear her a grudge because in *Aus Franzensbad* she had made some uncomplimentary remarks about members of their race. They understood her observations not as generally directed against the Jewish people but against the entrepreneurs who exploited the lower middle classes and were thus effecting deep structural changes in society. They knew that she admired Jewish resilience and shared it with them.[13] In her diary she once wrote the following anecdote: "Two rather insistent peddlers, one Christian, one Jewish, were thrown down a stairway by a beefy bouncer. The Christian collected his arms and legs and said: 'That is a fine end!' The Jew got up, rubbed his limbs, saying 'That is a fine beginning'" (Vesely 233). Marie von Ebner may have recognized herself in the Jewish hawker, because, like him, she had often started afresh in her life.

In her story "Der Vorzugsschüler" she lovingly describes a young Jewish huckster who, devoted to Georg Pfanner, the unhappy protagonist, provides him with a musical instrument that comforts him in times of despair. In her autobiography she finally emphasized, probably in reaction to the anti-Semitic atmosphere around her, how the priest and the Jewish doctor had worked together during a cholera epidemic in Zdislawitz. She also stressed how highly her father had regarded the Jewish physician. Her Jewish acquaintances also knew how grateful she was for having been accepted in their midst.

Once introduced to Ida von Fleischl-Marxow and her extensive network of Jewish friends, most of them scholars, writers, and medical doctors, Marie von Ebner-Eschenbach had soon felt at home among these people. They created an environment which was warm and welcoming to those who adopted its genuinely human values, comprising appreciation for family, for the arts, and for literature. In their midst she who had never really been at home in her own circles could develop her talent and rise above the repressive conventions of her class. By background and upbringing, educated Jews had much in common with the Austrian aristocracy. They had the same pride in family and ancestry, they respected the same code of behavior and valued etiquette. They likewise had a social support system which demanded that they care for the underprivileged of their race.[14]

On account of their desire to acculturate and to assimilate into Austrian society the Jews in Vienna had made an important contribution to its intellectual and cultural development. While monarchs like Maria Theresia and her son and successor Joseph II fostered music at their court, the succeeding rulers were averse to the arts and suspicious of people with a creative bent. Thus the bourgeoisie, and especially the educated Jewish classes, had to take over the role of patrons of the arts (Zweig).[15] Therefore artists and writers liked to gather in educated Jewish circles where they were able to talk shop and found a receptive audience for their new creations. Before publishing her works Ebner-Eschenbach read them to her Jewish friends, whose opinions and tastes she valued far more highly than those of her peers.

But apart from their passionate love for the arts and for culture, the Jews around Ebner-Eschenbach had even more in common with her. They had a great admiration for the House of Habsburg, respect for the Austrian aristocracy, for Liberalism and for German civilization. Like her they believed in German cultural hegemony, in progress through science and education and, like her, they saw hard work as the only means to personal and social improvement. Above all, Marie von Ebner and her Jewish friends had the same human, ethical, and moral values. They understood her humor and her sarcasm and truly appreciated her as a person. It is therefore no exaggeration to say that Marie von Ebner-Eschenbach's Jewish friends launched her career and, having been among the first to recognize and appreciate her narrative talent, made her famous in Austria and abroad. They were an extremely powerful group in Austrian culture, furthering it through their promotion and collaboration.

Marie von Ebner had made contact with Joseph Weil, Hieronymus Lorm, two well-known Austrian writers who had supported her, and with Julius Rodenberg, who had helped spread her fame in Germany. Another Jewish writer and editor who influenced her literary career in Austria in a very decisive way was Karl Emil Franzos, well known as the author of colorful stories from the Balkans. As editor of the *Wiener Illustrierte Zeitung* he asked Marie von Ebner-Eschenbach for contributions, thus helping her to become better known in Austria. After his appointment as editor of the periodical *Deutsche Dichtung* in 1885 he again invited her to contribute to the journal. There, her 1887 essay "Aus meinen Kinder- und Lehrjahren", was published for the first time (Schmidt 291). When Franzos asked her to extend the article for the purpose of including it it in his *Geschichte des Erstlingswerks,* she readily obliged. Once the book had appeared in print she wrote to Franzos: "(It) made me very happy; yesterday I read your preface and your own contribution with the greatest interest and I most heartily agree with you. May the book find many and only benevolent readers" (Schmidt 292).

Her own essay was published next to contributions by Felix Dahn, Ludwig Fulda, Paul Heyse, Ossip Schubin,[16] Conrad Ferdinand Meyer, Friedrich Spielhagen, and other acclaimed Austrian and German writers. By that time she had long won her literary spurs in Austria and knew that she owed her reputation to people like Karl Emil Franzos who had worked indefatigably to make Austria's and Germany's writers better known.

Another prominent Jewish personality must be mentioned who, though not a writer, helped in his own way to further Ebner-Eschenbach's fame in Austria: Victor Adler, later called the "father of socialism in Austria" (Johnston 99). In 1888 he founded *Die Zukunft,* a Social Democratic monthly for the educated classes. He further established the daily *Arbeiterzeitung,* first issued in 1889, whose circulation increased from 24,000 to 54,000 between 1900 and 1914 (May 124). It also published fiction by prominent Austrian novelists in order to reach a larger readership.

Adler had long been an admirer of Marie von Ebner-Eschenbach's work, having repeatedly asked her to give him permission to publish *Das Gemeindekind* in his daily. He particularly appreciated the part where she has the teacher praise the lower classes and predict that they will play a decisive role in the future development of the country:[17] "I tell you the best morality is the right one for you, you low-born ones, you are the most important of all! It is no longer possible to accomplish anything great without your aid—from you proceeds what will be the curse or the blessing of the future" (*Child of the Parish* 283). Although her publisher, Paetel, had some reservations at first, the novel was finally acquired by the *Arbeiterzeitung,* a fact which helped to make the writer known also in blue-collar circles.[18] From then on Adler kept in regular contact with her as one of her most enthusiastic fans. On her seventieth birthday he was among the congratulants, expressing his gratitude for her dedication and her empathy for the socially underprivileged (B II 240). When she received the message that her 1876 novel *Bozena* would be re-edited and that the working classes were taking an active interest in it, she knew that she owed this partly to Victor Adler's and his collaborators' efforts to educate the workers and to stimulate them to read her books.

CHAPTER 3:

"A BLISSFUL TOGETHERNESS FROM AFAR"

As much as Marie von Ebner-Eschenbach depended on her Jewish friends for being recognized as a writer of note in Austria and abroad, she in her turn meant a great deal to them as a friend and supporter. She never appeared in public to speak against anti-Semitism but she signed petitions for Jews (BC 121), invited them to her home and made it known through her membership in the Association for the Rejection of Anti-Semitism that she was firmly on the side of Jewry. All her Jewish confidants valued her personality, her tolerance and generosity of spirit and read her work in the light of the humanity and wisdom reflected in it. Especially the critic Moritz Necker, another man of letters who had helped launch her career in Austria, regularly emphasized in his reviews that her most important contribution to the literay scene was her "religion of belief in humankind" at a time when "hatred of all against all" was being propagated (*Neue Freie Presse*, 13. September 1900). He considered it a special privilege to know the writer personally and to correspond with her. Reading her work meant consolation and edification to him. Her wisdom became "a guiding light in difficult times" (Necker IX). On her seventieth birthday he wrote: "I have a deep need to wish you happiness on your birthday, personally, not as a reviewer; as one of those to whom you have shown goodness and goodness again" (RV I.N. 60972).[19]

He had been an admirer of Ebner-Eschenbach's work even before she became known to the larger public in Austria. In the early eighties Ferdinand von Saar had mentioned her name to him and had later made him aware of *Das Gemeindekind*. Although his superior, the editor of the journal *Grenzboten*, could not understand Necker's growing interest and enthusiasm for "the old lady" (Necker XI), the latter persisted in proclaiming her literary importance and in trying to bring her closer to the Austrian readership. In 1899 he published a very favorable review of her collection *Miterlebtes*, pointing out her high ethical standards and her positive attitude to life (Bittrich 252). From then on he became a staunch advocate of her work. By 1895, when Necker discussed the second edition of *Bozena*, he ranked its author firmly among the greatest German writers of the nineteenth century. He clearly saw an ever increasing maturity in her art, observing that she had achieved the much praised unity of "person and artist, of will and ability, of thought and creation" through tireless self-discipline and hard work (ibid.).

Marie von Ebner did not always appreciate his interpretation of her fiction and must have been quite annoyed with him at times, because in his congratulatory letter for her seventieth birthday he asked her to forgive him for his "bad moods and antics," assuring her that she was "the greatest fortune in (his) life" and that he remained her "poodle-loyal and poodle-crazy friend" (RV I.N. 60824). In September 1908 she again had occasion to be upset, because he had written in the *Tagblatt* that Bozena and Anna of "Totenwacht" were the result of her infatuation with George Sand. In her diary entry of September 27, 1908 she vehemently protested against such an insinuation, insisting: "I have never taken my figures from fiction, but always from life" (Rieder, *Weisheit* 123).

Because Necker's views sometimes clashed with her own, she may have declined his offer to write her biography as a tribute to her seventieth birthday. Was Necker too critical, too objective, not willing to paint her picture according to her own directions? There is no doubt that he had a genuine admiration for her as a person and as a writer. Still, she had more confidence in a colleague of Moritz Necker, a man considerably more experienced as a journalist and a biographer.

Anton Bettelheim had been a close friend since the 1880s, when Ebner had met him at a gathering at Ida Fleischl's. Later Betty Paoli, as his children's godmother, had sometimes asked her to accompany her on her visits to the Bettelheims' cottage in Döbling, and the Bettelheims in turn had come to St. Gilgen to spend a few days with Ebner-Eschenbach and Ida Fleischl at their holiday resort. Over the years a deep and lasting friendship developed. Bettelheim much appreciated the writer. Her work, as he once stated, always refreshed him "like hiking in pure mountain air" (B I, V). As editor of the *Zeitschrift für biographische Kunst und Forschung* he intended to publish a biographical essay on her. Convinced of his dedication and integrity, she entrusted to him her correspondence with Halm, Laube, and Louise von François. She also may well have suggested him as her biographer when in 1900 her publisher Paetel was looking for someone to create a literary portrait of her.

Bettelheim felt honored but at first hesitated to accept the offer, hoping that she herself would write her life which, in his view, would have rendered his own account unnecessary (B II, VII). However, at that time she was not ready to disclose bygone events. By nature reserved and eager to guard her privacy, she shied away from overt literary confessions and still preferred to look ahead towards the future instead of reminiscing about an often less than pleasant past. She did, however, provide Bettelheim with all the materials she wanted to have included in his work: information about her own and her husband's ancestors, correspondences with people in the literary world, manuscripts, and finally her diaries, which she took great pain to edit and to have copied by her secretary. She even rewrote part of her diaries, eager to omit intimate details. To Bettelheim she once remarked: "I am working away with zest at the diary excerpts. A bygone past is awakening, it is not always very pleasant. How much did I have to struggle for the sake of my art!" (B II 249).

At all costs she wanted to preserve the public image her readers had created of her as the kind, compassionate, self-sacrificing woman who lived according to the ideals presented in her work.[20] She was also concerned that her deceased relatives should be seen in a positive light and that living family members would not have any reason to be offended. While working on the biography, Bettelheim regularly consulted with her. As a true friend and admirer of her art, he intended to immortalize her literary achievement. He did not tire of praising her "purity of soul" and her "superiority of mind" (B I 101) and, as if trying to prevent his subject from being stigmatized as a bluestocking, he emphasized all her feminine qualities:[21] "Marie Ebner is a housewife as she should be" (B I 39). "It is not easy to find a more tender and solicitous aunt and great-aunt, a more helpful and motherly friend" (B I 41). Only after these assurances he pointed out that her "actual purpose in life was serving her art" (B I 42). She may indeed have asked her biographer to stress her womanly accomplishments. Often annoyed that her relatives considered her impractical, she wanted to prove to them that she had never neglected her domestic and social life. Bettelheim therefore stressed: "Marie Ebner never took her duties of representation easy, neither at the beginning of her marriage nor at any later time, nor did she neglect them. Everything went smoothly, nicely, noiselessly, as it should. She found time for everything" (B I 42).

Like most women writers at that time she harbored a lifelong guilt feeling on account of her urge to write, a propensity largely considered by her contemporaries as an aberration from true womanhood.[22] Having internalized the current ideals of femininity, Ebner-Eschenbach often found herself in a moral conflict, especially since her husband never approved of her work. Bettelheim's biography therefore partly served as vindication and as proof that his subject had successfully fulfilled her domestic duties. The work had, however, another purpose besides proclaiming Marie von Ebner-Eschenbach's greatness as a person and a writer. It was a means to propagate the myth that her marriage had been an extremely happy one, while in fact it was not.[23] Bettelheim therefore, especially in his second biography of 1920, tried very hard to depict her marital life as blissful. Proud to be her friend and confidant, he did everything to oblige her, to transform her into a person of heroic dimensions. His only goal was to spread the myth of her greatness and saintliness and to establish a public facade behind which the private Marie von Ebner could hide.[24]

She was truly grateful to him for his laudation. Easily offended by negative criticism and always on the alert not to reveal her intimate life, she rewarded Bettelheim's tact and discretion with a warm friendship. He, likewise devoted to her, further helped arrange for some of her theater pieces to be performed at the Burgtheater on the occasion of her seventieth birthday. He also may well have been instrumental in suggesting to the University of Vienna that she be nominated for the honorary doctorate, since he had close connnections to the academic world. In 1910 he helped organize the Ebner Fund in honor of the writer's eightieth birthday. In his congratulatory address he praised her as an "example of the most noble femininity" (B II 273), as an "unparalleled teacher and benefactress," as the "pride and glory of the fatherland" (274).

Much more objective and honest than Bettelheim in his characterization of Marie von Ebner-Eschenbach was Fritz Mauthner, another Jewish friend, who had been in contact with her since the 1880s. In his 1916 "Erinnerungen" he painted a portrait which reveals her humanity as well as the rougher edges of her personality. Mauthner remembered her "delightful, always subdued sarcasm," her great sense of humor and irony and her tendency to giggle about funny remarks. He further recalled that she was not free from jealousy.

How sharply she observed her fellow men may be seen from a diary entry which describes people attending a social gathering: "Louise Lodron, E. Barida, the parents, grandma and youth, and the deputy Graf with his good face, which looks tellingly like a cut-up cooked ham" (TB I 158). A visit to the Theatre du Chatelet in Paris ended with the following observation: "Costumes very beautiful, the actors vulgar, the singers have no voice but are bow-legged. Mme. Ugalde as Prince Charmant is quite unbearable" (TB I 186). While claiming that ill-will was foreign to her, Mauthner was convinced that she had "a good deal of the rascally teasing which the French call 'malice' " ("Erinnerungen" 2).

It must have been this very penchant for satire and ridicule which made Mauthner and Marie von Ebner such congenial friends. They met only twice personally, but after the second encounter the latter entered in her diary of February 20,1909: "This afternoon Fritz Mauthner paid me a visit. What a joy! I saw him only for the second time, but I felt as if had met an old friend again" (B II 270). As editor of the *Berliner Tageblatt* in the late 1880s he had asked her to contribute to his journal. She sent him her often rejected 1878 novella *Margarete* begging him to make as many changes as necessary. In contrast to other editors, like Julius Rodenberg and Karl Emil Franzos, Fritz Mauthner instantly liked the work (RV I.N. 57157). He also thought that the editors who had refused to publish "Margarete" ten years earlier "were apparently scared by the best in it, not by its romantic ending. The wonderfully drawn relationship between the baron and the seamstress was probably too real for the gentlemen" (RV I.N. 57160).

Since the appearance of *Das Gemeindekind* Mauthner had taken an active interest in Ebner-Eschenbach's work (RV I.N. 57144) and he became one of her most enthusiastic reviewers. He discussed her works with insight and appreciation in the *Berliner Tageblatt* and in *Deutschland*, a German weekly for the arts and sciences, which he also edited. She trusted his judgment so much that she began to approach him for literary advice. Unhappy about the lukewarm reception her novel *Unsühnbar* had received and intimidated by the disapproval of many critics, she turned to him for his opinion of her work. Mauthner advised her to "report some previously hidden detail about her protagonist Maria, which would make the reader better understand why she committed adultery. The writer promptly followed her critic's advice by describing Maria Dornach's emotions more in detail, trying to improve the second edition of *Unsühnbar* (I.N. 57150).

Through their correspondence Fritz Mauthner and Marie von Ebner became close friends, exchanging photographs of themselves and their loved ones and teasing each other on occasion. Once Mauthner pleaded with her: "Baroness, Poetess, Ebner-Eschenbach, please do not write again with such modesty. I solemnly declare that henceforth I shall understand every humble word directed at me as irony" (RV I.N. 57150). Around the time of his friend's sixtieth birthday he planned an "Ebner-evening" in Berlin by having her play, *Es wandelt Niemand ungestraft unter Palmen,* performed at a local theater. On account of his influence several other short pieces of hers ("Ohne Liebe," "Am Ende") were also successfully staged in Berlin.

Ebner-Eschenbach was extremely grateful for all her friends and always kept in touch with them, telling them about her work and showing a great interest in their private and professional lives. As she benefited from their advice and their influence in literary circles, they appreciated the fact that they had contact with an aristocrat, a member of the first society in Austria, well-connected with the most prominent families in the country. While she had a friendly and even cordial relationship with many men of letters, there was one writer, also of at least partly Jewish descent, who occupied a place closer to her heart than any of them: Paul Heyse. A reading of the correspondence between him and Marie von Ebner-Eschenbach reveals that he was the kindred soul for whom she had long been yearning. In an aphorism she once said: "Every artist will always long for a person who can identify with him and his work" (Rieder, *Weisheit* 74). Heyse filled the vacuum left in her heart since Grillparzer's death. He made her vibrate as a person and as an artist, as only a truly congenial person could do. In none of her correspondences is she so enthusiastic and affectionate as in her letters to him. Slowly and repeatedly she read every line of his, found it a "source of blissful wonder" and once admitted in a letter to him: "I should never have dreamed that such a treasure as I possess in the letters of my most highly revered writer would really become mine" (HC 287-288).

Paul Heyse was born in Berlin the same year as Marie von Ebner-Eschenbach. Encouraged by his father, who also would have liked to become a poet, he conceived poetry and dramas at the age of fifteen, and at seventeen firmly determined to make writing his career. He wrote prolifically. In his twenties he was already recognized as a great talent in Berlin and compared to the young Goethe. He was invited by the Bavarian King Maximilian II to become royal court poet in Munich and to teach at the university there. In 1871 he began editing *Deutscher Novellenschatz*, a collection of German novellas, in collaboration with his friend Hermann Kurz. He was always on the lookout for new German novellas to be included in his edition. Through a friend, a librarian in Württemberg, Heyse learned about Marie von Ebner-Eschenbach's novella "Die Freiherren von Gemperlein," a work he instantly liked because of its humor and pungent style.

Through a common acquaintance, Julie Schlesinger, the wife of the playwright Sigmund Schlesinger, Heyse sent Ebner-Eschenbach his greetings, assuring her of his admiration for her work. Moved and honored by his recognition, she replied in March 1882: "I now believe I know how a soldier feels who receives a medal on the battlefield; full of pride and happiness, and deeply moved as we always are upon seeing that we have reached a goal of which we have been dreaming, but which we have never dared hope to achieve" (HC 260). With this letter a thirty-six year epistolary friendship began, which enriched the life of two writers who were never meant to meet personally, but who deeply understood and valued each other as artists and as human beings.

In 1883 Heyse asked Marie Ebner for permission to include the "Gemperlein" in his *Neuer Deutscher Novellenschatz*, causing her to feel greatly honored. It was at the time when, utterly dispirited by the manifold rejections her two squires had received, she had laid them "full of resignation into the dark tomb (of a Year Book) where they were supposed to rest until all literature came to an end" (B I 100). To suddenly hear that Heyse was interested in her story and to be praised by him, a writer she had admired for years, meant bliss for her. When later reading Heyse's introduction to her "Gemperlein" in the *Novellenschatz* where he called the novella a "cabinet piece" and a "humoristic creation of the first rank" (9), she shed tears of happiness as she wrote to her benefactor: "I owe you a joy which will not fade as long as I live. From now on I am immune against indifference and envy, and it seems impossible to me that I will ever again lose courage" (HC 265-266). By 1885 the two writers were on such friendly terms that Heyse dropped the title "Baroness" in his address and replaced it with "dear, revered friend" (HC 273-274). She, in turn, no longer directed her letters to her "Revered doctor" but to her "revered" and even "highly revered friend" (HC 278-280).

She trusted him so completely that she sent him all her works, including her dramas, for his assessment. How proud she was when he expressed particular interest in *Marie Roland,* informing her that he, too, had initially wanted to become a dramatist and, like her, had to realize that readers valued him more as a writer of novels. "But," he predicted, "our last dramatic word has not yet been uttered, has it, my revered comrade in fate?" (HC 264), a promise they both fulfilled.

When Heyse first came across Marie von Ebner's novellas published in 1872 in the journal *Die Dioskuren*, he must have realized that he was dealing with an author whose Weltanschauung was much like his own. She shared his ethical and moral values and, like him, tried to make society aware of its responsibility toward the underprivileged. Like him she was a defender of the liberal cause. She was a dreamer like him and equally a searcher for truth. Her observational skills resembled his and, as he later found out, she was as interested in visual art as he was. She also had enjoyed drawing in her youth, an occupation he still cherished even in later years, when on his travels through Italy he sketched the scenery and all those women, whose features fascinated him (Krausnick 202). Ebner-Eschenbach also shared Heyse's love for antiquity, his compassion for animals, and his interest in women's emancipation, a topic he wrote about extensively in newspaper articles, once he was settled in Munich (Krausnick 278).

The longer the two writers corresponded, the more they felt how much alike they were in many ways.[25] They both affirmed life in their work. Not only did they believe in the nobility of mind and heart, they also both loved nature and had a keen eye for beauty. The one as well as the other had a strong aversion to naturalism, the literary movement that became fashionable in the 1880s (Petzet, XX). Like Heyse, Ebner considered art as sacred, having an almost ritual feeling toward it. The more the two writers studied and discussed each other's works, the closer they came as human beings. In 1886 Paul Heyse dedicated to her a collection of novellas containing "Himmlische und irdische Liebe," "F.U.R.I.A." and "Auf Tod und Leben." In his letters he declared his affection for her, an affection kindled by the fact that in her work he had discovered "the breath of a soul loyal and sure of herself" (HC 277). Henceforth he was able to entrust his problems to her, knowing that she understood him as only a true and kindred friend could. He considered it the good fortune of his life to have found Ebner-Eschenbach. Her letters were for him "a possession which constantly refreshes me anew" (HC 282). When he was plagued by doubts in his literary accomplishments she comforted him: "You could have articulated the beautiful even more beautifully, I do not doubt that, but why rob yourself by merciless self-criticism of the joy with one of your dearest and most magnificent novellas?" (HC 283/4). As a token of her friendship she sent him her latest work, *Neue Dorf- und Schloss-geschichten* with a personal dedication (HC 285).

Surrounded by writers and scholars in the "Münchner Dichterkreis" and involved in correspondences with Fontane and Storm, Heyse did not so much need the literary discussion with Ebner-Eschenbach but rather longed for her personal friendship. As he once confessed in a letter, when reading her work he did not admire her talent the most, but her personal warmth, kindness, and integrity: "I have a lively need to declare to you from time to time my love . . . in everything you write for me the most important thing is not the talent but the person" (HC 286-287). Reading such protestations of love and appreciation, she was filled with "blissfully happy astonishment" (HC 287). Never had she had a correspondent who wrote so openly, so exuberantly and with such overflowing affection.

In spite of his early fame in Berlin and his spreading recognition in literary circles in Munich, where he resided like a poet-king, Heyse seems to have needed his colleague's praise and adulation. At sixty-six he confided to her: "My dear, most precious friend, do you know that, while reading your letter, I blushed like a young girl at her first ball, like a girl who receives a bouquet from her secretly adored partner during the cotillion?" (HC 359). And after reassuring her of his love, he admitted: "I felt such an embarrassing, young and fresh joy on account of your manifold praise, as if it had been the first time that you overestimated me. If ever I needed it, although not being worthy of it, it is now" (HC 360).

Just then he felt very depressed and worried that he would never be able to create a work of value again. Her belief in him, her admiration for his work stimulated him and, although he often tried to discourage her from paying him so many compliments, he was extremely happy when she commended him for his achievement. Once she called him her "master" and remarked: "By the way, how long have I known that you are the greatest artist among all German writers and poets, not excepting anyone who ever lived" (HC 369), a statement Heyse must have relished. For Marie von Ebner-Eschenbach Paul Heyse's friendship was a godsend. Although she came in contact with him only in 1882, she had greatly admired him as a writer many years before. She adored his narrative skill and his style. To Natalie von Milde she once wrote: "Nobody, it seems to me, has been able to handle the German language as Paul Heyse does" (RV I.N.129013). Thus when she learned through her friend Bruno Walden (Florentine Galliny) that Heyse had praised one of her stories published in 1872 in *Die Dioskuren*, she was overjoyed. But, as she later confessed to Heyse on his seventy-fifth birthday: "The intoxication of bliss was followed by hangover-like doubts in the authenticity of the blessed news. Can it be ? Is it really possible that Paul Heyse reads and praises one of my stories?" (HC 394-395).

To have gained the friendship and trust of a writer she had valued highly for years was indeed a great joy for her. That he appreciated her work was more than she had ever imagined in her most daring dreams. In time she also came to love Heyse on account of his openness. In none of her correspondences is she as exuberant as in her letters to Heyse, letters which abound in superlatives and expressions of greatest enthusiasm. When replying to him she is not happy but "overjoyed," she "shouts with joy" and sometimes even has experiences of "ecstasy of joy" (HC 317). He was able to make a part of her vibrate which probably no one else had ever touched. He filled the gap left by her "most beloved Grillparzer" after his death in 1872 and caused her to be "enchanted" and "carried away" when reading his work (HC 311). He was able to draw her out of her reserve. Since he wrote to her of his "love" and his "admiration" for her, she adopted the same tone in her letters to him. In 1887 she even signed her letter of November 17 with: "Your friend who loves you very much" and added as a postscript: "I am already beginning to become reckless" (HC 306).

While sounding like a deeply caring mother in her correspondence with Saar, in her letters to Heyse Marie von Ebner comes across as a woman in love. She relishes the opportunity to open her heart, to vent her feelings of boundless admiration for someone she considered superior as an artist. Through Heyse's affection she felt transformed and valued, thus gaining more confidence in herself. Heyse's wife Anna[26] apparently was not jealous but often joined her husband in sending greetings. Once she wanted to visit the writer in Vienna but missed her because the latter was at her country estate. Anna Heyse also regularly conveyed New Year's greetings, reassuring her correspondent of her friendship and high regard. Through her niece who lived in Munich Marie Ebner once had flowers delivered, which Heyse's wife happily received. In her thank-you note she wrote: "I accept that joy as I accept everything that comes from you, without many words but with the warmest feelings of gratitude. How many beautiful things you have given us, and with what desire and even greater pleasure do I get hold of a book in which your name appears. I know in advance that I shall then have enjoyable hours" (HC 289).

In her letter of 29 February, 1888 Ebner called Heyse and his wife her "consolers and heart-liberators when I tend to get anxious, and self-doubts are overwhelming me" (HC 310). She was well aware how often she was depressed and disgruntled on account of her various ailments. Heyse's friendship gave her the strength to fight and to take up the daily battle with her many indispositions. Each of his letters was a "ray of sunshine," a panacea in times of physical and emotional suffering. Grateful for his sympathy when she was bed-ridden with influenza, she once dedicated a poem to him, in which she told him, using the familiar "Du," how much his letter meant to her: "It fills my heart with its golden glimmer and brings the sun into my darkened room" (HC 320).

As she welcomed each new work of his, so he considered each of her literary achievements a piece of true art coming from a person for whom he had the warmest regards. Every line she wrote was dear to him. He deeply admired her psychological insight and her observational skills. He appreciated her belief in humanity's innate goodness at a time when, in his view, mostly the obscene and the disgusting were glorified. In 1887 he included another story of hers in his *Novellenschatz*. Earlier he had chosen the "Gemperlein" because of its humor, this time he wanted a tragic tale and was wavering between "Er laßt die Hand küssen" and "Krambambuli." Finally he chose the latter. When he praised the story, Marie von Ebner was delighted and could not thank him enough for his approval. When he criticized her work, as he did for example with "Rittmeister Brand," a story he would have liked to see more rigorously structured (HC 344), she good-naturedly accepted his advice: "Up to now I did not recognize the flaws in my tale. But now! It is not pleasant, but it is healthy, and I express my gratitude, my highly revered, dear, benevolent Doctor" (HC 351). However, at times she also defended herself, explaining why she had employed certain literary devices and chosen a particular form for a story (HC 346).

For his sixtieth birthday she sent him a water-color painting of Bernini's colonnades in Rome, the very monument Heyse had described in his story "Gute Kameraden." It is unlikely that he had his Austrian friend in mind when in 1882 he conceived the figure of Gabriele von Berg, one of the protagonists of this novella. Yet the latter bears many of her traits. She has an aristocratic background, addresses Dr. Eberhard, in many ways a sketch of Heyse himself, with "Herr Doktor," has great observational skills, a sharp intellect, is rather unattractive, and well versed in artistic matters. When Gabriele von Berg and Dr. Eberhard engage in discussions about art, one feels reminded of Marie von Ebner-Eschenbach and her revered "Herr Doktor," who also regularly exchanged ideas of that nature. Yet, while Gabriele von Berg, deeply in love with Dr. Eberhard, prefers not to stay in touch with him upon returning home, because he is a married man, Ebner-Eschenbach remained Heyse's "good comrade" for the rest of his days, even becoming a friend of his wife.

Heyse felt extremely happy about Marie von Ebner's present. He thanked her for "the thoughtful choice and the inexhaustible good intentions which you showed again toward me. You know how often I think of you anyhow. But it is nevertheless a welcome enrichment of my joy of life daily to have something before my eyes which comes from you" (HC 313). Half a year after her friend, Marie Ebner turned sixty. Well before this event her relatives had asked her: "Aunt Marie, whose birthday greetings would you enjoy the most?" (HC 314). And she replied: "Well, of course, Paul Heyse's. And with every letter, every telegram, every bouquet that arrived, what curiosity, what expectation" (ibid.). He did not disappoint her but sent a big box containing a basket of flowers. On the card she could recognize "immediately the writing which I love" (HC 315), and once the flowers had withered, she kept the basket as a token of Heyse's friendship. In 1891 she dedicated her collection *Drei Novellen*, consisting of "Oversberg," "Der Nebenbuhler" and "Bettelbriefe," to her dearly beloved friend, knowing that he would understand these stories like no one else. He had already read one of them when it had appeared in serialized form and had been so much moved that he wanted to write her another "love letter." Later he commented: "I had read your 'Oversberg' and was again highly impressed by the power and grace of your art and nature, which form such an inseparable unity as I have found in no other writer of your gender" (HC 319).

Greatly honored by her dedication of the book, he wrote at the end of his reply: "I embrace you, dear precious friend, and am today and in all eternity your totally dedicated Paul Heyse" (HC 321). Reading these three novellas was for him not as if he had savored "sparkling wine," but "as if [he] had come back from a sunny walk through a vineyard in early fall and had enjoyed the ripeness and sweetness of the most noble grapes" (HC 324). Paul Heyse not only provided an emotional outlet and literary advice for Marie von Ebner, he also inspired her to write. In 1906 she completed "Novellenstoffe," a story in which she described a man and a woman, who at their first meeting fall in love and over many years keep in touch by correspondence. They never see each other again, because shortly before their long-desired rendezvous the woman, aware that she has aged and physically changed, decides not to leave the train that was to take her to the meeting with her friend. She realizes that he, whom she remembers as a young man, would be disappointed to see her again as an old, thickset matron. Therefore the two friends are not granted a second encounter but are able to preserve the image of each other that had been dear to them for all that time.

Paul Heyse and Marie von Ebner-Eschenbach never met personally, although the former had planned several times to visit his friend in Vienna and in St.Gilgen (HC 313). In 1898 he made definite plans to see her after taking the waters in Bad Kissingen. She wrote him from St. Gilgen, where she was staying with Ida von Fleischl: "Two little old women will from now on count the days to the end of your treatment in Kissingen. To see you face to face, highly revered friend, what an event for me. I shall stand at the station with a thumping heart" (HC 371). Yet Heyse's plan did not materialize, because the weather had become too hot to travel. Another time, when in Gmunden, he intended to make a trip to St. Gilgen but, just when he was about to leave, a friend arrived, preventing him from realizing his plan (B II 211). By that time Marie von Ebner may have felt like the protagonist of "Novellenstoffe," that it was better to preserve the ideal image of her friend intact instead of personally meeting him at a time when they were both old and physically less attractive. On the occasion of Heyse's eightieth birthday she wrote a poem for the friend she had never seen, but who was very close to her heart and soul. She assured him that being eighty was not as frightening as people think in their younger years and that "old age is the most beautiful age" for someone who has accomplished great things in art (HC 396). A few months later, on her eightieth birthday, Paul Heyse sent her the following lines: "I have never looked you in the eye, never heard your voice or pressed your hand, but I feel as close to you as if I had known you from childhood on. . . to the two of us was given a blissful togetherness from afar" (HC 396-397).

After Heyse's death in 1914, a sad Marie von Ebner wrote to her nephew Franz: "Heyse dead! I have never seen him, but there was a time when we were very close" ("Briefwechsel" 258). With him she had lost one of the most congenial and appreciative friends of her life.

NOTES:

1. Ebner-Eschenbach immortalized this sculptor in her story "Der Bildhauer" in "Altweibersommer" (B II 267).

2. In 1901 Isolde Kurz, in 1902 Emilie Mataja, in 1903 Hermine Villinger, in 1904 Enrica von Handel-Mazzetti, in 1905 Helene Böhlau won the prize (B II 289).

3. Lorm's novel is also set in Hungary, and there are likewise three characters by the name of Ilona, Stefan and Koloman. Furthermore, Lorm delineates in a very poetic way Ilona's relationship with her dearly loved son.

4. Carole Klein, a modern psychoanalyst, confirms this view in her study *Mothers and Sons*: "Sun and shadow, yin and yang, mind and body—all those qualities we try to balance in order to attain the richest expression of self—seem to find their most powerful fusion when a woman reaches out to a son" (7).

5. Isolde Kurz was the daughter of the Swabian writer Hermann Kurz, author of *Schillers Heimatjahre*. Her mother was the poet Baroness Marie von Brunnow (HC 362).

6. Bettelheim refers to the fact that Marie von Ebner, deeply concerned about a person's privacy, objected to Grillparzer's revelations in his autobiography (B II 249).

7. How much critics expected her to conform to the image of the "aristocracy of the mind," an image she had coined, may be seen by Rieder's statement: "She has lived this aristocracy of the mind and immortalized it in her work" (*Weisheit* 9).

8. Bettelheim states that Ebner's autobiography conceals more than it reveals (B II 30).

9. Ebner-Eschenbach had the same love-hate for Vienna as Beethoven, Grillparzer, Karl Kraus, and Arthur Schnitzler! Hermann Bahr, likewise attracted to and repelled by the city, once stated: "I often say to myself,

I say to myself daily: No, one can no longer live in Vienna. Away!"
Yet ultimately he came to the conclusion that "nowhere else would I
live as in Vienna, really live the life I wish" (qtd. in Johnston 126).

10. As Egon Schwarz remarks, the term "Jew" became a cipher. Jews
were held responsible for all the evil not only in Austria but everywhere
in the world, and every evil was associated with them (174).

11. Bertha von Suttner, nee Kinsky, was related to Marie Ebner through
marriage, since the latter's sister, Fritzi, had married Count August
Kinsky, a cousin of Bertha.

12. Richard Geehr points out that Stefan Zweig and Arthur Schnitzler
actually defended Lueger (171).

13. On the occasion of Marie Ebner's eightieth birthday Viktor
Klemperer honored her in an essay in the *Allgemeine Zeitung des
Judentums*, emphasizing her tolerance toward Jews (430).

14. Julian Straub convincingly argues: "Aristocracy and Jews are always
in the best accord. As an old and serene people the Jews are aristocrats
of the mind as well as of sensitivity. As such they are closer to the
nobility than to the 'unfermented' people'"(129).

15. Zweig observes that the Jews were "the real audience. They filled
the theatres and the concerts, they bought the books and the pictures,
and with their more mobile understanding, little hampered by tradition,
they were the exponents and champions of all that was new" (*The
World* 22).

16. Ossip Schubin's real name was Aloysia Kirchner.

17. By the time Ebner-Eschenbach wrote *Das Gemeindekind,* socialism
was rapidly gaining ground in Austria (Tapié 332).

18. Ebner-Eschenbach did not want to be linked to the Socialist Party.
When Viktor Adler's wife once asked her for a contribution to a
socialist publication she felt very reluctant to comply. Finally she
translated the poem "Guardian Angel" by Sládek from Czech into

German and submitted it to Frau Adler, knowing full well that it would not be welcome in a socialist paper (Vesely "EETL" 98).

19. Marie Ebner may have financially supported Necker, because in this same letter he mentions that she had acted "in a truly princely way in practical matters" toward him (RV I.N. 60972).

20. Moritz Necker remarks: "The public at large has an image of her personality, based more on feeling than on insight, which, however, all in all comes close to the truth. In this popular conception the reminiscences of high moral wisdom contained in Ebner's books set the tone" (50).

21. In his second biography Bettelheim also takes great pains to guard her mother, Marie von Vockel, from the suspicion of having been a bluestocking, assuring his readers that her "knowledge only increased the appeal and value of her femininity" (B II 50). He thus contradicts the then current notion that the "laborious learning and painful brooding . . . eliminate the advantage peculiar to girls" (qtd. in Mörsdorf 100).

22. As Robert Seidenberg aptly remarks: "The woman who seeks a professional identity in the world is faced with many hazards. They arise not only from a hostile and resentful environment, but also from her own inner doubts about what she is doing. Even when she reassures herself or is given support that her stand is proper and justified, she frequently manifests a feeling of guilt about not being in her proper place— the home" (Miller 320).

23. Up to now every scholar and critic who has written about Ebner's life has echoed Bettelheim's statement about the writer's happy marriage. Lilli Reinke writes in her 1910 essay about Ebner-Eschenbach: "Her first love most happily led to a harmonious marriage. Storms which have devastated many a woman's life remained foreign to her" (772). And Ingrid Cella in her 1988 afterword to Ebner's aphorisms observes: "The pair, which remained childless, lived in extraordinary harmony. This consisted not only in common intellectual interests and mutual tolerance but also in a critical view of the corruption in the Danube monarchy" (Reclam 64).

24. With the benefit of hindsight it must be pointed out that by depicting a more than life-size picture of his subject Bettelheim—he may have been under pressure from Ebner's relatives—did not render her a service. In a published lecture given on the occasion of the fiftieth anniversary of Ebner's death, Gertrud Fussenegger observed that the writer is now largely forgotten in Austria and Germany. "Her work," she says, "has never been critically analyzed because in her time critics bowed their knee before the kind lady, the beautiful soul" (12). And Kurt Benesch in the foreword to his fictionalized biography likewise states that in Austria readers refrain from reading the latter's work because they consider her to be "oozing out sentimentality" (XII).

25. A stylistic analysis of Heyse's and Ebner-Eschenbach's letters shows that both writers have a tendency to exaggerate. Both indulge in superlatives and like to use words with the prefix "un." She is, for example, Heyse's "unwandelbar getreue Marie Ebner"(HC 259), and his success does her "unbeschreiblich wohl" (HC 318). He in turn considers her "unschätzbar" and believes that the only thing that stands between them is Ebner's "unberechtigter Hang" to look up to him (HC 302).

26. Heyse's first wife Margarethe died young. In 1867 he married Anna Schubart, a native of Munich, who helped him to gain access to a large social circle in the Bavarian capital (Krausnick 278).

PART SIX

TO STRIVE UNTIL THE END (1910-1916)

> We can achieve nothing more beautiful in old age than a mild and unassuming tranquillity.

CHAPTER 1:

"THE MOST BEAUTIFUL WORLD I CREATE FOR MYSELF"

On her eightieth birthday Marie von Ebner-Eschenbach received many honors and congratulatory letters, and many friends and colleagues paid homage to her. Bettelheim's dedicatory address, in which he praised her work and attitude to life, was signed by more than five hundred people, among them Archduchess Marie Valerie, the Emperor's daughter, Archduke Rainer, the curator of the academy of sciences, and his wife, the association of Austrian Women Writers, the Viennese art school for women, and many art lovers, politicians, and scientists, not only from Austria but also from abroad. (B II 215). Marie Ebner's childlike vow had been realized: "I was a young girl, still almost a child, my fantastic opinions, my sympathies and antipathies changed like April weather; but one thing was always clearly and firmly in my mind, the conviction that I would not walk this earth without at least leaving a faint trace of my footprints upon it" (ZT 721).

Now she was overwhelmed by the signs of appreciation she received from far and wide. The emperor sent her the Elisabeth Orden Erster Klasse, a great distinction which she and her family highly treasured. A year before she had been made an honorary member of the Schillerstiftung when it celebrated the poet's 150th birthday, and also the Goethegesellschaft in Weimar had elected her a member. Had its constitution allowed women to join, Marie von Ebner-Eschenbach would at that time also have been made a member of the Austrian Academy of Sciences (B II 26). Hundreds of telegrams and letters arrived in Zdislawitz, where the octogenarian spent the great day. On the advice of her doctors she did not attend any public festivities. Overwhelmed by all the tokens of appreciation and praise she wrote from Zdislawitz to a friend:

> For eight days now I have been walking around as in a dream and every moment I think: now you will wake up, and I also become aware — how beautiful it all was. And a very pleasant aftertaste will remain from that dream. I have real difficulty to convince myself that I, Marie Ebner, am enjoying such honors, receive such ovations and, the most beautiful and enjoyable of all, such demonstrations of love. (NBV 933-934)

Unable to answer the numerous congratulatory notes, she sent a circular letter to all well-wishers with a poem, in which she expressed the hope that one day she might be able to thank them all much more profusely: "Let time, dear time, flow by; let me gratefully enjoy a new beginning. Once those ten times eight begin to move, I feel quite young again. Then perhaps my striving will yet lead to victory and may provide, what I must forego now, the opportunity to worthily offer you my thanks from the fullness of my soul" (B II 288).

Marie Ebner, like many of her protagonists, had seen life as a mission, putting into practice her motto: "If one considers one's existence a challenge, one is always able to endure it" (Reclam 10). In her work she had not only demonstrated great concern for human beings but also deep understanding for animals. This was acknowledged by the Weltbund für Tierschutz (World Association for the Protection of Animals), which in 1912 awarded her the silver Rothardt-Medaille (B II 291). She had written some of the most beautiful and moving stories about dogs, "Krambambuli" and "Die Spitzin," and had repeatedly voiced her concern about the maltreatment of helpless creatures.

In her 1893 novella "Glaubenslos?" she has Pater Leo show solicitude not only for the people in his parish but also for abused horses (272) and for a hen that had been tortured and buried alive by a hooligan (284). In *Meine Kinderjahre* she mentions a picture in her father's room which she could never observe without feeling tears well up in her eyes. It showed a French invalid who was about to bury his dog, his only friend and companion. Without his dog, so the young, compassionate Marie always thought, the poor man had no one left in this world (762).

How fond she was, especially, of dogs may also be seen from the following aphorism: "Among a hundred people I love just one; among a hundred dogs I love ninety-nine" (Rieder *Weisheit* 85).[1] In "Aus einem zeitlosen Tagebuch" she observed about a monkey: "A naked ape never evoked as much pity in me as one in a silk jacket with a beret on its head and a small rifle on its shoulder" (730). Annoyed with the cruelty to animals she had experienced in Italy, she told her friends the story of a merciful foreign lady in Rome, who once saved a donkey from abuse. She bought the animal from a villager and gave it to a monk under the condition that he employ it only for light labor and treat it kindly until the end of its days. With her typical "malice" Marie von

Ebner concluded the talk by remarking: "Thus a noble woman has rendered at least *one* ass in Rome happy" (B II 235).

The more famous and sought-after the writer became, the more she appreciated solitude. In her notebook she sighed: "Adoration, reverence, love: people, please grant all that to my memory" (Rieder, *Weisheit* 121) and further she pleaded "As long as I am still on earth, leave me alone" (ibid.). She also ultimately preferred Venice to Rome, because the people there bothered her less (B II 253). Yet she was proud of her success. She had proved to herself and to her incredulous relatives that she had talent and had been able to achieve her professional goal. In her work she had immortalized the Austrian aristocracy, the country population of her native place, and her family estate Zdislawitz.

Through her writing she had been able to come to terms with many fears and worries in her life and had found peace "in the little hut at the foot of the mountain top" (KL 279). She had brought honor to her husband's name, the name he had always been so concerned about. At last she had become famous.

But she did not care for fame, since it meant invasion of her cherished privacy.[2] She thought it a nuisance that people burdened her with demands for autographs, donations, contributions to journals, and recommendations for young, often untalented writers trying to get a start. At times she could hardly keep the critics and journalists at bay, who wanted to interview her for her opinion on current issues. To Natalie von Milde she once wrote: "Every little reviewer who has written a line about me, however tactless it may have been, feels entitled to steal an hour from me or drop a hint that he loves the life in a country house and would not mind accepting my brother's hospitality in Zdislawitz" (RV I.N. 129.255). And to Saar Marie Ebner complained: "I would have liked to spend at least a few months in my little home, but the demands, the schemes, and the soliciting to which I am now helplessy exposed, drive me away" (Kindermann 122). In "Altweibersommer" she further expressed how she felt about her fame: "You say you want to be famous and do not know what you are talking about. To be famous means to walk barefoot over scattered shards of glass" (666).

Her goal, as in previous years, still was to write and to strive for self-fulfillment and artistic perfection. She continued to get up at six o'clock every morning, in order to write and meditate about her work. The more she wrote, the better she came to know herself and the people around her. She had learned that, although she had meant well, some readers had always misunderstood her criticism of society and her call for reform (ZT 724). Once extremely judgmental, even harsh in her opinion of others, in old age she became more lenient toward her fellow men and tried to practice the greatest self-discipline: "The older we get, the stricter we have to be with ourselves. Our weaknesses, our faults, all our bad qualities, continue to live in us; the power to control them, however, diminishes" (ZT 735).

She also strove for intellectual and moral growth. So she continued to read voraciously, in order to learn from the wisdom of others. Having received Goethe's ten-volume *Gespräche* as a present, she happily wrote to Dr. Breuer: "And now I read, read, read. I sit in a swing, flying up and down; I hate, I love, I admire kneeling in the dust . . . Quite an excitement, such reading!" (BC 97). She also enjoyed Richard Hamdun's work on impressionism and Prentice Mulford's *Der Unfug des Sterbens*. With special interest she immersed herself again in Scheffel's *Ekkehard*, admiring the author's historical knowledge and his inventiveness (ZT 736). Trying to reach perfection as a human being gave her the greatest satisfaction.

Like many elderly people she had a tendency to praise the past as "the good old times" when authority was still respected and traditional values honored (*Kinderjahre* 765). Yet she also acknowledged the achievements of the present. She especially praised the fact that the relationship between parents and children, in her youth characterized by parental authoritarianism, had become more like friendship and partnership (ibid.). Toward modern authors, however, she remained often harsh and disapproving, partly probably because she knew that they looked down on her own achievement (Kindermann 154). Particularly the works of the naturalists with their seemingly too pessimistic Weltanschauung, their relentless description of crude reality, and of social and economic misery, filled her with horror ("Lotti, die Uhrmacherin" 923-924).

Her own conception of art had been shaped by the humanist tradition. Like Schiller[3] she believed that art as well as nature were the revelation of God. In accordance with Goethe and other neo-classicists she claimed that the artist had to combine imitation of reality and imaginative creation. She depicted conflicts and suffering in society but she always tried to solve whatever problems she described, through kindness, reason, and constant exhortation to renunciation and self-control (KL 743). She further strictly held to the principle that art had an aesthetic function and, although describing horrifying events as in the story "Er laßt die Hand küssen" and *Unsühnbar*, she tried to never offend her readers' aesthetic sensibilities (Alkemade 109).

Her occasional denial notwithstanding (Rieder, *Weisheit* 127), Ebner-Eschenbach's artistic intent was didactic. She firmly believed in educating her fellow men. In a letter she had planned to send, but never mailed, to Tolstoi she wrote: "If you wish to do something great and good, use your genius to educate your peasants" (Gladt, *Waldfräulein* 36). She believed she had received a divine mission to define the ethos of the community. Trying to create a reality susceptible to reason and to love, she detested works in which charity and compassion were ridiculed. She praised writers who extolled the virtues of selflessness and self-sacrifice (BF 73). Art, she claimed, in addition to its aesthetic purpose, also had an ethical function. The artist's vocation was to build a better world and to guide society in its endeavor to solve the problems of life.[4] In one of her letters to Helene Tafel she talked about the corruption of the Austrian press, pointing out how she personally coped with the shortcomings around her (RV I.N. 54416). According to her, an artist, endowed with a "divining rod," had the task of dreaming up a more desirable world (B II 108-109).[5] Art, in her view, had to reveal "the eternally beautiful" and "the eternally good" ("Spätgeborener" 669). In 1863, standing in front of a Mozart monument in Salzburg, she mused: "This is how an artist looks. 'I do not need you', he tells people, 'but I love you.' The most beautiful world I create for myself, but God's world is quite lovely, too" (TB I 11). And her artistically inclined baroness of *Bertram Vogelweid* confesses: ". . . if one has imagination, one dreams and slowly forms an ideal, a prototype of everything beautiful, everything perfect, and imagines oneself at its side" (Paetel, vol.8, 127).

Given Marie von Ebner's temperament, her basic conservatism and her strong belief in the values from which her artistic achievements grew, it is not astonishing that she had some reservations about the ideology of her younger colleagues. She rejected most of Gerhart Hauptmann's works—excepting *Biberpelz*, *Hanneles Himmelfahrt* and *Der arme Heinrich* (Alkemade 144)—and sarcastically noted in her diary about his play *Schluck und Jau*: "One feels like crying about the work and the author" (B II 251). Henrik Ibsen did not fare better. Although initially, after reading his first dramas, she had predicted for him a promising career, she later condemned his *Ghosts* as "ugly and mendacious" (qtd. in Alkemade 143). About *Die Wildente* she commented: "How can people like *Die Wildente*? This complicated obscenity! A Gordian knot: give me Alexander's sword! It may bubble in the head, but what is brought to paper must have been cleared" (qtd. in Vesely 222). And about the play's central figure she cuttingly observed: "I always think that a principal character whom I feel like massacring cannot be a hero; the protagonist whom I want to give a thrashing can never be a figure I am able to admire" (Vesely 222). Ibsen was the highly valued model and father figure of a group of avant garde writers known as "Das junge Wien" (Young Vienna), who regularly met at the Café Griensteidl to discuss their works.[6]

Toward Arthur Schnitzler, a member of this group, Marie von Ebner likewise had a strong aversion. She observed in her notebook after reading one of his works: "One of the ailments of our sick time: the penchant for an immersion in one's own person. To find oneself so terribly important, so mysterious, so strange and so precious that one tries to attract the interest of the entire world." And with her characteristic sarcasm she concluded: "The imaginary psychotic, entitled to a suite in the mental institution, in the end does not lack anything except someone who comes to lead him into it" (Rieder, *Weisheit* 124). Schnitzler's depiction of humankind's mental aberrations, psychological frustrations and scepticism toward traditional values, shocked and angered her. She could not relate to what she considered his pathological universe, a universe she thought marred by decadence and hedonistic egotism.

Saddened like him about the defeat of liberalism and the disintegration of society, she did not share his utter pessimism and his belief in the meaninglessness of all existence. His heroes were, in her view, unable to cope with life and to communicate emotionally and intellectually with their fellow men. They were diametrically opposed to her own protagonists. These fight for their values, show determination and assertiveness and try to rise above their selfish impulses. Her philosophy of life, shaped by nineteenth-century liberalism with its belief in rational man, whose progress in science and in moral self-control was to lead toward a perfect society, was too far removed from Schnitzler's fin-de-siècle mentality.[7]

Ebner-Eschenbach's ideals were stability, hard work and self-discipline. Any form of eccentricity and decadence was repulsive to her. She admired people who, having endured much, valiantly overcame their problems with strong determination and will-power and preserved a positive outlook on life. To Saar she once wrote: "All men who have suffered more than any tongue can utter, form a silent community whose members recognize each other at first glance, understand each other and loyally stay together" (Kindermann 13). Unable to mentally follow the younger writers, many of whom considered her own writing naive and escapist, on their flight into esotericism and melancholic resignation, she read and re-read the neo-classicist masters and her "ideal-realist" colleagues, whose art principles resembled her own. In her diary she commented about the despised modern literature: "To immerse oneself in the work of a modern author? It is as if one wanted to drown oneself in a wash-basin" (Vesely 220). Finally in "Aus einem zeitlosen Tagebuche" she observed: "A young literature is fiery and chaste. Our senile one has turned from passion to lust . . . from the beautiful to the grotesque. It searches for new art forms and finds new fads, and gruesome is the interaction between the books and the readers" (739).

As early as 1889 Marie von Ebner knew that some readers and critics regarded her writings as outdated, but she took it with a certain sense of humor.[8] Alluding to her beginning marginality as a writer, she once wrote to Dr. Breuer about an elderly lady who, instead of saying "Ite missa est" at the end of a mass, always uttered in French "Il y mit une anesse." When made aware of her error, the matron replied that she was too old to change her habits. Ebner continued: "I find myself in the very same situation vis-a-vis modern ingenuity. I hold with Feuchtersleben's sculptor who, 'while out there they announce new gods, continues his work, rounding off Diana's dress.' And if people want to degrade my Diana to an 'anesse,' I have to resign myself to it" (BC 21).

The older she became, the more she appreciated solitude. Gossiping visitors bored her. She found it even more trying than in her younger years to spend time with people who had no serious interests. As she once wrote in her diary: "There comes a visitor and says in a most regretful tone: 'You are all by yourself!' The poor man! If he only knew how well I was taken care of—till he came" (ZT 721). Many people must have found her reserved and aloof, causing her to write the following poem: "You consider me reticent, reluctant to trust?—if so, I am not aware of it . . . All my thinking, my hatreds and my loves are clearly written on my forehead. It is your own fault if you do not learn to read" (ZT 730).

But when she was really fond of people she longed to be open with them. One of the people to whom she felt particularly close was her brother Adolph, "the best of all brothers" ("Schattenleben" 464), her favorite since childhood. Courageous and adventurous like his sister, he often had joined in her childish pranks, cherishing her as his playmate during the summer holidays in Zdislawitz. Later he had often financially supported her and her husband at a time when they were not well off. Although Ebner-Eschenbach had found this rather humiliating, she always acknowledged that her brother had helped her because of love. One time she had entered in her diary: "Adolph, who brought me 18 guilders as a present (what shall I say?). The love that gives is more precious than the gift it bestows" (TB I 286). The same month another entry reads: "Besides, I had to accept 550 guilders from my much beloved brother Adolf, in spite of all resistance. His love makes me happy, his present makes me sad" (TB I 305). Once Adolph even bought a horse for his sister, because she enjoyed riding with him through the woods on his estate. When she was away to take the waters or to spend her summer holidays in St. Gilgen, he often sent chocolates to sweeten her life (TB I 122).

There had been a time when he, devastated by his first wife's death and worried that his sister would gain too much influence over his children, had treated her in a rather offensive way, hurting her deeply in the process (TB II 487). But gradually he began to appreciate that his sister was trying to help him care for his children. Once, when his daughter Stutzi was recovering from a severe illness and Marie helped nurse her back to health, Adolph gave the latter a little watch for her collection. Years afterwards she wrote the poem "Ein stiller Abend" about this event, praising her brother's "always alert love, which has changed many a phantom into golden reality for me" (Bucher 234). When renovating Zdislawitz, Adolph furnished a suite for her where she could write in peace and enjoy the beautiful view onto the park with the trees she loved so much. He also installed an Ebner-Eschenbach bust, created by the Viennese sculptor Robert Weigl for her seventieth birthday, in the park of Zdislawitz. Several times he accompanied her on her trips to Rome, bringing back Roman souvenirs for her to the country estate. Two mighty Roman lions, made of stone, placed at the entrance of the manor house, as well as a marble copy of the Vatican flora, gave ample evidence of his brotherly love.

In old age she often worried about Adolph, because he led a very hectic and strenuous life. For a while he was deeply depressed, thinking he suffered from an incurable heart disease. His sister, helplessly watching, wrote to Dr. Breuer, her confidant: "You should see and observe him often, that would be important. You, my best friend, can well imagine what worries he gives me, he, for whom I entertain more motherly than sisterly feelings" (BC 20). In June 1911 she had a strange vision in which she saw her brother in Zdislawitz, standing on a path in bright sunlight but seemingly shrouded in a veil. He looked at her and waved as if to bid farewell (B II 289).[9] On August 2 that same year he died, having undergone a goiter operation in Bern, from which he did not fully recover. His passing caused great heartbreak for Ebner-Eschenbach. She deeply mourned Adolph, finding it difficult to enter the crypt in Zdislawitz, where he was buried behind a marble slab. Still, during this time of suffering she did not rest idle. As so often before, writing helped her to conquer her pain, and she knew well by now that work was therapy.

In Italy she once helped a sculptor who had lost his son and was close to despair, by asking him to finish the bust of her he had earlier begun.[10] Working on this sculpture, which brought back memories of his late mother, made the sculptor forget his sorrow at least for a while. In the end he even received a prize for it from the government. Ebner-Eschenbach gratefully wrote: "What I felt, being able to experience this transition from paralyzing despair to the exercise of an artistic talent that strains all its powers, was pure joy, highest gratitude" (AW 693).

She herself found the longed-for distraction from her pain by writing the story "Herr Hofrat," published in 1915 in the collection *Stille Welt*.[11] Reading over the finished tale she commented: "Shall I wring my hands above my head because of the poverty of the little product which has come about? Well, in difficult days it deflected my thoughts, at least for a time, from the saddest experience, thus having fulfilled its purpose" (B II 291). What also helped her in this period of mourning was the fellowship of understanding people. All her adult life she had cultivated friendships, proud to count some of Vienna's most prominent artists among her closest friends. Yet one after the other died. The actress Luise Schönfeld-Neumann, perhaps her oldest confidante, passed away in 1905; Ferdinand von Saar committed suicide in 1906.

In an unpublished letter to Julius Rodenberg she once wrote: "The circle of loved ones grows ever smaller. With pain we see how one after another is stealthily moving out. May God preserve for us the dear loyal ones whom we still possess" (Alkemade 70). To the intimates yet left to her she clung with all her might, sharing their interests and deeply caring for each of their concerns.

CHAPTER 2:

"THERE IS NOTHING MORE HUMBLE AND MORE GRATEFUL THAN AN OLD ARTIST"

One relationship that warmed Ebner-Eschenbach's old age was her friendship with the Swabian writer Hermine Wilfried alias Hermine Villinger, who had made a name for herself with her Black Forest stories. Eighteen years Marie von Ebner's junior, Villinger had for many years admired her from distant Karlsruhe, before plucking up enough courage to send the writer her latest book *Kleinleben* as a token of appreciation for the story "Krambambuli". As Villinger recalls: "While I cried over 'Krambambuli' I decided: `You must thank that woman for all the many beautiful, good, and warm things she has given to you and to so many'" (Villinger 61). She finally put her thoughts into action, wrote to Ebner and soon received a very friendly, encouraging reply, which led her to comment: "It was the woman's whole and total generosity of heart which proffered to the beginner not only one hand but both hands in welcome" (Villinger 61).

Her first personal meeting with Marie von Ebner was an unforgettable experience: "I cannot describe her—only that much—a charm emanated from her to which my entire self succumbed" (Villinger 61). From the first moment she knew she could trust Ebner-Eschenbach and loved her like a mother. As she wrote later: "Throughout my life I had longed for motherliness. However, it is enough good fortune for me that heaven has given me Marie von Ebner-Eschenbach as a friend. Through her my soul has everything it needs" (Barck-Herzog 846).

After the first meeting in 1886 Villinger came every year to Vienna in order to spend some time with her friend. She accompanied her also to Zdislawitz and to her holiday resort St. Gilgen. She saw her surrounded by family and friends, marveling how she could write as much as she did while fulfilling her many social obligations. She was able to participate in some of the weekly tarok parties in Ida Fleischl's home and was also invited to the readings of Ebner's works. Sometimes she read from her own manuscripts, causing much laughter at the many humorous passages.

Marie von Ebner constantly encouraged the younger writer. She praised what she thought was well executed in her work, rejoiced with her about every literary success and recommended her stories to her acquaintances. After Villinger lost her mother, Ebner wrote to Natalie von Milde: "A while ago Betty Paoli mentioned a very pretty story by H. Villinger. That made me very happy. It would be a great misfortune for her if she were no longer able to write. Her mother died, as you know, and Hermine now depends more than fifty-fifty on the returns from her work" (RV I.N. 129.378). The more Hermine Villinger saw of her friend the more she missed her after returning to Karlsruhe. All the greater was her joy when she received a letter from her: "Yesterday your dear, dear letter arrived! Sunshine, sunshine" (Barck-Herzog 845).

Marie von Ebner decisively helped Villinger by recommending her work to Julius Rodenberg who, from 1896 onwards, published some of her pieces in *Die Deutsche Rundschau*. How sincerely the younger writer appreciated Ebner's support and friendship may be seen from the following enthusiastic lines: "You are the reward of my being. Your friendship is my crown. If I think of it, I am filled with joy" (Barck-Herzog 845). Through her Villinger also got to know Paul Heyse, whom she visited at the former's request in 1889 in Munich. For Ebner's seventieth birthday the younger writer dedicated to her a volume of her latest stories in gratitude for everything she was and had done for her. According to Villinger's statements Ebner was the center of her existence. When having problems she thought of her motherly friend, trying to imagine how she coped with life. Once she remarked to Ebner: "I cannot desist from the desire to become mind from your mind and soul from your soul. But I shall never reach my goal" (Barck-Herzog 849).

Villinger not only emulated Ebner-Eschenbach as a human being but also strove to imitate her art. When critics remarked on the resemblance between her own 1911 story "Lebensbuch" and Ebner's novella "Ein kleiner Roman," Villinger did not mind but was proud of her achievement (Alkemade 141). Yet, as much as the two women appreciated and liked each other, there was one topic on which they could never agree: the phenomenon of the creative impulse: "That she considered her talent, her urge to create as a severe pain" Villinger recalls," that was an opinion I could not share, and in spite of her head shaking I insisted: 'A talent is much more of a blessing than a curse'" (Villinger 64).

For Ebner-Eschenbach writing had always been a compulsive need. Early on she had called her creative urge a "demon" that possessed her, a power to whose dictates and relentless demands she had to give in.[12] Writing was a battle for her; to Dr. Breuer she once vividly described it in the following way: "Only when the shadows assume bodies and sit down, crying on the threshold, so that I cannot enter or leave without hearing their life-greedy noise, without seeing their life-greedy eyes, only then I engage them. It is a battle and I have never fought it to the end without coming away with a sense of defeat" (BC 43). A perfectionist, she wrote and rewrote each sentence several times, forever worrying how readers and critics would respond.[13]

She knew that her marriage had suffered because of her need to write, she also was aware that her nerves were "ruined" on account of her intense and strenuous literary occupation. Often she had wished to free herself of this "damned literature" (BC 49), especially when pressured by publishers to quickly finish or correct her works. Unlike Villinger, she had had to suffer humiliations from family and peers. In her younger years societal prejudice against writing women had been much stronger than at the time when Villinger started her career. Marie von Ebner knew much better of a woman writer's isolation, she was more aware of the price she had to pay for admission into the literary sphere. She also was familiar with the psychological problems a woman writer faced when creating a work (Mumbauer 27).

Because of her own sad experiences in the literary world, Ebner-Eschenbach never encouraged other women to enter the field. Still, once she recognized artistic ability in a woman, she gave her full support. Although by her own account rather timid and reluctant to approach an author whose work had impressed her, in 1903 she decided to contact a young writer in order to show her gratitude. The budding talent that had drawn her out of her usual reserve was Enrica von Handel-Mazzetti who, in due course, became like a daughter to her. While Marie Ebner's love for her "Herminele" was always mixed with a certain pity and amusement, her feelings for Handel-Mazzetti bordered on adulation. Soon after their first meeting she offered her new friend the informal "Du," claiming that both their souls were "on the Du-Fuß" (Mumbauer 43).[14]

Enrica von Handel-Mazzetti was born in Vienna in 1871 as the descendant of a Swabian family that had moved to Austria in the early nineteenth century (Siebertz 34). She received her first education at home, later entering a convent school in St. Pölten. She remained imbued with the Catholic faith, which shaped her more mature work above all. Her writing career began with the publication of a social novel called *Brüderlein und Schwesterlein*. Her historic work *Meinrad*

Helmpergers denkwürdiges Jahr made her widely acclaimed in Austria. Marie von Ebner-Eschenbach had read the novel with great fascination. A few years later, when a very positive review of it appeared, she sent the younger writer her novel *Agave* and an invitation to visit her. Handel-Mazzetti was given a warm reception: "How did I long to know you, my child. You are so young, I am so old, but I welcome you with joy as my colleague and my sister" (Mumbauer 26).

From their very first meeting the two friends felt extremely close. They belonged to the same social stratum, had had a similar upbringing and held the same values. They exchanged thoughts on literature and considered it a blessing to be able to talk openly about their professional projects and goals. Both writers had had a common friend whom they greatly admired: Dr. Robert Zimmermann, a professor of philosophy and ethics, and since 1886 rector of the University of Vienna. He and his wife Henriette had been Marie Ebner's staunchest supporters at a time when she still had to fight for recognition and her husband tried to prevent her from writing. In her diaries of the sixties she had mentioned Dr. Zimmermann as one of her best friends. He had believed in her talent as a dramatist, had praised her play *Das Geständnis* and had even written an essay about it (TB I 217-218). Enrica likewise had a great admiration for him as a scholar and teacher, since he had introduced her to important literary works. His widow was one of her closest confidantes.

Both Marie von Ebner and Enrica von Handel-Mazzetti were influenced by Zimmermann's aesthetics, based on neo-classical ideals. They were also great admirers of Schiller, the idol of their youth. As a youngster Marie von Ebner had declaimed the master's dramas among the spruce trees in the park of Zdislawitz and vowed to follow in his footsteps; Handel-Mazzetti had emphatically recited Schiller's "Der Taucher" in front of her fellow students. "Does it have to be so loud?" asked the teacher, shocked about her vehemence, whereupon she was told: "Yes it has to be like that." Then, unperturbed and in the same tone of voice, Enrica energetically continued to deliver the verses of her adored poet (Siebertz 37).

Besides their lasting interest in history, both writers possessed a gift for drawing their characters with penetrating psychological insight. In 1904 Ebner-Eschenbach attended a dress rehearsal of Enrica's play *Ich kauf mir ein Mohrenkind* ("I am going to buy myself a little black child"), in which Enrica herself participated, playing the role of the superior of a convent. After the performance Marie von Ebner hugged her protégée and praised her for her accomplishment: "This little piece is charming," she said, "who would have thought that Meinrada (a nickname Ebner-Eschenbach gave Enrica after the protagonist of her first major novel) can relate to the little ones in such a way! That she can do it is for me a new proof of her poetic mission" (Mumbauer 30-31). In their love for "the little ones," both friends further resembled each other very closely. Handel-Mazzetti, always claiming to have been influenced by Ebner-Eschenbach in her writing, may indeed have learned from her older friend to look deeply into children's souls. Time and again critics had praised Marie von Ebner as a master of child psychology and a champion of the child.[15]

In 1903 Dr. Leo Langer wrote the essay "Marie Ebner von Eschenbach und die Kinderseele" (Marie Ebner von Eschenbach and the soul of a child) in which he pointed out how deeply she understood children, sympathizing especially with those who, like herself, had lost their mother at an early age (125). Gabriele Reuter in her 1904 monograph likewise praised the writer's concern for children (74). At a time when society was just beginning to realize that young people, far from being immature adults, had their own intricate psyches, Ebner-Eschenbach was among the first Austrian writers to focus on their emotional and psychological problems and to insightfully describe their plight. In her poem "Ein stiller Abend" she explains her empathy for children as a consequence of her own childhood problems and of her long memory: "And because I am slow at forgetting, the old lady still is familiar with the child's pain" (Bucher 231). She had always loved children. In later years she asked her friend and physician, Dr. Josef Breuer, to collect stories about and sayings by his grandchildren, since she enjoyed them so much (BC 109). When in Rome in 1904, she made it a point to go to Aracoeli at Christmas in order to hear the customary children's sermons.

The longer Handel-Mazzetti knew her, the more she was struck by Marie Ebner's unusual modesty, an attitude she found all the more surprising, since she expected an aristocrat and a famous writer to show a good measure of arrogance and self-assurance (Mumbauer 33). Marie von Ebner had been brought up to be modest. According to the aristocratic code of behavior it was considered a sign of good breeding, especially for a girl, to be self-effacing, humble, and obedient. Yet values changed, so that the succeeding generation did not consider modesty such an asset any more, causing her, as a mature woman, to feel quite indignant about the change (TB I 137). She herself had always placed great importance on manners and etiquette. Still, what many of her acquaintances praised as her remarkable unassumingness was partly scepticism and fear of being criticized.

Highly sensitive and easily offended by negative reviews of her work, Marie von Ebner tended to run down her accomplishments before critics could even find fault with them. Thus, for instance, since she knew about the superficiality of some of her readers (Schmidt 178), she tried to prevent adverse remarks about *Meine Kinderjahre* by stating in her preface that she actually had lost her belief in her autobiographical sketches and was reluctant to send them into the world. Only when her publisher, Julius Rodenberg, protested, telling her she was too modest, did she conceive another conclusion for her introductory remarks. To Rodenberg she wrote: "As you wish!—I shall blow myself up somewhat at the end of the preface" (Schmidt 177). Ebner's so-called modesty therefore was accordingly a way of preventing criticism and of protecting herself from hurt.[16] Like many of her literary figures she adhered to the motto "humility is invulnerability" ("Beichte" 484) as a way of coping with life.[17] She herself gave another, likewise valid, reason for her submissive attitude in regard to her writing: "The basis of my so-called modesty is pride. I never compare my achievements with those of my inferiors but always with those of the great" (Rieder, *Weisheit* 121).

Handel-Mazzetti knew and understood this attitude well. She likewise practiced modesty by always acknowledging her indebtedness to her friend as her mentor and role model. Reading the latter's work had inspired her with themes, motifs, and values she later adopted for her own writing.[18] Everything she conceived she first sent to Ebner for her professional opinion, and the latter always welcomed each new accomplishment with joy. But she refused to be called Handel-Mazzetti's teacher. "You my pupil? If I could just imagine that! I cannot. Under my hand things do not come to life as much as under yours" (Mumbauer 49). And another time she commented: "Admirable! We live in the very time you evoke with ingenuous strength, we breathe the same air as your literary figures. O child, don't say that you can learn anything from me, it makes your old friend and admirer feel ashamed" (Mumbauer 52).

Through her friendship with Handel-Mazzetti, Marie Ebner, in her advanced age, was still able to participate in the literary debates of the time. The younger woman also filled an emotional void in her life. Having lost many relatives and most of her confidants from her own generation, Ebner appreciated this friendship as an outlet for the needs of her affectionate heart. As her circle of friends dwindled, she clung to Enrica with an almost childlike attachment, eagerly awaiting each of her visits: "I have been expecting you since the ninth every day, every hour, and hardly dared to leave the room " (Mumbauer 55).

In 1905 Handel-Mazzetti moved from Vienna to Steyr. She seldom visited her friend during the next eleven years. When she had to endure hostility from critics, among them Catholic clergy, who blamed her for describing Protestantism in too positive a way, Marie Ebner always stood by her young friend and reassured her as best she could. In 1911, during the conflict with Karl Schönherr, who accused Handel-Mazzetti of writing hysterical novels as only a woman could create them (Siebertz 465),[19] Ebner may have felt strongly reminded of her own struggles with male critics who, like Schönherr, had shown a derogatory attitude towards her as a woman. All her literary life she had feared critics because she had experienced their viciousness and lack of understanding. Even as a writer of note she worried after each publication about the verdict of those who presumed to have a right to pass judgment on her work. How little she appreciated most critics is revealed by the following note: "Today's critics, invited to pass judgment on a book, always ask first: 'Who has written it?' They are like people who have to be told who built the house in which they live, because otherwise they would not know whether it is a shack or a palace" (Rieder, *Weisheit* 125). She further wrote: "I have accepted the rudeness of well-meaning critics as a mother endures the roughness of a doctor when she has the expectation that 'it helps my child' " (Rieder, *Weisheit* 117). She knew she depended on her reviewers, having managed even to establish a cordial relationship with some of them. Nobody understood better than she what Handel-Mazzetti had to go through, and it was her friendship that gave the younger writer the greatest moral support. Above all else Handel-Mazzetti always remembered Marie von Ebner-Eschenbach's eyes: "They were gray, somewhat opalescent, and their expression was perfect goodness, paired with feminine charm and intelligence, and a grain of mischief" (Mumbauer 36).

Among the younger writers Marie von Ebner-Eschenbach also had a male fan, Felix Braun, who had approached her as a thirteen-year-old high-school student by sending her a card and a poem in which he asked her for an autograph. She was in Rome at that time and replied: "Do you know what I wish? That you, dear student Felix Braun, when you have matured to manhood, will not smile about the enthusiasm you once had as a boy for the writer Marie Ebner, but that you will fondly remember it" (Braun 231). Felix Braun later became widely known for his poetry, his novels, and novellas, and for his comedy *Till Eulenspiegels Kaisertum*. His dramas, especially *Kaiser Karl der Fünfte*, were largely influenced by Grillparzer, whom Braun purposely imitated (Nadler 514-515). In 1910 Braun became editor of the *Berliner Nationalzeitung*. As one of his first assignments he wrote a long essay about Ebner-Eschenbach's *Genrebilder*, which had just then been published. Thinking about his youthful eagerness to contact the writer, Braun later mused that Marie Ebner may have accepted his enthusiastic overtures "with the same smile that appears in so many of her works" (Braun 232). In the 1960s Braun, himself by then in his seventies and a few years older than Ebner-Eschenbach had been when he approached her for the autograph, wrote the "Nachwort" for the new Nymphenburg edition and was finally able to pay his respects to the writer, whose admirer he was as a young boy.

Marie Ebner was choosy by nature and very selective about the people with whom she wanted to socialize. Once she had taken someone into her confidence, though, she remained loyal all her life. One of her closest friends in old age was her physician Dr. Joseph Breuer. Ebner had been introduced to him in the 1870s by Ida Fleischl and her sons, who knew him as a colleague in the medical faculty at the University of Vienna. He soon became Marie Ebner's confidant. He met her relatives and friends, was invited to Zdislawitz and was a welcome guest in St. Gilgen, where she spent her summers in the 1880s and 90s (Kindermann 105). Since 1889 he also became Ebner-Eschenbach's regular correspondent and often acted as advisor, not only in medical matters, but also in questions concerning literature and art. Ebner had the fullest confidence in him as a physician and as a human being of great integrity. In one of her diary entries she mentioned that Dr. Breuer, twelve years her junior, was to her "like a loyal son" (B II 299), and in a rhymed dedicatory verse she wrote: "To Dr. Breuer, the friend who is dear to me, the doctor to whom I entrust the body, the mind, the soul" (*BC* 23).

Her letters to him are replete with reports about her ailments and with requests for medication. However, she also consulted him about medical information relating to her work. Thus she inquired whether what she had written in *Unsühnbar* in connection with Wolfi's death was medically plausible: "I feel embarrassed to face you and often turn crimson. How could I let this Wolfi die without asking you whether it is right. I implore you, please do me the favor and correct it for the book edition, which for me is the far more important one" (BC 20). Breuer gladly gave advice, which was then incorporated into the next edition. When he approved of her work, Marie Ebner felt as if a ray of sunshine had touched her heart: "Where does it come from? From the consciousness that you have given me good marks for my latest work" (BC 25). The physician always read her work with great interest and sympathy and thought about suggestions for improvement. After reading the novel *Glaubenslos?* he wrote to Marie Ebner: "These days, going around in my car, I have thought about a new fate for the priest in *Glaubenslos?*. He is certainly not at the end of his inner development. Something is going to happen to him again" (BC 44). Whereupon she responded by suggesting that each of them devise a sequel to the story and then, at their next meeting, exchange their ideas.

How thoroughly Breuer studied Ebner-Eschenbach's work is also seen from his comments on her parable "Menschenrassen," which he urged her to publish in the *Neue Freie Presse*. Somewhat embarrassed about his suggested changes to her work he wrote: "Truly, I feel stupid in my schoolteacher role vis-a-vis you; stupid and somewhat insolent. Yet friendship and dedication demand such sacrifice, too" (BC 54). But she was always grateful for his advice and did not publish anything for which she had not received his consent. Every line the two friends wrote to each other reflects their mutual regard and their ability to understand and empathize with each other's concerns. Often Ebner-Eschenbach confided to Breuer how worried she was about her friends and relatives. He always responded with a few words of comfort. Breuer belonged to that sort of family doctor who had a great concern for his patients' mental as well as physical well-being and who as a family doctor was at the same time "friend, advisor, and in many cases also a guide through the crises of life" (BC 12).

Breuer always encouraged her to publish and eagerly tried to show how much he believed in her literary talent. He once told her about a dream he had had in which her brother Adolph, during a theater performance, had turned to him, saying: "That is wholly my sister. In every word there is a grain of wheat; blessed, fruitful seed of thoughts" (BC 30). When Breuer woke up he felt that for once he had not dreamed nonsense "but a true and kind word" (BC 31). Later, when he sensed that his friend, by now in her eighties, felt frustrated about not being able to write as much as she used to, he tried to comfort her with the following suggestion: "When your present writing does not succeed, have all your printed works put on a desk; look at them and think to how many people you have given joy, consolation, hope, confidence" (BC 133).

Dr. Breuer professionally and personally cared about her physical well-being. He was concerned about the medication she should take and gave advice as to which spas in Austria and Germany she was to visit. Even his family took part in discussions about the best health resorts for her. Sometimes only Marie Ebner's relatives and Dr. Breuer knew when she was about to return home from her country estate, so that she would be spared annoying visitors. He understood his friend's aversion to boring social callers who had nothing to offer but gossip, depriving her of time and energy. He understood her well when she confided how much she always dreaded her return to Vienna: "I shudder when thinking of the feeling of insecurity in which I always find myself there. I can hardly read a book which interests me without thinking: before you turn the next page you will again be interrupted" (BC 108).

Although eager to contact Ebner and to know how she was doing, in later years he often refrained from writing, in order not to burden her. He knew that she would reply to every note he sent, but since she was often plagued by severe headaches he wanted to spare her the trouble of replying to him. He therefore asked that Angela, Marie Ebner's secretary, report to him every two weeks about his friend's condition. Still, Ebner-Eschenbach needed the contact with Dr. Breuer. She personally wrote to him as much as possible and invited him whenever she was in Vienna. During those visits the two friends discussed books they had both read and talked about political events in which they were interested. Marie Ebner was generally more pessimistic about Austria's fate than Joseph Breuer and clearly saw the rising nationalism as a sign of her country's pending demise. Both the writer and the doctor were admirers of Gustav Fechner, whose philosophy especially Breuer welcomed as the religion of the future.

Although of different backgrounds, Breuer and Ebner had similar tastes, and in most things they had the same opinion. However, about their notion of an artist they could never agree. The doctor did not believe that a creative person had to be of a good character in order to produce a masterpiece. Marie Ebner, on the other hand, never wavered from the firm conviction that only a perfect human being could create a flawless work of art (Alkemade 118). Imbued with Plato's and Schiller's concept of the artist as having a divine mission, she maintained that the creative genius had to be an exemplary personality in order to fulfill his artistic goal.

In 1909 Ebner published a collection of parables entitled *Altweibersommer,* which Dr. Breuer particularly liked and praised for its "smiling wisdom" (BC 104). Happy about this compliment, his friend replied: "Look, there is nothing more humble and more grateful than an old artist . . . If, instead of a rejection, she receives a warm welcome, she is extremely happy" (BC 105). In 1914 she sent her friend a plaster cast of her hand, a gift he valued as a token of a friendship which he considered one of the most beautiful things in his life (BC 119).

CHAPTER 3:

"BUT THE STRUGGLE IS NOT PLEASANT"

The greatest joy in Marie von Ebner-Eschenbach's old age were her nieces and nephews and their children, to whom she was greatly attached, and who gratefully returned her affection. The writer Marie Bunsen, having visited Marie Ebner in 1894 for an interview, saw her again as an octogenarian and observed: "She lived and aged quietly, but not lonely; she had a motherly love for growing youth, she who was childless meant much to them" (Bunsen, "Persönliche Eindrücke" 28). Marie Ebner's favorite niece was Maria Gisela, called Stutzi, the oldest daugther of Adolph and his first wife Sophie. After the latter's premature death, Ebner-Eschenbach became the substitute mother for her three children, lovingly watching over their physical and mental growth. With Stutzi, having been the first niece to live close to her—the children of Friederike and Julie were far away—"Tante Marie" had always had a special relationship. Like her, Stutzi loved nature and adored animals, like her, she was a "wild bumblebee" (Paetel 1901, I,177), racing through the courtyard with her younger brothers, and like her, she could be rather blunt and outspoken. By losing her biological mother at an early age Stutzi had a fate similar to that of her aunt and therefore probably also held a special place in the latter's compassionate heart. Marie Ebner particularly enjoyed Stutzi's sincerity, her loyalty and noble-mindedness, qualities the latter's mother, Sophie, had possessed in such rich measure (TB II 534). When married to Count Philip Kinsky, the son of Marie Ebner's sister Friederike and Count August Kinsky, Stutzi moved to the estate of Löschna and regularly invited her aunt during the summer. In her poem "Liebeserklärung" Ebner immortalized her love for Stutzi and her family, the circle in which she searched for and found her "purest happiness" (Paetel I, 1901, 178).

Stutzi's younger brothers, Viktor and Eugen, also were very dear to Tante Marie. In her diaries of the 1870s Ebner-Eschenbach regularly remarked how much she loved the three motherless children and how much she enjoyed visiting them every day. On December 16, 1878 she observed: "The children were well-behaved all day, and every day is beautiful which I can devote to them; more beautiful than the most beautiful day on which I am able to work" (TB II 599). Eugen soon became her problem child when, at the age of eight, a heart disease was diagnosed. He died in 1885. Four years later Ebner wrote her essay "Armer Junge" about him in the journal *Die Dioskuren*. She praised him for his steadfastness, his independence and strength of soul. She lamented the fact that he had to die so young without having been able to fulfill his dearest wish, namely, to become a hunter and a gentleman farmer (6). Later she immortalized him in the novel "Die arme Kleine" in the figure of young Franz who, like Eugen, has a heart disease and longs to dedicate his life to farming (685-686).

Viktor, in his childhood a rather temperamental and vehement boy who often made life difficult for his tutors, became Aunt Marie's "Providence disguised as a nephew" (BC 141), a great support in her old age. He visited her during her stay in Rome, accompanied her with her niece Marianne to Venice in 1907 and later kept her company during her summer visits in Zdislawitz. To Dr. Breuer she once remarked about him: "To be alone with my nephew Victor is heaven, because he carries you on his hands without letting you know it. In the whole wide world you will hardly find such kindness and selflessness" (BC 123).

A particularly intimate relationship existed between Ebner and her nephew Franz, son of her brother Adolph and his second wife, Countess Gisela von Palffy-Erdödy. Born on September 13 like his aunt Marie, Franz soon became the sunshine of her life. In her essay "Mein Neffe," published in 1885 in *Die Dioskuren*, she described him as an infant whose little heart belonged to his aunt. "When she enters the room, his big blue eyes begin to shine, his rosy mouth, as yet sparsely filled with teeth, opens with a laugh, his fat little arms spread, the whole little creature is moving toward the one who comes" (84). More than describing her nephew, Marie Ebner characterized herself in this essay as the devoted aunt who hungered for the little boy's love, wanting to be his favorite at all cost. She, who had no children of her own, clung to her nieces and nephews and vied for their affection. In 1889 she wrote to Natalie von Milde about Franz, whom she at first called "Bubi" and later "Feri": "Never was there a more tender aunt and never a more lovable nephew. His mother told him lately: 'It seems to me that you like Aunt Marie better than me.' He thought for a while and then replied very softly: 'Almost' . . . I am prouder of this love than of my best book" (RV I.N.129272).

Franz always remained special to her. As he described himself in his 1917 essay in *Die Neue Freie Presse*, he was a very inquisitive child, eager to find out what "Tante Marie" did when she was in her room in Zdislawitz and when people said she was not supposed to be disturbed. One day he could not contain his curiosity any longer and undertook a drastic effort to catch his aunt unaware by quickly and unexpectedly opening the door without knocking. When he saw Tante Marie sit at her desk he asked, full of disappointment: "When does she do something?" She smiled understandingly and drew him a picture with people and animals in the country. Next to this picture she wrote a poem about a little boy who was freed from his curiosity by a good fairy (16). Tante Marie also helped Franz to overcome his fear of ghosts and often delighted him by telling him fairy tales. She cured him as a nine-year-old from an arrogance he had developed toward those around him. Once, when he had called the cook "a mean person," his family was particularly upset and punished him. His aunt later used that incident to write the story "Hirzepinzchen," in which a little boy, arrogantly taking the love of his family for granted, even calling a fairy a "mean person," realized all of a sudden that his life depended on the affection of others. Hearing this story, Franz recognized that his aunt was stronger than he and he began to change his ways ("Erinnerungen 16). Marie Ebner, deeply moved, embraced her little nephew and later referred to him in her story "Fräulein Susannes Weihnachtsabend," where a young boy brightens the Christmas celebration of an old spinster.

In the following years an even closer bond developed between Marie Ebner and her nephew because of his literary interests and dramatic talent. At age seven, stimulated by a visit to Betty Paoli, Franz began to write poetry and secretly considered himself his aunt's colleague ("Briefwechsel" 251). During his summer holidays he often read stories to her from his children's books and from the adventures described by Karl May. She in turn acquainted Franz with poetry by Paul Heyse to whom she once wrote: "It would have made you happy, dearest friend, to see the impression which your poem made on the child. `Oh, that is magnificent' he said again and again; he had a crimson face, his deep-set eyes were bathed in tears" (HC 366). Eventually the young Heyse-fan bought the master's *Musenalmanach* with his pocket money and ever since shared his aunt's enthusiasm for the writer.

In St. Gilgen, where Franz visited her during the summer, he once aroused the envy of a lady who, considering herself a great poet, clamored for Marie von Ebner-Eschenbach's recognition. This lady was just visiting when Franz came to pick up his aunt for a walk along the lake. But, instead of leaving when the boy appeared, the visitor stayed on, ignoring him and her hostess' subtle hints that she wanted to be alone with her nephew. Finally, when Marie Ebner mentioned that Franz also was a poet, the lady started to pay close and somewhat annoyed attention to him ("Briefwechsel" 253). That same evening Marie Ebner asked her nephew to read from his first unfinished drama, praising him with tears in her eyes when he finished reading. In Franz she saw her own literary ambitions epitomized. She often told him to strive for greatness and originality in art and to apply the highest standards for himself. She jokingly reminded him of the St. Gilgen poet, Friederike Kempner,[20] who was not satisfied with mediocrity but produced totally bad art: "Because she is an individuality, because she is something whole, complete, and because she creates poems no one else could do so enjoyably badly. She certainly should not be our model, but we must admit that what she does she does thoroughly badly, and that is better in art than half good" (RV I.N. 153.170).

As Ebner also said in her poem "Der Halbpoet" (Paetel I, 1901, 169), mediocrity in art was the worst sin, in her eyes. She firmly held to her old belief that a great work of art could be created only by a mature human being of immaculate character. Gradually Franz understood his aunt's views and followed her advice. Finally, in 1916, his one-act play "Das Bild des Ramses" was performed at the Burgtheater in Vienna, an event which filled him and Tante Marie with great pride. In her nephew she saw the dream of her youth fulfilled, the dream of having her work performed at Vienna's most prominent theater.

At that time Marie Ebner was, however, like most of her contemporaries, highly preoccupied with the events of the World War. After the Austrian Archduke Francis Ferdinand and his wife had been assassinated by a Serbian nationalist at Sarajevo in 1914, Austria declared war on Serbia and, in due course, Europe's major powers were involved in one of the most brutal conflicts in history. Long before the war had begun, Ebner-Eschenbach had had forebodings of it, fearing that a power struggle among the Western countries was imminent. Like many Austrians she saw the assassination of Alexander of Serbia and his wife Queen Draga, in 1903, as the prelude to World War I (Mumbauer 28-29). She also considered the Balkan War of 1912 an immense threat to world peace. In her diary she wrote: "The now prevailing barbarization and stultification are necessary. People have to be prepared for the world war which is near at hand. They are now sharpening their teeth for the mutual devouring" (Rieder, *Weisheit* 36).

Marie Ebner had always been a pessimist. Although her readers and many of her critics praised her optimistic outlook on life, in her personal sphere she tended to see things in the gloomiest colors.[21] In her diary of 1864 she had written "I do not expect anything good, but if the worst happens, it will hit me nevertheless as a terrible surprise" (TB I 28). And another time she mused about human existence: "Poor life! Two duties: to be born and to die. Happy the one who can accomplish both in quick succession" (Vesely 217). Just as she had repeatedly predicted an early end to her career as a novelist,[22] she also had had some apprehensions about her country's fate. In 1887 she had shocked Louise von François with a letter "full of the most cruel war premonitions" (FMC 205), in which she had expressed the fear that Bismarck would conquer Austria and give Galicia and Moravia to Russia (ibid.). Even though this nightmarish prophecy did not come true, Marie Ebner always feared the worst and never trusted politicians. Still, after the assassination of Archduke Ferdinand, a man she detested because of his alleged arrogance, his authoritarianism, and his hatred of the Jews, she had hoped that the political situation would improve. Once the war had been declared she wrote to Dr. Breuer: "I had been convinced for a long time that this war was bound to come. One does not amass mountains of tinder for decades and then slink around it with cowardly knavery, reassuring everyone `I will not ignite it.' But that I experience it—that really surprises me!" (BC 156). Henceforth she was in constant worry about her relatives who, as soldiers or as assistants in hospitals, were all involved in the war effort, being at times even exposed to danger. Her brother Heinrich had been captured by the Italians on his estate Medea in Cormons, and for quite a while the family had no news from him. Finally, Marie Ebner learned that he was physically unharmed but held in a prison in Cremona (BC 163).

During this time of stress and uncertainty about his fate she suffered the most severe headaches which Dr. Breuer vainly tried to ease. Being in regular contact with her through correspondence, he finally admonished her not to reply to his letters anymore but have her secretary regularly send him a note about her state of health (BC 164). As soon as she stopped worrying about Heinrich, Ebner learned that her grandnephew Fritz Kinsky, Stutzi's son, had shot his hand while loading a Browning. Having bravely fought in Galicia, he now felt frustrated because he could not join his regiment. He was transferred to Tyrol far from his wife who had just given birth to a son.

News about her brother Viktor, who had been spending some time in Russia when the war began, further upset Marie Ebner. Her relationship with him had had its ups and downs, because of his alleged bluntness, his hard-headedness and his lack of understanding for her complaints about her health. He had always thought her too self-centerd and fastidious to really warm up to her. But all her life she nurtured for him "a love mixed with pain" (TB II 493). After receiving a telegram from Viktor in which he had informed her that he was well, Ebner again was plunged into despair when reading a few days later in the newspapers that he had had to interrupt his journey home "because he was not able to stand the strain" (BC 156). Viktor Dubsky eventually safely returned to Austria.

Even without immediate concerns for her relatives, Ebner-Eschenbach felt the burden of the war weigh heavily on her shoulders. Almost daily, trains brought severely wounded soldiers into the Austrian capital. The Prater, formerly a place of enjoyment, was converted into a training ground for the army. Theaters and music halls operated almost on a peacetime schedule, yet people all around were demoralized. There were food shortages; fuel and everyday necessities became scarce, a fact which likewise plunged the Austrian population into tired resignation and deep pessimism. The municipal government of Vienna conducted drives to collect clothes and medical supplies and asked for donations of metal, desperately needed by the army. Fundraising campaigns for war relief were held, and people were asked to perform many tasks connected with the war effort. Due to the unrestricted censorship, newspapers had to leave blank spaces where otherwise they would have reported about the war. This further angered and frustrated the population (May 144).

Dr. Breuer therefore collected articles for Ebner-Eschenbach from the socialist *Arbeiterzeitung,* which still dared to speak out against the government. That way she could inform herself about the state of affairs and the whereabouts of her relatives at the front. She was particularly upset to learn that even her private mail to Switzerland was censored. She corresponded regularly with Dr. Otto von Fleischl, Ida's son, who had moved from Rome to Switzerland. He and his wife Mina—Marie Ebner called the couple the "Minottos"—wrote to her every three or four days but never received the postcards sent from Zdislawitz (BC 163).

Writing to her friends was a great consolation at a time when the circle of her relatives drastically decreased. Friederike, with whom all her life she had had a warm and loving relationship, had died in 1895 after many years of suffering from a heart problem. In 1914 Ebner had lost her younger sister Julie, Duchess von Waldburg-Wurzach, and in 1915 her brother Viktor died. The writer had thus survived all her brothers and sisters except Heinrich, her youngest brother, and felt increasingly lonely. She fervently prayed for peace. To Enrica von Handel-Mazzetti, who worked as a nurse in a hospital in Linz, she wrote in 1915: "Do you not also have the feeling sometimes as if you perceived the soft sound of the wings of a dove of peace? I have this impression. This and the many great and magnificent things we experience in these horrible days sustain me" (Mumbauer 82).

She was referring to the people who worked with great dedication to help the wounded, trying to alleviate the misery in the war-torn country. Somehow she also hoped that the war would terminate the rivalry and hostility between Czechs and Germans. In her diary she noted: "In Prague they sing the national anthem in both languages. 'Common help in common need has established realms and states' (Grillparzer). If in this war the animosity between Germans and Czechs would be terminated, it would have brought forth a magnificent fruit" (Vesely 230). After the battle at Gorlice, where Germans, Austrians, and Hungarians had successfully fought as one, people in Austria hoped that the war would soon be over (Hantsch 522).

Ebner-Eschenbach was constantly preoccupied with the suffering, frequently entering her thoughts in her diary. She wrote: "We have now certainly awakened from our dream of the progress of civilization" (Rieder, *Weisheit* 113). The war had destroyed many hopes, many illusions, and many values. She took the situation very much to heart, and her health deteriorated. Sorrow and worries about loved ones taxed her energy.

But she still felt the urge to create. She would have been happy to accustom herself to idleness, but her "demon" was stronger; she had to write. A statement in "Aus einem zeitlosen Tagebuch" throws light on how she felt when the demon drove her: "To dig into one's work, to set one's hope on it, to despair of it, to struggle on to exhaustion, to self-annihilation—it is torture but very akin to bliss" (714). In 1915 she published her collection *Stille Welt.* She knew well that by now she was only a marginal writer and did not belong to the mainstream of Austrian literature any more. Authors like Gustav Meyrink, Richard Schaukal, Anton Wildgans and Franz Werfel dominated the literary scene, next to the members of "Das junge Wien," among whom Hugo von Hofmannsthal was prominent. But she still had much to say, and her publisher also urged her to keep writing. In 1909 Paetel printed 3,000 copies of "Altweibersommer" (BC 103). *Meine Kinderjahre* and the edition of collected works continued to sell well. In 1916 she completed "Meine Erinnerungen an Grillparzer," which she wanted to publish as a tribute to her late friend and literary mentor, for whom even in old age she still had the greatest admiration. She used material from her diary entries of the 1860s and 70s, written at the time when she had visited the master quite regularly. She also went to the city hall, where Grillparzer's room had been erected in memory of him, to study the environment again in which he had spent his final years. Nostalgically she looked at his desk and at the old chair in which he had died, and reminisced about the blissful hours she had been able to spend with him (B II 294-295).

Although Ebner-Eschenbach felt like an "ass" and thought she had "only dust in her head" (B II 294), she proved to be a skilled biographer, able to bring Franz Grillparzer to life by characterizing him with humor and empathy. She aptly portrayed him with his legendary gruffness, his pessimism and his proclivity for self-pity. Quite purposely, she did not write a eulogy but described her subject as she remembered him with his quirks and foibles, with his humanity. With a few strokes of the pen she delineated the poet's relationship with Kathi Fröhlich, the woman he loved but never married, pointing out his stubbornness, but also his goodness and generosity. At eighty-four she still had as much enthusiasm for her "beloved Grillparzer" as in younger years. She wished to pay tribute to the man who had been one of the first to recognize her literary talent, encouraging her to follow her call. But she also felt a need to help rehabilitate Kathi Fröhlich, often maligned and misunderstood, who, out of love for Grillparzer, had sacrificed her own career and had devotedly cared for him until his final hours (EG 915).

In 1916 Ebner-Eschenbach published "Aus einem zeitlosen Tagebuch," a collection of essays, anecdotes, reflections, poems, diary entries and aphorisms, which reveal her invincible humor, her sarcasm, her love of irony and wit, and her deep wisdom. The work shows her love of nature, her experience with the virtues and vices of her fellow men and expresses her lifelong desire for peace and quiet. In Rome she had found this peace in the cemetery for foreigners, where her friends Malvida von Meysenbug and Theo Schücking were buried; in Zdislawitz she always enjoyed the garden with its "most beautiful solitude, living, blissful, breathing quiet" (ZT 705), where she knew every tree whose destiny she considered linked to her own life.

As a child she had already felt a deep attachment to the trees in the park of Zdislawitz. She had anthropomorphized them, making them witness to her vow at thirteen to reform the German theater. Years later, when waiting for a reply from Devrient, to whom she had sent her manuscript of *Maria Stuart*, she had looked at the huge old linden trees in the park of Zdislawitz, comparing their leaves to her own state of feeling. Each of the leaves "had lived its own little life, each had considered itself the most important leaf on the whole tree. How stupid and poor they were—how stupid and poor had I been" (KL 278). As a septuagenarian she still observed those linden trees and noted how old and brittle they had become: "Once they formed an impenetrable wall and their tops went beyond the roof. Now they are dry and pruned, large gaps have formed in the canopy, the rotten limbs are groaning in the wind, the floor is covered with black, dry twigs, children of old age, born late and early departed" ("Schattenleben" 463).

At seventy-five, writing her autobiography, she again thought of the very same linden trees whose fate was so deeply interwoven with her own. In "Aus einem zeitlosen Tagebuch" she finally included some reflections on these trees which had been her faithful companions throughout life: "Here we stand and look at each other. What has become of us?" (710). She entered into a genuine dialogue with trees and saw her own destiny reflected in them. Wherever she had traveled she had noticed trees.[23] She had lovingly described the cypresses at the artists' cemetery in Rome and had made it a point to visit the impressive Tassilo oak on the Pincio (ZT 704). Yet the trees of the park in Zdislawitz always remained the most important: "One loves these trees, loves every branch, every leaf. The magic of one's home surpasses every other magic" (ESD 34).

In her last reflection, at the end of "Aus einem zeitlosen Tagebuch," entitled "Gedanken," she described how easily thoughts had come to her in younger years and had demanded to be expressed in writing. Now, when she was old, her thoughts were nothing but "pale shadows" which vanish before she can come to terms with them (ZT 746). She knew that this collection of diary entries and epigrams was to be her last work. Physically exhausted by old age and constant worries on account of the war, she felt that her days were numbered. Often she suffered from unbearable headaches and from a nerve-racking buzzing in her ears. Deeply depressed about it she wrote to her nephew Franz: "The most painful aspect of it is its inevitability. One can flee wherever one wants, one can plug one's ears, nothing helps; only a much stronger noise coming from outside, can outdo that revolt in one's own cranium" ("Briefwechsel" 259). Dr. Breuer tried to help with various medications but they caused unpleasant side efffects, like dizziness, so that she could not even read any more (Mumbauer 48).

She often dreamed at night, haunted by the thought that she was on a trip (B II 299). Yet she was prepared for death. In 1905, with the help of her secretary, Helene Bucher, she had established an archive in Zdislawitz, where she had deposited her own and her husband's literary estate, letters, diaries, and information about both their ancestors. Her concern for the well-being of those for whom she had cared during her life went beyond her death. She had decreed that her heir continue supporting the poorhouse in Zdislawitz with the royalties from her publications. She had put her clock collection up for sale with the intention of financing a kindergarten in her native place with part of the proceeds (B II 267). Dr. Max Ehrenreich, a judge of the district court and longtime friend and advisor in legal matters, was asked to be the executor of her will.

Marie von Ebner was not afraid of dying. From childhood on she had thought of death as a release from a harsh reality, as a means of being reunited with her late mother. In her 1892 prose poem "Schattenleben" she had said:

> How good is it to be, and how good also to vanish.
> Into nothingness? No! That much I have learned:
> everything is, except the void. No anxious dying, but
> a departing in greatest serenity. Whatever the way
> may be, universal wisdom has planned it, universal
> knowledge knows its aim. I enter it in blissful
> confidence, wihout fear of you, universal wisdom.
> (464)

She neither had to suffer a long last illness, nor was she surprised by a sudden death. Shortly after she had finished "Aus einem zeitlosen Tagebuch," which her publisher Paetel wanted to bring out in 1916 in the same volume as her "Erinnerungen an Grillparzer," Marie von Ebner-Eschenbach, weak from many sleepless, worrisome nights, developed pneumonia from which she was not to recover. Dr. Breuer, doing his best to cure her, wrote to Dr. Otto von Fleischl-Marxow: "Our old friend has overcome her cardiac weakness but is very run down and much bothered by coughing and sleeplessness. If she recovers she will have come down several floors. To me it seems probable that she will die while recovering" (BC 167).

Mindful of her imminent death, Ebner had prepared for the *viaticum* which the priest administered to her on March 12 in her apartment at Spiegelgasse No. 1. She had lived there during the winters with her unmarried niece Marianne Kinsky, the daughter of her sister Friederike. Solicitous for others, and full of humor to the very end, Ebner-Eschenbach showed the greatest concern that P. Rossmiller, her confessor of many years, might knock his head at the hanging lamp while giving her the last rites. A few hours later she died quietly and peacefully. Dr. Breuer informed his colleague Dr. von Fleischl by letter of the medical detail of his old friend's death, adding: "Her last word was, of course, 'I thank you all for everything,' her next-to-last word however, was: 'Has Angela sent the money to the seamstress?'" (BC 168).

With the philosopher Fechner she had believed that the dead remain in communication with the living. She accordingly had the countess of "Ob spät, ob früh" during a visit to a cemetery say: "One thinks of a loved, uncorporeal being who knows about us, for whom our desire makes a path to us, and whose nearness we feel" (411). And to Hermine Villinger she wrote in one of her last letters: "When I am dead, do not cry, Hermine, I am not far away, I am quite close" (Barck-Herzog 849).

From the Spiegelgasse the casket was taken to the Stephansdom where people could pay their respects. Enrica von Handel-Mazzetti recalled: "I saw her lying in state, so small and quiet and humble, almost disappearing under the mighty wreaths and the flowers, and I placed two bouquets of violets at her feet, the symbol of her sweet humility, which was the most beautiful of her features" (Mumbauer 39). After the funeral service, attended by family, friends, younger colleagues, and many dignitaries of Vienna, Ebner-Eschenbach's body was laid to rest, as she had wished, in her beloved Zdislawitz, next to her husband and his mother. All the major newspapers included reviews of her life and work. All obituaries stressed how much she had meant to so many people. In spite of early disappointments in her career as a dramatist, she had been fortunate to live long enough to see her work appreciated and publicly honored; she also had had the comfort of not outliving her reputation. Her relatives deeply mourned her. Shortly after her aunt's death, Marie Kinsky wrote to Dr. Breuer: "What we, and you with us, have lost by way of love and goodness is immeasurable. Countless people are mourning with us, but none of the others can imagine what those have had to part with who had the blessing of having been so close to her" (NBV 1056/16-1).

For the literary world Marie von Ebner-Eschenbach will live on in her work. As a chronicler of the Austrian aristocracy, as a proponent of women's emancipation, as a defender of children's rights, as an advocate of animals and nature, and as a woman with a firm devotion to her art she will continue to inspire future generations. Her great gift had been to closely observe herself and her contemporaries and to record the events of a world to which she was drawn. Her books were built around the central theme of her own life—the struggle of an unwavering will. When she handed her manuscript of "Aus einem zeitlosen Tagebuch" to her publisher, she expressed the hope of being able to see it in book form before her death. This wish was granted, giving her the pleasure of immersing herself in the published reflections about the beginning and end of her career.

When she wrote "Eine Heldin" and included it in her last work, she may not have been aware that in this little parable she had symbolically described her own artistic development. A spruce tree, struck down by a storm and almost totally destroyed, gains new strength from its strong, healthy nature and its indomitable will to endure. Henceforth it is able to brave life better than ever before. A new tempest cannot harm the regenerated tree because, thanks to its previous victorious battle with the elements, it has become invulnerable:

> Thus the heroine presents herself today, and when the other trees give way and bend in a storm, she lets herself be rocked playfully by it; and when her companions ache and groan, a low, almost threatening murmur arises from her dark branches. She clings with her roots, as if with iron ropes, to the mother

> soil and gently moves her evergreen head in quiet
> pride, while the storm rages all around her (709).

Looking back over the writer's life and career, considering the blows
she suffered, the obstacles she had to overcome in order to achieve her
goal, one recognizes the analogy between her own fate and that of the
defiant spruce tree. Similarly, her work as well bears resemblance to
this invincible, evergreen tree. Hers was a long life, a life that knew
tragedy and early disappointment, a life of hard work and determination,
a life that bore rich fruit for posterity. As a child she dreamed of
leaving some traces of her own on the face of the earth—and she was
able to realize this dream.

NOTES

1. In her diary of 1871 Ebner mentions having heard this saying from a friend by the name of Valerie Ziichy (TB II 14).

2. Otto Rank explains an artist's striving for success and his dislike for fame: "For the artist success is a way of returning to life when the work is completed, and fame is a sort of collective after-existence that even the greatest cannot dispense with, since there is no more individual after-existence. The tragedy lies in the fact that the collective continuation of existence . . . extends in the artist's case to a complete depersonalization" (*Myth* 233).

3. Schiller claimed: "The poet may, of course, also imitate bad nature, but in such a case his own beautiful nature must stand above the subject matter and the mean material must not pull down the imitator" (*Essays* 241).

4. Moritz Necker considered Ebner-Eschenbach an adherent of "poetic realism" (*Neues Wiener Tagblatt* February 2, 1895), and critics today still agree with this view (Binneberg 319). The term "poetischer Realismus" was first used by the philosopher Friedrich Schelling and then regularly applied by Otto Ludwig in his structural studies of dramatic and epic works (Preisendanz 69). Wolfgang Preisendanz defines poetic realism as a combination of mimesis and poesis, imitation of reality and creative imagination. He also considers humor an important aspect of this style of writing (206). The Russian critic Bielinski's definition of Turgenev's style also holds true for Ebner-Eschenbach's conception of art. He wrote to the master: "If I am not mistaken, your vocation consists in observing the phenomena of real life, in order to let them pass through your fantasy and then to reproduce them, but not relying only on fantasy (B I 136). Saar considered his own and his contemporaries' style of writing "Ideal-Realismus" (Kindermann 109), and Anzengruber thought of himself as a "Realistiker" (*Dorfgänge II*, Preface).

5. What Ebner thought about humankind may be inferred from her poem about a Donna Isabella who, professing not to believe in hell but

in people, is told by God: "In men—come to recover, O my child, from your wounds; you have already graduated from the very hell you deny" (qtd. in B I 199). Marie Ebner's belief in the perfectibility of humankind changed after 1890. Her earlier works were influenced by Adalbert Stifter's notionof the "gentle law," which was supposed to transform society through kindness and reason (Böschenstein 85). "Glaubenslos?" (1893), "Das Schädliche," "Totenwacht" (1894), "Verschollen" (1896) and "Das tägliche Leben" (1910) express a much more pessimistic attitude.

6. The term "Das junge Wien" was first used in 1892 by Michael Fels when he reported about the Austrian avant-garde writers in his journal *Freie Bühne* (Wunberg I, XL).

7. Heinz Rieder aptly remarks that liberalism was not only a political and economic creed but a way of life. Art had to provide aesthetic pleasure and in addition had to be a "textbook of life," providing counsel and guidance (*Liberalismus* 82).

8. In his essay in honor of Marie Ebner's eightieth birthday, Walter von Molo observed that the writer had never been "modern," and that her time was "eternal" (503).

9. Marie Ebner had a similar experience at the time of Ida von Fleischl's death. While sitting at the bedside of her dying friend, the writer had the impression that someone took her hand and shook it with deep sympathy (BC 170).

10. This was Zaccagnini, the sculptor recommended by Professor Emanuel Löwy.

11. The story "Der Herr Hofrat" was first called "Der Einbruch" (B II 198).

12. In a letter to Ebner-Eschenbach, Ferdinand von Saar calls his creative urge a "tiresome silkworm" (Kindermann 129).

13. To Mrs. Breuer Marie Ebner once confessed that each time she sent a manuscript off for publication she was filled with hatred and self-doubts (BC 56).

14. Ebner never offered Hermine Villinger the informal "Du," although she knew her for almost thirty years.

15. Twentieth-century critics still praise Ebner-Eschenbach for her psychological penetration into children's souls. Danuta Lloyd aptly remarks: "Her portrayal of children especially reveals a grasp of child psychology—predating even the work of Sigmund Freud—which projects her far beyond the literary tradition to which she is heir" (39). Reinhard Thum likewise refers to Ebner's valuable contribution to the delineation of children's psychological problems (30).

16. Fritz Mauthner characterizes Ebner's humility as "not the humility of stupidity, but the humility of the genius who, in happiness and fame, remains aware of her limitations" ("Erinnerungen" 2). Anton Bettelheim has the following explanation for Ebner-Eschenbach's modesty: "Her politeness of heart and the traditional civility of old aristocratic forms made her employ almost humble sounding tones in her letters to strangers or socially inferior persons" (B II 263). Heinrich Rüdiger Starhemberg points out that all Austrians and especially aristocrats have a "fear of men complex" and therefore tend to understate (Siegert 196).

17. Ingrid Aichinger is right in claiming that Ebner's humble and renouncing protagonists through this very attitude demonstrate a strength that renders them victorious in the struggle of life (485).

18. Anton Dörrer remarks on the similarity of Ebner-Eschenbach's and Handel-Mazzetti's values. He maintains that they both "stand in the consciousness of pure humanity and of classical education, above the contradictions of everyday life and of their country and profess the one gospel of love" (qtd. in Siebertz 407). Josef Nadler observes that in her early works between 1887 and 1897 Handel-Mazzetti wrote social novels resembling those of Ebner-Eschenbach (426). Enrica von Handel-Mazzetti in her turn influenced the twentieth-century authors Paula Grogger, Juliane von Stockhausen and Dolores Vieser (Siebertz 467/8). One writer who continued Ebner-Eschenbach's and Handel-Mazzetti's "Countess novels" was Edith von Salburg-Falkenstein, whom Nadler calls "the Countess without respect," in contrast to Ebner-Eschenbach, whom he sees as the "perfect Countess" (372).

19. Handel-Mazzetti had the impression that Schönherr had borrowed some material from her novel *Die arme Margaret*, whereupon Schönherr maligned her, sarcastically stating: "Baroness Handel-Mazzetti has written two novels which ooze out love strongly mixed with hysterics. A woman!" (qtd. in Siebertz 465).

20. Ebner-Eschenbach immortalized Friederike Kempner in her novella *Bertram Vogelweid* (79).

21. Gertrud Fussenegger calls Ebner-Eschenbach a "Kierkegaardian pessimist" (37). Jiri Vesely (ESD 41) and Ingeborg Geserick (57) have likewise observed the writer's tendency to conjure up worst-case scenarios. Böschenstein remarks about Stifter: "Optimism about life may be Stifter's wish, but pessimism is his conviction" (105). This statement would be true for Ebner as well. Yet her contemporaries praised her positive attitude in her work. In his review of *Stille Welt* Otto Zoff points out the writer's optimism and defines it as "crucial point of a feminine worldview, crucial point of all feminine creativity" (RV folder 77243). This may have been wishful thinking.

22. Ebner's diary entries in the 1870s reveal that she was easily discouraged, believed herself untalented and hoped to put an end to her writing (e.g., TB II 574).

23. Ebner-Eschenbach's work abounds with descriptions of trees. Heidi Beutin has pointed out the tree symbolism in *Bozena* (252). Christa Schmidt refers to the writer's regular use of tree metaphors (238). In "Die erste Beichte" Ebner likens the mind of her protagonist to a "strangely formed tree that stretches out its arms toward the lightning of heaven" (481). The protagonist of *Bertram Vogelweid* praises trees as the most beautiful things in the world (8).

EPILOGUE:

The world Marie von Ebner-Eschenbach describes in her work does not exist any more. Many of her ideals and principles have lost their relevance in our postmodern, postindustrial age. The Habsburg Monarchy to which she was deeply attached has disappeared from the stage of history. By declaring war on Serbia in 1914 after the assassination of Archduke Francis Ferdinand, the heir to the throne, the Dual Monarchy unleashed forces that ultimately led to its demise. The discontent of the various nationalities under Habsburg rule, the failure of the army to win a decisive victory, and the rapid deterioration of the economy brought about a crisis of morale, finally causing the dismemberment of the state.

When Emperor Francis Joseph died on November 21, 1916, his death was seen by many as a symbol of the extinction of the past. He had signified stability, adherence to tradition, and the willingness to survive. He had seen his role as a father who held his children, the different nationalities, together under one roof. His successor, Emperor Charles I, a young, mild-mannered, peace-loving man, realized that his country would be unable to win the war and tried to effect an armistice through secret negotiations with the Allies. But all his attempts failed, partly because of his inexperience in diplomatic matters, partly because of his advisors' indiscretion, and partly because Austria-Hungary refused to cede territories to other nations. Consequently the emperor's prestige suffered at home and abroad. Frustrated with the monarch and his government, the Entente powers supported the National Councils set up to help the different nationalities in the Dual Monarchy to gain equal rights and autonomy.

Public opinion in his country likewise turned against the emperor. People gradually became convinced that the state could not continue to exist in its prewar form, and that a new order had to be established. While still proclaiming their loyalty to the dynasty, the various nationalities, among them the Dalmatians, Croats, Czechs and Slovenes, asked for territorial modifications and the transformation of Austria into a federation of autonomous national states. Yet as much as the emperor was willing to acquiesce to these claims, as much as he tried to end the war, the people became increasingly demoralized and finally threatened with a social revolution. As strikes increased, with the respect for the imperial family diminishing, voices grew loud in demanding the abolition of the monarchy.

At the Social Democratic Congress on October 13, 1918 Hungary declared her independence from Austria. Later that month the Czechs and Slovaks seceded to form their own autonomous state, and the South Slavs likewise severed their ties with the Habsburg Monarchy to join the Kingdom of Serbia. Left on their own, the German-speaking countries of the former Dual Monarchy formed a Council of State under a socialist banner. Heinrich Lammasch, the emperor's last minister, yielded his powers to Karl Renner, the new president, instructing the commander of the Italian army to ask the Alliance for an armistice. Emperor Charles I renounced his constitutional rights, and on November 11, 1918 the Republic of Austria was proclaimed. Once the monarchy was dissolved, the framework within which the aristocracy had existed was destroyed. The social and political situation underwent a dramatic change, and prerogatives, accrued through birth, did not count any longer.

On April 3, 1919 the "Habsburg Gesetz," a law that decreed the abolition of the aristocracy, was enacted, forcing all noblemen to renounce their titles and coats of arms. Thus the social elite was integrated into the middle class. Formerly respected and endowed with cultural, political and social privileges, aristocrats suddenly were stigmatized and considered by many to be responsible for the corruption of the government, for the social injustice, and finally for the war. Although deprived of their status and influence, noblemen were permitted, however, to keep their family estates so that their economic existence was guaranteed. Zdislawitz castle, now no longer situated in Austria-Hungary but in newly formed Czechoslovakia which, like Austria, had anti-aristocratic laws, remained in the possession of the Dubskys. Viktor Dubsky, Marie von Ebner-Eschenbach's nephew, continued to live on his country estate where, as before, his relatives gathered for the summer and for special family reunions. They had to learn to adapt to the social restructuring and to find new meaning and purpose in their lives. Although they had lost their former privileges, they preserved their customs and traditions.

After Viktor Dubsky's death in 1932 the castle was sold. The Czechoslovak Republic, in a sense a multinational microcosm of the Habsburg Monarchy, at that time faced almost insurmountable foreign and domestic problems. Due to interference from Germany and Hungary, both trying to re-integrate their separated nationals, the country finally was dismembered in 1938. It was divided into the independent Slovak Republic and the Protectorate of Bohemia-Moravia, which became part of the German Reich. The Czechs, considered by the German authorities as culturally and racially inferior, were brutally exploited. In 1940 the Nazis even made plans to completely destroy the Czech nation through assimilation, deportation and extermination. But the Czechs formed a resistance and an underground movement, uniting with the Slovaks who likewise feared Hitler and a German invasion of their country. In 1944 the Czechs and Slovaks organized a national uprising against the German dictatorship. Although it failed, Czechs and Slovaks, having decided to join forces in a renewed Czechoslovakian state, received the support of Russia and were finally liberated from the German oppressors.

Unlike other castles owned by German-speaking aristocrats and now considered hated symbols of the feudal past and of the recent German persecution, Zdislawitz was not destroyed during or after World War II. However, it was vandalized. Paintings and furniture were auctioned off, books were given to a paper mill. Valuable objects, left to Christian Kinsky after Viktor Dubsky's death, were stolen by Russian communists, who ransacked Löschna castle, his family estate. Marie von Ebner-Eschenbach's library, consisting of many books given to her by friends and colleagues, had been transferred from Zdislawitz to Mork-ovice, the estate of her great-niece, Countess Therese Spiegelfeldt. But again the communists looted the castle and burned all the books in the courtyard.

Zdislawitz castle was first turned into a training center for political functionaries and later converted into an asylum for mentally deranged women. Ebner-Eschenbach's "old nest," her beloved home, to which she owed numerous inspirations and happy memories, has thus found a purpose of which the writer would wholeheartedly approve. All her life she had been concerned about humanity and social justice, all her life she had tried to help women in need. When she came to Zdislawitz she always visited the destitute, and in 1900 she established a poorhouse, a symbol of her solicitude and interest in the well-being of the community.

As she had long foreseen, the state, instead of the aristocracy, has now assumed the protection of the people. While before and even still during the nineteenth century the insane and mentally retarded were treated almost as animals and kept like prisoners behind bars, they are now looked after with respect for their human dignity. Zdislawitz, a link between past and present, keeps Marie von Ebner's memory alive. It is presently the home of more than a hundred mentally challenged women, and it truly reflects the message of "Ein Edelmann," in which a noble-man turned commoner advises his son:

> And when you see your house decay, your pos-
> sessions diminish, feel edified by the thought that out
> of the ruins of your castles you will build huts for the
> homeless; that, by virtue of your example, you be-
> queath your ancestors' best legacy, the noble-mind-
> edness, the benevolent heart, at least to some indi-
> viduals, for the benefit of all. (DS 65)

WORKS CITED

Primary Sources:

Ebner-Eschenbach, Marie von. *Das Gemeindekind. Novellen. Aphorismen.* Vol. 1. Ed. Johannes Klein. München: Winkler, 1978.

—. *Kleine Romane.* Vol. 2. Ed. Johannes Klein, München: Winkler, 1978.

—. *Erzählungen. Autobiographische Werke.* Vol. 3. Ed. Johannes Klein. München: Winkler, 1978.

—. *Aus Spätherbsttagen.* Berlin: Paetel, 1901.

—. *Gesammelte Schriften.* Berlin: Paetel, 1901.

—. *Meine Kinderjahre.* Berlin: Paetel, 1907

—. *Die unbesiegbare Macht. Der Erstgeborene. Jhr Beruf.* Berlin: Paetel, 1905.

—. *Margarete.* Stuttgart: Cotta, 1906.

—. *Sämtliche Werke.* Berlin: Paetel, 1920.

—. *Gesammelte Werke.* Hafis Ausgabe. Leipzig, 1928.

—. *Genrebilder.* Leipzig: Fikentscher Verlag, n.d.

—. *Gesammelte Werke.* Ed. Edgar Gross. München: Nymphenburger Verlagsbuchhandlung, 1961.

—. "Ein Edelmann." *Die Dioskuren.* Vol. 2, 1873.

—. "Es wandelt niemand ungestraft unter Palmen." *Die Dioskuren.* Vol. 10. 1881.

—. "Schattenleben." *Deutsche Rundschau* 86.1

—. *Kritische Texte und Deutungen.* Gen. ed. Karl Konrad Polheim. Vol. 1: *Unsühnbar.* Ed. Burkhard Bittrich. Bonn: Bouvier, 1978. Vol. 2: *Bozena.* Ed. Kurt Binneberg. Bonn: Bouvier, 1980. Vol. 3: *Das Gemeindekind.* Ed. Rainer Baasner, Bonn: Bouvier, 1983. Vol. 4: *Autobiographische Schriften. Meine Kinderjahre. Aus meinen Kinder- und Lehrjahren.* Ed. Christa-Maria Schmidt. Tübingen: Niemeyer, 1989.

—. *Tagebücher I.* 1862-1869. Eds. Karl Konrad Polheim and Rainer Baasner. Tübingen: Niemeyer, 1989

—. *Tagebücher II.* 1871-1878. Eds. Karl Konrad Polheim, Markus Jagsch, Claus Pias and Georg Reicherd. Tübingen: Niemeyer, 1991.

—. *Aphorismen.* Nachwort von Ingrid Cella. Stuttgart: Reclam, 1988.

—. *Aphorisms.* Translated by G.H. Needler. Toronto: Burns & McEachen, 1959.

—. *Letzte Worte. Aus dem Nachlaß.* Ed. Helene Bucher. Wien: Rikola, 1923.

—. *Weisheit des Herzens*. ed. Heinz Rieder. Graz: Stiasny, 1958.

—. *Aus Franzensbad*. Ed. Karlheinz Rossbacher. Wien: Österreichischer Bundesverlag, 1985.

—. *Aphorismen. Erzählungen. Theater*. Ed. Roman Rocek. Graz: Böhlau, 1988.

—. *Seven Stories*. Trans. Helga H. Harriman. Columbia: Camden House, 1986.

—. *Das Waldfräulein*. ed. Karl Gladt. Wien: Belvedere, 1969.

—. *The Child of the Parish*. Trans. Mary A. Robinson. New York, 1893.

—. "Mein Neffe." *Die Dioskuren*. Vol. 14, 1885.

—. "Armer Junge." *Die Dioskuren*. Vol. 18, 1889.

—. "Louise von François." *Velhagen und Klasings Monatshefte*. March, 1894.

—. "Betty von Paoli." *Neue Freie Presse. Morgenblatt*. July 22, 1894.

—. "Meine Uhrensammlung." *Velhagen und Klasings Monatshefte*. January 1896.

Marie von Ebner-Eschenbach und Hieronymus Lorm. "Aus Briefen an einen Freund." *Deutsche Rundschau* 249, 1936.

Marie von Ebner-Eschenbach und Ferdinand von Saar: Briefwechsel. Ed. Heinz Kindermann. Wien: Wiener Bibliophilen Gesellschaft, 1957.

Marie von Ebner-Eschenbach und Dr. Josef Breuer. Ein Briefwechsel, 1889-1916. Ed. Robert A. Kann. Wien: Bergland, 1969.

Secondary Sources:

Abraham, Karl. "Die Stellung der Verwandtenehe in der Psychologie der Neurosen." *Jahrbuch für Psychoanalytische und Psychopathologische Forschungen* 1, 1900.

Adam, Ingrid and Gisela Preuss, Gen. eds. *Meyers Handbuch über die Literatur*. 2nd ed. Heidelberg: Winter, 1970.

Aichinger, Ingrid. "Harmonisierung oder Skepsis? Zum Prosawerk der Marie von Ebner-Eschenbach." *Österreich in Geschichte und Literatur*, 16, no. 9 (1972):483-495.

Alkemade, Mechtild. *Die Lebens- und Weltanschauung der Freifrau Marie von Ebner-Eschenbach*. Mit Briefwechsel zwischen Paul Heyse und Ebner-Eschenbach. Graz: Wächter, 1935.

Anzengruber, Ludwig. *Dorfgänge II.* Vol. 4 of *Gesammelte Werke,* 3rd ed. Stuttgart: Cotta, 1896.

Aschenbrenner, Viktor. "Marie von Ebner-Eschenbach." Ein Gedenken zum 50. Todestag, 1830-1916. *Sudetendeutscher Kulturalmanach* 1967.

Balzer, Bernd and Volker Mertens, eds. *Deutsche Literatur in Schlaglichtern.* Mannheim: Meyers Lexikonverlag, 1990.

Barchilon, Jacques and Peter Flinders. *Charles Perrault.* Boston: Twayne, 1981.

Barck-Herzog, Lisa. "Hermine Villinger—Marie von Ebner-Eschenbach: Eine Dichterfreundschaft, Nach Briefen von Hermine Villinger dargestellt." *Deutsche Rundschau* 87 (1961): 845-849.

Baym, Nina. *Woman's Fiction. A Guide to Novels by and about Women.* Ithaca, NY: Cornell UP, 1978.

Benesch, Kurt. *Die Frau mit den hundert Schicksalen.* Wien: Österreichischer Bundesverlag, 1966.

Berkley, George E. *Vienna and Its Jews. The Tragedy of Success 1880s-1980s..* Cambridge, MA.: Madison, 1988.

Berlin, Isaiah. "Fathers and Children." Romanes Lecture in: Ivan Turgenev, *Fathers and Sons.* London: Penguin, 1965.

Bettelheim, Anton. "Ida von Fleischl-Marxow." *Münchner Allgemeine Zeitung.* Beilage June 9, 1899.

—. *Marie von Ebner-Eschenbach.* Biographische Blätter. Berlin: Paetel, 1900.

—. *Ferdinand von Saars Leben und Schaffen.* Leipzig: Hesse, 1908.

—. ed. *Allgemeine deutsche Biographie.* 56 vols. Leipzig: Duncker, 1875-1912.

—. "Emilie Exner." *Biographenwege.* Berlin: Paetel, 1913.

—. *Marie von Ebner-Eschenbach's Wirken und Vermächtnis.* Leipzig: Quelle und Meyer, 1920.

—. ed. *Louise von François und Conrad Ferdinand Meyer.* Berlin: de Gruyter, 1920.

—. ed. *Neue Österreichische Biographie 1815-1918.* Wien: Amalthea Verlag, 1928.

Beutin, Heidi. "Marie von Ebner-Eschenbach: Bozena. Die wiedergekehrte 'Fürstin Libussa'." *Romane und Erzählungen des Bürgerlichen Realismus. Neue Interpretationen.* Ed. Horst Denkler. Stuttgart Reclam, 1980.

Bietak, Wilhelm. "Marie von Ebner-Eschenbach." *Österreich in Geschichte und Literatur*, 10, no. 9 (1966):482-500.

Böschenstein, Hermann. *German Literature of the Nineteenth Century*. London: Arnold, 1969.

Bovenschen, Silvia. *Die imaginierte Weiblichkeit*. Frankfurt/M: Suhrkamp, 1980.

Bramkamp, Agatha. *Marie von Ebner-Eschenbach. The Author, Her Time and Her Critics*. Bonn: Bouvier, 1990.

Brandt, Helmut. "Marie von Ebner-Eschenbach und die Deutsche Rundschau." *Die österreichische Literatur. Ihr Profil von der Jahrhundertwende bis zur Gegenwart (1880-1980)*. Vol.2. Ed. Herbert Zeman. Graz: Akademische Druck- und Verlagsanstalt, 1989.

Braun, Felix. "Marie von Ebner-Eschenbach—Ein Lebensbild. "*Gesammelte Werke*. Vol. 9. München: Nymphenburger Verlagshandlung, 1961. Pp. 215-233.

Bunsen, Marie von. "Marie von Ebner-Eschenbach, unsere erste Schriftstellerin." *Die Frau*, 1, (1893):29-35

—. "Marie von Ebner-Eschenbach." Persönliche Eindrücke. *Die Frau*, 23 (1916):25-28

Copleston, Frederic. *A History of Philosophy*. 9 vols. New York: Doubleday, reprint 1985

Cysarz, Herbert. *Schiller*. Darmstadt: Wissenschaftliche Buchgesellschaft, 1967.

Dalsimer, Katherine. *Female Adolescence. Psychoanalytic Reflections on Works of Literature*. New Haven: Yale University Press, 1986.

Davidson, Cathy N. and E.M. Broner, eds. *The Lost Tradition*. New York: Ungar, 1980.

Daymond, Douglas and Leslie Monkman, eds. *Canadian Novelists and the Novel*. Ottawa: Borealis, 1981.

Dubsky, Franz. "Erinnerungen an Marie von Ebner-Eschenbach." *Neue Freie Presse*, December 25, 1917.

—. "Aus meinem Briefwechsel mit Marie von Ebner-Eschenbach." *Mährisch-Schlesische Heimat* 10, 1965.

Dunlop, Marilyn. *Body Defenses: The Marvels and Mysteries*. Toronto: Irwin, 1987.

Ebner-Eschenbach, Moritz von. "Aus den Erinnerungen des k.k. Feldmarschall-Leutnants a. D. Moriz Frhrn. Ebner v. Eschenbach." Ed. Marie von Ebner-Eschenbach. *Münchner Allgemeine Zeitung*. Beilage 1899. Nr. 225-227.

—. *Zwei Wiener Geschichten.* "Hypnosis Perennis." "Ein Wunder des heiligen Sebastian." Stuttgart: Cotta, 1897.

Edel, Leon. "Biography and the Science of Man." *New Directions in Biography.* Ed. Anthony M. Friedson. Honolulu: University Press of Hawaii for Biographical Research Center, 1981.

Endres, Elisabeth. "Marie von Ebner-Eschenbach." *Frauen: Porträts aus zwei Jahrhunderten.* Ed. Hans Jürgen Schultz. Stuttgart: Kreuz Verlag, 1981.

Fechner, Gustav Theodor. *Zend-Avesta oder über die Dinge des Himmels und des Jenseits.* Leipzig: Leopold Voß, 1854.

Flügel, J.C. *The Psycho-Analytic Study of the Family.* London: Hogarth, 1939.

Fraenkel, Josef, ed. *The Jews of Austria. Essays on Their Life, History and Destruction.* London: Valentine, Mitchell, 1970.

Freud, Sigmund. *An Outline of Psychoanalysis.* New York: Norton, 1949.

Fuchs, Eduard. *Sozialgeschichte der Frau.* Frankfurt/M: Verlag Neue Kritik, 1973.

Fussenegger, Gertrud. "Marie von Ebner-Eschenbach oder Der gute Mensch von Zdisslawitz." *Schriftenreihe der Künstlergilde.* Vol. 9. eds. Ernst Schremmer and Hans Gottschalk. München: Delp, 1967.

Gardiner, Judith Kegan. "On Female Identity and Writing by Women." *Critical Inquiry.* Winter 1981: 347-361.

Garnett, Edward. *Turgenev. A Study.* London: Collins, 1917.

Garraty, John A. *The Nature of Biography.* New York: Knopf, 1957.

Geehr, Richard. *Karl Lueger: Mayor of Fin-de-Siècle Vienna.* Detroit: Wayne State University Press, 1990.

Geiger, Ludwig. *Die Deutsche Literatur und die Juden.* Berlin: Reimer, 1910.

Gerhard, Adele. "Mädchenerziehung und Rassenhygiene." *Neue Freie Presse.* September 1, 1910.

Geserick, Ingeborg. "Marie von Ebner-Eschenbach und Ivan Turgenev." *Zeitung für Slawistik,* 3(1958):43-64.

Gillie, Christopher. *A Preface to Jane Austen.* London: Longman, 1974.

Gladt, Karl. "Ein Skizzenbuch der Marie von Ebner-Eschenbach." *Librarium.* Vol. 10, 2, 1967.

Gnüg, Hiltrud and Renate Möhrmann, eds. *Frauen. Literatur. Geschichte. Schreibende Frauen vom Mittelalter bis zur Gegenwartt.* Stuttgart: Metzler, 1985.

Goetz, Philip W., gen. ed. *Encyclopedia Britannica* 15th ed. 29 vols. to date. Chicago: University of Chicago Press, 1988.

Grun, Bernard. *The Timetables of History.* New York: Touchstone, 1963.

Guglia, Eugen. *Das Theresianum in Wien. Vergangenheit und Gegenwart.* Wien: Schroll, 1912

Halasz, Nicholas. *Captain Dreyfus.* New York: Simon and Schuster, 1955.

Hantsch, Hugo. *Geschichte Österreichs 1648-1918.* Vol. 2. Graz: Styria, 1961.

Harriman, Helga H. "Marie von Ebner-Eschenbach in Feminist Perspective." *Modern Austrian Literature* 18, no. 1 (1985):27-38.

—. "Talent Is Only Another Word for Power. A Letter from Marie von Ebner-Eschenbach (1830-1916)." *Women's Studies International.* No. 3, 1984.

Hartwig, Otto. "Zur Erinnerung an Louise von François." *Deutsche Rundschau.* December 1893.

Heyse, Paul and L. Laistner, eds. *Neuer Deutscher Novellenschatz.* Vol. 1. Berlin: Globus, n.d.

Hinz, Evelyn J. "A Speculative Introduction: Life-Writing as Drama." *Mosaic.* 20, no 4. Fall 1987.

Historische Kommission bei der Bayrischen Akademie der Wissenschaften. *Neue Deutsche Biographie.* 16 vols. to date. Berlin: Duncker und Humblot, 1952-1990.

Hoffmann-Krayer, E., ed. *Handwörterbuch des deutschen Aberglaubens.* Vol. IV. Berlin: de Gruyter, 1931/32.

Hogsett, Charlotte. *The Literary Existence of Germaine de Staël.* Carbondale: Southern Illinois University Press, 1987.

Horney, Karen. *Neurosis and Human Growth. The Struggle toward Self-Realization.* New York: Norton, 1950.

Istituto per la collaborazione culturale. *Enciclopedia Filosofica.* 4 vols. Venezia, 1957.

Janik, Allen and Stephen Toulmin. *Wittgenstein's Vienna.* New York: Simon and Schuster, 1973.

Johnston, William M. *The Austrian Mind: An Intellectual and Social History.* Berkeley: University of California Press, 1972.

Kabel, Rolf, ed. *Eduard Devrient. Aus seinen Tagebüchern.* Karlsruhe 1852-1870. Weimar: Böhlau, 1964.

Kann, Robert A. *A History of the Habsburg Empire 1526-1918.* Berkeley: University of California Press, 1974.

Klein, Carole. *Mothers and Sons.* Boston: Houghton Mifflin, 1984.

Klemperer, Victor. "Religion und Konfessionen bei Marie von Ebner-Eschenbach." *Allgemeine Zeitung des Judentums.* Berlin, September 9, 1910.

—. "Marie von Ebner-Eschenbach und ihre Frauengestalten." *Die Frau,* 17(1910):711-719.

Knowles, Anthony Vere. *Ivan Turgenev.* Boston, Twayne, 1988.

Kössler, Gottfried. *Mädchenkindheiten im 19 Jahrhundert.* Gießen: Kemp, 1979.

Krausnick, Michail. *Paul Heyse und der Münchener Dichterkreis.* Bonn: Bouvier, 1974.

Kris, Ernst. *Psychoanalytic Explorations in Art.* New York: International Universities Press, 1952.

Langer, Leo. "Marie von Ebner-Eschenbach und die Kindesseele." *Münchener Allgemeine Zeitung.* Beilage. June 5, 1903.

Laube, Heinrich. *Das Wiener Stadttheater.* Leipzig, 1875.

Lernet-Holenia, Alexander. "Der österreichische Adel." *Der Monat* 9, February 1957.

Lessing, Doris. *The Golden Notebook.* New York: Knopf, 1973.

Lloyd, Danuta. "Waifs and Strays: The Youth in Marie von Ebner-Eschenbach's Village Tales." Karl S. Weimar, ed. *Views and Reviews of Modern German Literature.* Festschrift for Adolf D. Klarmann. München: Delp, 1974.

—. "Dorf und Schloss: The Socio-Political Image of Austria as Reflected in Marie von Ebner-Eschenbach's Works." *Modern Austrian Literature,* Vol. 12, nos. 3-4, 1979.

Lorm, Hieronymus. *Ein Schatten aus vergangenen Tagen.* Stuttgart: Deutsche Verlangsanstalt, 1882.

Lothar, Rudolph. *Das Wiener Burgtheater.* Leipzig: Seemann, 1899.

Mann, Golo. *Deutsche Geschichte des 19. und 20. Jahrhunderts.* Frankfurt/M: Fischer, 1975.

Marxow, Ernst Fleischl von. *Gesammelte Abhandlungen.* Ed. Otto von Fleischl-Marxow, Leipzig: J.A.Barth, 1893.

Maurois, André. *Aspects of Biography.* Trans. Sidney Castle Roberts. Reprint 1919 New York: Arden, 1977.

Mauthner, Fritz. "Erinnerungen." *Berliner Tageblatt,* April 2, 1916.

May, Arthur J. *Vienna in the Age of Franz Josef.* Norman: University of Oklahoma Press, 1966.

Meyer, Richard M. "Marie von Ebner-Eschenbach: Zum siebzigsten Geburtstage." *Velhagen und Klasings Monatshefte,* 15 no. 1 (1900): 57-60.

—. *Die Deutsche Literatur des 19. Jahrhunderts.* Berlin: Bondi, 1912.

Milde, Natalie von. "Marie von Ebner-Eschenbach und ihre Bedeutung für die Frauenbewegung." *Centralblatt des Bundes deutscher Frauenvereine,* 2 (1900):90.

—. "Von den Männern und Frauen." *Hamburgischer Correspondent.* April 21, 1901.

Miller, Jean Baker, ed. *Psychoanalysis and Women.* Baltimore: Penguin, 1973.

Minor, Daisy. "Marie von Ebner-Eschenbach." *Dokumente der Frauen.* Vol. 33, 1900.

Mitterhofer, Bettina. "Moritz Ebner von Eschenbach - Erfinder und Literat. Ein Mann im Schatten seiner Frau." Diss. Universität Wien, 1986.

Möhrmann, Renate. *Die andere Frau.* Stuttgart: Metzler, 1977.

—. "Die lesende Vormärzautorin. Untersuchungen zur weiblichen Sozialisation." *Literatur und Sprache im historischen Prozeß.* Ed. Thomas Cramer. Vol. 1, Tübingen: Niemeyer, 1983.

Molo, Walter von. "Marie von Ebner-Eschenbach." *Grenzboten* 3, 1910.

Mörsdorf, Josef. *Gestaltwandel des Frauenbildes und Frauenberufs in der Neuzeit.* München: Delp, 1958.

Mumbauer, Johannes, ed. *Der Dichterinnen stiller Garten. Marie von Ebner-Eschenbach und Enrica von Handel-Mazzetti. Bilder aus ihrem Leben und ihrer Freundschaft.* Freiburg, Brsg.: Herder, 1918.

Nadler, Josef. *Literaturgeschichte Österreichs.* Salzburg: Müller, 1951.

Necker, Moritz. "Marie von Ebner-Eschenbach." Zum siebzigsten Geburtstag. *Neue Freie Presse.* Feuilleton. September 13, 1900.

—. *Marie von Ebner-Eschenbach. Nach ihren Werken geschildert.* München: Müller, 1916.

Olsen, Tillie. *Silences.* New York: Delacorte, 1978.

Peters, H.F. *Lou Andreas Salomé. Das Leben einer außergewöhnlichen Frau.* München: Heyne, 1962. 2nd ed. 1989.

Petzet, Erich. "Vorwort." Paul Heyse, *Gesammelte Novellen.* Stuttgart: Cotta, 1923.

Piaget, Jean. *The Child's Conception of the World*. London: Paul, Trench and Truebner, 1929.

Polheim, Karl Konrad, ed. *Ferdinand von Saar. Ein Wegbereiter der literarischen Moderne*. Bonn: Bouvier, 1985.

—. ed. *Theorie und Kritik der deutschen Novelle*. Tübingen: Niemeyer, 1970.

Politzer, Heinz, ed. *Grillparzer über sich selbst. Aus seinen Tagebüchern*. Frankfurt am Main: Insel Verlag, 1965.

—. *Franz Grillparzer. Oder das abgründige Biedermeier*. Wien-München-Zürich: Fritz Molden, 1972.

Poulet, Dom Charles. *A History of the Catholic Church*. Transl. Sidney A. Raemers, vol. 1, London: Herder, 1935, reprint 1957.

Preisendanz, Wolfgang. *Wege des Realismus*. München: Fink, 1977.

Rank, Otto. *The Myth of the Birth of the Hero*. New York: Knopf, 1959.

Redinger, Ruby V. *George Eliot. The Emergent Self*. New York: Knopf, 1975.

Reinke, Lilli. "Annette von Droste-Hülshoff und Marie von Ebner-Eschenbach." *Eckart*. Vol. 4 (1910):169-182.

Reuter, Gabriele. *Ebner-Eschenbach*. Berlin: Schuster, 1904.

Rieder, Heinz. *Liberalismus als Lebensform*. Germanische Studien. Berlin: Matthiesen, 1939. Reprint 1967.

Rodenberg, Julius. *Wiener Sommertage*. Leipzig: Brockhaus, 1875.

—. *Heimaterinnerungen*. Berlin: Paetel, 1882.

—. *Aus der Kindheit*. Berlin: Paetel, 1907.

Rozenblit, Marsha. *The Jews of Vienna 1867-1914. Assimilation and Identity*. Albany: State University of New York Press, 1983.

Saar, Ferdinand von. "Begegnungen mit Marie von Ebner-Eschenbach." *Die Gartenlaube*. (1900): 503-505.

—. "Marie von Ebner-Eschenbach." *Illustrierte Frauenzeitung*. Vol.13, January 1, 1886.

Sagarra, Eda. *Tradition und Revolution. Deutsche Literatur und Gesellschaft 1830-1890*. München: List, 1972.

Salter, William Mackintire. *Die Religion der Moral*. Trans. Georg von Gizycki. Leipzig, 1885.

Schiller, Friedrich. "Aesthetical and Philosophical Essays" in *Complete Works*. 8 vols. New York: Collier, 1911.

Schlossar, Anton, ed. *Anastasius Grün. Sämtliche Werke*. Leipzig: Hesse, 1907.

Schorske, Carl E. *Fin-de-Siècle Vienna: Politics and Culture.* New York: Knopf, 1980.

Serke, Jürgen. *Frauen schreiben.* Frankfurt/M: Fischer, 1982.

Siebertz, Paul. *Enrica von Handel-Mazzettis Persönlichkeit, Werk und Bedeutung.* München: Kösel, 1930.

Siegert, Heinz. *Adel in Österreich.* Wien: Kremayr, 1971.

Spiero, Heinrich. *Julius Rodenberg. Sein Leben und seine Werke.* Berlin: Paetel, 1921

Stekel, Wilhelm. *Dichtung und Neurose. Grenzfragen des Nerven- und Seelenlebens.* Heft 65. Wiesbaden: Ritter, 1937.

Straub, Julian. *Hieronymus Lorm als Prosaist.* München: Rother, 1959.

Suttner, Bertha von. *Memoirs. The Records of an Eventful Life.* Vol. 2, Boston: Ginn and Co., 1910.

Szczepanski, Paul von. "Vom Schreibtisch und aus der Werkstatt." Erinnerungen an Louise von François und Marie von Ebner-Eschenbach. *Velhagen und Klasings Monatshefte.* February 1920.

Tapié, Victor-L. *The Rise and Fall of the Habsburg Monarchy.* Trans. Stephen Hardman. New York: Praeger, 1971.

Thum, Reinhard. "Parental Authority and Childhood Trauma: An Analysis of Marie von Ebner-Eschenbach's 'Die erste Beichte.'" *Modern Austrian Literature.* Vol. 19, no. 2 (1986):15-31.

Turgenev, Ivan. *First Love.* Harmondsworth, UK: Penguin, 1977.

Tyrolt, Rudolf. *Chronik des Wiener Stadttheaters 1871-84.* Wien: C. Konegen, 1889.

Vesely, Jiri. "Marie von Ebner-Eschenbach, Saar, David: Tschechische Elemente in ihrem Werk und Leben." *Lenau-Forum.* 1. no. 3-4 (1969): 25-45.

—. "Marie von Ebner-Eschenbach und die tschechische Literatur." *Germanistica Pragensia,* 6 (1972):91-100.

—. "Tagebücher legen Zeugnis ab: Unbekannte Tagebücher der Marie von Ebner-Eschenbach." *Österreich in Geschichte und Literatur,* 15 (1975):211-241.

Villinger, Hermine. "Wie ich Marie von Ebner-Eschenbach kennenlernte." *Velhagen und Klasings Monatshefte.* (September 1890):61-64.

Wagman, Richard J., ed. *The New Complete Medical and Health Encyclopedia.* Vol.2. Chicago: Ferguson, 1989.

Weilen, Alexander von. *Der Spielplan des neuen Burgtheaters 1888-1914.* Nendeln: Kraus Reprint, 1975.

Weininger, Otto. *Geschlecht und Charakter.* Wien: Braumüller, 1904.

Winter, Ingelore. *Der Adel*. Wien: Molden, 1981.

Wunberg, Gotthart. *Das Junge Wien*. Vol. 1, 1887-1896, Vol. 2, 1897-1902. Tübingen: Niemeyer, 1976.

Wurzbach, Constantin. *Biographisches Lexikon des Kaiserthums Österreich*. New York: Johnson Reprint Corp., 1966.

Wydenbruck, Nora. "Komtessen und Stiftsdamen." *Der Monat*. 9, February 1957.

Zweig, Stefan. *The World of Yesterday*, Lincoln: University of Nebraska Press, 1964.

INDEX

ARIADNE PRESS
Studies in Austrian Literature, Culture and Thought

Major Figures of
Modern Austrian Literature
Edited by Donald G. Daviau

Austria in the Thirties
Culture and Politics
Edited by Kenneth Segar
and John Warren

Stefan Zweig:
An International Bibliography
By Randolph J. Klawiter

Of Reason and Love:
The Life and Works of Marie
von Ebner-Eschenbach
By Carl Steiner

Franz Kafka
A Writer's Life
By Joachim Unseld

Kafka and Language: In the
Stream of Thoughts and Life
By G. von Natzmer Cooper

Robert Musil and the Tradition
of the German Novelle
By Kathleen O'Connor

Implied Dramaturgy:
Robert Musil and the Crisis
of Modern Drama
By Christian Rogowski

Introducing Austria
A Short History
By Lonnie Johnson

Major Figures of
Turn-of-the-Century
Austrian Literature
Edited by Donald G. Daviau

Austrian Writers
and the Anschluss:
Understanding the Past—
Overcoming the Past
Edited by Donald G. Daviau

"What People Call Pessimism":
Sigmund Freud, Arthur Schnitzler
and Nineteenth-Century
Controversy at the University
of Vienna Medical School
By Mark Luprecht

Arthur Schnitzler and Politics
By Adrian Clive Roberts

Structures of Disintegration:
Narrative Strategies in
Elias Canetti's Die Blendung
By David Darby

Blind Reflections:
Gender in Elias Canetti's
Die Blendung
By Kristie A. Foell

ARIADNE PRESS
New Titles

Walk about the Villages
By Peter Handke
Translated by Michael Roloff

The Giant File on Zwetschkenbaum
By Albert Drach
Translated by Harvey I. Dunkle

Woman's Face of Resistance
By Marie-Thérèse Kerschbaumer
Translated by Lowell A. Bangerter

Ice on the Bridge
By Erich Wolfgang Skwara
Translated by Michael Roloff

"It's Up to Us!"
Collected Works of Jura Soyfer
Selected, Edited and Translated
By Horst Jarka

The House of the Linsky Sisters
By Florian Kalbeck
Translated by Michael Mitchell

Springtime on the Via Condotti
By Gustav Ernst
Translated by Todd C. Hanlin

Against the Grain
New Anthology of Contemporary Austrian
Prose
Selected by Adolf Opel

The Final Plays
By Arthur Schnitzler
Translated by G.J. Weinberger

New Anthology
of Contemporary
Austrian Folk Plays
Edited by Richard H. Lawson

Shooting Rats, Other Plays and Poems
By Peter Turrini
Translatedy by Richard Dixon

Dirt
By Robert Schneider
Translated by Paul F. Dvorak

Rilke's Duino Elegies
Edited by Roger Paulin
and Peter Hutchinson

Phantom Empires
The Novels of Alexander Lernet-Holenia
and the Question of Postimperial
Austrian Identity
By Robert Dassanowsky

Waking the Dead
Correspondences between Walter
Benjamin's Concept of Remembrance and
Ingeborg Bachmann's Ways of Dying
By Karen Remmler

ARIADNE PRESS
Translation Series

Lerida
By Alexander Giese
Translated by Lowell A. Bangerter

Three Flute Notes
By Jeannie Ebner
Translated by Lowell A. Bangerter

Siberia and Other Plays
By Felix Mitterer

The Sphere of Glass
By Marianne Gruber
Translation and Afterword
by Alexandra Strelka

The Convent School
By Barbara Frischmuth
Translated by
G. Chapple and J.B. Lawson

The Green Face
By Gustav Meyrink
Translated by Michael Mitchell

*The Ariadne Book of Austrian
Fantasy: The Meyrink Years
1890-1930*
Ed. & trans. by Michael Mitchell

Walpurgisnacht
By Gustav Meyrink
Translated by Michael Mitchell

The Cassowary
By Matthias Mander
Translated by Michael Mitchell

Plague in Siena
By Erich Wolfgang Skwara
Foreword by Joseph P. Strelka
Translation by Michael Roloff

Memories with Trees
By Ilse Tielsch
Translated by David Scrase

Aphorisms
By Marie von Ebner-Eschenbach
Translated by David Scrase and
Wolfgang Mieder

Conversations with Peter Rosei
By Wilhelm Schwarz
Translated by Christine and
Thomas Tessier

*Anthology of Contemporary
Austrian Folk Plays*
By V. Canetti, Preses/Becher,
Mitterer, Szyszkowitz, Turrini
Translation and Afterword
by Richard Dixon

Try Your Luck!
By Peter Rosei
Translated by Kathleen Thorpe

ARIADNE PRESS
Translation Series

ARIADNE PRESS
Translation Series